THE PIVOT

STANDING ON TRUTH

Everett L. Blaylock

A DIVINE SPARK
PUBLISHING

A DIVINE SPARK PUBLISHING

Ignite the Light Within.

Published by
A Divine Spark Publishing, LLC
Houston, Texas, USA

© 2025 Everett LaMar Blaylock
All rights reserved.

No part of this book may be reproduced, stored in a retrieval system, or transmitted in any form or by any means—electronic, mechanical, photocopying, recording, or otherwise—without prior written permission from the publisher, except for brief quotations in critical articles and reviews.

All Scripture quotations are from the New American Standard Bible (NASB1995) unless otherwise noted.

Scripture quotations taken from the
NEW AMERICAN STANDARD BIBLE®, 1995 Edition (NASB®)
Copyright © 1960, 1962, 1963, 1968, 1971, 1972, 1973, 1975, 1977, 1995 by
The Lockman Foundation.
Used by permission.
www.lockman.org

Cover Design: A Divine Spark Publishing Creative Department
Interior Layout: A Divine Spark Publishing Production

Printed in the United States of America
ISBN: 979-8-9943571-0-1

For more resources, visit:

@PastorELBlaylock
@ADivineSparkPublishing
@ ABeaconOfLightHTX.com
www.ADivineSpark.com

This book is dedicated to the foundations of my faith and purpose: to my late grandmother, **Dorothy "Madea" McCall**, whose life first pointed me toward God; to my mother, **Bobbie J. Blaylock**, my steady rock and living example of strength; and to my children, **Evan, Emersyn,** and **Everett II**, whose lives became the reason I fully surrendered mine to God.

Foreword

..., and over the years we grew into best friends.
.ok us to different places…college, careers,
,mehow stayed neighbors in spirit and in truth. We
.nrough life's ups and downs side by side, and by God's
.'e both still standing… and now standing on purpose. He is
.iter's godfather, and I know this man of God deeply and
.ally.

.is devotional is not theory for him. It is the overflow of a sacred .ieart and a disciplined life. I am encouraged daily by his unwavering pursuit of his calling…the daily 6 a.m. men's discipleship call, his hospice, youth, gym and prison ministries, the weekly Bible lessons he has written faithfully for five years, and the way he lives his out assignment with intention and integrity.

You will feel that same authenticity in these pages. Every devotion carries purpose, wisdom, and the kind of clarity that only comes from communion with God. This work is an extension of the life he already lives…one marked by obedience, consistency, and a desire to move humanity closer to its God-given place.

My prayer is that as you read, you feel what I've witnessed for decades: a servant of God whose life and words lead us toward clarity, toward purpose, and toward the lives we were created to live.

Dr. Carla Brailey

A pivot is not random.
It is not reckless.
It is not without purpose.

A pivot is the moment you realize that **change is necessary** in order for you to attain success.

A pivot is God protecting the promise by redirecting your path.

Proverbs 3:5–6
Trust in the Lord with all your heart
And do not lean on your own understanding.
In all your ways acknowledge Him,
And He will make your paths straight.

Table of Contents

JANUARY

January 1 • Driven by Purpose • **Proverbs 16:3**
January 2 • The Rewards of Sacrifice • **1 Corinthians 3:8**
January 3 • Let Your Smile Change the World • **Philippians 4:5**
January 4 • Die to Rise • **John 3:3**
January 5 • Rise Again • **Proverbs 24:16**
January 6 • Discipline Determines Destiny • **Proverbs 13:4**
January 7 • One Step at a Time • **2 Corinthians 5:7**
January 8 • Wake Up: Don't Be the Walking Dead • **Ephesians 5:14**
January 9 • The Rhythm of Becoming • **Colossians 3:17**
January 10 • Bold Moves Require Bold Faith • **Joshua 1:9**
January 11 • Doing Less, But Doing Better • **Philippians 4:12**
January 12 • Truth That Heals • **John 8:32**
January 13 • Living Beyond the Conscious • **Matthew 16:24**
January 14 • Give Freely, Live Abundantly • **Acts 10:38**
January 15 • Remove What Stops Growth • **Hebrews 12:1**
January 16 • You Are the Equation • **Proverbs 21:5**
January 17 • You Cannot Love God Without Loving Others • **1 John 4:20–21**
January 18 • For Him, Not For Us • **Colossians 1:16**
January 19 • Look, Listen, and Learn • **Proverbs 4:20–21**
January 20 • In the Huddle • **Jeremiah 29:11**
January 21 • Service: The Secret to Greatness • **Matthew 25:40**
January 22 • Choose Your Company Wisely • **1 Corinthians 15:33**
January 23 • The Fulfillment of the Law Is Love • **Matthew 5:17**
January 24 • Stay Honestly Free • **Ephesians 4:25**
January 25 • Compassion: The Heart That Heals • **Ephesians 4:32**
January 26 • Gratitude: The Key to Elevation • **1 Thessalonians 5:18**
January 27 • Through Devotion • **Psalm 37:4**
January 28 • Consistency: The Steady Drip of Success • **Galatians 6:9**
January 29 • Patience: The Power of the Wait • **James 1:4**
January 30 • Focus: Eyes Fixed on Purpose • **Proverbs 4:25**
January 31 • Integrity: Wholeness in Action • **Proverbs 11:3**

FEBRUARY

February 1 • Winning Where It Matters Most • **1 Timothy 5:8**
February 2 • Stay Light So You Can Take Flight • **Psalm 51:10**
February 3 • Soul Over Selfie • **1 Samuel 16:7**

February 4 • Be Bright On Purpose • **Matthew 5:16**
February 5 • You vs YOU • **Galatians 5:17**
February 6 • Stop Chasing Sand • **Matthew 7:24**
February 7 • Struggle Is the Assignment • **1 Peter 5:10**
February 8 • The Smallest Shift, The Biggest Life • **Romans 12:2**
February 9 • No Enemies? • **Luke 6:26**
February 10 • The Healing Power of Kindness • **Hebrews 13:16**
February 11 • The Sacred Struggle • **James 1:12**
February 12 • Greatness in Solitude • **Matthew 14:23**
February 13 • The Power of Hope • **Proverbs 13:12**
February 14 • Love: The Greatest of All • **1 Corinthians 13:13**
February 15 • The Will to Win • **Philippians 2:13**
February 16 • A Distracted Mind Never Builds an Intentional Life • **Psalm 119:37**
February 17 • Change Habits → Change Your Life • **Colossians 3:9–10**
February 18 • Just Plant the Seed • **1 Corinthians 3:6**
February 19 • Appreciate the Detour • **Proverbs 3:5–6**
February 20 • Will Your Sacrifice Be the Reason Your Family Flourishes? • **Genesis 12:3**
February 21 • Discipline: The Pathway to Purpose • **Hebrews 12:11**
February 22 • Joy Is an Inside Job • **Nehemiah 8:10b**
February 23 • Your Next Move Matters More Than Your Last Mistake • **Philippians 3:13–14**
February 24 • Looking Forward • **Isaiah 43:18–19**
February 25 • The Cheat Code of Breath • **Genesis 2:7**
February 26 • Called to Be Light, Not Liked • **1 John 1:6–7**
February 27 • Faith That Finds Peace • **Philippians 4:7**
February 28 • Which Wolf Are You Feeding? • **Romans 8:6**
February 29 • A Church Serious About Souls • **James 5:19–20**

MARCH

March 1 • The Power of Being Present • **Matthew 6:34**
March 2 • Power of Thought, Word, and Presence • **Proverbs 23:7**
March 3 • Dying to Live Divine • **1 John 2:16**
March 4 • Mastered by Time • **Psalm 37:7**
March 5 • How You Love Is Your Superpower • **John 13:35**
March 6 • When You Can't Feel Him, Trust Him • **Hebrews 13:5b**
March 7 • Don't Wait to Be Great • **Psalm 139:14**
March 8 • Be the Energy You Want to Attract • **Galatians 6:7**
March 9 • A Still Pond Reflects the Sun Perfectly • **Psalm 46:10**
March 10 • Your Value Isn't in Your Bank … It's in Your Vision • **Matthew 6:33**

March 11 • The Ladder of Consciousness • **2 Corinthians 3:18**
March 12 • Drawn to the Light • **Ephesians 5:8**
March 13 • One Purpose • **Matthew 6:33**
March 14 • On Earth As It Is In Heaven: Roots & Reach • **Matthew 6:10**
March 15 • If You Ain't Giving, You Ain't Living • **Acts 20:35**
March 16 • When Two Become More Than Two • **Ecclesiastes 4:9**
March 17 • The Lord Saves Us From… • **Luke 19:10**
March 18 • Hard Work Works • **Colossians 3:23**
March 19 • From Worry to Wonder • **Philippians 4:6–7**
March 20 • The Power of Small Acts • **Galatians 6:9**
March 21 • Change Your Mind, Change Your Life • **Romans 12:2**
March 22 • The Only Person Coming to Save You • **Philippians 2:12–13**
March 23 • When the Storm Comes • **Matthew 7:24–25**
March 24 • The Enemy Wants More than Casualties • **1 John 3:8**
March 25 • The Gospel Means More Than Blessings … It Means Change • **2 Corinthians 3:18**
March 26 • Change Born from Love • **Ezekiel 36:26**
March 27 • Grace Over Performance: Entering the Kingdom by Faith • **Ephesians 2:8–9**
March 28 • The Illusion of a Compromised Gospel • **Galatians 1:6–7**
March 29 • The Illusion of Money: The Price of Nothing • **Luke 12:15**
March 30 • Peace Is Power • **John 14:27**
March 31 • Guarding Your Peace • **Proverbs 4:23**

APRIL

April 1 • Happy New Year April Fool • **Exodus 12:2**
April 2 • Refined for Elevation • **Zechariah 13:9a**
April 3 • Ready Is a Decision, Not a Feeling • **2 Corinthians 5:7**
April 4 • Build the Builder Before You Build the Business • **Ephesians 2:10**
April 5 • I Didn't Come to Go Along; I Came to Create a New Song • **Psalm 96:1**
April 6 • Public Praise Flows from Private Worship • **Matthew 6:6**
April 7 • To Get to the Promise • **Deuteronomy 2:3**
April 8 • Habits Shape Your Horizon • **Galatians 6:9**
April 9 • Choose Daily Discipline • **1 Corinthians 9:27**
April 10 • Mastering Your Three Currencies: Knowledge, Time, Money • **Proverbs 2:6**
April 11 • Heal the Parent, Protect the Child • **Exodus 20:5**
April 12 • He Is Everything to Me • **Colossians 1:18**
April 13 • The God-Shaped Hole in Your Heart • **Ecclesiastes 3:11**
April 14 • A Divine Spark Within • **Genesis 2:7**

April 15 • Resonating with Heaven's Frequency • **John 10:27**
April 16 • A Peace of Mind vs. A Mind of Peace • **Isaiah 26:3**
April 17 • Prayer That Starts in Heaven • **Romans 8:26**
April 18 • Faith Makes Miracles • **Matthew 17:20**
April 19 • Faith Receives Before It Sees • **Mark 11:24**
April 20 • Spiritual Beings, Holy Assignment • **Colossians 3:10**
April 21 • Growth Demands Challenge • **James 1:2–4**
April 22 • The Call to Virtue: Moral Excellence in Action • **2 Peter 1:5**
April 23 • The Power of Letting Go • **1 Peter 5:7**
April 24 • Don't Wait; Life Moves Faster Than You Think • **James 4:14**
April 25 • Love Yourself Enough to Care for Your Temple • **1 Corinthians 6:19**
April 26 • Make Your Food Your Medicine • **Proverbs 23:20–21**
April 27 • Knowing God by Doing His Work • **James 1:22**
April 28 • Wisdom That Speaks, Works That Show • **James 3:13**
April 29 • Standing Firm in a Shifting Culture • **John 17:17**
April 30 • When God Co-Signs • **Joshua 1:9**

MAY

May 1 • The Greatest Love Letter Ever Written • **Psalm 119:105**
May 2 • Seek First • **Matthew 6:33**
May 3 • Ambition Without Action Becomes Anxiety • **Proverbs 13:4**
May 4 • Distractions in Disguise • **Proverbs 4:25–27**
May 5 • Sacrifice: The Currency of Elevation • **Romans 12:1**
May 6 • Living by a Creed • **Psalm 19:14**
May 7 • The Beginning of Solitude • **Luke 5:16**
May 8 • Truth Breaks Chains • **John 8:32**
May 9 • The Loneliness of Leadership • **Isaiah 63:3**
May 10 • A Mother's Sacred Influence • **Proverbs 31:26–28**
May 11 • Vanity or Virtue • **Proverbs 31:30**
May 12 • Kindness Is Godly • **Galatians 5:22**
May 13 • When Kindness Is a Mask • **Romans 12:9**
May 14 • What's Behind Your Smile? • **Proverbs 15:13**
May 15 • Shine • **Matthew 5:14**
May 16 • Change Requires Change • **Romans 12:2**
May 17 • One Small Decision Away from Breakthrough • **Proverbs 3:5–6**
May 18 • Our Heavenly Reconciliation • **John 17:17**
May 19 • The Ride Matters • **2 Corinthians 5:10**
May 20 • You Are Not the Fixer • **1 Corinthians 3:7**
May 21 • Seeing Beyond the Surface • **Matthew 13:29–30**
May 22 • Warned & Ready: Guard Your Soul from Silent Distractions • **John 10:10**

May 23 • The Measure of Love Is Sacrifice • **John 3:16**
May 24 • United We Stand, Divided We Fall • **Matthew 12:25**
May 25 • The Cost of Becoming New • **Romans 12:2**
May 26 • Sow Wisely: You Get What You Give • **Galatians 6:7**
May 27 • Don't Feed Your Babies the Same Lies You Ate • **2 Timothy 3:15**
May 28 • God's Order: God > Jesus > Man > Woman > Children • **Isaiah 3:12**
May 29 • Disconnected Youth, Defeated Generation • **Judges 2:10**
May 30 • Not the Woodpecker … But the Termite • **2 Corinthians 6:16**
May 31 • Love Covers a Multitude of Sins • **1 Peter 4:8**

JUNE

June 1 • Grace: God's Resources at Christ's Expense • **Ephesians 2:8**
June 2 • Let Go and Let God • **Isaiah 43:18–19**
June 3 • Lessons in the Fall • **Proverbs 24:16**
June 4 • What Happens Inside Matters Most • **Proverbs 23:7a**
June 5 • To Me and Through Me • **Philippians 2:13**
June 6 • Jesus: My Master, Savior, Ruler, Redeemer, Provider • **Isaiah 54:5**
June 7 • Master Your Desires to Manage Your Destiny • **Proverbs 25:28**
June 8 • Stop Letting Satan Romance You to Death • **2 Timothy 4:3–4**
June 9 • Sin Separates; Obedience Unites • **Isaiah 59:2**
June 10 • God Never Asked You to Audition • **Romans 8:38–39**
June 11 • True Freedom • **2 Corinthians 3:17**
June 12 • One With God • **Genesis 1:26**
June 13 • Joy Cultivated in Christ • **Nehemiah 8:10**
June 14 • Heaven in Your Design • **Psalm 139:14**
June 15 • Built for Eternity • **James 1:3–4**
June 16 • Anointed for Peace • **Psalm 23:5**
June 17 • Called to Transform, Not Perform • **Matthew 23:27–28**
June 18 • The Strength of Stillness • **Psalm 46:10**
June 19 • The Hard Path Builds the Unshakable Life • **James 1:12**
June 20 • A Problem for Every Solution • **1 Corinthians 15:33**
June 21 • A Father's Holy Weight • **Proverbs 20:7**
June 22 • Shut the Door and Pray • **Matthew 6:6**
June 23 • The Gift of Giving • **Proverbs 11:25**
June 24 • Integrity Over Impressing • **Proverbs 11:3**
June 25 • The Power of Showing Up • **James 2:26**
June 26 • Energy Multiplies When We Reflect Light Together • **Romans 14:19**
June 27 • Light Your Cornor • **Matthew 5:14–16**
June 28 • The Gift of Serenity • **Philippians 4:7**

June 29 • Love That Disciplines • **Proverbs 13:24**
June 30 • Marriage: Built to Last • **Psalm 127:1**

JULY

July 1 • Authentic by Design • **Psalm 139:14**
July 2 • The Kingdom Within • **Luke 17:21**
July 3 • Called to Be "Twice-Born" in a Once-Born World • **John 3:3**
July 4 • When a Nation Forgets God • **Proverbs 14:34**
July 5 • No Free Rent • **2 Corinthians 10:5**
July 6 • Ask. Seek. Knock. • **Matthew 7:7**
July 7 • Cheerful Obedience • **Jeremiah 17:10**
July 8 • Where Attention Flows, Energy Grows • **Colossians 3:2**
July 9 • The Power of Oneness • **John 17:21**
July 10 • The Call to Overcome • **Revelation 2–3**
July 11 • Don't Miss Today's Blessings • **Isaiah 43:18–19**
July 12 • Just Can't Help It • **Acts 4:20**
July 13 • Be Patient in the Process • **Luke 21:19**
July 14 • From Venting to Victory • **Proverbs 16:24**
July 15 • The Battle for Your Mind • **Romans 12:2**
July 16 • Guarding Your Energy • **Proverbs 4:23**
July 17 • Life Is Not About Magic, It's About Management • **1 Corinthians 4:2**
July 18 • Get Comfortable Being Uncomfortable • **James 1:2–3**
July 19 • Seated in Heavenly Places • **Ephesians 2:6**
July 20 • The Power of Humility • **James 4:10**
July 21 • Steward Your Temple • **1 Corinthians 10:31**
July 22 • The Diligence of Self-Discipline • **Luke 9:23**
July 23 • Freedom Starts on the Inside • **John 8:36**
July 24 • Full Custody, Not Visitation • **Colossians 3:3**
July 25 • Don't Be Like the Dead Sea • **Proverbs 11:25**
July 26 • Helping People Is Godlike • **Luke 6:36**
July 27 • Be Still & Let God Fight • **Exodus 14:14**
July 28 • Bob & Weave: Lessons From My First Coaches • **Proverbs 24:16**
July 29 • What the Thief Comes to Steal • **John 10:10**
July 30 • Joy Inside, Happiness Outside • **Philippians 4:4–5**
July 31 • The Gift of Joy Carriers • **Proverbs 17:22**

AUGUST

August 1 • Unity: Gang Up on the Problem, Not Each Other • **Genesis 11:6**
August 2 • Don't Play in the Gray • **Matthew 6:22**

August 3 • Who's Driving? • **Romans 8:14**
August 4 • Wait for the Wind • **Isaiah 40:31**
August 5 • Goliath Was the Gift • **1 Samuel 17:37**
August 6 • Righteousness Over Loyalty • **1 Corinthians 15:33**
August 7 • HALT Before You Fall • **1 Peter 5:8**
August 8 • Wisdom in Small Things • **Proverbs 6:6–8**
August 9 • Procrastination Isn't Your Friend • **Psalm 90:12**
August 10 • Who You Are in Christ, and Who Christ Is in You • **Galatians 2:20**
August 11 • The Download of Wisdom • **Joshua 1:8**
August 12 • Get Off the Wrong Train • **Proverbs 14:12**
August 13 • The Power of De-Escalation • **Proverbs 16:32**
August 14 • Getting Over You • **Ephesians 4:23–24**
August 15 • When the Word Hurts • **Hebrews 4:12**
August 16 • Abound to Enlightenment • **2 Peter 1:19**
August 17 • The End of Self • **Jeremiah 17:10**
August 18 • God Will Provide • **Philippians 4:19**
August 19 • Suddenly, The Light • **2 Peter 1:19**
August 20 • The Keys to Shining Your Light • **Matthew 16:19**
August 21 • Love Looks Like Sacrifice • **John 15:13**
August 22 • From Fearless in Foolishness to Fearless in Faith • **Jeremiah 29:11**
August 23 • Light Up the Darkness • **Matthew 5:14–16**
August 24 • Wisdom in Action • **Proverbs 3:19**
August 25 • Get in the Game • **Ephesians 6:12**
August 26 • A Shepherd and His Sheep • **Psalm 23:1–3**
August 27 • With God, Any Is Plenty • **Philippians 4:12–13**
August 28 • Discipline Is a Must • **Proverbs 22:15**
August 29 • Covered in His Dust • **1 John 2:6**
August 30 • End of Self, Rise in Christ • **Romans 6:6**
August 31 • What Temptation Tests • **James 1:13**

SEPTEMBER

September 1 • Righteous Hearted • **James 5:16b**
September 2 • Our Daily Bread • **Matthew 6:11**
September 3 • The Key of Prayer • **Matthew 7:7**
September 4 • God Is Near When You Call • **Psalm 145:18–19**
September 5 • Trust Me, I Have It Under Control • **Psalm 46:10**
September 6 • Sheep or Shepherd • **John 10:11**
September 7 • The War Within • **Romans 7:23**
September 8 • Freedom Is an Inside Job • **John 8:36**
September 9 • Sacrifice Required • **Ecclesiastes 1:18**

September 10 • In His Likeness • **2 Corinthians 3:18**
September 11 • Love Set Apart • **1 Thessalonians 4:3–4**
September 12 • Birthed Out of the Darkness • **Isaiah 45:3**
September 13 • On Earth as It Is in Heaven • **Matthew 6:10**
September 14 • When the Lights Went Out, Power Showed Up • **Acts 1:8**
September 15 • You Get What You Give • **Matthew 7:12**
September 16 • Built Low to Rise High • **James 4:6**
September 17 • The Power Already Within You • **John 8:36**
September 18 • A Good Man Leaves an Inheritance • **Proverbs 13:22**
September 19 • Purpose Is the Impact You Leave • **1 Peter 4:10–11**
September 20 • The Eyes, Ears, and Heart of Christ • **Galatians 6:2**
September 21 • Live Together or Perish Together • **1 John 4:7–8**
September 22 • Letting Go of Being Right • **Philippians 4:6–7**
September 23 • Freedom Ain't There • **2 Corinthians 3:17**
September 24 • The Equation of Divine Alignment • **Ephesians 4:23–24**
September 25 • Don't Open the Door • **Galatians 5:19–21**
September 26 • The Blessing of Being a Blessing • **Acts 20:35**
September 27 • Washed Away • **Psalm 103:12**
September 28 • Free Behind Bars • **John 8:36**
September 29 • Stay Light So You Can Take Flight • **Hebrews 12:1**
September 30 • Disciplined Growth • **Hebrews 12:11**

OCTOBER

October 1 • The Hard That Builds • **Hebrews 12:11**
October 2 • Don't Lose Your Soul Chasing the Gold • **Mark 8:36**
October 3 • Beyond the Classroom • **Colossians 2:2–3**
October 4 • Saved, But Still in Chains • **Isaiah 58:6**
October 5 • The Enemy Inside • **2 Corinthians 10:3–5**
October 6 • Blessed to Be a Blessing • **Luke 6:38**
October 7 • Spiritually Intelligent • **1 Corinthians 2:14**
October 8 • A Temple Divided Cannot Stand • **1 Corinthians 3:16**
October 9 • The Point of No Return • **Genesis 19:17**
October 10 • Peace Through Righteousness • **Isaiah 48:22**
October 11 • The Mirror That Demands Change • **James 1:23–24**
October 12 • Kindness, Not Weakness • **Romans 12:21**
October 13 • The Quiet Power of Knowing Who You Are • **Colossians 3:3**
October 14 • The Origin of the Word Helper • **Genesis 2:18**
October 15 • Love Beyond Convenience • **1 Corinthians 16:14**
October 16 • From Perform to Transform • **Ephesians 4:22–24**
October 17 • One Human Family, One Origin • **Genesis 1:27**
October 18 • Guard Your Legacy • **Proverbs 4:23**
October 19 • The Call Back to Surrender • **Galatians 2:20**

October 20 • Saved From Foolishness • **Ephesians 2:4–5**
October 21 • Awake from the Prison of Distraction • **1 Thessalonians 5:6**
October 22 • Mastery Through Calm • **Proverbs 25:28**
October 23 • Transformed by Choice • **Colossians 3:10**
October 24 • What Does Your Attitude "Smell" Like? • **Ephesians 4:31–32**
October 25 • When You Move, The Way Appears • **2 Corinthians 5:7**
October 26 • More Than 24 Hours: The Power of Divine Teamwork • **Matthew 4:18–22**
October 27 • Be Still and Know: From Beta to Alpha • **Psalm 46:10**
October 28 • It's All a Gift • **James 1:17**
October 29 • Don't Build Your Barns First • **Luke 12:20–21**
October 30 • Single and Rooted in Worth • **Psalm 139:14**
October 31 • Light in the Darkness • **John 1:5**

NOVEMBER

November 1 • Windows and Mirrors • **Matthew 7:3–5**
November 2 • Sin Is Poison to the Elevated Soul • **James 4:1**
November 3 • The Obstacle Is the Way • **James 1:2–4**
November 4 • Forgiven As I Forgive • **Matthew 6:12**
November 5 • Created to Create • **Genesis 1:27**
November 6 • Trained for Greater • **1 Samuel 17:39–40**
November 7 • Joy Beyond Happiness • **John 15:11**
November 8 • Strength in His Joy • **Nehemiah 8:10**
November 9 • Be a Conduit and Not a Cul-de-Sac • **John 7:38**
November 10 • Go Get It and Come Back With It • **Deuteronomy 11:24**
November 11 • Professing Is Not Possessing • **Matthew 7:21–23**
November 12 • The Power of "I AM" • **Proverbs 23:7a**
November 13 • True Life • **1 John 5:12**
November 14 • From Spectators to Disciples • **Hebrews 5:14**
November 15 • Focus Sets the Frequency • **Colossians 3:2**
November 16 • Training Wheels and the Teacher Within • **2 Timothy 3:16–17**
November 17 • The Rhythm of God • **1 Corinthians 14:33**
November 18 • Consistency Beats Creativity • **1 Corinthians 4:2**
November 19 • Passing the Baton • **2 Timothy 2:2**
November 20 • Invincible Ignorance vs. Visible Wisdom • **James 1:22**
November 21 • A Weight Too Heavy to Carry • **1 Peter 3:18**
November 22 • Forged in the Fire, Beautified from Brokenness • **Romans 5:3–5**
November 23 • Depth Determines Connection • **Proverbs 20:5**
November 24 • Why Consistency Is Everything • **Galatians 6:9**
November 25 • The Courage to Continue • **Galatians 6:9**

November 26 • Enlightenment as a Way of Life • **2 Peter 1:19**
November 27 • Love from the Level of Healing • **2 Corinthians 3:18**
November 28 • You Were Created for Connection • **Genesis 2:18**
November 29 • Rules to Upgrade Your Life • **1 Timothy 4:7–8**
November 30 • Supported from the Inside Out • **Psalm 46:10**

DECEMBER

December 1 • Refined in the Fire • **Isaiah 48:10**
December 2 • Take Responsibility, Stop Complaining • **Philippians 2:14–15**
December 3 • Set the Setting • **Galatians 5:22–23**
December 4 • Three Solutions • **Proverbs 3:5–6**
December 5 • To Love and Let Go • **Matthew 19:29**
December 6 • Be Still and Breathe • **Psalm 46:10**
December 7 • Beyond Your Ability but Within His Grace • **1 Corinthians 15:10**
December 8 • The Church Is a Hospital, Not a Hospice • **Psalm 147:3**
December 9 • Change Your Soil to Bloom • **Isaiah 32:15–16**
December 10 • It's Not the Arrow, It's the Archer • **2 Corinthians 4:7**
December 11 • What Would You Ask For? • **Matthew 7:7**
December 12 • Come as You Are, But Don't Stay as You Are • **2 Corinthians 5:17**
December 13 • Live for the Audience of One • **Galatians 1:10**
December 14 • Don't Get Distracted • **Psalm 16:8**
December 15 • Compassion That Breaks Our Hearts • **Matthew 9:36**
December 16 • Your Story Becomes a Survival Guide • **2 Corinthians 1:3–4**
December 17 • Thank You Father, for Saving My Life • **Psalm 28:7**
December 18 • The Battlefield of the Mind • **2 Corinthians 10:3–5**
December 19 • When Charity Becomes Toxic • **2 Thessalonians 3:10**
December 20 • Unshackled: From History to Destiny • **Philippians 3:13**
December 21 • Hidden Worship, Public Weapons • **Matthew 6:6**
December 22 • Failure Is Part of It, and the Start of It • **Proverbs 24:16**
December 23 • Secrets of Sincere Love • **Jeremiah 33:3**
December 24 • Handcuffed to History or Free for Destiny • **Isaiah 43:18–19**
December 25 • The Languages of Love • **1 Corinthians 13:13**
December 26 • Why the Shift Feels Like Rejection • **2 Timothy 3:12**
December 27 • Purposely Bright • **Philippians 2:15**
December 28 • A Beacon of Light • **Matthew 5:14**
December 29 • Training the Inner Man • **1 Timothy 4:8**
December 30 • Your Greatest Project • **Ephesians 2:10**
December 31 • Shutting the Door on Yesterday • **Philippians 3:13–14**

January 1

Driven by Purpose

Proverbs 16:3
Commit your works to the LORD and your plans will be established.

Reflection

Most people are distracted with pleasure … not because they are rebellious, but because they are living without purpose. When a person does not know why they were created, anything can entertain them, and everything can derail them.

Purpose changes that.

Purpose wakes you up with excitement.
Purpose gives your steps direction.
Purpose removes confusion and replaces it with clarity.

When you live without purpose, pleasure becomes your compass. But when you know your assignment, discipline becomes your strength. You begin to plan your work and work your plan because you understand that destiny requires structure.

The truth is simple: When a person is not excited to wake up, it is usually because they are not clear about why God woke them up. But once purpose is discovered, even small tasks feel sacred.

Application
- Identify the distractions that most often pull you away from your God-given assignment.
- Write down one plan … just one …that aligns with your purpose, and commit it to God.
- Take one step today that moves you toward living intentionally, not aimlessly.

Prayer

Lord, align my life with Your purpose. Strip away every distraction that keeps me from my assignment. Teach me to plan with wisdom, work with discipline, and walk with intention. Make me excited to rise each day … not for pleasure, but for purpose. In Jesus' name, **Amen.**

January 2
The Rewards of Sacrifice

1 Corinthians 3:8
Now he who plants and the one who waters are one, but each will receive his own reward according to his labor.

Reflection

The truth is … your rewards in life are directly correlated to your level of sacrifice.

You might see the word "sacrifice" and think of loss, hardship, giving up … but in the Kingdom it's actually a means of investment … like planting a seed.

God honors what you surrender, what you give, what you build from faith. When you step into sacrifice … serving when you'd rather rest, giving when you'd rather hold back, loving when you'd rather protect yourself … you're placing yourself in the position to receive from God.

Scripture says your labor is not in vain, because God sees and rewards what is done for Him. This doesn't mean sacrifice always leads to instant financial gain or worldly recognition … sometimes it leads to character development, depth, faith, and eternal reward. God recognizes, remembers, and will increase. What you give determines what you grow.

Application
- List one thing you're hesitant to sacrifice.
- Choose one act of sacrifice today.
- Invest boldly, trusting that your labors in the Lord are never wasted.

Prayer

Father, thank You that You see the unseen … every sacrifice, every moment of faith, every act of love. Help me to give not for applause but because You are worthy. Align my heart with Your Kingdom, where sacrifice is sowing and reward is growing. In Jesus' name, **Amen.**

January 3
Let Your Smile Change the World

Philippians 4:5
Let your gentle spirit be known to all men. The Lord is near.

Reflection
Someone once said: "Let your smile change the world ... but don't let the world change your smile." Your smile is more than a gesture ... it's your heart speaking out loud.

In a world full of bitterness and strife, a genuine display of joy reflects the presence of Christ within you.

When you allow the pressures, disappointments, and failures of life to harden your expression, you silence the hope that God intends to broadcast through you.

But when you guard the inner joy God has given, your smile becomes a powerful testimony ... announcing, "I have peace, I have purpose, I have a Father."

Ships don't sink because of water around them. Ship sink because of the water that gets in them. Don't let what's happening around you get inside you and weigh you down.

Don't let the world's noise steal your joy. Let your heart speak, let your smile shine, let your life reflect hope. Your joy may be the light someone else is in need of.

Application
- Pause for a moment: How often do I allow the world (its stress, its injustice, its rejection) to steal my smile?
- Choose today to give someone a genuine smile ... without speaking, just presence. Let that simple act reflect the hope you carry in Christ.
- Declare: "My heart is full of life. My smile is a witness. The world will see ... and God will get the glory."

Prayer
Father, thank You for placing Your joy inside me. Help me not to let the world change my smile or steal the expression of Your heart. Let my life reflect Your hope. Let my smile speak of You. In Jesus' name, **Amen**.

January 4
Die to Rise

John 3:3
Jesus answered and said to him, "Truly, truly, I say to you, unless one is born again he cannot see the kingdom of God.

Reflection
I had to die to my old self ... so that I could rise. The truth is ... we all do.

You cannot carry the old you into a new life. Your past patterns can't enter your promised land. Your old mindset can't walk in a new anointing. Being born again is not a suggestion ... it is not optional ... it is essential. It is a death followed by a rising.

You die to pride. You die to ego.
You die to lust, anger, fear, and the need to control.
You die to the version of you that survived ... so you can become the version of you that will thrive.

God is not trying to improve the old you ... He is crucifying it.
Because resurrection power only shows up where something has died. The cross is not just what Jesus carried ... it is what you must carry too. And when you release who you were, the Spirit awakens who you were always called to be.

When you let the old self go, the new self in Christ rises with power, clarity, identity, and purpose.

This is the Gospel. This is transformation. This is rebirth.

Application
- Ask the Holy Spirit to show you one old pattern that must die today.
- Replace old thinking by speaking God's truth over yourself.
- Make one decision today that reflects the new identity Christ has given you.

Prayer
Father, I surrender the old me. Every habit, every thought pattern, every fear, every desire that does not honor You ... I lay it down. Crucify what is not from You and resurrect what is. Help me to walk in the power, clarity, and identity of the new life You have given me. Let the old self die, and let Christ rise in me today. In Jesus' name, **Amen.**

January 5
Rise Again

Proverbs 24:16
For a righteous man falls seven times, and rises again,
But the wicked stumble in time of calamity.

Reflection
Nelson Mandela once said, "The greatest glory in living lies not in never falling, but in rising every time we fall." He echoed a biblical truth that God established long before the world honored his wisdom.

Falling is not failure. Staying down is.

Scripture teaches that the righteous fall repeatedly ... but what makes them righteous is not their perfection... it's their resilience. Their ability to rise again. Their refusal to let a fall become their final chapter. God never asked you to avoid every stumble. He asked you to abide in Him so He could give you the strength to rise.
Like the phoenix rises from ashes, believers rise from their brokenness ... but not by sheer willpower. We rise because Christ upholds us.

His Word rebuilds us.
His Spirit restores us.
His love lifts us.
Every time you get up, you testify that grace is stronger than guilt, purpose is stronger than pain, and God's power is greater than your past. Your rise is your glory. Your rise is your testimony. Your rise is the proof that Christ lives in you.

Application
- Stay connected to Christ ... through Scripture, prayer, worship, and obedience ... so the Holy Spirit can strengthen your inner man.
- Ask yourself today: "Where is God calling me to rise again?"
- Rise again today by trusting God's grace and taking one confident step forward in faith.

Prayer
Father, thank You for being the God who lifts me when I fall. Give me the courage to rise again ... stronger, wiser, and more surrendered than before. Let Your Word rebuild me, Your Spirit empower me, and Your love sustain me. In Jesus' name, **Amen**.

January 6
Discipline Determines Destiny

Proverbs 13:4
The soul of the sluggard craves and gets nothing,
But the soul of the diligent is made fat.

Reflection
Desire is easy. Discipline is rare.

Many people want a better life, a stronger walk with God, a healthier body, a thriving business, or deeper wisdom. But desire alone has never built a destiny.

The Bible says the lazy person "craves" … they desire, dream, wish, and imagine … but they receive nothing. Why? Because spiritual desires without spiritual discipline lead nowhere. Your destiny is not shaped by what you feel … but by what you repeat.

It is your daily habits, not your momentary emotions, that shape who you become.

Desire stirs you for a moment, but discipline builds you for a lifetime. Desire inspires; discipline transforms. Desire starts the engine; discipline takes you to the destination. Every great man or woman of God had to practice this truth.
Daniel prayed three times a day consistently. David sought God early in the morning repeatedly. Jesus withdrew to pray regularly. Not because they felt like it every day… but because their destiny required discipline. Your destiny is hidden in your daily routine.

Application
- Identify one spiritual discipline you must strengthen (prayer, reading, fasting, silence, obedience, consistency).
- Replace emotional motivation with God-centered commitment.
- Create a daily routine that aligns with where the God is taking you.

Prayer
Father, thank You for the reminder that destiny is not driven by emotion but by obedience and diligence. Shape my habits, strengthen my discipline, and make me consistent in the areas that matter most. Help me to walk intentionally, and persistently. In Jesus' name, **Amen.**

January 7
One Step at a Time

2 Corinthians 5:7
For we walk by faith, not by sight.

Reflection
Sometimes we're so focused on the horizon that we miss what God has placed right in front of us.

We stare at the size of the dream, the height of the mountain, or the weight of the task ... and it feels impossible. But the Lord never called us to finish it all in one leap. God calls us to take one step at a time ... because our victory is in the details and the diligence.

Life, like faith, unfolds one bite at a time. It's not ten thousand goals ... it's ONE.

One goal.
One objective.
One task.

The enemy wants you to see your calling as an elephant ... too big, too heavy, too much. But through Christ, it becomes bite-sized ... manageable, possible and achievable. Not by your strength, but by His power.

Remember: Jesus multiplied five loaves and two fish, and He can multiply your small steps into supernatural outcomes when you allow Him to join you in your work.

Application
- Ask yourself today: What is the one thing God is asking me to do right now?
- Break down your dream into steps, and faithfully take the next one.
- Instead of being overwhelmed by the "elephant," see it as bread ... daily provision you eat piece by piece.

Prayer
Father, thank You for reminding me that life is not meant to be swallowed whole, but lived step by step. Help me focus on the "one" You've placed before me today ... one task, one step, one act of love. Give me faith to walk forward without fear and to trust that You will multiply my steps into Your glory. In Jesus' name, **Amen.**

January 8

Wake Up: Don't Be the Walking Dead

Ephesians 5:14
For this reason it says, 'Awake, sleeper, And arise from the dead, And Christ will shine on you.

Reflection
We live in a generation that has been lulled to sleep.

The glow of entertainment, the comfort of luxury, and the lusts of the flesh have sedated countless souls into spiritual unconsciousness.

Many walk through life breathing but not living ... functioning bodies with dormant spirits. Like the walking dead, they chase pleasures but miss purpose, pursue comfort but lose calling.

The Bible is urgent: Wake up! (Romans 13:11). Time is short. Salvation is nearer now than when we first believed. The enemy doesn't need to destroy you outright if he can distract you long enough to keep you spiritually asleep.

Jesus calls us to rise from the deadness of sin, from the trance of distractions, and from the slumber of complacency. To awaken is to see clearly, live soberly, and walk faithfully. When we open our eyes to Christ, His light pierces the darkness, and His life resurrects us from within.

Application
- Ask yourself: Am I awake to God's voice, or asleep in the world's lullabies?
- Limit the distractions of entertainment, comfort, or lust that numb your spirit.
- Begin each day with prayer, Scripture, and surrender—letting God reset your mind and spirit.

Prayer
Lord, wake me up. Deliver me from the sleep of sin, the distraction of pleasure, and the numbness of this world. Let Your light shine on me, and make me fully alive in You. Keep me watchful, sober, and alert until the day You return. In Jesus' name, **Amen.**

January 9

The Rhythm of Becoming

Colossians 3:17
Whatever you do in word or deed, do all in the name of the Lord Jesus, giving thanks through Him to God the Father.

Reflection
Life is not built on moments alone … it is built on rhythms.

Who you are becoming is not the result of one great event or one powerful prayer; it's the fruit of what you repeatedly do.

Habits are more than motions. They are seeds planted in the soil of your soul, watered daily by your choices.

The truth is, what you do in the quiet will echo in the crowd. Your patterns will preach louder than your words.

Excellence is not a single act of greatness but a rhythm of faithfulness. And discipline is not punishment … it's preparation for destiny.

God's Spirit invites us into a rhythm where prayer is not occasional but daily bread, where worship is not performance but posture, where obedience is not optional but natural. This is the rhythm of becoming … the process of being transformed day by day into the likeness of Christ.

Application
- Identify one daily habit that pulls you away from God's rhythm, and replace it with one that draws you closer to Him.
- Reflect on how your unseen patterns … your prayer life, your thoughts, your study … are shaping your future more than your public words or works.
- Practice one intentional habit today …prayer, gratitude, or obedience … that aligns your daily rhythm with Christ

Prayer
Father, align my rhythm with Yours. Help me to walk in patterns that reflect Your Spirit and discipline that honors my destiny. Teach me to sow seeds in faith, water them with consistency, and trust You for the growth. May the rhythm of my becoming glorify Christ in both the quiet and the crowd. In Jesus' name, **Amen.**

January 10
Bold Moves Require Bold Faith

Joshua 1:9
Be strong and courageous! Do not be terrified nor dismayed, for the Lord your God is with you wherever you go.

Reflection
Much in life is about faith… and much of it is about resilience. Faith gives you the vision to see beyond the obstacles, and resilience gives you the strength to keep moving when the obstacles don't move. One believes, the other endures. Together, they carry you into every promise God has spoken over your life."

Life will test you with locked doors, closed opportunities, and voices that say "you can't." But faith doesn't stop at the closed door … it looks for the window, the rooftop, the path nobody else sees. Faith is both knowledge and action: knowing God's Word and then executing that Word strategically and diligently.

Resilience means you don't quit when the road is blocked. You press forward, even when others fold or deny. You keep believing in the God who believes in you. He has plans that were written before you were born (Jeremiah 29:11). And if God wrote the plan, no man can erase it.

Bold moves require bold faith. This season is not about performance but perseverance. Not about what's flashy on the outside, but about being faithful on the inside. If God is for you, you already have the victory.

Application

- Identify one "closed door" in your life and ask God to reveal the hidden opportunity behind it.
- Choose one bold step of faith to take this week, even if it scares you.
- Remind yourself daily: "My faith is bigger than my fear."

Prayer
Lord, give me the courage to move with bold faith. Teach me to see beyond closed doors and trust that You are opening the right ones. Strengthen me to persevere with resilience, and let my bold steps honor You. **Amen**.

January 11

Doing Less, But Doing Better

Philippians 4:12
I know how to get along with humble means, and I also know how to live in prosperity; in everything and in all things I have learned the secret both to be full and to hunger, both to abound and to be in want.

Reflection
Sometimes the solution isn't doing more … it's doing less better.

We live in a world where "more" seems the answer: more tasks, more responsibilities, more things to check off. But the spiritual life invites another rhythm. Jesus taught that the Kingdom's math often looks backwards to the world: less can be more.

Paul wrote that he knew how to live with little or much … and his secret wasn't quantity … it was alignment, faith, purpose.

The real shift isn't adding more tasks; it's refining the tasks you already have. It's aligning your actions with your calling, doing fewer things but investing your heart deeper into each one.

So ask: Are you adding more things to your schedule, hoping that will fix something? Or are you choosing to reduce the clutter and do the essential with excellence?

Application
- Choose one area where you're spread thin … too many commitments, too many goals.
- Decide to stop something today … or tomorrow … and instead focus your energy on one task you'll do well.
- Declare: "I will not measure success by how much I do, but by how well I do what aligns with God's purpose for me."

Prayer
Father, thank You for the wisdom of simplicity. Help me to stop racing in more, and instead walk steadily in better. Show me what to release, what to refine, and what to invest with my whole heart. Let my life honor You not by the volume of my duties, but by the value of my devotion. In Jesus' name, **Amen.**

January 12

Truth That Heals

John 8:32
And you will know the truth, and the truth will set you free.

Reflection
Many people today aren't looking for truth … they're looking for something that won't hurt their feelings.

They want comfort, acceptance, words that don't challenge, messages that fit their preference rather than their purpose. But the Gospel wasn't given to soothe our vanity … it was given to redeem our hearts.

Truth sometimes hurts, because it asks more of us than we want to give. But that hurt is not destruction … it's cleansing.

The Scriptures teach that: truth sets you free (John 8:32) and love without hypocrisy demands we hate evil and embrace what is good (Romans 12:9).

If you only listen to what pleases you, you risk missing what saves you.

The enemy loves a religion of "feelings and emotions only" … because it keeps us comfortable, but it doesn't keep us real.
Today invite yourself: Am I looking for soothing words or searching for truth?
Truth may sting … but what is broken in you craves truth more than comfort.

Application
- Ask: "What truth is my heart avoiding because it's uncomfortable?"
- Commit: Choose one correction, one truth you'll align with today …even if it challenges your comfort.
- Today reflect: "Did I choose comfort over change? Did I cling to what pleases me or what redeems me?"

Prayer
Father, forgive me for chasing messages that stroke my pride rather than shape my character. Give me ears to hear Your truth … even when it hurts … and is hard to embrace. Let Your truth not just fill my ears, but change my life. In Jesus' name, **Amen.**

January 13

Living Beyond The Conscious

Matthew 16:24
Then Jesus told His disciples, 'If anyone would come after Me, let him deny himself, take up his cross, and follow Me.

Reflection
Most of us live at the level of conscious intention ... we serve, we pray, we attend church, we contribute. That's good. But it's not the fullness of what God has called us to. True maturity moves beyond being consciously active for God to being unconsciously surrendered to God.

In other words:
The mature believer doesn't stop being aware of God ... they simply stop being aware of themselves being used by God.

They don't live for applause, visibility, or recognition. They live for presence, for obedience, for the invisible work of God in and through them.

When you still think of your service as "what I do for God", you haven't yet stepped into "who I've become in God". The goal isn't to notice your own activity ... it's to obey Christ quietly and consistently until your life is shaped more by Him than by your own agenda. Let God use you so seamlessly, you don't even have to think about the use ... you simply live in the flow of His purpose. We must move past the stage of intentional serving to total surrender.

Application
- Ask yourself: Am I operating from performance or from presence?
- Choose one small moment today to surrender your agenda to God's agenda.
- Declare: "I will stop performing. I will start abiding. I will be used ... unknown, unseen, but deeply aligned."

Prayer
Father, thank You that You don't just call me to serve You ... but to become like You. Forgive me for the times I've made my service about visibility instead of submission. Help me to move from intention to surrender ... from doing for You to living in You. Use me quietly, powerfully, and faithfully for your glory alone. In Jesus' name, **Amen.**

January 14

Give Freely, Live Abundantly

Acts 10:38
You know of Jesus of Nazareth, how God anointed Him with the Holy Spirit and with power, and how He went about doing good and healing all who were under the power of the devil; for God was with Him."

Reflection

Do good without expecting anything. Life has a way of surprising you with more than you gave.

Our calling as followers of Christ isn't to give so someone owes us ... it's to give because He first gave to us.

In Christ's ministry we see this pattern: He went about doing good without tallying the return. When you give without expectation: You reflect the heart of Christ ... kindness without calculation. You step into God's economy, where giving is not measured by what you see, but by what He sees. You open yourself to a surprise return ... not always monetary, but in character growth, opened doors, deeper relationships, multiplied peace.

Give freely.
Love boldly.
Serve humbly.

Let your life be marked by generosity, not obligation; grace, not expectation.

Application
- Today, identify one act of kindness or service without planning for praise or return.
- Say: "Lord, I give because You gave, not because I expect."
- After the act, pause and reflect: What happened inside me when I gave without keeping score?

Prayer
Father, thank You for the free gift of grace and love You poured out in Christ. Help me to give freely ... not out of obligation, but out of gratitude. Let my generosity be a reflection of Your heart. Surprise me with growth, peace, connection, and purpose. In Jesus' name, **Amen.**

January 15
Remove What Stops Growth

Hebrews 12:1
Therefore, since we have so great a cloud of witnesses surrounding us, let us also lay aside every encumbrance and the sin which so easily entangles us, and let us run with endurance the race that is set before us.

Reflection
A man once asked his gardener why his plants grew so beautifully. The gardener replied, "I don't force them to grow. I remove what stops them."
—Unknown

That is wisdom for life. Growth is not about pressuring yourself to become more or pretending to be something you are not. It is about clearing away the things that choke your purpose. Bad habits that drain your energy. Toxic environments that stunt your potential. Wrong relationships that pull you off course. Negative thought patterns that sabotage your identity. Unhealed wounds that keep you cycling in the same struggles.

These are the weights Hebrews warns us about … the unnecessary burdens and entangling sins that slow our pace and blur our vision. You cannot run freely while carrying what God never intended you to hold.

You do not need to push your destiny; you need to protect it. The race God crafted for you becomes lighter when the clutter is removed. When distractions are silenced, clarity returns. When excess is cut away, what God planted in you can finally breathe, stretch, and flourish. Just like a plant, your growth was designed into your DNA … your job is to clear the soil.

Sometimes the breakthrough is not found in doing more. It is found in letting go … releasing what no longer serves your future so the life God placed in you can rise to its full expression.

Application
- Ask God to reveal what is hindering your growth.
- Make a decision today to remove one unhealthy influence.
- Trust that pruning is preparation, not punishment.

Prayer
Father, thank You for caring enough to prune my life. Give me the courage to let go of what no longer serves Your purpose in me. Remove every hindrance so I can grow freely and fully into what You have planted. In Jesus' name, **Amen.**

January 16
You Are the Equation

Proverbs 21:5
The plans of the diligent lead to profit as surely as haste leads to poverty.

Reflection
Success is not an accident; wealth is not a coincidence. It is science, and you are the equation.

Success isn't random.
It's not a result of luck, fame, or mere hope.
It's the outcome of intentional choices ... discipline, vision, and belief.

Just as the strategies of God's kingdom work with precision and consistency, our lives follow spiritual laws.

Your habits, your mindset, your focus ... they're the variables in the equation of your destiny. When you align those with Kingdom principles, you activate divine multiplication.

Remember: prosperity in God is not just financial ... it's spiritual, emotional, relational.

Let your life reflect His order, His design, and His steadfast abundance.

Application
- Evaluate your variables: What habits or mindsets need adjustment to better align with God's design?
- Intentionally invest your energy: Make choices ... daily acts of faith, discipline, prayer ... that compound over time.
- Declare: "God's wisdom guides my strategy, and His grace multiplies my efforts."

Prayer
Heavenly Father, thank You that success under Your Kingdom isn't random ... it's designed. Help me align my thoughts, habits, and actions with Your truth. Teach me to steward my life as an equation that you multiply for Your glory and my good. In Jesus' name, **Amen.**

January 17

You Cannot Love God Without Loving Others

1 John 4:20–21
If someone says, 'I love God,' and hates his brother, he is a liar; for the one who does not love his brother whom he has seen, cannot love God whom he has not seen. And this commandment we have from Him, that the one who loves God should love his brother also.

Reflection
Loving God cannot be divorced or separated from loving His children … everyone is created in His image. You cannot truly love God unless you love the others.

John is unapologetically direct: anyone who claims to love God but harbors hatred toward a brother or sister is living a lie in the Kingdom. Loving someone you've seen is evidence that you genuinely love the One unseen.

This is not about fleeting emotions but deliberate action. One author reminds us that love is a verb … not merely a warm feeling but a choice to act lovingly, even toward those who have hurt us or whom we find difficult to relate to.

God's love is not dormant … it flows to us first, then through us to others.

Our love for people is not optional; it is the only tangible demonstration of our love for God.

Application
- Look beyond your comfort zone. Identify someone you struggle to love or perhaps disagree with. Pray for a loving posture toward them today.
- Love as Jesus loved. Let agape love … not emotions … lead your actions. Serve, forgive, and honor, even when it's hard.
- Reflect His love. Ask yourself: Am I loving God in how I treat His children?

Prayer
Father, You are love … and Your love streams into my life every day. Teach me to love as You love. Help me see others through Your eyes, and to lovingly act toward them … not because I feel like it, but because You command it. May my love for others be the clearest expression of my love for You. **Amen.**

January 18

For Him, Not For Us

Colossians 1:16
For by Him all things were created, both in the heavens and on earth, visible and invisible, whether thrones or dominions or rulers or authorities … all things have been created through Him and for Him.

Reflection
So many people have this backwards! GOD DOES NOT EXIST FOR US … WE EXIST FOR GOD!

Too often, faith is approached like a vending machine: insert prayer, expect blessing. We treat God like a genie, expecting Him to fulfill our plans, our dreams, our comfort. But that mindset flips creation on its head. He is not our accessory … we are His creation.

You were not made to chase blessings … you were made to glorify God and be a blessing.

He is the Author, we are the story.
He is the Potter, we are the clay.

The sooner we shift from "God, bless my plans" to "God, show me Yours," the sooner we align with our true identity and calling.

That "for Him" part in Colossians 1:16 changes everything. You are created through Him and for Him. Your gifts, your influence, your resources, your very breath … all exist for His glory.

Application
- Examine your prayers this week: are they mostly about God serving your desires, or about you surrendering to His?
- Start your day by asking: "Lord, how can I glorify You today?"
- Rewrite one of your personal goals in God-centered language: instead of
- "I want to succeed," pray "Lord, let this success point others to You."

Prayer
Father, forgive me when I treat You like You exist for me. Remind me that I was created for You … to bring You glory, serve You faithfully, and walk in the purpose You designed. Help me to surrender my plans, my will, and my desires. Teach me to live for Your will and not my own. Use me for Your glory. In Jesus' name, **Amen.**

January 19

Look, Listen, and Learn

Proverbs 4:20–21
My son, give attention to my words; Incline your ear to my sayings. Do not let them depart from your sight; Keep them in the midst of your heart.

Reflection
Growth in God begins with awareness.

To look is to notice what He is showing you in His Word and in your daily walk.

To listen is to quiet the noise long enough to hear His Spirit guiding you.

To learn is to take what you've seen and heard and put it into practice.

Many stumble not because God is silent, but because they never slow down to look or listen. Learning is the natural fruit of paying attention. Every trial, every blessing, and every correction is a classroom.

If your eyes are fixed on Him and your ears are tuned to His voice, then wisdom becomes your teacher and Christ your model.

Application
- Set aside five minutes today to look at God's Word with undivided focus.
- Practice listening by silencing distractions and inviting the Holy Spirit to speak.
- Record one truth you've learned today and apply it in action before the day ends.

Prayer
Father, give me eyes that see beyond the surface, ears that discern Your voice, and a heart that is willing to learn. Teach me through Your Word, through my experiences, and through Your Spirit, that I may walk in wisdom and grow into the likeness of Christ. In Jesus' name, **Amen.**

January 20

In the Huddle

Jeremiah 29:11
For I know the plans that I have for you,' declares the Lord, 'plans for welfare and not for calamity, to give you a future and a hope.

Reflection
Life is not a pickup game; it's a divine playbook. When God calls the huddle, He has already drawn up the perfect play for your victory.

Too often we break from the huddle and try to run our own routes ... only to end up frustrated, off course, or missing the blessing that was meant for us.

Like a wide receiver waiting on the quarterback, your role is to trust the play and run the route.

If God says, "Go long," then stretch your faith and go! The ball will come your way in His timing, because He never calls a play without a purpose.

His plan is already designed for your good, your future, and your hope.

Application
- Pause and ask: Am I following the play God gave me, or am I making up my own?
- Commit to studying His playbook daily ... the Word ... so you know His voice in the huddle.
- Run your route with faith, even when you can't see the ball yet. Trust that God delivers on time.

Prayer
Father, thank You for being the ultimate Coach and Author of my playbook. Forgive me for running my own routes outside of Your huddle. Help me to trust Your calls, run with faith, and believe that what You have purposed for me will come in due season. I receive the future and hope You've already planned. In Jesus' name, **Amen**.

January 21

Service: The Secret to Greatness

Matthew 25:40
And the King will answer and say to them, 'Truly I say to you, to the extent that you did it for one of the least of these brothers or sisters of Mine, you did it for Me.

Reflection
The Kingdom flips the script ... greatness isn't about how many serve you but how many you serve.

Service multiplies impact and reflects Christ's heart.

The world seeks crowns; Jesus stooped to wash feet. True greatness is measured in humility, not hierarchy.

When you serve, you step into divine purpose ... because in serving others, you're serving Christ Himself.

Every act of service plants eternal seeds that outlive the moment, echoing in Heaven long after the applause of men fades away.

Don't grow weary in well doing.

Application
- Look for one opportunity today to serve someone without recognition.
- Ask: "How can I bless rather than impress?"
- Declare: "Service is my strength, not my sacrifice."

Prayer
Lord, make me a servant like You, shaping my heart to reflect Your humility and compassion. Teach me to measure my life not by what I accumulate, but by what I willingly pour out for others. Open my eyes to the overlooked and the hurting, reminding me that every act of love toward them is service unto You. Guide my hands, my words, and my steps today so that my service brings You glory alone. **Amen.**

January 22
Choose Your Company Wisely

1 Corinthians 15:33
Do not be deceived: 'Bad company corrupts good morals.'

Reflection
Eighty percent of your success has nothing to do with talent, timing, or opportunity… It has everything to do with who you choose to walk with. Because people are spiritual environments … they either feed you or drain you, sharpen you or dull you, strengthen you or sabotage you. You can have a great plan, a pure heart, and a God-given assignment… and still miss destiny simply because you stayed connected to the wrong people.

Bad company doesn't just corrupt your morals … it corrupts your mindset, your momentum, your money, and your mission. The wrong circle can make you doubt what God said, delay what God started, and diminish what God placed in you. Some people are not evil … just misaligned. Some are not wicked … just wrong for where you're going. And some connections cost more than they give.

God will often change your circle before He changes your life … because elevation always requires separation. You cannot run after purpose while entertaining people who celebrate your dysfunction. You cannot pursue destiny while holding onto company that is comfortable with your bondage.

Choose your company like your future depends on it … because it does. Walk with the wise → you rise. Walk with fools → you fall. Your circle is your ceiling. Guard it with discernment, courage, and truth.

Application
- Evaluate your circle: Who consistently drains your faith, focus, or peace? Who pushes you closer to God?
- Set one boundary today with a person who pulls you away from purpose.
- Pray for divine connections … people who sharpen your character, fuel your growth, and honor your calling.

Prayer
Lord, give me the courage to choose my company wisely. Remove every relationship that corrupts my purpose, delays my development, or distracts my discernment. Surround me with people who sharpen my spirit, honor my calling, and align with Your will for my life. Teach me to value peace over popularity and purpose over comfort. In Jesus' name, **Amen.**

January 23

The Fulfillment of the Law Is Love

Matthew 5:17
Do not presume that I came to abolish the Law or the Prophets; I did not come to abolish, but to fulfill.

Reflection
Jesus made it clear ... He did not come to erase the law but to embody it.

The law was always pointing us toward something greater: love. The fulfillment of the law is not in rituals or rule keeping but in God's love flowing through us until we ourselves become love and light to all mankind.

In the Old Testament, the focus was on doing and not doing ... sacrifices, ceremonies, and strict observance of the commandments. But the New Testament shifts the focus from performance to transformation. Through Christ, we are called to become ... to abound in God's divine nature and purpose.

This becoming is not about checking boxes, but about allowing the Spirit to shape us from the inside out. It is about becoming holy, becoming sanctified, and ultimately becoming love. When God's love fills our hearts, obedience is no longer a burden; it is the overflow of who we are in Him.

The law sets the boundaries, but Christ reveals the goal ... to be conformed to His image, reflecting the Father's love and shining His light in a dark world. The call of the gospel is not just to do differently, but to be different.

Application
- Ask the Holy Spirit to shape your character today so your obedience flows from love, not obligation.
- Look for one opportunity to reflect Christ's love to someone who needs light, patience, or kindness.
- Examine your actions and motives to ensure they align with becoming more like Christ, not just doing Christian things.

Prayer
Lord, thank You that Jesus fulfilled the law and showed us the fullness of love. Transform me by Your Spirit so that I may not just follow rules, but become love and light to those around me. May my life reflect Your divine nature and purpose in everything I do. **Amen.**

January 24
Stay Honestly Free

Ephesians 4:25
Therefore, laying aside falsehood, speak truth each one of you with his neighbor, for we are members of one another.

Reflection
Honesty builds trust and reflects Christ, who is Truth Himself.

Lies enslave, but truth liberates. A half-truth is a whole lie, but honesty is the foundation of authentic relationships and Kingdom credibility.

Truth is not just something we speak … it's something we embody and live.

When we choose honesty, we choose freedom.
When we choose deception, we choose bondage.

Truth doesn't just cleanse our lips; it purifies our character.
It strengthens our witness.
It guards our integrity.

And it creates a space where real love, real healing, and real accountability can thrive.

Every time we tell the truth … even when it's uncomfortable … we align ourselves with the God who cannot lie. And when we commit to living truthfully with one another, we build a community where masks come off, hearts open up, and Christ is revealed through our authenticity.

Application
- Commit to complete honesty today … even in the small things.
- Ask: "Does what I'm saying align with God's truth?"
- Declare: "I live in truth, and truth sets me free."

Prayer
Lord, cleanse my lips and heart of deceit. Make me a person of truth who honors You with integrity. Give me the courage to speak truth in love, even when it costs me, and shape my character to reflect Your holiness in every word I say. **Amen.**

January 25
Compassion: The Heart That Heals

Ephesians 4:32
Be kind to one another, compassionate, forgiving each other, just as God in Christ also has forgiven you.

Reflection
Compassion literally means to suffer with … from 'com,' meaning with, and 'passion,' meaning to suffer … reminding us that true compassion chooses to enter another's pain rather than avoid it.

Compassion moves us beyond sympathy into action. It feels deeply, but it also responds tangibly. Jesus was "moved with compassion" before He healed, fed, and taught. Compassion is not weakness … it is Heaven's strength flowing through the human heart.

True compassion remembers what God did for you first. It humbles you, softens you, and stretches your capacity to love people who may not "deserve" it.

Compassion says, "I see your pain, and I refuse to walk past it."

It looks like patience with the difficult, grace for the wounded, and forgiveness for the guilty.

When we choose compassion, we choose to mirror the heart of Christ … the One who forgave us long before we ever got it right. Compassion is not simply an emotion; it's a Kingdom response that brings healing, unity, and restoration wherever it flows.

Application
- Notice someone's struggle today and offer practical help.
- Forgive someone who doesn't "deserve" it.
- Declare: "I carry the compassion of Christ wherever I go."

Prayer
Lord, soften my heart to feel what others feel and give me the courage to step into their pain with Your compassion. Teach me to love, forgive, and respond the way Christ has responded to me … with mercy, patience, and grace. Let Your healing flow through my life so that others encounter Your kindness through my actions. **Amen.**

January 26

Gratitude: The Key to Elevation

1 Thessalonians 5:18
In everything give thanks; for this is the will of God for you in Christ Jesus.

Reflection
Gratitude is your best attitude and will change your altitude.

Gratitude lifts the soul, empowering you to climb into higher realms of holiness.

Gratitude shifts the heart from lack to abundance. It heals bitterness, fuels joy, and strengthens resilience.

To thank God in everything … even hardship … is to trust His sovereignty.

Gratitude doesn't ignore reality; it redefines it through Heaven's lens. It takes your eyes off what's missing and opens them to what God is already doing. A grateful spirit silences complaint, disarms envy, and creates room for peace to dwell.

Gratitude transforms trials into testimonies and setbacks into stepping stones, because it sees life not as random chaos but as the unfolding of God's good plan.

When your perspective elevates, your gratitude elevates with it.
Stay grateful, think higher, live lighter.

Application
- List three things you often overlook and thank God for them.
- Express appreciation to one person today.
- Declare: "Gratitude is my attitude … and it lifts my altitude."

Prayer
Lord, cultivate in me a heart of gratitude that sees Your hand in every season. Teach me to thank You not only for what is good, but also in what is difficult, trusting that every moment is woven with purpose. Lift my spirit above negativity and complaint, and fill me with a thankful heart that honors You, strengthens me, and elevates my life. **Amen.**

January 27

Through Devotion

Psalm 37:4
Delight yourself in the Lord; and He will give you the desires of your heart.

Reflection
Devotion is more than a feeling ... it is love expressed through loyalty, obedience, and discipline.

Earth, Wind & Fire once sang: "Through devotion, blessed are the children... your devotion opens all life's treasures and deliverance from the fruits of evil." While those words rang out in song, the Scriptures give us the eternal truth: true devotion begins with God.

Jesus modeled this devotion. He loved and served others. He obeyed the Father perfectly. He lived a life disciplined, surrendered, and fully aligned with His Father's will: "I have come down from heaven, not to do My own will, but the will of Him who sent Me" (John 6:38).

This kind of devotion transforms us. Paul reminds us that we are not our own, but bought with a price (1 Corinthians 6:19–20). To call Jesus Lord means to accept Him as Boss ...not consultant. Romans 12:1–2 urges us to present ourselves as living sacrifices, refusing conformity to the world and choosing transformation through the renewing of our minds.

And what does transformation produce? Revelation. As we grow in the image of Christ, His Word and Spirit unlocks a deeper knowledge of His will, His power, and His peace. This is how we overcome the world (1 John 5:4) ... not by striving in our own strength, but by faith in Christ and devotion to His commands.

The secret to a successful life is not luck or hustle ... it is devotion to God.

Application
- Where do I need to deepen my devotion today?
- How will I delight in the Lord first?
- What must I surrender to grow closer to Christ?

Prayer
Father, I delight in You today. Teach me to walk in love, to obey without hesitation, and to discipline my heart to stay devoted to You. Transform me by Your Spirit until my life reflects Christ. May my devotion shine as a light to others and glorify You in all I do. In Jesus' name, **Amen.**

January 28

Consistency: The Steady Drip of Success

Galatians 6:9
Let us not lose heart in doing good, for in due time we will reap if we do not grow weary.

Reflection
Consistency is the bridge between desire and destiny.

One prayer may move the heart, but a consistent prayer life transforms the soul.

One act of kindness can inspire, but consistent kindness builds trust.

The world often celebrates intensity, but God honors faithfulness. It's the steady drip of obedience, day by day, that shapes the rock of character. Just as rivers carve valleys and stones are polished smooth over time, so too does consistency carve Christlike character within us.

Desire sets the direction, but only disciplined faithfulness gets you to the destination. God doesn't just look at what we do once in a moment of passion; He measures the rhythm of our walk, the daily steps of trust, and the long obedience in the same direction.

True transformation isn't in quick bursts of excitement … it's in the steady flame of faith that never goes out.

Application
- Choose one small but meaningful action (Scripture reading, gratitude journal, exercise) and commit to doing it daily.
- Resist the urge to measure progress by speed; measure it by steadiness.
- Declare: "I will not quit. My consistency will produce my harvest."

Prayer
Lord, strengthen my spirit to walk in steady, unwavering faithfulness. Help me to show up daily … praying, trusting, obeying … even when the results seem slow. Shape my character through consistency, and let every small step of obedience draw me closer to the harvest You have promised. **Amen.**

January 29
Patience: The Power of the Wait

James 1:4
But let patience have its perfect result, so that you may be perfect and complete, lacking in nothing.

Reflection
Patience is not passivity ... it is active trust in God's timing.

It is the quiet confidence that God is working, even when nothing seems to be moving. Long-suffering is strength, not weakness, because it takes a Spirit-controlled heart to remain steady when circumstances feel slow, delayed, or uncertain.

Waiting is not wasted when it becomes worship ... when you choose to praise instead of panic and trust instead of forcing your own way.

Patience is the training ground of faith. It stretches us, shapes us, and strips us of the illusion that we control outcomes.

In the waiting, God refines motives, purifies desires, and strengthens character. This is why James says patience makes us "perfect and complete" ... because something happens in us while we wait that could never happen if God gave us everything when we asked.

Patience isn't just surviving the delay; it's becoming more like Christ in the delay. When patience finishes its work, you emerge whole, grounded, and ready for the blessing God has prepared.

Application
- Surrender one situation where you're tempted to rush.
- Practice stillness for 10 minutes, inviting God's peace.
- Declare: "I trust God's timing more than my own."

Prayer
Lord, help me trust Your timing even when I feel rushed or impatient. Strengthen my heart to remain steady, believing You are working in ways I cannot see. Let patience complete its work in me so I become more like Christ in every season of waiting. **Amen.**

January 30

Focus: Eyes Fixed on Purpose

Proverbs 4:25
Let your eyes look directly ahead and let your gaze be fixed straight in front of you.

Reflection
Distraction is the enemy of destiny.

One of Satan's greatest weapons isn't destruction ... it's diversion.

If he can't break you, he will try to busy you. If he can't stop your anointing, he will try to scatter your attention. That's why focus is spiritual warfare. Focus clears the noise, sharpens vision, and anchors your heart in what truly matters.

Jesus modeled this perfectly. Scripture says He "set His face toward Jerusalem," meaning His mind, His heart, and His steps were locked in on the cross. Undistracted. Unwavering. Unshaken. His focus fueled His obedience, and His obedience fulfilled His mission. Likewise, your fixation will determine your future. Your direction follows your attention.

The enemy knows he doesn't need to destroy you if he can simply distract you. One glance backward, one compromise sideways, or one obsession with the trivial can delay what God is trying to do in your life. Every great calling requires great concentration. When your eyes are fixed on God's purpose, the temporary loses its pull, and the eternal gains its weight.

Focus is mastery of attention. And what you focus on will either drain your destiny or drive you toward it. Guard your gaze. Guard your attention. Guard your mind. Your future is tied to your focus.

Application
- Write down your top 3 priorities for today and remove one distraction.
- Begin and end your day by focusing your mind on God's Word.
- Declare: "My focus is my power ... I fix my eyes on Jesus."

Prayer
Lord, fix my eyes on the purpose You've placed before me and silence every distraction that pulls me away from Your will. Strengthen my focus so I walk with clarity, conviction, and courage. Keep my heart anchored in Your Word and my vision locked on Jesus, the Author and Finisher of my faith. **Amen.**

January 31
Integrity: Wholeness in Action

Proverbs 11:3
The integrity of the upright will guide them, but the crookedness of the treacherous will destroy them.

Reflection
Integrity is doing right when no one is watching … being the same person in the dark that you are in the light.

Integrity means living whole … without duplicity, without secret compromises, without hypocrisy. It is the alignment of your heart, your words, and your actions under the authority of God. Integrity becomes your internal GPS, guiding you when the path is unclear and protecting you from decisions that could sabotage your destiny.

Without integrity, success is fragile. It may shine for a moment, but it cannot stand the weight of pressure, temptation, or time. But with integrity, your life becomes a testimony that withstands storms, criticism, temptation, and spiritual warfare. Integrity builds trust with people and credibility with Heaven. It keeps your conscience clean, your character strong, and your steps steady.

The crooked may seem to rise quickly, but their foundation is hollow … and hollow things collapse. The upright may rise slower, but they rise steadier, because integrity is a safeguard, a covering, and a compass. When integrity guides you, you don't have to manipulate outcomes, defend lies, or fear exposure. You walk in freedom, clarity, and confidence because your life is rooted in truth.Integrity doesn't make life easier … but it makes life stronger. And strong lives last.

Application
- Evaluate one area where your actions don't match your words. Correct it today.
- Let your "yes" be yes and your "no" be no.
- Declare: "I walk in integrity … my life aligns with God's truth."

Prayer
Lord, shape my heart to love truth and strengthen me to live with integrity in every place, seen and unseen. Expose anything in me that is misaligned, and give me the courage to correct it quickly. Guide my steps with Your wisdom, keep my character steady under pressure, and let my life reflect the wholeness and honesty that honor You. In Jesus' name, **Amen.**

February 1
Winning Where It Matters Most

1 Timothy 5:8
But if anyone does not provide for his own, and especially for those of his household, he has denied the faith and is worse than an unbeliever.

Reflection
We're winning at work. We're winning with peers. But are we winning at home?

Too often we celebrate public victories while suffering private defeats. We can get applause in the boardroom and silence in the bedroom. We can post wins online but live in brokenness offline. But God does not measure success by platform ... He measures success by faithfulness, and faithfulness begins in the home.

The real scoreboard isn't promotions, followers, or awards. The scoreboard starts at the dinner table, in the hallway conversations, in the prayers whispered over our children, and in the ways we serve our families without applause. Marriage is a battleground. Family is sacred territory. And the enemy knows that if he can corrupt the foundation, the entire structure will collapse ... no matter how beautiful it appears publicly. This is a call to husbands and wives, mothers and fathers, and believers of all ages: Do not succeed publicly while failing privately. Fix the foundation.

Stop neglecting what matters most.
Start praying with and for your spouse.
Rebuild what you have allowed to break.

Peace doesn't come through perfection ... it comes through presence, persistence, and prayer. True success begins at home.

Application
- Evaluate honestly: What area of your home life needs your presence, repentance, or intentionality?
- Prioritize connection: Pray with or encourage one family member today.
- Declare: "I win where it matters most ... at home, in integrity, and in love."

Prayer
Father, heal our homes and restore our foundations. Strengthen our marriages, our families, and the private places no one sees but You. Give us wisdom, humility, and courage to be faithful where it matters most. Make our private lives holy, whole, and aligned with Your truth. In Jesus' name, **Amen.**

February 2
Stay Light So You Can Take Flight

Psalm 51:10
Create in me a clean heart, O God, and renew a steadfast spirit within me.

Reflection
In ancient Egyptian belief, a soul was judged by the "Weighing of the Heart." The heart was placed on one side of a scale, and the Feather of Ma'at ... symbolizing truth and righteousness ... was placed on the other. If the heart was lighter, the soul could enter paradise; if heavier, it was devoured and lost.

We don't embrace that system, but the symbolism speaks loudly: a heavy heart cannot rise. Sin is heavy. Guilt weighs the soul down. Bitterness, lies, pride, un-forgiveness, and secret sins sink the heart to the ground. But righteousness, truth, humility, and purity lighten the load. A clean heart is a free heart.

David cried out, "Create in me a clean heart, O God..." ... and Jesus answered that cry at the cross. He didn't come to weigh your heart; He came to wash it. He came to lift the weight off your soul so you could live light, walk free, and rise above everything that once held you down.

A pure heart doesn't just behave differently ... it flies differently.
It sees God clearly. (Matthew 5:8)
It carries a lighter burden. (Matthew 11:30)
It lives unchained, unburdened, unhindered.

Stay light. Stay humble. Stay right with God.
Because the lighter your heart, the higher your spiritual flight.

Application
- Identify what is weighing your heart down ...sin, guilt, resentment, or worry ... and release it to God in prayer.
- Choose one act of purity today: forgiveness, confession, honesty, or humility.
- Declare: "My heart stays light because God keeps it clean."

Prayer
Father, search my heart and remove anything that makes it heavy. Cleanse my spirit, renew my mind, and free me from every weight that keeps me grounded. Help me walk in purity, humility, and truth so I can rise higher in You. Lord, keep my heart light so my life can take flight. In Jesus' name, **Amen.**

February 3
Soul Over Selfie

1 Samuel 16:7
But the Lord said to Samuel, 'Do not look at his appearance or at the height of his stature, because I have rejected him; for God sees not as man sees, for man looks at the outward appearance, but the Lord looks at the heart.'

Reflection
The mirror was never the problem ... our obsession with it was.

Humanity began to drift when we became more fixated on the image than the imago Dei ... the image of God within. Mirrors reflect truth, but never the full truth. They show the body, but remain silent about the soul.

We live in a mirror culture: polished, filtered, curated, and self-branded. The world tells us to chase approval through appearance, performance, and perception. But God calls us to live from identity ... an identity rooted in who He created us to be, not in how people perceive us.

When image becomes an idol, identity becomes distorted. The soul shrinks under the weight of self-obsession. The more we chase applause, the emptier we feel. God is still looking ... not at the angles, outfits, highlights, or platforms, but at the heart.

Your reflection may get likes, but only your soul can be loved. So let go of the pressure to perform. Step away from the mirror of public opinion and return to the God who formed you in the secret place and knows you beyond the surface.

You weren't created merely to be seen ...
You were created so that God might be seen through you.

Application
- Identify one place you've prioritized image over character.
- Choose one soul-strengthening action today: prayer, Scripture, worship, or silence.
- Declare: "I value who I am in God more than how I appear to others."

Prayer
Lord, search my heart and free me from the pressure to perform for people. Restore my identity in You and shape my character from the inside out. Help me value purity over popularity and depth over image so that Your glory ... not mine ... is what others see. In Jesus' name, **Amen.**

February 4
Be Bright On Purpose

Matthew 5:16
Let your light shine before men in such a way that they may see your good works, and glorify your Father who is in heaven.

Reflection
Light doesn't apologize for shining.

When Jesus said, "Let your light shine," He wasn't offering a suggestion ... He was issuing a charge. You were never meant to blend in. You were created to brighten, to illuminate, to reflect the presence and power of God in dark places.

But life has a way of dimming us. Critics, insecurity, failure, distraction ... even the slow grind of routine ... can put a bushel over the flame God lit within you. That's why you must be bright ... on purpose.

Purposeful brightness means speaking when silence would be easier ... serving when selfishness would be justified ... loving when judgment feels deserved. Your light isn't for attention ... it's for direction. Your glow is not about you ... it's about leading others to Him.

Let the world see your good works ... not for applause, but for God's glory. Your excellence at work ... your kindness under pressure ... your peace in chaos ... your courage when tested ...these are your beacons. Keep them lit.

So today, don't flicker. Don't hide. Don't dim.

Be bright on purpose.

Application
- Identify what dims your light most ... fear, distraction, or people's opinions.
- Choose one act of purposeful brightness today ... serve, speak, or encourage.
- Declare: "My light shines for God's glory ... not my own."

Prayer
Lord, thank You for the light You've placed within me. Strengthen me to shine with courage, humility, and joy. Let my life reflect Your glory so others are drawn to You. In Jesus' name, **Amen.**

February 5

You vs YOU

Galatians 5:17
For the flesh sets its desire against the Spirit, and the Spirit against the flesh; for these are in opposition to one another, so that you may not do the things that you please.

Reflection
The greatest fight of your life isn't with the devil.
It's not with your enemies, your past, or the culture.

It's you vs YOU.

There is a war inside every believer. One part of you craves holiness … the other craves indulgence. One part of you wants to pray … the other wants to scroll. One part of you desires peace … the other wants payback. This is the ancient battle between flesh and Spirit, and the battleground is your soul.

The flesh is the old you … self-centered, impulsive, rebellious.
The Spirit is the new you … God-conscious, surrendered, renewed.
And your soul … your mind, will, and emotions … is the prize.

If the flesh wins, sin gains ground.
If the Spirit wins, righteousness rules.
This is why Paul said, "I discipline my body and make it my slave…"
because he understood that the greatest victory isn't external … it's internal.

You cannot win this war by willpower alone. But if you surrender to the Holy Spirit, He strengthens you to overcome the old you.

Walk by the Spirit … and you won't carry out the desires of the flesh.

Application
- Identify one area where your flesh is winning more often than your spirit.
- Choose one daily discipline to strengthen your spiritual life.
- Declare: "I walk by the Spirit … and I win the war within."

Prayer
Lord, I surrender every part of me to You. Strengthen me by Your Spirit to overcome the battles within and walk in victory. Take my mind, my will, and my heart, and align them with Your truth. In Jesus' name, **Amen.**

February 6

Stop Chasing Sand

Matthew 7:24
Everyone who hears these words of Mine and acts on them will be like a wise man who built his house on the rock.

Reflection
Stop chasing sand.

Sand looks promising ... sunlit, soft, and easy to move. But try to stand on it during a storm and it collapses beneath you. Try to build your life on it and it crumbles under the winds of pressure, opinion, and pain.

Many of us chase sand without realizing it ...
Quick success without structure ...
Relationships without covenant ...
Status without substance ...
Feelings without faith.

Jesus said the wise build on rock, but the foolish build on sand. The good news is this ... God can transform the sand. All it needs is Living Water.

When you add Jesus ... the Living Water ... to what was once shifting and unstable, it begins to solidify. Just as water mixed with sand becomes concrete, the Word and the Spirit can take scattered pieces of your life and form a firm foundation.

He takes unstable places and makes them unshakable.
He turns wastelands into worksites.
He doesn't erase the sand ... you just needed the right mix.

You weren't made to chase sand. You were made to stand on the Rock.

Application
- Identify one area of your life where you've been building on sand.
- Invite the Living Water ... Jesus .. into that place today.
- Declare: "I build my life on the Rock ... not shifting sand."

Prayer
Lord, reveal every place where I've been chasing what won't last. Pour Your Living Water into my weakness and make my foundation strong. Help me build my life on Your truth, Your Word, and Your presence. In Jesus' name, **Amen.**

February 7
Struggle Is the Assignment

1 Peter 5:10
After you have suffered for a little while, the God of all grace ... will Himself perfect, confirm, strengthen, and establish you.

Reflection
"Struggle is the meaning of life. Defeat or victory is in the hands of God ... but struggle itself is man's duty and should be his joy."

Struggle = Assignment.
Struggle = Refinement.
Struggle = Purpose.

We often treat hardship like an interruption ... as if struggle is something to escape rather than something to embrace. But what if the struggle is the curriculum? What if the valley is where the real transformation happens?

Diamonds don't form in convenience ... they form under crushing pressure. In the same way, spiritual maturity is not developed in comfort, but in endurance. God never wastes the hard things. He uses pressure to stretch you, suffering to strengthen you, and struggle to sanctify you.

This season may not feel good ... but it is producing something God calls good. So don't just go through it ... grow through it. Every tear, every test, every tension is forming spiritual muscle you will need for the next level.

Embrace the process.
Endure the tension.
Struggle with purpose, knowing the hands forming you are divine.

Application
- Identify one struggle you are currently facing and surrender it to God.
- Look for one character trait God may be refining through this season.
- Declare: "My struggle has purpose ... and God is strengthening me through it."

Prayer
Lord, help me see my struggle as part of Your assignment for my growth. Strengthen my heart to endure the pressure with faith and expectation. Use every challenge to shape me, refine me, and draw me closer to You. In Jesus' name, **Amen.**

February 8
The Smallest Shift, The Biggest Life

Romans 12:2
And do not be conformed to this world, but be transformed by the renewing of your mind, so that you may prove what the will of God is, that which is good and acceptable and perfect.

Reflection
The smallest shift in your mind can unlock your biggest life.

Most of us think our breakthrough is out there somewhere … a new job … a new relationship … a new opportunity … But the Kingdom doesn't work from the outside in … it works from the inside out. God is far more interested in renewing your mindset than rearranging your circumstances.

One small shift … one new thought … one healed belief … one renewed perspective … can break chains that years of striving could never touch. Because most of our battles aren't on the job … they're not in our bank account … they're not even in the people around us … they're in our thinking.

Sometimes God doesn't send a storm to change things … He sends a whisper. A nudge. A gentle adjustment in how you see yourself, your future, and your God. You're waiting on a "big move," but Heaven is waiting on a "small yes" in your mind.

Don't overlook the small changes. Don't despise the small shifts. The smallest key can open the largest door. The enemy wants to keep you locked in old patterns … old stories about who you are, what you deserve, and what is possible. But the Holy Spirit wants to rewrite those stories with truth. Keep growing. Keep shifting.

Application
- Identify your "stuck thought" and write it down.
- Replace it with God's truth and speak it aloud today.
- Declare: "My mind is being renewed … and my life is being transformed."

Prayer
Father, thank You that transformation begins in my mind, not just my circumstances. I surrender every old pattern … fear, doubt, shame, and smallness. Renew my mind by Your Word and shift my perspective until I see myself and my future through Your truth. Let one small shift in my thinking open big doors of purpose and peace. In Jesus' name, **Amen.**

February 9
No Enemies?

Luke 6:26
Woe to you when all men speak well of you, for their fathers used to treat the false prophets in the same way.

Reflection
If you've lived long enough to take a stand for righteousness, chances are … you've made an enemy or two. And that's not a bad thing.

In his bold poem "No Enemies," Charles Mackay delivers a timeless challenge:

"You have no enemies, you say?
Alas! my friend, the boast is poor…"

To stand for truth is to stand against lies.
To pursue justice is to confront injustice.
To follow Christ is to challenge the crowd.

The more your light shines, the more it exposes what has been hiding in the dark … and not everyone will thank you for it.

Jesus Himself warned that being universally praised is not the mark of a prophet … but of a counterfeit. When no one is offended by your faith, it may be because your faith isn't confronting anything. Real love tells the truth even when it costs comfort. Real courage risks rejection for the sake of righteousness.

So if you've ruffled feathers, rejoice. You are likely standing on the right side of history … and His story.

Application
- Ask yourself whether you are seeking to be liked or to be light.
- Identify one truth God is calling you to speak with courage.
- Declare: "I stand for truth … even when truth stands alone."

Prayer
Lord, give me the courage to speak truth with love, even when it's unpopular. Strengthen my heart to stand firm in righteousness and not bow to the pressure of public opinion. Help me live boldly, faithfully, and authentically for You. In Jesus' name, **Amen.**

February 10
The Healing Power of Kindness

Hebrews 13:16
Do not neglect to do good and to share what you have, for such sacrifices are pleasing to God.

Reflection
Kindness heals mind, body, and soul.

Science now reveals what scripture declared long ago … kindness is not just emotion … it is healing medicine. Whether we give it, receive it, or simply witness it, our bodies respond in remarkable, God-designed ways.

Receiving kindness boosts serotonin, lowers blood pressure, and strengthens the immune system. Giving kindness produces the same biological benefits … sometimes even stronger … elevating mood, immunity, and heart health. Observing kindness releases oxytocin and serotonin, lowering stress and inflammation … like a natural antidepressant that lifts the spirit and softens the heart.

Kindness is Heaven's ripple effect. It restores us. It reconnects us. It reflects God's heart in the simplest ways.

Be generous with kindness … Be gracious in receiving it … Be attentive in noticing it.

God designed kindness not only as an act of love … but as a pathway to physical, emotional, and spiritual restoration. When we reflect His compassion in small moments, we light up our world.

Let kindness become your daily medicine.

Application
- Take one intentional step of kindness today … hold a door, encourage someone, or bless a stranger.
- Receive a kind gesture without deflecting or minimizing it.
- Declare: "Kindness is healing me … and healing the world through me."

Prayer
Father, thank You for the healing power of kindness. Teach me to give it freely, receive it humbly, and notice it intentionally. Let every gesture of care reflect Your heart and bring restoration to those around me. In Jesus' name, **Amen.**

February 11
The Sacred Struggle

James 1:12
Blessed is the man who remains steadfast under trial ... for once he has been approved, he will receive the crown of life which the Lord has promised to those who love Him.

Reflection
In God's Kingdom, achievement is about getting comfortable being uncomfortable.

Life is not meant to be a series of comfort zones strung together by spiritual naps. The very definition of growth implies resistance, pressure, and yes ... struggle. Struggle is not a sign of failure ... it is a sign of faith in motion.

God never promised a painless journey, but He did promise His presence. That means the very thing you're pushing through right now may be His divine tool shaping your destiny.

God is sovereign over the outcome ... but you are responsible for the effort. The struggle is sacred ... not merely because of what it produces, but because of who you become in the wrestling. Like Jacob in the night, your limp may become your legacy. Like Paul's thorn, your weakness may become your strength.

You were not called to comfort ... but to calling.
Not to drift ... but to discipline.
Not to avoid the valley ... but to walk through it with Him.

Don't run from the tension ... lean into it.
God often births purpose in the very places we try hardest to escape.

Application
- Identify one discomfort you've been avoiding and face it with faith.
- Ask God to show you how your struggle is refining your character.
- Declare: "My struggle is sacred ... and God is shaping me through it."

Prayer
Lord, teach me not to fear the struggle, but to embrace it as a place where You meet me. Help me trust You with the results, knowing You are shaping something eternal in me. Give me courage to stay faithful in the fight and steady in the process. In Jesus' name, **Amen.**

February 12
Greatness in Solitude

Matthew 14:23
After He had sent the crowds away, He went up on the mountain by Himself to pray; and when it was evening, He was there alone.

Reflection
When you decide to become yourself, you become lonely.

True leaders often walk alone ... not because they are antisocial, but because greatness is forged in quiet places. The world celebrates the spotlight, but destiny develops in the shadows.

Solitude isn't failure ... it's preparation. William Deresiewicz once observed that "the position of the leader is ultimately an intensely solitary, even intensely lonely one."

Leadership demands conviction, and conviction is shaped in silence. It is in the still hours ... far from applause ... where character becomes clear and calling becomes cemented.

In Ecclesiastes, Solomon reminds us that every purpose has its season ... including the season of being hidden. These quiet stretches are not punishments ... they are sacred workshops of soul and strength. The noise of crowds can cloud your identity, but solitude brings clarity. What feels like isolation may actually be incubation.

Embrace the quiet.
Honor the hidden season.

Greatness grows in the soil no one sees.

Application
- Embrace your season of solitude as preparation, not rejection.
- Use your quiet moments to pray, plan, write, or dream.
- Declare: "God is building greatness in me ... even in the silent places."

Prayer
Father, teach me to value the season of solitude You've allowed. Build in me what only quiet can strengthen ... depth of character, clarity of calling, and conviction of heart. Help me trust the hidden work You are doing and prepare me to lead with wisdom and humility. In Jesus' name, **Amen.**

February 13
The Power of Hope

Proverbs 13:12
Hope deferred makes the heart sick, but a longing fulfilled is a tree of life.

Reflection
God didn't create us to sink ... He created us to swim.

In the 1950s, Johns Hopkins professor Curt Richter discovered something remarkable. Rats placed in water quickly drowned ... not because their bodies failed, but because their hope did. Yet if those same rats were rescued once and then placed back into the water, they swam for up to 60 hours ... not because of physical strength, but because they believed rescue was possible.

This isn't just a rat story ... it's a parable of the human soul.

When life overwhelms us, despair whispers that the end is near. But even a single glimpse of God's grace ... an answered prayer, a timely encouragement, a quiet breakthrough ... can revive hope, renew strength, and unleash supernatural endurance far beyond our natural limits.

Hope is fuel.
Hope is oxygen.
Hope is spiritual survival.

And God is the Giver of hope.

Remembering one moment of His rescue can help you keep swimming through seasons that would have drowned you before. And your kindness, your words, your presence may be the lifeline someone else needs to stay afloat.

Application
- Recall a moment when God "rescued" you and let it renew your hope.
- Look for one sign of God's faithfulness today and hold onto it.
- Declare: "Hope is alive in me ... and God will carry me through."

Prayer
Father, remind me of Your past faithfulness when I feel overwhelmed. Fill me with hope that strengthens my spirit and renews my endurance. Help me keep swimming in faith ... and help me become a lifeline of hope to others. In Jesus' name, **Amen.**

February 14
Love: The Greatest of All

1 Corinthians 13:13
Now abide faith, hope, love, these three ... but the greatest of these is love.

Reflection
Love is the glue that holds everything together. Love is God's nature ... Christ's example ... and the believer's highest calling.

Love is the atmosphere of the Kingdom ... the very environment where spiritual growth thrives. You can have knowledge, gifting, charisma, influence, and even spiritual power ... but without love, it all collapses into noise. Love purifies motive. Love stabilizes calling. Love transforms obedience from duty into delight. It is impossible to walk with God deeply without walking in love, because "God is love."

Love is not passive emotion ... it is intentional action. It is patient when it could rush ... kind when it could react ... gentle when it could judge. Love sacrifices, covers, restores, and pursues. Love makes us look like Jesus. Every miracle He performed flowed from love. Every lesson He taught was shaped by love. And every wound He endured was healed through love.

Faith may move mountains ... hope may anchor the soul ... but love changes hearts.

This is why love is "the greatest of all." It outlasts spiritual gifts, achievements, sermons, and seasons. Love is the only thing you can carry from earth into eternity. When everything else falls away, love remains.

So choose love ... over ego, over offense, over pride, over convenience. Choose the path that looks like Jesus. Because the world will know you belong to Him ... not by your gifts, but by your love.

Application
- Spend intentional time today expressing love to God through prayer and worship.
- Show one act of selfless love to someone who needs encouragement.
- Declare: "Above all, I will walk in love."

Prayer
Father, fill me with Your love today. Teach me to love You fully and to love others genuinely. Let everything I do flow from a heart anchored in Your love. In Jesus' name, **Amen.**

February 15
The Will to Win

Philippians 2:13
For it is God who is at work in you, both to will and to work for His good pleasure.

Reflection
Talent is a gift. Opportunity is a blessing.
But will ... the inner resolve to keep moving forward ... is the difference between potential and purpose fulfilled.

Many doors open in life. Some are held wide by favor, others by skill, and still others by divine timing. But only the willing walk through and endure what waits on the other side. You don't just need a dream ... you need the discipline and drive to finish the race when you're tired, discouraged, or unseen.

The will of a person is not loud or flashy. It is formed in silence ... in prayer ... in hidden hours of obedience. Willpower wakes you up when motivation fades. It gets back up after failure. It chooses faithfulness over comfort, growth over ease, and purpose over excuses.

Success doesn't come to the wishful ... it comes to the willing.

The willing press forward.
The willing sacrifice.
The willing surrender their will to God's will ... and that is where spiritual power is born.

Passion may start the race ...
but a surrendered will finishes it.

Application
- Examine one area where you've relied on talent instead of discipline.
- Identify where God is asking you to press forward even when it's uncomfortable.
- Declare: "Lord, align my will with Yours ... I am willing to finish what You started."

Prayer
Father, align my will with Your will. Strengthen me to not only desire Your purpose, but to pursue it with everything in me. Build in me a will that endures, obeys, and stays faithful in every season. In Jesus' name, **Amen.**

February 16
A Distracted Mind Never Builds an Intentional Life

Psalm 119:37
Turn my eyes away from looking at worthless things, and revive me in Your ways.

Reflection
You can't build a strong house with scattered bricks ... and you can't build a meaningful life with a scattered mind.

Distraction is subtle sabotage. You think you're making progress ... but you're really just making noise.

In a world full of pings, posts, and endless options, it's easy to drift. But drifting never builds destiny. Greatness isn't stumbled into ... it's pursued on purpose. You won't find your calling while scrolling. You won't fulfill your assignment while chasing everything. You must focus your faith ... and guard your gaze.

The Word says, "Let your gaze be fixed." That means spiritual vision, mental clarity, and emotional discipline. Every great building starts with a blueprint ... and your life is no different. You cannot lay bricks of faith on a mind distracted by fear, guilt, entertainment, or ego.

Don't be fooled. Distraction isn't just inconvenient ... it's dangerous. It delays development. It weakens your witness. It distorts your discernment.

Today, silence the noise and strengthen your mind.
Focus isn't optional for those building something eternal.

Application
- Identify the one distraction that has been pulling your focus the most.
- Choose one intentional action to fix your gaze on God's purpose today.
- Declare: "My mind is disciplined ... my focus is fixed ... my life is intentional."

Prayer
Lord, renew my focus and guard my mind from drifting. Help me fix my eyes on what You've called me to do and reject the distractions that steal purpose. Teach me to walk in discipline, clarity, and divine direction. In Jesus' name. **Amen.**

February 17
Change Habits → Change Your Life

Colossians 3:9–10
Do not lie to one another, since you laid aside the old self with its evil practices, 10 and have put on the new self who is being renewed to a true knowledge according to the image of the One who created him …

Reflection
Godly transformation is not just subtraction … it's substitution.

We often believe spiritual growth is about stopping sin or cutting off distractions. But real transformation happens not just when you remove something … but when you replace it with something better, wiser, and aligned with God's design.

You don't just stop old habits … you swap them. Godly growth is not only about what you subtract … but what you substitute.

Consider these personal exchanges …

Netflix Marathons → Sleep. Entertainment overload brings escape, but it steals rest. **Fast Food → Home-Made Food.** Convenience can cost your health. Your body is a temple. **Toxic Friends → Mentors.** Let go of people who drain your soul. **TV → Exercise.** Movement becomes worship when done with purpose. **Complaining → Gratitude.** Shift your speech. Gratitude is the language of trust. **Overthinking → Action.** Faith doesn't overanalyze … it obeys. **Blame → Responsibility.** Own your story. No excuses.

Every holy exchange is a decision to align more deeply with Christ … one habit at a time.

Application
- Identify one habit God is calling you to replace today.
- Choose a spiritual substitution instead of just subtraction.
- Declare: "I am being transformed … one holy habit at a time."

Prayer
Father, I surrender my excuses and my patterns. Help me replace what drains me with what develops me. Form me into the image of Christ … one habit and one holy exchange at a time. In Jesus' name, **Amen**.

February 18
Just Plant the Seed

1 Corinthians 3:6
I planted, Apollos watered, but God was causing the growth.

Reflection
We preach. We pray. We teach. We pour out.

But sometimes we forget ... we don't produce the harvest.
We only plant the seed.

Ministry becomes heavy when we confuse our role with God's role. When someone doesn't change, we question our calling. When they ignore wisdom, we wonder if we did enough. When they drift, we feel like failures. But hear this clearly: You are a messenger, not the Messiah. You carry the seed, not the outcome.

Paul reminds us in 1 Corinthians 3 that planting and watering are human assignments... but transformation is divine. Only God can soften a heart. Only God can open blind eyes. Only God can break chains, shift mindsets, and produce spiritual growth. Your calling is simple: Plant faithfully. Water consistently. Trust completely.

The ground may look hard today, but the seed is alive. The soil may look stubborn, but God is patient. The harvest may seem distant, but Heaven is not in a hurry. No seed planted in love is ever wasted.

Release the pressure. Release the guilt. Release the outcome.

Stay faithful in the planting... and let God be faithful in the growing.

Application
• Identify one person you've been trying to fix instead of faithfully serve.
• Pray for them today ... not with pressure, but with peace.
• Declare: "I plant. I water. God brings the growth."

Prayer
Father, thank You for trusting me with seeds of truth, grace, and love. Help me to embrace my role with humility and release the outcomes into Your hands. Free me from carrying burdens You never assigned. Teach me to plant faithfully, to water gently, and to trust You completely with the harvest. Make my work light, my heart surrendered, and my spirit aligned with Your purpose. In Jesus' name, **Amen**.

February 19
Appreciate the Detour

Proverbs 3:5–6
Trust in the Lord with all your heart and lean not on your own understanding; in all your ways acknowledge Him, and He will make your paths straight.

Reflection
We love momentum. We love control. We love when life follows our script. But God is not committed to our plans … He is committed to our purpose. And sometimes the only way to protect your purpose is to interrupt your plan.

Detours feel frustrating, but they are often divine. What looks like delay may actually be deliverance. What feels like rejection may be redirection. God sees danger, traps, and disappointment long before we do, and in His mercy He shifts the path before the path can break us. Detours develop what shortcuts can't. They stretch your patience. Forge your faith. Correct your vision. And deepen your trust until you stop leaning on your own understanding and start leaning on God's sovereignty.

From Moses trapped at the Red Sea to Jesus "accidentally" passing through Samaria, detours have always been the birthplace of destiny. The route you didn't choose may be the road God uses to reshape you into who you must become.

You don't just survive detours … you grow in them. Appreciate the pause. Honor the redirection. Trust the God who sees the whole road. He's not just guiding your steps… He's guarding your soul.

Application
- Identify one detour you're resisting and ask God what He's showing you.
- Practice gratitude by thanking God for closed doors and new directions.
- Declare: "God's detours aren't delays … they're protection and preparation."

Prayer
Father, thank You for every detour wrapped in Your wisdom. Help me surrender my plans and embrace Your path, even when it feels unclear. Protect me from what I cannot see, prepare me for what You have planned, and make me patient in the pauses You allow. Redirect my steps, reshape my heart, and keep me aligned with Your perfect will. In Jesus' name, **Amen.**

February 20
Will Your Sacrifice Be the Reason Your Family Flourishes?

Genesis 12:3
In you all the families of the earth will be blessed.

Reflection
Some seeds don't break the soil until after you're gone.
Some blessings don't bloom in your lifetime …
they bloom in the lifetime of the ones who come after you.

God told Abraham his obedience would bless nations, yet Abraham died without ever seeing the multitudes. He didn't witness the generations. He didn't hold the promise in his hands. But his faith laid a foundation his family would stand on forever. That's legacy.

Your obedience today can be the reason your family walks in freedom tomorrow. Your sacrifice can become the spiritual inheritance your children didn't earn but desperately need. Your private surrender can produce a public harvest for generations.

Legacy is never built through convenience. It's built through commitment. Through choosing discipline over desire. Through saying "yes" to God when everything in you wants to cling to comfort.

You may not see the full harvest, but your family will. God does not waste obedience. He takes your surrender, your sacrifice, your faithfulness … and turns it into generational blessing. Live with vision. Obey with purpose. Sacrifice with eternity in mind. What you lay down today may become the ground your family rises from.

Application
- Identify one area where God is calling you to sacrifice for future generations.
- Speak a blessing over your family and declare God's promises over them.
- Declare: "My obedience outlives me; my sacrifice strengthens my family."

Prayer
Father, give me faith big enough to think beyond myself. Show me what to surrender so that generations after me may flourish. Let my obedience plant seeds of blessing, protection, and purpose for those who come behind me. Use my sacrifices to break cycles, build foundations, and establish a legacy rooted in Your truth. May my life be a bridge that leads my family into promise. In Jesus' name, **Amen.**

February 21
Discipline: The Pathway to Purpose

Hebrews 12:11
No discipline seems pleasant at the time, but painful; later on, however, it produces a harvest of righteousness and peace for those who have been trained by it.

Reflection
Discipline isn't God punishing you … it's God preparing you.
It is His loving process of pruning what distracts you, correcting what derails you, and strengthening what defines you. Discipline is the training ground of destiny. No one drifts into purpose … you grow into it through intentionality, consistency, and surrender.

The undisciplined life is scattered, reactive, and easily shaken. But the disciplined life is focused, resilient, and anchored in truth. Just as an athlete trains daily to master their craft, the believer trains the mind, subdues the flesh, and aligns the spirit to walk in Kingdom purpose.

Discipline is evidence that God loves you too much to leave you unshaped. His correction is compassion. His training is transformation. His pruning is progress.

You cannot walk in God's purpose without embracing God's process.
And discipline is the process.

When you choose discipline, you choose destiny.
When you embrace structure, you embrace strength.
When you commit to training, you commit to becoming.

Application
- Identify one habit that is hindering your growth and intentionally replace it with a God-honoring practice.
- Take one negative thought captive today (2 Corinthians 10:5) and submit it to Christ.
- Declare: "Discipline is not my enemy… it is my pathway to destiny."

Prayer
Lord, help me see discipline not as restriction but as Your divine training for purpose. Strengthen my will, purify my habits, and align my heart with Your truth. Make me consistent in obedience and faithful in practice, so that my life produces a harvest of righteousness and peace. Shape me through Your discipline into who You've called me to be. In Jesus' name, **Amen**.

February 22
Joy Is an Inside Job

Nehemiah 8:10b
The joy of the Lord is your strength.

Reflection
IMMA SIT THIS RIGHT HERE FOR SOMEBODY.
Because many are waiting for joy to arrive like a package on the doorstep … when God designed it to flow from the inside out.

You've been searching through the window of your eyes for something God placed in the jar of your soul. Joy was never meant to be hunted externally… it was meant to be cultivated internally.

This joy is not emotional … it's spiritual. It's not built on circumstances … it's built on Christ. It doesn't rise and fall with people's actions, your finances, or a "perfect day." It is rooted in the Lord, not the world.
And here's a truth that confronts us all: If you're depending on others for your peace, your progress, or your purpose… you're handing them keys to a car God told you to drive.

Some give more responsibility to a spouse, a boss, a church, or a childhood wound than to their own spiritual stewardship. But joy begins with ownership. Growth begins with responsibility. Freedom begins with surrender.

Real joy says: "I refuse to be a prisoner to circumstances. I choose to manage what God placed inside me." No magic. Just management.
God gave you the jar … now protect it, nurture it, and keep it full.

Application
- Identify one area where you've expected others to create joy for you instead of cultivating it yourself.
- Practice gratitude today … name three blessings God has already placed inside your life.
- Declare: "Joy is my responsibility. Strength is my portion. Christ is my source."

Prayer
Lord, restore the joy of Your salvation in me. Help me stop searching outside for what You planted within. Teach me to take ownership of my peace, my purpose, and my spiritual health. Strengthen me to guard the joy You've given and to live from the fullness of Your presence. In Jesus' name, **Amen**.

February 23
Your Next Move Matters More Than Your Last Mistake

Philippians 3:13–14
"...forgetting what lies behind and reaching forward to what lies ahead, I press on toward the goal..."

Reflection
Everybody stumbles. Everybody falls. But the power of the Gospel isn't only that God cleanses you ... it's that He calls you even after the fall.

The enemy wants your last mistake to become your final identity. But grace has a pen too. And God is still writing.

Your past may explain how you got here, but it does not define where you're going. Your failure may have humbled you, but it does not disqualify you. What Heaven is watching right now is not your last misstep... but your next move.

Ask Moses ... his anger cost him, yet God still sent him.
Ask David ... his sin was great, yet God still called him a man after His own heart.
Ask Peter ... his denial was public, yet his restoration was powerful.
Ask Paul ... his past was violent, yet his purpose was unmatched.

You are not the exception to redemption. You are a candidate for it.

Shame can only sabotage you if you let it stay. Scars may remind you where you've been, but they cannot dictate where you're going. You are one decision away from a new direction. One step away from momentum. One "yes" away from legacy. Your next move matters more than your last mistake.

Application
- Identify the one mistake you've allowed to shape your identity ... and release it to God today.
- Take one step of faith toward the future you've been avoiding.
- Declare: "My past is forgiven. My present is redeemed. My next move is aligned with purpose."

Prayer
Lord, I surrender every past mistake, every failure, and every place of shame. I pick up grace today and move forward ... not because I am perfect, but because You have redeemed me. Establish my steps, renew my courage, and write legacy through my obedience. In Jesus' name, **Amen.**

February 24
Looking Forward

Isaiah 43:18–19
Forget the former things; do not dwell on the past.
Behold, I am doing a new thing!

Reflection
I heard an elderly woman once say, "I am 105 years old... and I'm looking forward." And those words hit harder than a sermon.

Because many younger than her ... full of time, talent, and potential ... are stuck. Not because God hasn't opened a door, but because they can't stop replaying what's behind them.

Some are paralyzed by past wounds. Some haunted by heartbreak. Some addicted to old versions of themselves... like Lot's wife looking back, or Israel wandering in circles they were never meant to die in.

But here is the Kingdom truth: You cannot move forward while clinging to yesterday. God doesn't live in your rearview ... He reigns in your future. And His voice still calls from ahead: "Behold, I am doing a new thing!"

Stop rehearsing what God has healed. Stop revisiting what God has closed. Stop replaying what He's already redeemed. If a 105-year-old woman can look forward, what's stopping you?

Your new season is not waiting on a new miracle... it's waiting on a new mindset. Forward faith always begins with forward focus.

Application
- Identify one memory, mistake, or moment you must release in order to move forward.
- Write down one "new thing" you sense God calling you into ... and take one small step toward it.
- Declare: "My past is behind me. My future is before me. God is not done with me yet."

Prayer
Lord, give me forward faith. Help me release what no longer serves my purpose and receive what You are doing now. Free me from the weight of old seasons and fix my eyes on the future You have prepared. You are not done with me, and I choose to walk with hope, courage, and expectation. In Jesus' name, **Amen.**

February 25
The Cheat Code of Breath

Genesis 2:7
Then the Lord God formed man of dust from the ground, and breathed into his nostrils the breath of life; and man became a living being.

Reflection
Sometimes the most spiritual thing you can do… is breathe.

From the very beginning, God built restoration into your design. Before He gave Adam a task, a calling, or a garden … He gave him breath. That breath wasn't just oxygen; it was ruach … God's Spirit, God's presence, God's life entering human dust. And yet, in our world of hurry, anxiety, and constant pressure, we forget the simplest gift God ever gave us: the ability to pause.

Breath is God's cheat code. With every inhale, He reminds you He is near. With every exhale, He invites you to release what He never asked you to carry.

Stress may scream, but stillness strengthens. Life may rush, but breath resets. Your next breakthrough may not require more effort … just a deeper inhale.

When you slow your breathing, your body calms, your mind clears, and your spirit reconnects to the Source. Breath doesn't just keep you alive… it keeps you aligned. It centers you, grounds you, and brings you back to the God who breathed life into your lungs.

Every deep breath is a quiet reminder: I am His… and He is here.

Application
- Set aside 60 seconds today to breathe slowly, intentionally … prayerfully.
- When anxiety builds, stop and breathe His name … inhale "Yah," exhale "weh."
- Declare: "My breath is not just natural … it is spiritual. God breathes peace into me."

Prayer
Lord, thank You for the breath that sustains my life and centers my soul. Teach me to pause more often and to breathe with intention. Calm my anxious thoughts, quiet my restless spirit, and draw me back into Your presence with every inhale and exhale. Let each breath reset my focus, restore my peace, and remind me that I belong to You. In Jesus' name, **Amen.**

February 26
Called to Be Light, Not Liked

1 John 1:6–7
If we say that we have fellowship with Him and yet walk in the darkness, we lie and do not practice the truth; but if we walk in the Light as He Himself is in the Light, we have fellowship with one another, and the blood of Jesus His Son cleanses us from all sin.

Reflection
God never called you to fit in … He called you to shine.
And shining will always cost you something.
Light doesn't blend in. Light doesn't apologize. Light doesn't negotiate with darkness. Light simply reveals what darkness tries to hide.

In a culture obsessed with approval, affirmation, and applause, it's easy to confuse being liked with being effective. But walking in the light will not always make you popular … it will make you purposeful. When Jesus declared, "You are the light of the world," He wasn't extending an invitation… He was giving a commission.

Light exposes. Light confronts. Light heals. And yes, light makes people uncomfortable … because truth makes people uncomfortable.
Too many believers shrink to avoid rejection. They dim their light to maintain access, approval, or relationships. But you cannot carry divine truth and live for human applause. The two cannot coexist.

Here's the Kingdom reality: When you walk in the light, you may lose some circles … but you gain real fellowship. When you walk in the light, you may face resistance … but you gain cleansing. When you walk in the light, you may be misunderstood … but you walk with God. Don't trade divine calling for human comfort. Don't sacrifice holiness to be harmless. You weren't designed to be liked. You were created to be light.

Application
- Identify one area where you've been dimming your light for acceptance.
- Take one bold step today to live in truth … even if it costs you comfort.
- Declare: "I choose light over likes. I choose truth over approval."

Prayer
Lord, strengthen my heart to walk boldly in the light. Free me from the need to be approved by people, and anchor me in the truth of who You've called me to be. Let my life shine with conviction, compassion, and clarity. In Jesus' name, **Amen**.

February 27
Faith That Finds Peace

Philippians 4:7
And the peace of God, which surpasses all comprehension, will guard your hearts and your minds in Christ Jesus.

Reflection
Faith isn't proven when life is clear … it's proven when life is confusing. Anybody can trust God when everything makes sense, but real faith stands firm when nothing does. Real faith breathes when the pressure rises. Real faith rests when fear whispers. Real faith chooses confidence in God over clarity in circumstances.

We often convince ourselves that peace requires answers… but Scripture teaches the opposite. Peace doesn't come from understanding everything around you … it comes from trusting the God who reigns above you. His peace is not logical. It's not predictable. It's not earned by effort. It is given by grace and guarded by Christ.

When you stop demanding explanations and start embracing God's sovereignty, something shifts. Confusion loses its power. Anxiety loses its voice. The unknown loses its sting. You no longer walk by what you can figure out … you walk by who you know.

Peace is not the absence of problems… It's the presence of trust.
It's the quiet confidence that God is in control … even when you aren't.
Let go of the pressure to understand everything. Hold tightly to the God who understands you.

Application
- Identify one area where you've been desperate for answers and release it to God.
- Pray aloud: "Lord, I don't see the outcome… but I trust You."
- At the first sign of stress or doubt this week, pause, breathe, and declare "Your peace holds me. Christ guards me."

Prayer
Father, thank You that I don't have to know the outcome to trust Your plan. Guard my heart and mind with a peace that rises above understanding. When questions swirl and uncertainty pulls at me, anchor me in Your presence. Teach me to rest, to release, and to rely on You fully. In Jesus' name, **Amen.**

February 28
Which Wolf Are You Feeding?

Romans 8:6
"...the mind set on the flesh is death, but the mind set on the Spirit is life and peace."

Reflection
Inside every believer lives a daily battle ... a tug-of-war between flesh and Spirit. It's the same truth echoed in the old Cherokee parable of two wolves fighting within: one driven by anger, envy, pride, and fear; the other shaped by love, peace, patience, humility, and truth.

The grandson asked, "Which wolf will win?" The answer was simple: "The one you feed."

That story mirrors the spiritual reality Paul describes in Romans 8. The flesh always pulls you downward ... toward chaos, confusion, reaction, and regret. But the Spirit pulls you upward ... toward clarity, peace, self-control, and purpose.

Your mind is the feeding ground. Your thoughts are the meals. Your choices are the portions. Every prayer, every surrender, every moment you choose truth over temptation is a meal for the Spirit. Every grudge, every impulse, every indulgence of old patterns is a meal for the flesh.

You are becoming what you consistently feed. The life you want... the peace you crave... the growth you desire ... they will always be the result of feeding the right wolf. Choose the Spirit today. Choose life. Choose peace.

Application
- Pause and ask honestly: "Which wolf have I fed most today ... flesh or Spirit?"
- Choose one intentional act that feeds the Spirit: prayer, gratitude, kindness, or resisting a negative thought.
- Declare: "I will feed the Spirit, not the flesh. I choose life and peace."

Prayer
Father, thank You for placing Your Spirit within me. I confess that at times I feed the wrong desires ... fear, anger, pride, and self. Today I choose to feed what brings life. Strengthen my mind, purify my heart, and train my habits so that I walk in Your Spirit with consistency and clarity. Let peace grow where chaos once lived. In Jesus' name, **Amen.**

February 29
A Church Serious About Souls

James 5:19–20
My brethren, if anyone among you wanders from the truth and someone turns him back, let him know that he who turns a sinner from the error of his way will save a soul from death and cover a multitude of sins.

Reflection
There is a sobering truth many churches quietly ignore: A church that is not serious about saving souls is silently saying, "Go your own way ... even if the path leads to death."

If we preach everything except repentance... If we create spaces that comfort the saved but never confront the lost... If we gather weekly but never extend the Gospel message clearly...Then we have drifted far from Christ's mission.

James tells us plainly ... turning a sinner from error is not a small act; it is saving a soul from death. This is eternal work. Weighty work. Kingdom work.

The early church understood this. They preached with urgency. They prayed with tears. They lived with a burden. Somewhere, in the comfort of modern Christianity, that urgency cooled. But the stakes never changed.

A church serious about souls will: Pursue the wandering. Declare the truth unapologetically. Love fiercely and rescue boldly. The love of Christ compels us ... not to entertain, not to impress, but to intercept eternal death with eternal life. This is not cruelty. This is compassion. This is the Gospel. Let us be a church ... let us be believers ... who refuse to let souls perish on our watch.

Application
- Ask yourself: Do I pursue the lost or just comfort the found?
- Pray today for one person far from God.
- Declare: "I won't be silent ... I'll speak, love, and help rescue."

Prayer
Father, thank You for the Gospel that saves. Forgive me for every moment I treated salvation lightly or ignored the urgency of eternity. Make me serious about souls ... serious about truth, serious about compassion, and serious about rescue. Let Your church burn again with a passion for the lost, and let my life reflect that same fire. Give me boldness to speak, love, and lead people toward You. In Jesus' name, **Amen.**

March 1
The Power of Being Present

Matthew 6:34
Therefore do not worry about tomorrow, for tomorrow will worry about itself. Each day has enough trouble of its own.

Reflection
The true gift of life lies in the present.

Being present in every conversation, every room, and present with the Spirit of God ... this changes everything.

Stress and depression often stem from dwelling too long in the past. Anxiety pulls us into the future. But God lives in the now ... that is why the present is a gift. Worry does not take the sorrow out of tomorrow but it will take the joy out of today. Don't pull tomorrow's clouds over today's sunshine. Worrying is burying blessings.

As believers, we're invited to let go of regret and worry and anchor ourselves in the present moment God has given us. When you stay present with the Spirit ... regardless of the task or setting ... you find peace, clarity, and alignment with His purposes.

The past is for lessons, not chains. The future is for faith, not fear. God's presence is available right now ... that's why the present is sacred.

Staying present with the Spirit empowers focus, reduces stress, and deepens connection. Living in the now anchors us to God's peace and keeps us from worry.

Application
- Identify one area where worry has pulled you out of the present and release it to God today.
- Practice being fully present in one conversation or moment and invite the Holy Spirit into it.
- Declare that today is a gift and choose to live in the peace God provides right now.

Prayer
Holy Spirit, help me to live in the present moment You've given me. Let me be present in every conversation, every space, and always aware of Your presence. Free me from the weight of the past and the fear of the future.
Amen.

March 2
Power of Thought, Word, and Presence

Proverbs 23:7
For as he thinks within himself, so he is.

Reflection
Once you realize the power of your thoughts, you won't just think anything.

Your mind is a battleground. Every thought plants a seed ... for peace or for destruction, for faith or for fear. When you understand that your thoughts shape your reality, you will guard them like treasure. Philippians 4:8 teaches us to think on what is true, honorable, pure, lovely, and of good report.

Once you realize the power of your words, you won't just say anything. Death and life are in the power of the tongue (Proverbs 18:21). Your words carry spiritual weight ... they can build faith, break hearts, heal wounds, or release harm. Matthew 12:36–37 reminds us that even careless words echo in eternity.

Once you realize the power of your presence, you won't just be anywhere. Where you stand, who you stand with, and what you stand around speaks volumes about your priorities and your spiritual alignment. Presence is agreement ... and proximity is influence. Psalm 1:1 calls us to walk away from ungodly counsel, and 2 Corinthians 6:17 calls us to separate ourselves so our witness remains pure.

The truth is simple:
Your life will rise or fall on these three disciplines ... what you think, what you speak, and where you stand. Guard them. Steward them. Surrender them to God.

Application
- Identify one unhealthy thought you've been carrying and replace it with God's truth.
- Speak one faith-filled declaration today that aligns with Scripture.
- Evaluate one environment or relationship that is shaping you ... and step toward godly alignment.

Prayer
Lord, purify my thoughts, sanctify my speech, and direct my steps. Help me think what is true, speak what is life-giving, and stand where Your presence leads. Shape my mind, my mouth, and my movements until they reflect Your truth and Your character. In Jesus' name, **Amen.**

March 3

Dying to Live Divine

1 John 2:16
For all that is in the world ... the lust of the flesh, the lust of the eyes, and the pride of life ... is not from the Father, but is from the world.

Reflection
You don't have to physically die to enter Heaven ... but you do have to die metaphorically.

Die to the lust of the flesh.
Die to the lust of the eyes.
Die to the pride of life.

These are the tangled weeds that choke out the flourishing of your divine nature. Every believer walks a daily road toward a personal Golgotha ... a place where the old self is surrendered so the new self can rise.

Just as Christ carried His cross, we must carry ours. We lay down self-indulgence, worldly cravings, and self-centered pride so we can rise into the identity God has woven into us. The cross does not only save ... it transforms. It crucifies what is false and resurrects what is divine.

Dying to self is not punishment; it is the pathway to your true life in Christ. As you release the old man, you rise into Kingdom living ... empowered, awakened, renewed, and aligned with His divine nature.

This is the mystery of the Gospel:
You die to what is lesser so you can live in what is greater.

Application
- Identify one fleshly desire or worldly pull you need to surrender at the cross today.
- Practice a simple act of self-denial and offer it to God as worship.
- Declare that your old nature is crucified and your new life in Christ is rising today.

Prayer
Lord Jesus, teach me to die daily to the lust of the flesh, the allure of the eyes, and the pride of life. Help me carry my cross with courage and surrender so I may rise in Your divine nature. Transform me from the inside out until my life reflects the newness of Christ. In Your name, **Amen.**

March 4
Mastered by Time

Psalm 37:7
Rest in the LORD and wait patiently for Him…

Reflection
Some things burn when rushed. Others become a masterpiece with time.

In a culture obsessed with speed, God often works in seasons. He develops, He shapes, He refines… slowly. Not because He is delaying your destiny, but because He is preparing you for the destiny He already designed.

Rushing what God is refining will always lead to disappointment.
Impatience ruins what obedience could have perfected.
Haste destroys what wisdom would have protected.

But trusting His timing changes everything.
Pressure becomes preparation… and preparation becomes purpose.

Masterpieces aren't microwaved.
They're crafted, stretched, molded, and detailed in due season.
Even when you can't see progress, Heaven is at work behind the scenes, shaping something only time can reveal.

The truth is simple:
When you slow down and surrender to God's pace, you stop fighting the process and start becoming the masterpiece.

Slow down. Let God work. Your masterpiece is already in motion.

Application
- Identify one area of your life where you've been rushing God's process.
- Surrender the timeline to Him and write down what patience looks like today.
- Take one small, faith-filled step that aligns with trust… not hurry.

Prayer
Lord, teach me to trust Your timing. Deliver me from the urge to rush what You are refining in me. Help me see that Your pace is perfect, Your process is intentional, and Your timing is always on time. Shape me, mold me, and prepare me until my life reflects the masterpiece You designed. In Jesus' name, **Amen.**

March 5
How You Love Is Your Superpower

John 13:35
By this all men will know that you are My disciples, if you have love for one another.

Reflection
How you love is your superpower ... because love is what makes you most like God.

Love isn't just something you do; it's who you become when you walk in divine purpose. Since God is love (1 John 4:8), every act of love is a revelation of His nature flowing through you. It's not your gifting, your intellect, your status, or your achievements that make you resemble God. It's how you forgive, how you show kindness, how you serve, how you respond to those who don't deserve it. Love is the clearest evidence that Christ lives within you.

When you forgive when it's undeserved, you manifest God.
When you show kindness when it's inconvenient, you manifest God.
When you serve when it costs you something, you manifest God.

The truth is simple:
Love is your superpower.
Love is what made God give.
Love is what made Jesus stay on the Cross.
And love is what makes you spiritually unstoppable.
When you choose to love like God, you don't just imitate Him ... you reveal Him.

Application
- Identify one person who needs love from you today, especially where it costs something.
- Practice one act of kindness that reflects God's heart, not your mood.
- Declare that love ... not pride, wounds, or fear ... will lead your decisions today.

Prayer
Lord, fill my heart with Your love until it overflows into everything I think, speak, and do. Help me forgive freely, serve willingly, and love sacrificially. Make my life a living expression of Your heart so that others see You through me. In Jesus' name, **Amen.**

March 6
When You Can't Feel Him, Trust Him

Hebrews 13:5b
I will never leave you, nor will I ever forsake you.

Reflection
There will come a moment ... if it hasn't already ... when the presence of God seems hidden. The silence is heavy. Prayers feel like they bounce back unanswered. In these moments, you'll be tempted to measure God by your emotions. But your feelings are not your faith, and your perception is not your foundation.

It is in the seasons when we cannot feel God that we must stand on what we know of Him. Feelings fluctuate, but His faithfulness does not. His presence is not dependent on your mood, your strength, or your understanding. He is the same God in the silence that He is in the sanctuary.

The enemy thrives in emotional instability. He whispers lies into the fog: "You're forgotten... you're forsaken... you're invisible." But God has already sealed His promise in eternity: "I will never leave you nor forsake you." That is not a possibility ... it's a covenant.

The truth is simple:
When God feels absent, He is often working most deeply.
When you can't trace Him, you can still trust Him.
And when emotions fail you, His Word will anchor you.

Don't cling to what you feel today ... cling to what He said.
Trust the God who stays, even when He seems silent.

Application
- Identify one lingering emotion that has made you question God's nearness and surrender it to Him.
- Choose one Scripture today to anchor your soul when your feelings waver.
- Declare: "God is with me, even when I cannot feel Him."

Prayer
Lord, teach me to trust You beyond what I feel. When my emotions rise and Your presence seems distant, anchor me in Your unchanging Word. Silence every lie of abandonment and strengthen my heart with the truth that You never leave, never forsake, and never withdraw Your love. Help me walk by faith, not feelings. In Jesus' name, **Amen.**

March 7

Don't Wait to Be Great

Psalm 139:14
I praise You, for I am fearfully and wonderfully made;
Wonderful are Your works, and my soul knows it very well.

Reflection
Your greatness is not waiting in some distant future. You are not "almost" great, "on your way" to great, or "preparing" to be great. You are great right now … not because of accomplishments, applause, or external validation, but because the God who formed you is great, and He made you in His image (Genesis 1:27).

Too often, we delay bold living by telling ourselves we need more preparation, more perfection, or more proof before we move. But greatness is not a graduation you earn; it is an identity you carry. The enemy loves to trap people in delay … calling it preparation … so they never step into what God has already approved.

Jesus didn't wait for the disciples to qualify before He called them.
God didn't wait for David to mature before He anointed him king.
And God is not waiting for you to hit some invisible milestone before He uses you.

The truth is simple:
God's greatness in you is a present reality, not a future potential.
You were designed to reflect Him today… not someday.

Stop waiting to be great. Walk in what God already placed inside you.

Application
- Identify one dream, assignment, or responsibility you've delayed because you didn't feel "ready."
- Take one bold action today that reflects the greatness God already placed in you.
- Declare: "God's greatness in me is active now … not later."

Prayer
Father, thank You for reminding me that my greatness comes from You, not from anything I achieve. Help me walk boldly in the identity You've already spoken over my life. Remove hesitation, silence insecurity, and awaken courage. Let my words, actions, and presence reflect the greatness of the God who lives within me … today. In Jesus' name, **Amen.**

March 8
Be the Energy You Want to Attract

Galatians 6:7
Do not be deceived: God is not mocked. For whatever a man sows, this he will also reap.

Reflection
The atmosphere around you is rarely random ... it is often a reflection of the atmosphere within you. Scripture tells us that whatever we sow ... we will also reap. This truth stretches far beyond actions ... it reaches into attitudes, tone, and spiritual posture.

If you want peace, walk in peace.
If you want joy, radiate joy.
If you want love, give love freely.

Energy is spiritual currency. The seeds you release through your words, your presence, and your responses become the harvest that returns. You are not merely a thermometer reacting to the temperature around you ... you are a thermostat empowered to set it.

Chaos cannot silence a believer who carries peace.
Coldness cannot freeze a heart that has chosen kindness.
Darkness cannot withstand a soul anchored in light.
So stop waiting for the room to change.
Be the one who shifts the room.
Be the energy you want to attract ... and watch Heaven multiply it back to you.

Application
- Practice one intentional shift today ... respond with peace where you would normally react.
- Speak life into at least one environment you enter ... home, work, church, or conversation.
- Declare: "I set the atmosphere around me by the truth that lives within me."

Prayer
Father, align my inner world with Your Spirit so that what flows from me reflects Your heart. Purify my thoughts ... steady my emotions ... and fill my words with grace. Make me a carrier of peace, joy, and love in every space I enter. Let my life sow the kind of seed that brings glory to You and blessing to others. In Jesus' name, **Amen.**

March 9
A Still Pond Reflects the Sun Perfectly

Psalm 46:10
Be still, and know that I am God…

Reflection
Imagine a pristine lake at dawn … calm, glass-like, mirroring the rising sun with flawless clarity. As long as the waters remain still, the reflection remains perfect. But the moment the wind stirs, the image blurs. Your soul is no different. When your inner world is restless, hurried, or unsettled … God's light doesn't shine through your life as clearly.

A still soul is a surrendered soul. "Be still" is not merely a command to stop moving … it is an invitation to trust, to release control, and to rest in God's sovereign presence. As Psalm 23:2 reminds us, He leads us beside still waters … places of restoration where He clears our vision and renews our strength.

Like the moon, you are not the source of light … you are the reflection of it. When you cultivate quietness before God, the radiance of Christ is seen in you with greater purity. Stillness is not the absence of storms … it is peace in the storm. It is the disciplined choice to anchor your heart in God despite the winds of worry, conflict, or pressure.

Let your soul become the calm pond that reflects His presence with clarity.

Application
- Identify the "ripples" in your soul today … fears, stresses, or conflicts that are distorting your peace.
- Pause and pray … invite God to calm the winds within you.
- Reflect His light … choose one action today that shows Christ through your stillness.

Prayer
Lord Jesus, make my soul like a still pond … quiet, surrendered, and open to Your presence. Calm every inner wind … worry, noise, haste … and let Your truth, beauty, and goodness shine clearly through me. Restore my peace, center my heart, and help me reflect You to everyone I encounter today.
Amen.

March 10

Your Value Isn't in Your Bank ... It's in Your Vision

Matthew 6:33
But seek first His kingdom and His righteousness, and all these things will be provided to you.

Reflection
Real kings don't just lead to the bag ... they lead to the Throne.
In a culture where manhood is often defined by money, image, and influence, Jesus recalibrates the metric. He reminds us that our true worth does not flow from what we accumulate ... but from what we align with. Kingdom alignment is the real wealth.

Hear this clearly ... money is low-hanging fruit. It is not difficult for a man who walks in obedience, stewardship, and vision to access it. Money flows to those who are faithful ... it follows divine favor. But money without mission is empty, and power without purpose is dangerous. The world teaches men to grind for gold ... but the Spirit teaches us to reign with righteousness.

Your value isn't in your bank ... it's in your vision. The Kingdom is the treasure. Righteousness, peace, and joy in the Holy Ghost (Romans 14:17) are riches that never crash with markets and never fade with inflation.

Kingdom men build altars before they build empires. They cover their families, disciple their sons, strengthen their communities, and carry the presence of God wherever they go. A real king is never threatened by another man's crown ... because his identity comes from God, not from gold.

Stay grounded. Stay guided.
Lead not just to success ... but to salvation.

Application
- Examine your motivations today ... are you chasing money, or chasing God?
- Identify one area where your leadership can point others toward Christ instead of culture.
- Declare: "My value is in my vision ... and my vision is Kingdom."

Prayer
Father, teach me to lead like Christ ... not for riches, but for righteousness. Purify my motives ... strengthen my vision ... and align my steps with Your purposes. Make me a king after Your own heart, and may those who follow me find You through me. In Jesus' name, **Amen.**

March 11
The Ladder of Consciousness

2 Corinthians 3:18
But we all, with unveiled face, beholding as in a mirror the glory of the Lord, are being transformed into the same image from glory to glory…

Reflection
Every day, you are climbing … not a ladder made of influence, income, or applause, but a spiritual ladder of consciousness. This is the soul's ascent from survival to surrender … from fear to faith … from ego to divine alignment. Paul says we are being transformed from glory to glory … meaning transformation is progressive, intentional, and upward.

Believers often get stuck in the lower realms of shame, guilt, and fear … places that distort identity and keep the soul bound. Shame says "I'm unworthy," guilt says "I can't recover," and fear says "I'm not safe." Yet Scripture reminds us there is no condemnation, forgiveness is available, and God has given us power, love, and a sound mind.

As God lifts us, we enter the middle realms … the spaces of awakening and alignment. Here the journey shifts as courage rises, willingness opens the heart, and acceptance trusts God's plan above our own. This is not passive surrender but a conscious choice to align with Him. In these realms, the soul begins to cooperate with transformation instead of resisting it.

The higher realms reflect true spiritual maturity. Wisdom brings clarity, love flows without condition, and oneness grows as we abide in Christ. This leads to a Spirit-led life where Christ lives through us and we rest deeply in His presence. Here, the soul moves from struggling to becoming … fully awake and aligned with who we are in Him.

Application
- Identify the realm you're operating from today … shame, fear, courage, wisdom, or love.
- Ask the Holy Spirit for one next step toward a higher rung.
- Declare: "I am being transformed from glory to glory … I will climb higher."

Prayer
Lord, elevate me. Lift me out of shame into sonship … out of fear into faith … out of guilt into grace. Lead me upward from glory to glory until all that remains in me is You. Transform my consciousness, purify my vision, and anchor my identity in Your presence. **Amen.**

March 12
Drawn to the Light

Ephesians 5:8
For you were formerly darkness, but now you are Light in the Lord; walk as children of Light.

Reflection
Let me share a secret with you ... everything is drawn to light.

If you're single and searching, the best thing you can do isn't to chase love ... it's to become light. When the light of Christ radiates from within you, the right people, opportunities, and blessings are naturally drawn to your life.

But here's the part we don't always talk about ... weeds grow toward the light just like roses do.

Light attracts life, but it also exposes and pulls in things that may look appealing at first glance but are harmful beneath the surface. This is why discernment becomes a non-negotiable spiritual tool.

When you begin walking in God's light, expect both divine connections and deceptive distractions to show up. The same sun that nourishes flowers also empowers the thorns.

Your responsibility is to walk in the Spirit, stay rooted in the Word, and allow God to sharpen your discernment so you can distinguish fruit that feeds you from weeds that choke you.

Light is attractive. But wisdom is protective.

Application
- Remember: just because something is drawn to you doesn't mean it's aligned with you.
- Ground your growth in Scripture so your roots stay deep and stable.
- Pray for spiritual discernment ... it is one of God's greatest forms of protection.

Prayer
Lord, make me a vessel of Your light. Draw toward me everything that is aligned with Your purpose, and give me the wisdom to release everything that is not. Strengthen my discernment so I never confuse weeds for wheat or thorns for fruit. Let my walk reflect Your truth and keep me rooted in Your presence. **Amen.**

March 13

One Purpose

Matthew 6:33
But seek first His kingdom and His righteousness, and all these things will be added to you.

Reflection
You were not created for multiple callings, divided loyalties, or scattered living. You were created for one purpose ... oneness with God. Not two. Not three. Not four. One.

He made you in His image (Genesis 1:26).
He called you to dwell in His presence.
He sent His Son to restore the intimacy sin fractured.

When Jesus said, "Seek first the Kingdom ..." He wasn't offering a suggestion ... He was revealing the blueprint of life itself. Your job, your title, your platform, your opportunities ... these are not your purpose. They are the overflow of it.

Your purpose is simple and singular:
Seek Him. Abide in Him. Align with Him.

When your soul is aligned, your life becomes ordered.
When your heart abides, your fruit becomes evident.
When your eyes are fixed on the Kingdom, your needs are met.

The world says, "Find your purpose." The Word says, "Seek His Kingdom." Your purpose is His presence, and when you find Him ... you find everything else.

Application
- Identify one area of your life where you've been chasing secondary purposes.
- Redirect that energy toward seeking God first in prayer, Scripture, and surrender.
- Declare: "I was made for one purpose ... oneness with God."

Prayer
Lord, I release every divided pursuit and every scattered desire. Bring my heart into alignment with Your Kingdom. Teach me to seek You first ... to abide in You deeply ... and to walk in the oneness for which I was created. Let every part of my life flow from intimacy with You. **Amen.**

March 14
On Earth As It Is In Heaven: Roots & Reach

Matthew 6:10
Your kingdom come. Your will be done, on earth as it is in heaven.

Reflection
When Jesus taught us to pray "on earth as it is in heaven," He wasn't pointing us merely upward … He was pointing inward. He revealed a divine rhythm … what happens in the unseen shapes what appears in the seen. Heaven influences earth … spirit influences flesh … roots influence fruit.

Creation confirms it.

Every tree grows through two simultaneous forces. Gravitropism … roots pulled downward into the dark, anchoring and nourishing what will one day be seen. Phototropism … branches pulled upward toward the light, stretching into visibility and bearing fruit.

Your spiritual life works the same way.
Private disciplines produce public fruit.
Inner alignment leads to outer elevation.
The work done in the dark is what manifests in the light.

A storm may bend the branches and shake the trunk … but if the roots remain, the tree rises again … reaching upward, stretching toward its source.

So hear this clearly … stay rooted in truth, and keep reaching for the light. Heaven is not just a destination … it is a pattern. When your inner world aligns with God, your outer world begins to reflect His order, His peace, and His power. This is one true meaning of "on earth as it is in heaven."

Application
- Strengthen your "roots" today … prayer, stillness, Scripture, worship in private.
- Examine whether your outward reach matches your inward depth.
- Declare: "As I align with Heaven inwardly … my life will reflect Heaven outwardly."

Prayer
Father, align my inner world with Your will. Deepen my roots in truth, steady my heart in Your presence, and lift my life toward Your light. Let what is done in me secretly produce fruit that honors You publicly. Make my life a reflection of Heaven … on earth, as it is in Jesus' name. **Amen.**

March 15
If You Ain't Giving, You Ain't Living

Acts 20:35
..."*It is more blessed to give than to receive.*"

Reflection
Let's be real ... if you're not giving, you're not truly living ... not in the Kingdom, not in the Spirit, not in the life God designed for you.

Giving is not just an action ... it is a posture. It is how you breathe life into others, and how God breathes life back into you. The world is obsessed with getting, keeping, and storing up ... but Heaven moves on generosity.

God so loved that He gave. Jesus so loved that He gave. So how can a Kingdom citizen live fully without stepping into the rhythm of divine generosity?

This isn't just about money. It's forgiveness. Time. Encouragement. Presence. Compassion. Obedience.
Seed is bigger than dollars ... it's anything you release for God's glory.

Here's the truth: every seed has a season, and every seed comes up.
You cannot sow bitterness and reap peace.
You cannot sow selfishness and expect abundance.
You cannot sow nothing and expect something.

But when you plant good seed ... in faith, in love, in obedience ... harvest is inevitable. Not accidental. Not occasional. Inevitable. Because harvest doesn't lie ... it reflects what was sown.

Application
- Examine your life today: What seeds have you been planting ... in words, actions, and attitudes?
- Choose one intentional act of giving ... time, forgiveness, service, or generosity.
- Declare: "I am a giver ... and because I sow good seed, I will see good harvest."

Prayer
Lord, teach me to give like You give — freely, joyfully, and intentionally. Make me a sower of good seed, and help me trust Your timing for the harvest. Turn my life into a stream, not a reservoir ... a vessel through which Your generosity flows. In Jesus' name, **Amen.**

March 16
When Two Become More Than Two

Ecclesiastes 4:9
Two are better than one, because they have a good reward for their toil.

Reflection
When two minds come together, they don't just add ... they create a third, invisible yet tangible mind.

This is the essence of synergy: when two harmonious energies unite, the result is greater than each working alone.

In relationships, partnerships, friendships, ministry teams ... when hearts are aligned, words are honest, and purposes match, something extraordinary happens. The whole becomes greater than the sum of its parts.

But this only works when there is trust, openness, shared direction. If one mind is closed, self-centered, or disconnected, that third mind never forms and the power of togetherness is lost.

You are invited to join with another: spiritually, emotionally, purposefully. When you do, you'll find that you're not just two people walking side by side ... you are co-creating something new.

That new thing could be: deeper insight, greater influence, a stronger call, a clearer path. Don't settle for being isolated. Embrace synergy.

Application
- Think of one person with whom you are aligned in purpose (in ministry, business, or personal life).
- Reach out and say: "Let's work together toward what God has called us to."
- Ask: In what area can our combined strength produce what we cannot do alone?

Prayer
Father, thank You for creating us for relationship ...not just with You, but with one another. Let me not live alone when You intended us to co-labor, co-create, and co-walk. Unite my mind with someone of kindred spirit, align our hearts in Your purpose, and birth through our union a greater mind, a greater calling, a greater impact for Your Kingdom. In Jesus' name, **Amen.**

March 17
The Lord Saves Us From...
In Honor of Rev. Theodore Johnson

Luke 19:10
For the Son of Man has come to seek and to save that which was lost.

Reflection
Jesus is not simply your Savior from hell ... He is your Rescuer from everything that attempts to steal your peace, distort your identity, and derail your destiny. When we say "Lord and Savior," we aren't repeating a church cliché ... we are declaring that Christ holds full authority to save us from anything that seeks to destroy us ... including ourselves.

Salvation is not merely an event ... it is an ongoing rescue. Every day Christ is drawing you out of what harms you and into what heals you. He seeks you, saves you, restores you, and transforms you. That's why Luke 19:10 is more than a verse ... it's a lifeline.

The Lord rescues us from far more than we often recognize. He saves us from **condemnation**, freeing us from a past that no longer defines us (Romans 8:1). He delivers us from **ignorance**, bringing us out of darkness into His light (John 8:12). He breaks the power of **fear**, giving us power, love, and a sound mind (2 Timothy 1:7). He even saves us from **ourselves**, teaching our will to bow to His (Luke 22:42). He frees us from **sin**, both forgiving us and breaking its hold (Matthew 1:21), and from **Satan**, moving us from darkness into light (1 John 3:8). He protects us from **this evil age**, reminding us we are in the world but not of it (Galatians 1:4). He lifts us from **hopelessness**, anchoring us in eternal hope (Hebrews 6:19). He brings us from **spiritual death** to life in Christ (Ephesians 2:5). And He saves us from **emptiness**, offering abundant life in Him (John 10:10).

Application
- Identify one area today where you still need Christ's rescue ... fear, guilt, distraction, or internal struggle.
- Surrender that area in prayer and declare His Lordship over it.
- Remind yourself: "Jesus is still saving me ... from what tries to destroy me."

Prayer
Lord, thank You for saving me ... not just once, but daily. Deliver me from anything that is not like You, and lead me into the fullness of the life You purchased for me. Be my Lord. Be my Savior. Be my Everything. In Jesus' name, **Amen.**

March 18
Hard Work Works

Colossians 3:23
Whatever you do, do your work heartily, as for the Lord rather than for men.

Reflection
Struggle is not the proof that you're failing … it's the evidence that you're growing.

The meaning of life isn't avoiding challenge … it's engaging the battle with faith, discipline, and perseverance. Victory or defeat rests in God's sovereign hands, but the struggle with self … pushing past laziness, fear, and comfort … that part is your responsibility.

Hard work works because it transforms you from the inside out. It's less about the trophies you earn and more about the character you develop. God uses your effort, your diligence, and your refusal to quit as chisels that shape Christlikeness in you.

When you embrace the struggle with joy, something powerful happens. The grind stops feeling like punishment and becomes preparation. The battle becomes your teacher. The work becomes worship. Your job is to show up with excellence … God's job is to decide the outcome.

And He honors those who work heartily … because hard work is not just physical effort … it is spiritual obedience.

Application
- Identify the area where you are the biggest obstacle … procrastination, fear, inconsistency, or comfort.
- Commit to one act of disciplined effort today as worship unto the Lord.
- Declare: "Effort is my responsibility … the outcome belongs to God."

Prayer
Father, thank You for giving me the strength to work and the opportunity to grow. Help me to see hard work not as a burden, but as a blessing. Give me the discipline to push past my limits with joy, knowing You are shaping me through every challenge. Form Christ in me through every effort. In Jesus' name, **Amen.**

March 19

From Worry to Wonder

Philippians 4:6–7
Be anxious for nothing, but in everything by prayer and supplication with thanksgiving let your requests be made known to God. And the peace of God, which surpasses all comprehension, will guard your hearts and your minds in Christ Jesus.

Reflection
Worry and wonder often sit on opposite sides of the same thought. When you worry, you imagine what might go wrong. When you walk in faith, you imagine what God might do.

The difference is a mindset shift.

Worry looks at tomorrow through the lens of fear. Wonder looks at tomorrow through the lens of faith. Worry drains you; wonder fuels you. Worry shrinks possibilities; wonder opens doors.

God never called us to be prisoners of "what if." He called us to be carriers of "even if." Even if tomorrow is uncertain, God is certain. Even if the outcome is unclear, His promises are sure.

When your mind starts racing with anxiety, you have a choice. Will you imagine disaster, or will you expect destiny? Will you rehearse problems, or will you anticipate miracles?

Every time you choose wonder over worry, you honor the God who holds tomorrow in His hands.

Application
- Write down one thing that you're tempted to worry about today.
- Then rewrite it as a faith-filled expectation. (Example: Instead of "I'm worried I won't have enough," declare, "I'm excited to see how God will provide.")
- Begin practicing this daily shift ... move from "what if" fear to "what if" faith.

Prayer
Lord, renew my mind so I no longer live in the shadow of worry. Teach me to expect good things from You, because You are faithful. Help me replace every anxious thought with anticipation of Your glory. **Amen.**

March 20
The Power of Small Acts

Galatians 6:9
And let us not grow weary of doing good, for in due time we will reap, if we do not give up.

Reflection
You have more power than you know. Not the kind that headlines newspapers or fills stadiums … but the kind that transforms someone's day … and sometimes, their life.

Kindness is Kingdom currency. It rarely looks impressive on the surface, yet in the hands of God, it multiplies. A smile, a gentle word, a moment of patience, a prayer whispered over someone's hidden pain … these are not wasted gestures. They are seeds. And seeds never stay seeds … they grow into hope, healing, strength, and reminders that Heaven still sees and cares.

You may not be able to fix the whole world today … but you can change someone's world. That's how revival begins … not always through sermons or platforms, but through compassion. Through presence. Through small acts of love that carry eternal weight.

As Senator Cory Booker said, "We may not be able to change the world, but we can make a world of change in one person's life."

Amen and Amen.

Application
- Ask God to show you one person who needs a small act of kindness today.
- Look for one simple way to serve … a word, a prayer, a gesture.
- Declare: "My small acts carry Kingdom impact."

Prayer
Father, use me today in quiet ways that make eternal impact. Open my eyes to the one who needs encouragement, kindness, or compassion. Let my hands reflect Your heart, and let every small seed I sow become a testimony of Your love. In Jesus' name, **Amen.**

March 21
Change Your Mind, Change Your Life

Romans 12:2
Do not be conformed to this world, but be transformed by the renewal of your mind, that by testing you may discern what is the will of God, what is good and acceptable and perfect.

Reflection
If you want to change your life, you must begin with your thoughts.

The world says, "Change your circumstances." God says, "Change your mind." Transformation starts inward long before it ever shows up outwardly.

Changing what you think changes how you feel.
Changing how you feel changes how you act.
Changing how you act … changes your life.
But the root of it all is what you believe to be true.

This is why the enemy wages war in the arena of the mind. If he can distort your beliefs, he can hijack your behavior. If he can pollute your thinking, he can paralyze your purpose. But when your thoughts are renewed by the Word of God, your life begins to align with His will.

Mindset is mission-critical in the Kingdom.
You cannot walk in peace with a polluted mind.
You cannot pursue purpose while entertaining lies.

Do not let culture shape your thinking.
Let Christ do the renewing.

A transformed mind leads to a transformed life.

Application
- Identify one limiting belief or toxic thought pattern that has been shaping your behavior.
- Replace it with a truth from Scripture … write it, speak it, meditate on it.
- Declare: "Lord, renew my mind … and align my life with Your truth."

Prayer
Lord, renew my mind. Rewire my thinking. Uproot every lie, every fear, and every thought that is not from You. Fill my mind with Your Word so I can live in alignment with Your will. Transform me from the inside out … thought by thought, truth by truth. In Jesus' name, **Amen.**

March 22
The Only Person Coming to Save You

Philippians 2:12–13
Work out your own salvation with fear and trembling; for it is God who is at work in you, both to desire and to work for His good pleasure.

Reflection
The only person coming to save you is the version of yourself who finally gets tired of your current situation.

God has already given you His Spirit, His promises, and His presence. But transformation won't begin until you decide that staying where you are is no longer an option.

Israel couldn't remain in Egypt and walk into the Promised Land.
The prodigal son couldn't stay in the pigpen and return to his father's embrace.

You cannot remain in cycles of comfort, compromise, or complaint and still expect breakthrough.

Deliverance always begins with a decision.
The Holy Spirit empowers you … but you must agree with Him.
Sometimes the greatest miracle is not that God moves the mountain … but that you finally get tired enough to climb it.

Breakthrough waits on participation. God invites, but He will not drag you into your destiny. You must rise, step, and align.

Application
- Identify one situation in your life that no longer aligns with who God is calling you to become.
- Choose one practical step today to partner with the Spirit's work in you … a phone call, a decision, a boundary, a commitment.
- Declare: "I refuse to stay stuck … I rise with the power of God working in me."

Prayer
Lord, make me dissatisfied with anything less than Your will. Give me the courage to rise from where I am and walk with You into the life You prepared for me. Empower the version of me that agrees with Your Spirit. Let today mark a turning point. In Jesus' name, **Amen.**

March 23

When the Storm Comes:

Matthew 7:24-25
Therefore everyone who hears these words of Mine and does them, will be like a wise man who built his house on the rock; ... the rain descended, the floods came, the winds blew and beat against that house, and it did not fall, for it was founded on the rock.

Reflection
Every storm that hits your life carries two purposes: to destroy what isn't solid and to reveal what is. It rips away the structures built on weak ground ... habits, relationships, identities, parts of life that weren't anchored in truth, integrity, or faith.

It exposes what remains: what stands strong when the wind blows, the rain falls, the floods rise. What remains is proof of what is built to last.

As Jesus taught, the wise person builds on the rock so that when the storm comes, the house stands. The foolish build on sand, and when the storm hits, everything crashes. These storms don't just happen to test you ... they reveal where your foundation is.

So don't let this season of trial just define you ... let it refine you.

Let what falls away free you.
Let what remains become your testimony.

Application
- Ask: "What parts of my life are built on weak ground ... comfort, neglect, compromise?"
- Make a decision: "I will build on the Rock ... Christ ... so I stand firm."
- Take one step today: a confession, repentance, a renewed commitment to truth, a conversation you've avoided.

Prayer
Father, thank You that You stand as my Rock. When the storms hit ... and they will ... help me to see that You aren't the cause of my destruction, but the anchor of my deliverance. Reveal where I'm built on weak ground, and help me rebuild on You. Let what remains in me after the storm be strong, true, and pleasing in Your sight. In Jesus' name, **Amen.**

March 24
The Enemy Wants More than Casualties

1 John 3:8
He who makes a practice of sinning is of the devil; for the devil has sinned from the beginning.

Reflection
The enemy doesn't merely want casualties … he wants converts. He doesn't want people broken in defeat; he wants people bound in allegiance. While he could destroy you, his deeper victory comes when he draws you into his kingdom of darkness, making you his follower rather than simply his victim.

Jesus warns in John 10:10 that the thief comes to steal, kill, and destroy … but He came so that we may have life, and have it in abundance. In other words: the enemy's goal isn't just damage … it's dominion.

In 1 John 3:8 we learn that continuing in sin characterizes someone who is aligned with the devil. He doesn't merely strike superficially … he slips into identity, system, practice.

When you realize the strategy of evil isn't just "messing you up" but "making you one of his," it changes the stakes. You're not just fighting storms … you're guarding your allegiance. Are you holding your life loosely?

Is your identity rooted in Christ or drifting in the wind of compromise?

Application
- Reflect: Where have I been treated as a casualty and still trapped? Where have I accepted forms of allegiance that don't align with Christ?
- Commit to one concrete step today: remove a habit, realign a relationship, bring a formerly secret struggle into light … so allegiance to Christ becomes clear.
- Declare: "I will not simply survive … you'll not make me your casualty. I belong to Christ and I will live in His freedom."

Prayer
Father, thank You for sending Your Son to bring life … not next to death, but through victory. I confess any allegiance I've given to the schemes of darkness, any compromise where I became more than a casualty. I ask You now: break every invisible contract, uproot the lies, free my identity so I stand fully aligned with You. Let me live as a convert to Your Kingdom, not a casualty of the enemy. In Jesus' name, **Amen.**

March 25
The Gospel Means More Than Blessings ... It Means Change

2 Corinthians 3:18
And we all, with unveiled face, beholding the glory of the Lord, are being transformed into the same image from one degree of glory to another.

Reflection
The gospel wasn't given simply to serve us ... it was given to transform us. It's not just about gaining privileges, feeling better, or receiving blessings. It's about becoming new.

The true power of the gospel (good news) lies in its ability to change hearts, minds, and lives.

When we reduce the gospel to what it does for us ... comforts, protects, rewards ... we miss what it does in us.

The message of Christ is: "You are new, you are changed, you are being made like Me."

Transformation isn't optional for believers
... it's the evidence of the gospel's power.

If your life looks the same as it did before Christ, something's off.

The gospel is not merely your ticket ... it's your transformation.

Application
- Reflect: "What part of me has not yet been changed by the gospel?"
- Choose one area you'll let the gospel transform today ... perhaps your attitude, your habits, your speech.
- Declare: "I don't just believe the gospel ... I let it change me."
- At day's end: Ask: How did I respond to the gospel today ... not just receive it, but let it work in me?

Prayer
Father, thank You for the gospel that does more than save ... it changes. I receive Your power, I yield to Your transformation. Let more of You show up in me. Let the old fade, and the new shine. In Jesus' name, **Amen.**

March 26

Change Born from Love

Ezekiel 36:26
And He will give you a new heart, and a new spirit I will put within you.

Reflection
Here's a truth worth remembering: God does not change us so He can love us; He loves us so He can change us.

His love for us isn't conditional upon performance …
His love is the foundation from which transformation flows.

While we may live believing we need to become something different before God will accept us, the Gospel says the opposite: He loves us first, and then by His love, He begins to remake us.

The pathway of change isn't a list of things you must do to earn His affection … it's the outflow of receiving His affection.

When you rest in the reality of His love, the heart becomes fertile soil for His work. God's love allows you to change and grow into the person He wants you to become.

So stop living under the weight of trying to be "good enough" for Him. Let His love lift you into the space where change isn't forced … it's formed by relationship.

Application
- Close your eyes and say this: "God, I receive Your love for me right now. I yield to Your work of change in me."
- Identify one area where you've tried to change by willpower alone rather than by love. Invite God's love into it instead of guilt.
- Declare: "Because You love me, I will change …not to earn Your love, but because Your love is shaping me."

Prayer
Father, You loved me long before I knew You. Thank You for Your initiating love that changes my heart, renews my mind, and frees my life. I cease striving to make myself acceptable and simply receive the love You already poured out. Change me, shape me, by Your love … not by my efforts. In Jesus' name, **Amen.**

March 27

Grace Over Performance: Entering the Kingdom by Faith

Ephesians 2:8-9
For by grace you have been saved through faith; and this is not from yourselves, it is the gift of God ... not by works, so that no one may boast.

Reflection
The Kingdom of God isn't about ticking boxes, earning points, or hoping you've done enough. It's about believing and receiving.

When you try to climb in God's favor through merit, you miss the heart of the Gospel.

Grace doesn't work like a treadmill ...it's a doorway. Scripture says salvation is "not by works, so that no one may boast."

Think about it:
You don't climb your way into God's presence ...you trust your way in.
You don't work for His love ... you welcome it.
You don't qualify yourself ... He already called you.

Religion says: Do more. The Kingdom says: Believe Me.

When you stop striving to be "good enough," you finally meet the God who is more than enough.

Drop the performance. Receive the grace. Live free.

Application
- If you're exhausted by self-effort, pray: "Lord, I receive Your grace. I abandon the pedestal of performance and rest in Your finished work."
- Identify one area where you've hustled for God's approval ... say: "Today I will lean on faith, not on feeling worthy."
- Declare: "I am in the Kingdom by faith. I believe. I receive. I live free."

Prayer
Father, thank You for saving me by grace through faith ... not by what I've done, but by what You did. Help me to live from the place of receiving, not trying to earn. Teach me to rest in Your love, walk in Your calling, and serve from my freedom, not my performance. In Jesus' name, **Amen.**

March 28

The Illusion of a Compromised Gospel

Galatians 1:6-7
For I am astonished that you are so quickly deserting the one who called you in the grace of Christ and are turning to a different gospel ...which is not another gospel; but there are some who trouble you and want to distort the gospel of Christ.

Reflection
Thankfully, we serve a God who does not change, whose Word remains pure and powerful. Yet many churches and many messages today have compromised that Word. The enemy has found a foothold in a gospel preached too liberally." The danger of a watered-down gospel.

We have romanticized and compromised the Word of God. Instead of presenting the full truth, we've softened, sweetened, and repackaged it so it aligns with culture, pleases ears, and avoids offense. Meanwhile, the enemy steps in through what appears safe, acceptable, and popular ... shaping hearts with a gospel that lacks power and purpose.

The Gospel isn't primarily about comfort ... it's about transformation. But when the message shifts from "Be changed" to "Be comfortable," from "Follow Christ" to "Feel good," we lose the potency of the Word. Churches trade depth for reach, doctrine for presentation; the Word becomes diluted, the message becomes pliable, and the call to holiness becomes optional.

Don't just worship the Word ... let the Word change you. Don't just receive comfort ... be transformed by the truth. Because a gospel compromised in message leads to lives compromised in power.

Application
- Ask: Which part of the Gospel have I softened to make life easier?
- Choose one truth you've ignored because it was uncomfortable ... then respond: repentance, obedience, step of faith.
- Declare: "I will not accept the gospel that pleases me more than it changes me."

Prayer
Father, forgive me for being content with a gospel that sounds good but lacks power. Forgive the times I chose ease over truth, comfort over conviction, popularity over purity. Renew in me the hunger for Your Word in full ... its depth, its challenge, its transforming power. Let Your Gospel ... not mine ... shape me, lead me, and send me out. In Jesus' name, **Amen.**

March 29
The Illusion of Money: The Price of Nothing

Luke 12:15
Then He said to them, 'Beware, and be on your guard against every form of greed; for not even when one has an abundance does his life consist of his possessions.'

Reflection
We were told money makes the world go round. Yet, look at creation: trees don't pay rent, the sun doesn't invoice for light, and God never charged you for your first breath.

Still, we spend our lives chasing past what Heaven gave freely. We confuse value with valuation, making paper and digits our security instead of Him.

Jesus' warning in Luke 12:15 rings clear: life is not measured by how many possessions you accumulate.

Greed, or the unending grasp for more, destroys our soul, distracts our purpose, and draws us away from the eternal to the ephemeral.
When you chase money as your identity, you sell your time, your peace, and your life for a marker that can vanish overnight.

Maybe the real wealth is everything money can't buy … presence, purpose, peace, love, and the legacy of serving rather than accumulating.

Application
- Reflect on your habits today: Is my focus on acquiring … or being?
- Identify one area where money or possessions are driving my decisions. Ask: Is this aligned with God's kingdom or my comfort zone?
- Declare: "I will place my security in God, not in the numbers. I will treasure what lasts."

Prayer
Father, forgive me when I placed more worth on wealth than on You. Let my value be found in You, not in possessions. Guard my heart from greed, reshape my mind toward kingdom treasures, and lead me in the freedom of Your provision. In Jesus' name, **Amen.**

March 30
Peace Is Power

John 14:27
Peace I leave with you; My peace I give to you; not as the world gives do I give to you. Do not let your heart be troubled, nor let it be fearful.

Reflection
When you lose your peace, you lose your power.

Peace is not the absence of conflict … it is the presence of God ruling your heart and mind. It's the calm center in the middle of chaos, the inner stillness that keeps you steady while everything else around you shifts and shakes.

The enemy knows the strength of a peaceful heart … that's why he stirs offense, fuels drama, and ignites fear. A restless heart is a distracted heart … and a distracted heart is a powerless one.

When Jesus said, "My peace I give to you," He wasn't offering a feeling … He was handing you a spiritual weapon.

Peace sharpens your discernment. Peace steadies your emotions. Peace positions you to hear from God and act with wisdom.

When you guard your peace, you guard your power. But when you forfeit your peace, you surrender the strength that helps you overcome.

Heaven fights for the believer who stands still in peace.

Application
- Guard your peace like treasure … it is your spiritual power source.
- Refuse emotional bait … not every conflict deserves your energy or response.
- Stay rooted in prayer … it shifts your focus from circumstances to God's control.

Prayer
Father, thank You for the gift of Your peace. Help me to hold it, protect it, and walk in it no matter what happens around me. Remind me daily that by keeping my peace, I keep my power. Fight for me as I stand still and trust You. In Jesus' name, **Amen.**

March 31
Guarding Your Peace

Proverbs 4:23
Watch over your heart with all diligence, for from it flow the springs of life.

Reflection
Do not let the behavior of others destroy your inner peace.

You cannot control the words, choices, or reactions of people ... but you can always control how you respond.

Your peace is not optional ... it is a spiritual safeguard. It is the environment where faith grows, joy thrives, and God's voice becomes clear.

When you hand your peace over to someone else's attitude, you give them access to a place in your spirit that belongs only to God. That is why the enemy tries so hard to provoke you ... constant reacting, emotional instability, and inner agitation weaken your spiritual footing.

But Scripture calls you higher. "As far as it depends on you," live in peace. That means setting boundaries, guarding your heart, and refusing to let another person's chaos pull you into their storm.

Peace is not passive ... it is a weapon.

When you protect it, you protect the flow of God's life within you.

Application
- Pause before reacting ... let the Holy Spirit guide your response.
- Pray for those who disturb your peace ... it disarms offense and frees your heart.
- Stay rooted in the Word ... lasting peace is sustained by truth, not circumstance.

Prayer
Lord, teach me to guard my heart with diligence. Keep me unshaken by the actions or emotions of others, and strengthen me to remain in the peace that only You can give. Let my responses honor You and protect the springs of life flowing within me. In Jesus' name, **Amen.**

April 1
Happy New Year April Fool

Exodus 12:2
This month shall be the beginning of months for you; it is to be the first month of the year to you.

Reflection
The world celebrates a new year in the cold of January ... but God marked His New Year in the warmth of spring.

In Scripture, the year begins in Abib ... Nisan (March/April) ... the season of Passover, deliverance, resurrection, and new life. While the world is still chasing resolutions, Heaven is quietly announcing a divine reset.

Spring is when God told Israel, "This month shall be the beginning of months for you." In that same season, He broke chains in Egypt, led His people through the Red Sea, brought manna from Heaven, crossed them into the Promised Land, and, allowed Jesus to be crucified and raised with resurrection power. Nisan is God's month of pivots ... when old stories end and new chapters begin.

For me, April 1 is my natural birthday ... but more than that, it is a prophetic picture: new beginnings, fresh starts, divine alignment, and transformation ... right in the middle of what others call "spring time."

So if you feel late, behind, or stuck in cycles that should have ended long ago, hear this truth deep in your spirit: you are not late ... you are right on time for God's spring. Today isn't just another day ... today is a pivot point, a divine reset, an invitation to begin again. Today represents a God appointed turning point when He says, "This will be the beginning of months for you."

Application
- Identify one area where you need a true, God-sized new beginning
- Declare aloud: "I align with God's timing and step boldly into my new season."
- Write three testimonies that prove God has brought you out before.

Prayer
Father, thank You that new beginnings flow from Your timing, not man's calendar. As You marked Nisan as the first month, mark this day as a holy reset in my life. Renew my mind, break old cycles, and align my steps with Your purpose. Let resurrection power rise in me and spring forth something new. I step into Your season with faith and obedience. In Jesus' name, **Amen.**

April 2
Refined for Elevation

Zechariah 13:9a
I will put this third into the fire, and refine them as silver, and test them as gold is tested.

Reflection
When God sets His eyes on elevating you, the process often begins not with a crown ... but with a break.

He doesn't pamper you first; He prepares you.

He stretches your faith beyond comfort zones, shakes you from complacency, and places you in the fire ... not to destroy you, but to refine you. Just as a blacksmith keeps silver and gold in the flames until he can see his own reflection, God holds you in His refining fire until His image begins to appear in you. Only then does He pull you out ... because now you are ready, strengthened, and fit for His use.

Every tear, every test, every trial becomes part of that refining. Nothing is wasted. The heat that feels unbearable is burning away impurities, revealing a stronger, purer version of who you were always meant to be.

So don't resist the process. Power doesn't come from ease; it's born in endurance and transformation.

Let God forge you in the fire until you can stand unshaken ... shining as a reflection of His image.

Application
- Identify one challenge you're facing and ask God to show you how He is using it to prepare you for what's ahead.
- Declare with faith: "Lord, I yield to Your refining ... make me pure, prepared, and powerful for what You've promised."
- Take one bold step of obedience today and trust that God is shaping you through the process, even before you see the outcome.

Prayer
Father, I thank You that You don't skip the preparation when You're preparing me for something great. Help me to embrace the refining fire. Remove the dross of self-reliance, ease, and comfort. Build strength where I'm weak, faith where I falter, and purpose where I settle. I trust You to elevate me ...not on my terms, but on Yours. In Jesus' name, **Amen.**

April 3
Ready is a Decision, Not a Feeling

2 Corinthians 5:7
For we walk by faith, not by sight.

Reflection
Most people wait until they "feel ready" to move. They wait for the confidence, the clarity, the comfort. But that kind of waiting often turns into a lifetime of hesitation.

The truth is: ready isn't a feeling … it's a decision.

You don't step out because you feel fearless or perfect … you step out because you decide: "This is my moment."

Faith calls for obedience before emotion, commitment before comfort.

Motivation might spark the start, but discipline, decision and divine purpose carry you through.

So if you're waiting on a feeling, you may wait forever.
Instead … make a decision.
Step when you're called.
Move when God says go.

He'll meet the decision with His strength, even as your feelings catch up.

Application
- Take a look at your life and ask: What am I waiting for before I act?
- Choose one next step today … even if you don't feel ready … just decide: "I will move."
- Declare: "I will not delay because I'm not comfortable; I will move because I'm committed."

Prayer
Father, thank You that You honor my decision even when I don't feel ready. Help me to trust that You will supply what I lack … strength, clarity, courage. I choose obedience over comfort, decision over delay. Let me walk forward in faith, knowing You go with me. In Jesus' name, **Amen.**

April 4

Build the Builder Before You Build the Business

Ephesians 2:10
For we are God's handiwork, created in Christ Jesus for good works, which God prepared beforehand that we should walk in them.

Reflection
Entrepreneurship isn't just about the business you launch … it's about the person you become in the process.

It's easy to download a business plan, register an LLC, post content, or buy inventory. But becoming the version of you who can sustain the dream? That's the real work.

Articles on entrepreneurship repeatedly point out: "Your business can't grow if you yourself aren't growing." You must develop discipline you've never had, faith you've never walked in, consistency you've never shown.

The business will eventually reflect your growth … or expose your lack.

So ask: Are you investing in your character, mindset, and habits? Because the business simply can't outgrow its builder.

Application
- Identify one area in your life that needs growth: time management, self-discipline, faith-walk.
- Choose one small but consistent step today: read 15 minutes, journal your vision, pray through one fear.
- Declare: "I commit to building myself before I build my business."

Prayer
Father, thank You for the dream You've placed in me. Help me to recognize that before the business thrives, I must grow. Develop in me discipline, focus, faith, and consistency. Let the person You're shaping become strong so the venture You give can stand strong. In Jesus' name, **Amen.**

April 5

I Didn't Come to Go Along; I Came to Create a New Song

Psalm 96:1
Sing to the Lord a new song; sing to the Lord, all the earth.

Reflection
Today you may hear the call: "Go along to get along." But deep down, you know you weren't created merely to fit in ... you were designed to stand out for God's glory.

The phrase "sing a new song" in the Psalms carries the idea of something fresh, something distinct that rises out of new experience, new victory, and new identity.

The word sanctified means "set apart."

When God sets you apart, He doesn't just ask you to repeat what's been done ... He invites you to compose what's never been done or heard.

You weren't made to echo the culture, the crowd, or the comfort zone. You were made to carry a unique melody of purpose, faith, service, and love.

So if you feel the stirring in your spirit that you're meant for more than routine ... welcome it. It's the song that only you can sing, the mission only you can live, the difference only you can make.

Application
- Ask: What old song am I still singing ... beliefs, habits, voices ... that keep me from creating the new song God has placed in me?
- Choose one step today that aligns you with the fresh song: a bold act of faith, a new idea of service, a change of mindset.
- Declare: "I will not go along; I will create. I will let my life compose a new song of God's power and purpose."

Prayer
Father, thank You that You don't call me to conformity but to creativity in You. Help me to stop singing the old refrains of fear, insignificance, and comfort. Compose in me a new song ... one of courage, boldness, and grace. Let my life be a melody that honors You and inspires others. In Jesus' name, **Amen.**

April 6

Public Praise Flows from Private Worship

Matthew 6:6
But you, when you pray, enter into your inner chamber, and having shut your door, pray to your Father who is in secret; and your Father who sees in secret will reward you.

Reflection
Here's a truth: we often struggle to praise and worship God publicly because we haven't worshipped Him privately.

When our worship is only surface-level ... what others see ... we miss the deep encounter in the "Holy of Holies", the hidden place where we meet God alone. If our worship begins in the public pew but never originates in the quiet whisper of our heart, our praise is hollow. We can sing the songs, raise the hands ... but the heart remains untouched, unprepared, un-transformed.

Private worship does more than prepare for Sunday ... it cultivates authenticity, establishes a rhythm of surrender, and enables our public praise to be genuine. You cannot give what you don't receive in private.

When you spend time alone with God ... reading His Word, speaking with Him, listening ... it shapes your spirit so that when you stand before others, your worship is heard, felt, and real.

Application
- Set aside 10 minutes today in a quiet place where no one sees you. Read a short Psalm or chapter. Pray it through.
- Ask: "Am I more comfortable praising in front of people than pouring out in private?"
- Make a simple commitment: "This week I will cultivate a 'secret place' so that my public praise will flow from genuine encounter."

Prayer
Father, I thank You that You see me in secret and invite me into Your presence. Forgive me for times I've worshipped for show but neglected the chambers of my heart. Help me to cultivate private worship so that my public praise is honoring, real, and powerful. Transform me in the quiet so when the songs rise in company, You receive genuine adoration. In Jesus' name,
Amen.

April 7

To Get To The Promise

Deuteronomy 2:3
You have circled this mountain long enough; now turn north.

Reflection
There's a reason many believers stay stuck: they carry a wilderness mindset into their promise land.

The wilderness mindset is built on survival, fear, comparison, and past limitations. It thinks small and lives in repeat loops. As one teaching put it: "We go around and around the same mountain instead of making progress."

But the promise land mindset is different.

It trusts God's provision, embraces growth, steps forward in faith, and leaves yesterday in the rearview.

When you try to live by wilderness thinking in your season of promise, you risk forfeiting what God has already prepared for you.

Remember: the land flowing with milk and honey required a different walk than wandering in the desert. If your mindset's still stuck in the desert … you'll never claim the abundance on the other side.

Application
- Identify one "wilderness thought" today … fear of lack, old identity, survival mode.
- Replace it with a promise thought: "God has already provided. I walk in abundance. I am His."
- Take one action that steps toward your promise land: perhaps a bold move of faith, a new initiative, or a heart shift from scarcity to abundance.

Prayer
Father, thank You for the promises You've placed before me … the lands of fruitfulness, purpose, and peace. Forgive me for carrying a survival mindset into my season of promise. Renew my mind, shift my perspective, and give me the courage to step into what You've prepared. I choose to walk in Your abundance, not my lack; in Your presence, not my fear. In Jesus' name,
Amen.

April 8

Habits Shape Your Horizon

Galatians 6:9

*And let us not grow weary of doing good, for in due season we will reap, if we do not give u*p.

Reflection

Successful people have habits that lazy people are too lazy to develop.

The difference isn't luck … it's discipline. While many wait for "motivation" or "chance," those who succeed lean into habits that build character and momentum.

Here's what sets them apart:
They act before they feel like it. Discipline is choosing the right step when you don't feel like it.

They build small, consistent habits rather than waiting for grand transformation. "Tiny tasks kept" builds trust in self.

They guard their environment, their rhythms, their energy … so that the right actions become easier.

When you don't develop these habits the lazy ignore, you surrender your future to randomness. The horizon becomes what happens to you, rather than what you shape. But when you diligently build good habits, you steer your destiny rather than drift into the abyss of life.

Application

- Choose one habit today … even a small one (for example: wake 15 minutes earlier, write one gratitude note, set your priorities).
- Commit: "I will keep this habit for 7 days straight and track it."
- Ask yourself: "What habit am I neglecting because it doesn't feel urgent, but it matters long-term?"

Prayer

Father, give me the strength to build habits that honor You … habits of discipline, focus, and obedience. Help me not to be lazy in what matters most. Mold my daily rhythms so my life aligns with Your purpose, and let the small things I do today prepare me for the harvest You have planned. In Jesus' name, **Amen.**

April 9
Choose Daily Discipline

1 Corinthians 9:27
No, I discipline my body and make it my slave, so that after preaching to others I myself will not be disqualified.

Reflection
Motivation gets you started ... but discipline keeps you going.

Motivation is a feeling.
Discipline is a decision.

Feelings come and go. They are like waves ... they rise, they crash, they fade. But discipline holds steady when your emotions have changed.

Discipline is consistency in motion: the daily training of your will, obedience to your purpose, and commitment to your plan.

The Christian life doesn't rely on "feeling godly" but choosing to honor God even when you don't feel like it. Discipline is worship beyond emotion, and it reveals faith that lasts.

When you schedule your quiet time, set your priorities, serve when no one sees ... you're not relying on the spark of motivation ... you're walking in steadfast discipline.

You'll start strong with motivation ... but you'll finish victorious with discipline.

Application
- Decide today: What one habit will I discipline, even if I don't feel like it?
- Schedule it: Write it down, set a reminder, prepare your mindset ahead of time.
- Declare: "I will not rely on how I feel. I will act because I've committed to God's purpose."

Prayer
Father, thank You that You reward steadfastness. Help me not to rely on fleeting motivation, but to walk in disciplined obedience. Shape my habits, strengthen my will, and align my actions with Your purpose. Even when I don't feel it, let my discipline honor You and bring forth lasting fruit. In Jesus' name, **Amen.**

April 10

Mastering Your Three Currencies: Knowledge ,Time, Money

Proverbs 2:6
For the Lord gives wisdom; from His mouth come knowledge and understanding.

Reflection
In life, you hold three primary currencies: Knowledge, Time, and Money. When you lack one, you can often leverage the other two to obtain it. This principle isn't just for business ... it's for your walk of faith and purpose.

Knowledge unlocks insight, opens doors, and informs your decisions. Time is finite and irreplaceable; how you spend it shapes your destiny. Money offers access, freedom, and ability ... but it isn't the only way.

Example: If you lack money, you can use time (work, serve) and knowledge (skill, wisdom) to generate it. If you lack knowledge, you can use time (study, listen) and money (invest in learning) to acquire it. If you lack time, you can use knowledge (efficiency, prioritization) and money (delegate, automate) to free it.

In your spiritual life:
If you feel you lack wisdom (knowledge) for a challenge, invest time in prayer and scripture and use your resources to access mentorship or study.

If you feel constrained by time for service or growth, use your knowledge to streamline your schedule and your resources to support your efforts.

If you feel restricted by money, use what you know (faith, gifting) and give of your time ... God often multiplies what's invested.

Application
- Choose one currency you feel you're lacking today.
- Ask: Which of the other two can I use to acquire it?
- Commit: "I will use my time and knowledge to invest in this area," or "I will use my money and time to develop my knowledge," etc.

Prayer
Father, thank You for the resources You entrusted me with ... my mind, my hours, my finances. Help me to steward them wisely. When I'm lacking in one area, give me wisdom to use the others. Let my use of knowledge, time, and money honor You and further Your Kingdom. In Jesus' name, **Amen.**

April 11

Heal the Parent, Protect the Child

Exodus 20:5
For the sins of the fathers are visited on the children to the third and the fourth generations of those who hate Me.

Reflection
The child's first enemy is an unhealed parent.

This statement isn't an attack on parents … it's a revelation about pain. When a mother or father carries unresolved wounds … fear, trauma, anger, abandonment, insecurity … those wounds often spill over into the atmosphere their child grows up in. Not out of malice … but because hurt people tend to hurt people.

An unhealed parent reacts from pain rather than love. Their child ends up fighting battles that belonged to generations before them. Sometimes the child isn't wrestling with their own identity … but with the unprocessed shadows of the parent's past. The Bible shows us this reality through generational patterns … cycles that continue when they're not confronted, but break when Christ heals. Through Christ, the old can truly pass away, and the new can come. We must heal and turn our pain into purpose.… because pain that does not get transformed, gets transferred.

This truth reframes everything:
The parent is not the enemy … unhealed pain is. The question then becomes: Will I pass down my wounds … or my healing?

Application
- Reflect: Identify the pain or patterns that may be shaping those you lead or love.
- Invite: Ask God to heal what could overflow into the next generation.
- Declare: The cycle stops with me I will pass down healing, not hurt.

Prayer
Father, heal every wound in me that has the power to touch the next generation. Break every unhealthy pattern, silence every inherited lie, and restore what was damaged in my childhood or my parent's childhood. Make me whole so I can lead, love, and nurture from a place of wholeness. Let the healing You begin in me become a shield of protection around my children and their children. In Jesus' name, **Amen.**

April 12
He Is Everything to Me

Colossians 1:18
And He is the head of the body, the church; He is the beginning, the firstborn from the dead, so that He Himself will come to have first place in everything.

Reflection
There's a powerful quote attributed to Adrian Rogers: "When you think you are something, that means that God is not your EVERYTHING."

This truth exposes the subtle ways pride, self-reliance, and identity creep into places only Christ should occupy.

Whenever I elevate my abilities, my titles, my success, or even my spiritual progress, I unintentionally dethrone the One who deserves first place in all things. Christ cannot simply be important; He must be Supreme.

God desires to be my EVERYTHING ... my source, my strength, my direction, my identity. Not my backup plan when life gets heavy, not my occasional refuge when things fall apart, but my all in all. When Jesus truly becomes first in my life, everything else finds its rightful place beneath Him.

And when He covers every part of your life ... as Savior who redeems you, as Lord who leads you, as Friend who walks with you, and as Provider who sustains you ... you are no longer defined by performance, status, or the opinions of others. You are defined by Him. His supremacy becomes your stability. His presence becomes your peace. His identity becomes your identity.

Application
- Quietly declare: "Jesus, You are everything to me.
- Choose one area today where you've carried the weight of being something. Surrender it to Him and invite Him to be your all in that place.
- Reflect on this: What changes when I stop proving myself and simply rest in Him being everything?

Prayer
Father, You are so much greater than I often live as if You are. Help me to relinquish my striving, my self-identity apart from You. Let You be my everything ... my identity, my worth, my purpose. In Jesus' name, **Amen.**

April 13

The God-Shaped Hole In Your Heart

Ecclesiastes 3:11
He has made everything appropriate in its time. He has also set eternity in their heart, yet so that man will not find out the work which God has done from the beginning even to the end.

Reflection
Inside every human heart is a longing that nothing in this world can satisfy.

We try to fill it with success, relationships, pleasure, or possessions ... but no matter how much we gain, the hunger remains. That emptiness is the God-shaped hole in every believers heart that only God can fill.

Blaise Pascal once said, "There is a God-shaped vacuum in the heart of every man which cannot be filled by any created thing, but only by God the Creator, made known through Jesus Christ."

This longing is not a flaw ... it's divine design. God placed eternity in our hearts so we would never be content with temporary things. The thirst you feel, the restlessness in your soul, is not meant to drive you deeper into the world ... it's meant to draw you closer to Him.

Jesus told the woman at the well: "Whoever drinks of the water that I will give him shall never be thirsty; but the water that I will give him will become in him a fountain of water springing up to eternal life" (John 4:14).

Only God can fill the hole He created. Until He does, you will always feel and be incomplete.

Application
- Identify one thing you've been trying to use to fill your inner emptiness (success, approval, comfort, etc.).
- Surrender that space to God today. Invite Him to fill the longing with His presence.
- Remember: the God-shaped hole is a daily reminder that your heart was made for Him.

Prayer
Lord, I confess that I have tried to fill my emptiness with things that cannot satisfy. Today, I invite You to be the center of my heart. Fill the void with Your presence and make me whole in You. **Amen.**

April 14

A Divine Spark Within

Genesis 2:7
Then the LORD God... breathed into his nostrils the breath of life, and man became a living being.

Reflection
From the very beginning, when God breathed into Adam, something holy ignited inside humanity... a divine spark. This spark is more than motivation or emotion ... it is the breath of God, the imprint of His Spirit, and the seed of His creative power resting inside every believer. And that spark is still in you.

It is the reason your spirit refuses to settle for average.
It is the inner fire that nudges you toward destiny.
It is the quiet reminder that you were created on purpose, with purpose, and for purpose. But a spark unattended grows cold.

Paul told Timothy to fan it into flame ... to stir it, guard it, fuel it... because what God places in you must be awakened by you. When your divine spark is alive, clarity rises, courage grows, and your life becomes a light that shifts atmospheres.

Beautiful people, you are not waiting for greatness. You are carrying it. You are breathing it. You are walking with the very fire of God within. Let that truth reorder your day, your decisions, and your direction.

This cold world needs the flame God placed inside you.

Application
- Acknowledge the divine spark within you ... say out loud, "God breathed His life into me."
- Choose one ordinary moment today (a commute, a chore, a conversation) and ask, "How can God's fire guide this?"
- Take one intentional step ... worship, obedience, service ... that fans your spiritual flame.

Prayer
Lord, thank You for breathing Your life into me and placing a divine spark within my spirit. Help me to fan that flame with discipline, worship, and obedience. Let Your fire guide my thoughts, my choices, and my steps today. Make my life a light that reveals Your presence wherever I go. In Jesus' name, **Amen.**

April 15
Resonating with Heaven's Frequency

John 10:27
My sheep hear my voice, and I know them, and they follow Me.

Reflection:
Resonance ... whether in music, physics, or the human body ... is the phenomenon where two frequencies align and the energy between them multiplies. Spiritually, the same principle applies. Your spirit has been created to respond to God's voice, and when your inner frequency aligns with His, something powerful happens: His voice becomes clearer, stronger, and unmistakably present.

Beautiful people, when your heart's frequency matches God's ... through worship, stillness, prayer, or Scripture ... the resonance is undeniable. Your spirit begins to "vibrate" with His truth. As one writer noted, *"spiritual resonance is the recognition of the divine spark within all things... a sense of coming home."* It's that deep inner knowing that you are in sync with the One who created you.

But we must also recognize that not all resonance is holy. Just as bridges can collapse under destructive vibration, our hearts can collapse under the weight of negative, fearful, or toxic frequencies. Worry, bitterness, comparison, or chaos each have a frequency ... and if we let them, they can tune our hearts away from God.

That's why we must be intentional about alignment ... guarding our atmosphere, filtering our inputs, and tuning our spirit to the dominant vibration of God's presence. When His frequency becomes the loudest in your life, everything else must come into order.

Application:
- Tune In: Set aside a quiet moment today and breathe a simple prayer: "Lord, align my heart with Yours."
- Filter Out: Identify one negative frequency ...fear, comparison, or chaos ... and silence it by replacing it with Scripture.
- Stay Aligned: Choose one practice (worship, stillness, or gratitude) that helps your spirit resonate with God, and commit to it today.

Prayer:
Father, tune my heart to Your frequency. Help me hear Your voice clearly in the noise, and let my spirit resonate with the life and light You bring. May Your voice be the song that echoes in me today. In Jesus' Name, **Amen.**

April 16

A Peace of Mind vs. A Mind of Peace

Isaiah 26:3
You will keep him in perfect peace, whose mind is stayed on You, because he trusts in You.

Reflection
There's a difference between peace of mind and a mind of peace.

"Peace of mind" is a calm feeling, a moment of quiet, maybe a break from stress. Good ... but often fragile, dependent on circumstances.

A "mind of peace" is the presence of deep, abiding calm that flows from aligning your mind with God. It doesn't just show up when things go well ... it stands strong when storms come.

Philippians 4:7 promises: the peace of God will guard your mind when you are in Christ. It's active. It watches. It shields.

Isaiah 26:3 states that a mind fixed on the Lord will be kept in perfect peace. The peace doesn't just come ... it stays when the mind stays.

You may have the fleeting peace of mind: a vacation, a moment of rest, a quiet day. But if your mind is still chasing approval, chasing comfort, chasing calm ... then when pressure hits, the peace might vanish.

A mind of peace, however, is built when you anchor your thoughts, your trust, your identity in God. You're not just seeking peace ... you are rooted in it.

Application
- Choose: Which am I living in today ... peace of mind (momentary) or a mind of peace (rooted)?
- Action step: Take five minutes of stillness. Pray: "Lord, fix my mind on You. I receive a mind of peace, not just a moment of calm."
- Declare: "My mind will be aligned with You, so Your peace becomes my mindset."

Prayer
Father, thank You for Your peace ... a peace that guards, a peace that holds, a peace that lasts. Forgive me when I depend on fleeting calm instead of resting my mind on You. Help me build a mind of peace ... anchored in You, unaffected by the storms, unwavering in trust. In Jesus' name, **Amen.**

April 17
Prayer That Starts in Heaven

Romans 8:26
Likewise the Spirit also helps our weakness; for we do not know what to pray for as we should, but the Spirit Himself intercedes for us with groaning too deep for words.

Reflection
Praying in the Spirit is not about beginning with our own words, feelings, or desires ... it is about joining in with what God has already spoken in heaven.

True prayer begins with the Father's heart.

The Holy Spirit takes what originates in heaven, plants it in our spirit, and draws it out of us in prayer. Then, as incense rising, it returns to the Father in perfect agreement with His will.

Prayer is heaven's holy sport ... finding the Father's desire, letting it become our desire, and sending it back through our lips to His throne.

This is why we must serve and surrender to God daily; only a yielded life can be filled with the Spirit. When you pray this way, you are no longer just requesting things from God ... you are echoing His will on earth as it is in heaven.

Prayer doesn't start with us ... it starts with God. Our role is to yield so the Holy Spirit can flow.

Application
- Before praying, pause and ask: "Holy Spirit, what is on the Father's heart today?"
- Let the Word of God shape your prayers, since Scripture reveals His desires.
- Notice when your prayers shift from asking for your will to aligning with His.

Prayer
Father, teach me to pray in the Spirit. Plant Your desires deep in my heart. Let my words be an echo of heaven, returning to You in worship and trust. May my prayer life be a holy exchange between Your heart and mine. **Amen.**

April 18

Faith Makes Miracles

Matthew 17:20
So Jesus said to them, 'Because of your little faith. For truly I say to you, if you have faith like a grain of mustard seed, you will say to this mountain, "Move from here to there," and it will move; and nothing will be impossible to you.

Reflection
There are moments in life when everything you see argues against everything God has spoken. Logic says stop; fear says wait; circumstances say don't even try. But faith speaks a language that the natural mind cannot translate.

Faith is the courage to believe God when nothing around you agrees with Him. "Faith doesn't make sense. It makes miracles." — Tony Evans

Scripture is full of people who moved beyond reason and stepped into the realm of the supernatural: Noah built an ark before clouds ever formed. Abraham lifted the knife believing God would raise his son. The woman with the issue of blood pressed through a crowd without seeing power ... but she touched a miracle.

Faith doesn't ignore reality ... it just refuses to be ruled by it. Faith doesn't always make sense ... but it always makes room for God. And when faith stands up, mountains sit down.

The kingdom principle is simple:
When you choose trust over evidence, you unlock the impossible.
If you feel the tension between what God said and what your eyes see, don't shrink back. You're closer to a miracle than you realize.

Application
• Ask: Where am I letting logic lead when God is calling me to trust?
• Take one step today that aligns your feet with your faith.
• Declare: "I will not be guided by sight. I will be grounded in faith."

Prayer
Father, thank You that miracles are not reserved for the extraordinary ... but for the believing. Teach me to trust Your voice above my feelings and Your promise above my logic. Strengthen my faith until doubt loses its grip and mountains lose their power. Let my life testify that nothing is impossible with You. In Jesus' name, **Amen.**

April 19
Faith Receives Before It Sees

Mark 11:24
Therefore I say to you, all things for which you pray and ask, believe that you have received them, and they will be granted you.

Reflection
Jesus challenges us to pray with a mindset that defies natural logic. He doesn't merely encourage hope or patience … He calls us to believe that we have already received what we're asking for.

This is not wishful thinking; it's rooted trust in God's character and promises.

When we pray, we're not begging a reluctant God … we're partnering with a loving Father.

Faith speaks in past tense because it's certain of God's future fulfillment.

This is the spiritual posture that honors Him most: not waiting to see before believing, but believing before we see.

Faith that receives ahead of time shifts our posture from anxiety to peace, from striving to thanksgiving. It's the kind of faith that Jesus modeled and commended … a faith that says "Amen" before the answer arrives.

Application:
- Thank God today as though your prayer has been answered … declaring gratitude births expectation and readies your heart for breakthrough.
- When doubt whispers "not yet," choose faith instead: speak God's promise over your situation and live like His answer is already working.
- Let your everyday words, choices, and attitude line up with the faith of your prayer … trust in God's timing, but walk now as though victory has already come.

Prayer
Father, thank You that You hear me when I pray. Strengthen my faith so I can believe … not just that You will answer, but that You have already answered according to Your perfect will. Teach me to live with joyful expectation and patient trust. In Jesus' name, **Amen.**

April 20

Spiritual Beings, Holy Assignment

Colossians 3:10
"and have put on the new self, which is being renewed in knowledge after the image of its Creator"

Reflection
You are not merely flesh and blood … you are an image-bearer of God. Formed with divine intention, you carry His likeness, His breath, and His purpose. Your identity isn't rooted in earthly labels or temporary experiences… it's rooted in the God who created you.

In Genesis 1:26, God entrusts humanity with dominion … not domination … calling us to steward His creation with wisdom, justice, compassion, and love. You were never meant to rule from ego, but to reflect His character in how you lead, serve, and influence.

Genesis 2:7 reveals the beauty of our dual nature: we are dust, yet animated by the breath of God. We live in a physical body, but our true origin is spiritual. You are a heavenly being navigating an earthly assignment, a living vessel where the divine and the natural meet.

This understanding reshapes how you live, pray, and perceive others. When you recognize yourself … and your neighbor … as image-bearers, worship becomes more intentional, work becomes more meaningful, and relationships become sacred spaces where God's presence is revealed.

So live today with heaven's agenda. You weren't crafted merely for dust … you were designed to carry God's glory into every place you step.

Application
- Live each moment remembering you are God's "new self," renewed in His image … so treat even small tasks as sacred assignments.
- When old habits or negative thoughts arise, "put them off" and choose to respond as the renewed image-bearer you are.
- Use your time, talents, and relationships as stewardship … reflecting God's character and purpose in everything you do today.

Prayer
Father, thank You for your image in me. As I live today, let me steward my time and words with spiritual awareness. May my breath and actions reflect You. In Jesus' name, **Amen.**

April 21

Growth Demands Challenge

James 1:2–4
Consider it all joy, my brethren, when you encounter various trials, knowing that the testing of your faith produces endurance. And let endurance have its perfect result, so that you may be perfect and complete, lacking in nothing.

Reflection
REMEMBER: You asked God for growth. You prayed for strength, for wisdom, for patience, for deeper faith. But those qualities don't appear overnight like a gift on your doorstep … they are forged in the fire of challenge.

Don't be surprised when life stretches you.

God answers prayers for growth by sending opportunities to endure, to trust, to overcome. Trials are not punishments; they are platforms. The very thing that feels like resistance is often God's training ground for resilience.

Like an athlete builds muscle by lifting weight, your faith grows under the weight of adversity.

The test is not designed to break you but to build you. So, when you find yourself pressed, remember: you are in God's obstacle course, and every hurdle has purpose.

Application
- When life presses you hard … don't ask "Why me?" … ask "What is God building in me through this?"
- Let every challenge refine your faith, knowing endurance under pressure is God's training ground for spiritual strength.
- Respond to hardship with faith and perseverance, trusting that testing strengthens character and shapes hope.

Prayer
Father, thank You that You never waste a challenge. Teach me to see growth in the pressure, purpose in the pain, and Your hand in every obstacle. Help me to endure with joy, knowing You are shaping me for Your glory. **Amen.**

April 22
The Call to Virtue: Moral Excellence in Action

2 Peter 1:5
For this reason also, applying all diligence, in your faith supply virtue; and in your virtue knowledge.

Reflection
Virtue means moral excellence, righteousness, and goodness.

It's not just a vague idea ... it refers to qualities or behaviors that show high moral standards: honesty, courage, kindness, patience, humility, self-control.

In your walk of faith, virtue is the bridge between belief and behavior. Knowing the truth is important ... but living it is essential.

Scripture tells us to supply virtue in our faith, meaning we actively grow in these traits.
When you live virtuously:

You reflect the character of God (He is the standard of virtue). You become trustworthy, kind, courageous ... people see more than your words; they see your life. You build a testimony not on what you say, but on who you are.

Virtue isn't natural without nurture. It grows when you submit to God, walk in the Spirit, choose what's right the moment you could choose otherwise.

If you aim only for comfort or convenience you'll miss the mark. Virtue is demanding, and it demands something of you.

Application
- Choose one virtue today .. like patience, humility, or self-control.
- In your next challenge, ask: "How can I respond with this virtue rather than reacting with what comes naturally?"
- At the end of the day reflect: "Where did I reflect moral excellence? Where did I fall short? What will I adjust tomorrow?"

Prayer
Father, thank You for calling me to a life of moral excellence. Help me to grow in virtue ... not for my glory but for Yours. Teach me to be honest when it's hard, courageous when I'm afraid, kind when it's easier to dismiss, humble when I could boast, self-controlled when I'm tempted. Let my life bear witness to Your goodness. In Jesus' name, **Amen.**

April 23
The Power of Letting Go

1 Peter 5:7
Cast all your anxiety on him because he cares for you.

Reflection
Sometimes our greatest struggle isn't the battle in front of us ... it's the weight we refuse to release. We hold tight to what hurts us, confuses us, or overwhelms us ... believing, somehow, that clinging to it gives us control. But God invites us into something far better: release.

The call to cast our cares isn't an invitation to apathy, but a bold act of trust ...choosing God's sovereignty over our anxiety, His strength over our striving, and His wisdom over our need to understand. Scripture is clear: He cares for you. Not in theory ... in detail. Not from a distance ... with intimacy.

Yet holding onto past hurts, regrets, disappointments, or unfulfilled hopes can cloud our vision of what God is doing now. When our hands are gripping yesterday, they cannot receive what God is offering today. But surrender ... moment by moment, breath by breath ... opens us to His freedom, His clarity, and His new beginnings.

Letting go is not weakness; it is spiritual courage. It activates faith, and faith moves us forward into kingdom living.

When we release what was, we make room for what God is preparing. And His peace ... steady, healing, and complete ... meets us in the space where our burdens once lived.

Application
- Whisper to God today, "I release this to You," and watch how surrender clears the way for His peace.
- Choose to drop one burden ... a fear, regret, or memory ... and walk forward expecting God's new beginning.
- Let letting go become your first act of faith, opening your heart for God to move in what you no longer carry.

Prayer
Father, thank You that Your arms are wide enough to hold my brokenness. I surrender my fears, memories, and unmet expectations to You now. Renew me for what's ahead. In Jesus' Name, **Amen.**

April 24

Don't Wait; Life Moves Faster Than You Think

James 4:14
Yet you do not know what your life will be like tomorrow. You are just a vapor that appears for a little while and then vanishes away.

Reflection
Life passes faster than we often realize ... like mist at dawn, visible only for a brief moment before it disappears.

Too many of us wait. We wait for the "right time," the "perfect moment," the "better circumstances." But that waiting is often a silent thief ... stealing our moments, our opportunities, our potential to live fully.

We were not made for pause. We were made for purpose. Our hearts were given dreams, our hands were given work, our voices were given messages worthy of sound. Every breath is a chance ... a sacred window to act, to speak, to love, to step into what God has for us.

Jonathan Edwards once resolved: "to live with all my might, while I do live."

The brevity of life doesn't demand fear ... it demands urgency. Not a frantic scramble, but a faithful seizing of the day God has entrusted to us.

Today isn't a dress rehearsal. It's showtime. Every heartbeat is an invitation ... to live boldly, love deeply, serve selflessly, and step into purpose without regret.

Application
- Live like today counts ... don't wait, because your life is as fleeting as a vapor.
- Take a step now toward that dream, that calling, that conversation ... don't assume "later" will come.
- Let faith lead your actions today, not fear of failure or waiting for a "perfect moment."

Prayer
Father, help me to see the preciousness of this moment. Replace my hesitation with courage, my regret with action. May I live with purpose, not pause for perfection. I surrender today to You. In Jesus' name. **Amen.**

April 25

Love Yourself Enough to Care for Your Temple

1 Corinthians 6:19
Or do you not know that your body is a temple of the Holy Spirit within you...?

Reflection
If you truly want to show the world how much you love yourself, start by caring for your health.

Self-love is more than affirmations ... it's stewardship. When you move your body, nourish it with whole foods, breathe deeply, pray, meditate, and rest, you're not just investing in your physical frame; you're honoring the very life God breathed into you. Regular physical activity strengthens more than muscles ... it strengthens confidence, resilience, and mental clarity. It reminds you that your body was designed to carry purpose, not just survive. Nutrition is more than calories and cravings; it shapes your mood, focus, energy, stress levels, and even your ability to hear God clearly.

Stillness, prayer, and intentional rest reconnect you with your Creator. They slow the noise, restore your soul, and realign your spirit so you can respond to life with wisdom instead of exhaustion.

When you neglect your body, you diminish your capacity to serve, love, lead, and live with excellence. But when you honor your body as God's temple, you reflect self-respect, gratitude, and spiritual maturity. You show the world ...and yourself ... that you are committed to living the abundant life God intends for you.

Application
- Choose one simple act today: a walk, a healthy meal, or 10 minutes of prayer.
- Ask where your body is being neglected, then make one practical change.
- Declare: "My body is God's temple ... I will move it, nourish it, and rest it well."

Prayer
Father, thank You for the gift of this body, this temple entrusted to me. Help me to honor You by caring for it well ... through movement, nourishment, rest and communion with You. Shape my habits so that my body, mind and spirit reflect Your will. Let my health be a testimony to my self-love, my stewardship, and my devotion to You. In Jesus' name, **Amen.**

April 26
Make Your Food Your Medicine

Proverbs 23:20–21
Do not join those who drink too much wine or gorge themselves on meat, for the drunkard and the glutton will come to poverty, and drowsiness will clothe them in rags.

Reflection
Too often, the gifts meant to sustain us become the chains that entangle us.

The saying goes: "If we don't make our food our medicine, then our medicine will become our food." Food, a fundamental blessing, can become an idol ... driving us toward gluttony, which the Bible warns against.

Our bodies are not just vessels ... they're temples of the Holy Spirit:

"Or do you not know that your body is a temple of the Holy Spirit... you were bought with a price. So glorify God in your body."

Satan seeks to steal, kill, and destroy. Sometimes he uses food and ignorance ... turning nourishment into an anchor that drags us away from spiritual clarity and self-control.

Food becomes medicine when it restores health, honors God, and aligns with stewardship.

On the contrary, when it dominates your thoughts or emotions, it becomes your master.

Application
- Whisper to God: "I release this to You," and let go of what's weighing down your spirit.
- Choose to drop one burden today ... a regret, fear, or memory ... trusting God to carry it.
- Live today expecting God's new beginnings, no longer chained to what once held you back.

Prayer
Lord, help me see food as You intended: a gift to nourish and sustain, not to consume or control. Guard my heart from gluttony and teach me to honor You with all that I eat. May my body remain a holy temple, my mind focused on You, and my appetite aligned with Your will. **Amen.**

April 27
Knowing God by Doing His Work

James 1:22
But prove yourselves doers of the word, and not merely hearers who delude themselves.

Reflection
Ray Anderson once remarked, "There are things you simply cannot know about God unless you are in ministry." His words remind us that God is not revealed by speculation alone, but through participation. Academic study is valuable, but it is not enough.

True knowledge of God is discovered in the trenches of obedience ... in serving, in teaching, in loving, in walking with the broken, in proclaiming the gospel.

God's character shines through His actions. He fed the hungry, healed the sick, wept with the grieving, touched the untouchable, and forgave the sinner. To know Him is to join Him in those same rhythms of grace. The more we take part in God's ministry, the more clearly we see His heart.

Faith matures not in the classroom alone but in the field of service. To know God better, we must do God's work.

It is when we pour ourselves out that we discover His endless supply.
It is when we love the unlovable that we taste His love more deeply.
It is when we serve in weakness that we experience His power made perfect.

Application
- Reflect: Where in your life are you actively participating in God's work? Where are you simply observing?
- Choose one act of service this week that puts your faith into motion. It could be encouraging someone, feeding the hungry, or offering forgiveness.
- Journal: What did that act teach you about God's character?

Prayer
Father, thank You that You reveal Yourself not only through Your Word but also through Your work. Draw me into the activity of Your Spirit so I may know You more fully. Teach me to serve, love, and give in such a way that my hands become Your hands, my words Your words, my heart Your heart. As I do Your work, let me discover more of who You are. In Jesus' name, **Amen.**

April 28
Wisdom That Speaks, Works That Show

James 3:13
Who is wise and understanding among you? By his good conduct let him show his works in the meekness of wisdom.

Reflection
Family, listen ... your words matter, but your works matter even more.

People should hear God in your wisdom, but what they experience through your actions reveals God's heart. Solely speaking the truth without living it rings hollow.

As James reminds us, true wisdom must be evidenced in gentle, humble behavior ... our works must confirm what our words proclaim.

God's wisdom emerges not just from knowing His Word but from walking it out daily. We can speak the truth boldly, but if our lives don't align, the message loses its power.

Scripture, the Spirit, prayer, and godly counsel all feed our insight ... but they must surface in our relationships, conversations, and service.

Imagine someone encountering you ... should they leave having only heard your sermon, or should they have felt Jesus through your kindness, patience, and love? That's what generosity in both speech and action looks like.

Application
- Consider an area where your words may outpace your actions ... like forgiveness, patience, kindness.
- Ask the Holy Spirit, "Where can Your wisdom become visible through me today?"
- Do one small act of kindness that reflects God's character ... no announcement, just authentic reflection of His love.

Prayer
Father, may Your wisdom flow through me ... not only in words but in my everyday life. Help me to walk gently, serve humbly, and speak truth with love. Let others see You in my actions, and may my works validate what I say. **Amen.**

April 29
Standing Firm in a Shifting Culture

John 17:17
Sanctify them in the truth; Your word is truth.

Reflection
Every generation of believers faces cultural pressures, but ours seems particularly loud and persuasive. From identity to sexuality, from materialism to distorted views of justice, society constantly invites us to compromise biblical truth for acceptance. The danger is real: some churches water down God's Word to appear relevant, while others withdraw completely and lose their witness to the world.

Jesus showed us another way. He did not conform to culture, but neither did He isolate Himself from it. He lived in the world while remaining sanctified by truth. He loved people with compassion yet never compromised the Father's will.

As the church, our challenge is the same. We are called to hold fast to God's Word without apology and also extend grace without judgment. We must be light in darkness, not a mirror of the darkness ... nor a bunker hiding from it. Standing firm in truth while walking in love is not easy ... but it is the way of Christ.

Application
- Renew Your Mind Daily: Immerse yourself in Scripture so you can discern truth from cultural distortions.
- Practice Both Grace and Truth: Don't compromise God's standards, but let your convictions be clothed in compassion.
- Engage, Don't Escape: Look for ways to be salt and light in conversations, workplaces, and communities without blending in or bowing down.

Prayer
Lord, in a world that pulls at my convictions, keep me rooted in Your Word. Protect me from compromise that weakens my witness and from isolation that hides my light. Teach me to walk as Jesus walked ... full of grace and truth. May my life reflect both Your holiness and Your love, drawing others to You. In Jesus' name, **Amen.**

April 30
When God Co-Signs

Joshua 1:9
Have I not commanded you? Be strong and courageous! Do not be terrified nor dismayed, for the Lord your God is with you wherever you go.

Reflection
Many people's opinions are often rooted in their own pre-understandings, presumptions and fears, not in God's promises. If you aren't careful, their doubts will become your ceiling.

But God did not call them to your assignment …He called you. He didn't give them the vision … He gave you the vision.

David understood this when he refused Saul's armor. Saul wanted David to fight in a way that made sense to man, but David had already been equipped by God. The sling and stones that defeated Goliath were not ordinary tools … they were divine instruments in the hands of a man who trusted God's call.

Many remain stuck in mediocrity because they choose to follow man's opinion rather than God's voice.

Extraordinary lives are birthed when we stop waiting for approval from others and step boldly into what God has already affirmed.

When God co-signs, no other signatures are required.

Application
- Silence the Noise: Identify whose voices have created fear or doubt in your life. Submit those voices to God.
- Walk in Your Equipping: Like David, use what God has already placed in your hands instead of trying to imitate someone else's armor.
- Move Boldly: Write down the vision God gave you and take one courageous step today toward it, regardless of others' opinions.

Prayer
Father, thank You for the vision You have given me and the calling You have placed on my life. Forgive me for the times I allowed other people's opinions and fears to hold me back. Strengthen me to walk in courage like David, trusting the tools You have placed in my hand. I declare today that when You co-sign, I need no other approval. In Jesus' name, **Amen.**

May 1
The Greatest Love Letter Ever Written

Psalm 119:105
Your word is a lamp to my feet and a light to my path.

Reflection
The Bible is not just a book ... it is God's personal love letter to His children.

From Genesis to Revelation, every page reveals His heart, His promises, and His plan for redemption.

Just as God fed Israel with manna daily in the wilderness, He has given us His Word to feed our spirits every day.

When we neglect Scripture, our souls grow weak and malnourished. But when we open its pages, the Holy Spirit uses it to strengthen, guide, and transform us.

The Bible is living and active ... it comforts in sorrow, convicts in sin, and directs us into truth. It is the divine road map to our identity, purpose, and freedom in Christ.

Reading the Bible once is not enough; like daily bread, it must become our constant source of nourishment. Each time we return to it, we find fresh revelation, deeper wisdom, and renewed strength for the journey ahead.

The Bible is daily manna for the soul ... feed on it, and you will live in the fullness of God's love.

Application
- Don't let your Bible sit closed ... open it daily.
- Read with expectation, knowing God wants to speak to you.
- Treat Scripture as your daily bread ...not a snack, but a feast for your soul.

Prayer
Lord, thank You for giving us the living Word, the greatest love letter ever written. Stir in us a hunger for Scripture, that we may not live by bread alone but by every word that proceeds from Your mouth. Help us to treasure it, obey it, and walk in the freedom it declares. **Amen.**

May 2

Seek First

Matthew 6:33
But seek first His kingdom and His righteousness, and all these things will be provided to you.

Reflection
God's abundant blessings and favor are not scattered randomly ... they are reserved for those who make Him their top priority.

The Lord has never called His people to fit Him into their schedules; He calls us to build our lives around Him.

Yet how often do we treat God as an afterthought, giving Him what's left of our time, our energy, or our devotion?

Scripture makes it clear: anything we put before God ... whether success, relationships, money, or even ministry ... becomes an idol. And God will not share His glory with idols.

True worship is ordering life properly: the Creator above creation.

When God is first, everything else finds its rightful place. When He is not, chaos and futility follow.

"When God is your priority, everything else becomes provision."
— Anonymous

Jesus taught us that the pathway to provision, peace, and purpose is simple: seek first the kingdom of God and His righteousness.

Application
- Evaluate your priorities this week ... does God come first, or is He an afterthought?
- Remove anything in your life that has taken God's rightful place.
- Begin each day seeking His presence before pursuing anything else.

Prayer
Father, forgive me for the times I have placed other things above You. Teach me to order my life around Your kingdom and Your righteousness. Help me to worship the Creator, not creation, and to trust that when I put You first, all else will fall into place. **Amen.**

May 3
Ambition Without Action Becomes Anxiety

Proverbs 13:4
The soul of the sluggard craves and gets nothing, but the soul of the diligent is made fat.

Reflection
Ambition is not the problem. God Himself plants vision, desire, and holy fire in our hearts. But when ambition is left to sit unwatered …when it receives no steps of faith, no movement in obedience, no action that matches the dream …it turns sour. What once stirred you begins to suffocate you. Dreams deferred become dread. Hopes without hands become heaviness. Potential without pursuit becomes pressure.

Much of the anxiety we carry doesn't come from the size of the dream but from the distance between what God showed us and what we refuse to step toward. That gap becomes a battlefield.

The dream God gave you will not build itself. Heaven equips, but earth must respond. Faith without works is dead (James 2:17), and ambition without action eventually mutates into anxiety.

Think of Peter on the water: when he responded to Jesus' call, he stepped into the miraculous. The impossible became possible because obedience matched faith. But when he froze in fear … when his focus shifted from the Caller to the chaos … he began to sink.

Vision must meet obedience; otherwise, it decays into worry and weighs down the soul. Remember: God doesn't bless intentions … He blesses obedience. Ambition without action becomes anxiety. But ambition with obedience becomes advancement.

Application
- Write down one ambition God has placed in your heart.
- Ask yourself: What step of action can I take today in faith?
- Replace the cycle of waiting and worrying with walking and working in obedience.

Prayer
Lord, deliver me from the paralysis of inactive ambition. Help me to move when You say move, to build when You give vision, and to trust You with each step. May my diligence turn my dreams into testimony and my ambition into answered prayers. **Amen.**

May 4
Distractions in Disguise

Proverbs 4:25-27
Let your eyes look straight ahead; fix your gaze directly before you. Give careful thought to the paths for your feet and be steadfast in all your ways. Do not turn to the right or the left; keep your foot from evil.

Reflection
"Distractions don't look like distractions until they finish distracting you."

Solomon teaches us that staying focused protects our calling from unseen detours and silent drift. Focus is not just about attention ... it's about direction, discipline, and discernment.

The truth is this: distractions rarely show up wearing a warning label. They often walk in wearing disguises.
They look like opportunities. They feel like necessities.
They present themselves as blessings. Sometimes they even sound spiritual.

They don't shout; they whisper. They don't pull violently; they nudge gently. And by the time you realize it, your mission has been delayed, your clarity has been clouded, and your momentum has been stolen inch by inch ... day by day.

Even Jesus faced subtle distractions. In Matthew 4, Satan used Scripture itself to tempt Him off the Father's path. Not every "good thing" is a God thing. Not every open door is Heaven's assignment.

Discerning distraction means slowing down long enough to measure each moment, each opportunity, each invitation against the mission God has placed in your heart. It means asking not, "Is this wrong?" but "Is this right for where God is taking me?"

Application
- Pause now. What feels "good" but may be steering you off course?
- Ask: "Is this building me toward my calling or simply passing time?"
- Respond with a focused "no" or a redirected "yes," then move ... today, not later.

Prayer
Father, clear my vision and guard my heart from distractions dressed as blessings. Help me discern what truly aligns with Your assignment and keep my feet walking steadfast in Your light. In Jesus' name, **Amen.**

May 5
Sacrifice: The Currency of Elevation

Romans 12:1
I urge you therefore... present your bodies a living sacrifice, holy and acceptable to God, which is your spiritual worship.

Reflection
The rewards you receive in life are directly proportional to the level of sacrifices you're willing to make.

Paul reminds us that laying down our comforts is not extraordinary ... it's expected worship.

Sacrifice isn't just a motivational quote ... it's a spiritual law woven from Genesis to Revelation. From Abraham leaving home (Genesis 12:1–2) to Jesus enduring the cross (Philippians 2:8–9), every great elevation in God's narrative demands surrender and sacrifice.

It's true in farming too ... you can't reap without sowing. Likewise, spiritual harvest demands seeds sown through time, comfort, pride, or relationships laid down in faith. This is the currency of elevation.

Sacrifice proves our seriousness, unlocks purpose, and bridges the gap between where we are and where God is taking us.

Application
- Pause and reflect: What is God asking you to release today? It could be time, a comfort zone, or a relationship.
- Write it down and pray: "Lord, I release this offering back to You. Use it for Your purposes." Let your surrender invite His next level.
- Take action today: Choose one small step of obedience ... serve someone, give something, or deny a comfort ... and offer it to God as a seed toward your next season.

Prayer
Father, teach me that what I lose in surrender, I gain in You. May my sacrifices be holy worship that opens doors to Your promises. I choose obedience over ease. In Jesus' name, **Amen.**

May 6

Living by a Creed

Psalm 19:14
Let the words of my mouth and the meditation of my heart be acceptable in Your sight, O LORD, my rock and my Redeemer.

Reflection
Every believer needs a creed ... not just pretty words, but a daily declaration that checks your spirit and sets your daily standard.

A creed is how you remind your soul who you really are. It's how you shut down the lies the enemy whispers before your feet even hit the floor. It's how you walk into your day with alignment, not confusion; conviction, not chaos.

You must make up your mind to ride with Jesus all the way, no turning back, no shrinking down, no switching sides. It's a statement that says: My present is intentional. My future is already covered.

Affirmations built on Scripture remind you of your real identity: That you belong to Christ, That you're led by the Spirit, That no weapon formed against you can prosper, and that nothing ... absolutely nothing ... can separate you from His love.

Your creed becomes your compass. It keeps you steady when storms try to shake you... focused when distractions try to pull you... and bold when pressure tries to break you. Because when you know who you are ... and Whose you are ... you walk different. You talk different. And you live with a confidence hell can't cancel.

Application
- Write a personal affirmation of faith that aligns with Scripture.
- Speak your creed each morning before you start your day.
- Let it remind you: you are a disciple of Christ, equipped by His Spirit, and unashamed of the Gospel.

Prayer
Lord, let my words agree with Your Word. Teach me to rise each day with a declaration of who I am in You. May my creed be my compass, my strength, and my testimony. Keep me steadfast and immovable until the day You call me home. **Amen.**

May 7

The Beginning of Solitude

Luke 5:16
But Jesus Himself would often slip away to the wilderness and pray.

Reflection
When a man begins to wake up spiritually, something inside of him shifts.

Conversations that once seemed satisfying now feel shallow. He notices how much of life is built on performance ... status updates, gossip, complaints, and the constant search for validation.

Without announcing it, he steps back. Not because he thinks he is better, but because he no longer needs the illusions that once held him.

This is the beginning of solitude ... the sacred space between who he used to be and who God is shaping him to become.

Silence, once uncomfortable, becomes a sanctuary. The need for applause fades, replaced by a hunger for truth. He stops pretending, stops chasing, and starts seeing clearly. The world may not understand the distance, but the shift is undeniable.

Solitude is not isolation ... it is consecration. It is the place where God peels away the noise and reveals what is real, lasting, and eternal.

Application
- Ask yourself: Where am I still performing for acceptance instead of resting in God's approval?
- Practice stepping back from conversations or habits that drain your spirit.
- Carve out intentional solitude this week to hear God's voice above the noise.

Prayer
Lord, teach me the beauty of holy solitude. Free me from the need to perform, to be praised, or to be constantly validated. Let my silence be filled with Your presence, and may my transformation be a testimony that speaks louder than words. **Amen.**

May 8
Truth Breaks Chains

John 8:32
… And you will know the truth, and the truth will set you free.

Reflection
It's a powerful thing to realize: every belief, idea, or assumption we hold that is not truth has the capacity to bind us. Emotional, mental, spiritual… these are realms where lies can imprison us. But the Bible doesn't leave us powerless. Jesus says that once we know the truth, it sets us free.

To "know the truth" isn't just to intellectually agree with facts … it's to let truth sink into your heart, to live by it, to allow it to displace lies you've believed about yourself, others, or God. These lies might sound like: "I'm not good enough," "No one loves me," "God won't forgive me," or fears like "I'll always fail." These lies suppress you.

Truth, on the other hand, exposes them. When you bring these lies into the light of Scripture, when the Holy Spirit unveils them to you, they lose power. You begin to see what's real: who God says you are, what He's done, what you're forgiven of, and what your purpose is. And from that place, real freedom begins.

Don't stop now. God is not finished, and your harvest is still on the way. Stay faithful, stay courageous, and keep going … because those who continue are the ones who reap.

Application
- Identify one lie you've believed about yourself (mentally, emotionally, or spiritually). Write it down.
- Find a Scripture that contradicts that lie. Meditate on it, memorize it if possible.
- Pray and ask the Holy Spirit to reveal truth in your heart. Then, every time the lie pops up, consciously replace it with the truth.

Prayer
Father, thank You for the truth that sets me free. I invite You now to reveal the lies I've carried. Shine Your light into every part of my mind, emotions, and spirit. Help me to know, live, and guard Your truth. May that truth break the chains of fear, shame, and guilt. I believe You are making me free indeed. In Jesus' name, **Amen.**

May 9
The Loneliness of Leadership

Isaiah 63:3
I have trodden the wine trough alone, and from the peoples there was no one with Me.

Reflection
To be a leader is to be lonely ... not because you're unwanted, but because you're out ahead alone. Leadership often means maintaining unity while walking where others won't go.

You're out front when others aren't, you carry burdens others can't see, and you make decisions that impact many. Leadership is lonely because the responsibilities weigh heavier, the vision stretches further, and few people share the load.

Jesus Himself walked that path. Even surrounded by people, He carried the weight of the mission alone while the world misunderstood Him. His seat was up front, but His journey was one of solitude and surrender.

If you've been leading ... at work, at home, in ministry ... and you feel alone, know two things: You're not alone in your loneliness. It's part of the calling. The loneliness is not the end ... it's the backdrop to strength, resilience, and spiritual maturity.

You don't lead by popularity, but by purpose; you don't lead by comfort, but by conviction. The one called to lead walks where others won't, stands when others sit, and stands firm ... even when standing solo.

Application
- Ask: Where am I leading today?
- Choose one act of courage: speak truth no one else will, hold to your values when it's unpopular, walk your purpose even if you walk alone
- Declare: "I will lead ... and I will live with the cost of being out front.

Prayer
Father, thank You for calling me to lead ... for giving me a vision bigger than myself. When I feel alone at the front, remind me You are with me. Grant me strength to walk the path You've laid, courage to carry the weight You've given, and joy in the solitude that brings clarity. Let my leadership reflect Your heart ... not the applause of crowds, but the whisper of Your Spirit. In Jesus' name, **Amen.**

May 10
A Mother's Sacred Influence

Proverbs 31:26–28
She opens her mouth in wisdom, And the teaching of kindness is on her tongue. She looks well to the ways of her household, And does not eat the bread of idleness. Her children rise up and bless her; Her husband also, and he praises her.

Reflection
A woman's influence stretches far beyond what she sees in a single day. Her words can build or break, her prayers can cover or wither, and her presence can anchor or scatter. God has entrusted her with the ministry of shaping hearts … whether as a mother, a mentor, or a spiritual mother to many.

She does not have to be flawless to be faithful. She is called to be present, to speak wisdom with grace, and to love with a courage that reflects Christ. Her beauty is not measured by appearance but by her devotion, by the strength of her hands, and by the light of her heart.

When a woman walks in the Spirit, her household feels it, her community notices it, and her children will one day thank God for it. She becomes a living testimony that God's love is best expressed through a life poured out for others. A godly woman carries a quiet power that echoes into generations. Her wisdom plants seeds, her kindness heals wounds, and her faith becomes a refuge for those she loves. When she lives surrendered to the Spirit, her life becomes a legacy … one her children will rise to honor and heaven itself will celebrate.

Application
- Speak life daily, knowing your words carry the power to shape hearts and futures.
- Cover your household in prayer, inviting God's wisdom and peace into every room.
- Lead with quiet strength and consistent love, reflecting Christ through your presence and actions.

Prayer
Lord, thank You for the gift of womanhood and the sacred role You have given to women. Strengthen every mother, wife, daughter, and sister to walk in wisdom and kindness. May her influence bring life, her prayers bring breakthrough, and her faith leave a lasting legacy for generations to come.
Amen.

May 11

Vanity or Virtue

Proverbs 31:30
Charm is deceitful and beauty is vain, but a woman who fears the LORD is to be praised.

Reflection
In this world there are two kinds of people: those of vanity, and those of virtue.

The people of vanity chase the wind, build their lives around appearances, self-praise, comparison, and the fleeting applause of others. Scripture warns that vanity is empty, a vapor, something that ultimately disappears.

The people of virtue build on what lasts: integrity, humility, truth, God-fearing character. Proverbs says the one who fears the Lord is truly to be praised … because she values what matters, not what looks gold on the surface.

Which path are you walking today? Vanity distracts you with "how it looks"; virtue anchors you in "how it is." Vanity pits you against others. Virtue serves others, honors God, and reflects Him.

Let the mirror of your heart reveal whether you're pursuing breath (vanity) or building a foundation (virtue). Choose reason. Choose substance. Choose God's way.

Application
- Ask: "In what area of my life am I pursuing vanity … seeking approval, status, looks, or fleeting praise?"
- Choose one decision today that reflects good reason over vanity: a humble act, a truth spoken, a motive examined.
- Declare: "I will walk in good reason, not hollow vanity. My life will reflect what matters, not what fades."

Prayer
Father, thank You that You call me to a life of virtue, not vanity. Show me where I've built on shifting sand … on praise, appearance, self-elevation. Help me rebuild on You … on humility, truth, service, fear of You. Purify my motives, redirect my gaze, and shape my life so others see not my vanity, but Your glory. In Jesus' name, **Amen.**

May 12

Kindness Is Godly

Galatians 5:22
But the fruit of the Spirit is… kindness.

Reflection
Kindness is more than a pleasant attitude; it is a supernatural indicator that the Holy Spirit is actively transforming us from the inside out. It is not performance … it is proof. Proof that God is reshaping our instincts, renewing our responses, and maturing our character.

We live in a culture that celebrates toughness, quick comebacks, dominance, and emotional armor. But Kingdom strength looks different. In the world, kindness is seen as soft; in the Spirit, kindness is a sign of deep courage. It takes far more strength to stay gentle than to retaliate. Anybody can react … only the Spirit-led can respond with grace.

Kindness is not passive; it is powerful.
Choosing compassion over cruelty, patience over provocation, peace over pride … this is the work of a yielded heart. It requires spiritual maturity, emotional self-control, and a surrendered will. This kind of kindness is not natural; it is cultivated by the Spirit.

When the Holy Spirit fills us, kindness becomes our weapon … not a weapon to wound, but a weapon to heal. Not to dominate, but to lift. Not to silence, but to soothe. Kindness becomes a light in dark places, a salve in wounded spaces, and a testimony that God is alive within us.

Scripture is clear: kindness isn't just a trait … it's fruit. And fruit doesn't grow by accident. It grows because the root is healthy, the soil is cared for, and the Spirit is at work. Kindness on the outside is always the result of God working on the inside.

Application
- Respond gently today, even when irritation rises.
- Show intentional kindness to someone overlooked.
- Extend grace to someone who has hurt or frustrated you.

Prayer
Father, teach me that true strength looks like love, humility, and grace. Let my actions reflect the kindness of Your Spirit … even when the world demands toughness. Empower me to be bold with love. In Jesus' name, **Amen.**

May 13
When Kindness Is a Mask

Romans 12:9
Let love be without hypocrisy. Abhor what is evil; cling to what is good.

Reflection
There are people in this world whose evil hides behind good deeds and friendly faces.

Evil can pretend to be good and kind ... yet true kindness cannot pretend to be evil. So when you sense evil behavior in someone, believe it ... because over time, character reveals itself.

We serve a God who sees the heart and knows what's real. The Lord wants us to walk in integrity, not deception.

In our interactions:

Be aware when kindness feels conditional or manipulative. Recognize that genuine goodness is transparent, consistent, humble. Understand that someone can wear a mask ... but the truth of their heart won't stay hidden forever.

God calls us to love without hypocrisy, to hate what is evil and hold tightly to what is good. If we ignore hidden evil because it looks like kindness, we compromise our integrity and ignore God's warning.

Application
- Reflect today: "Where have I accepted surface kindness without checking the character beneath?"
- Pray: "Holy Spirit, give me discernment to see beyond the mask and wisdom to respond with truth and love."
- Commit to one action: respond to someone with authentic kindness ... but stay alert. Guard your heart, and refuse to be deceived.

Prayer
Father, thank You that You see my heart and the hearts of others. Forgive me when I've ignored hidden evil because it looked nice. Help me to love without hypocrisy, to abhor what is evil and cling to what is good. Grant me insight, courage, and compassion to walk in truth today. In Jesus' name,
Amen.

May 14
What's Behind Your Smile?

Proverbs 15:13
A joyful heart makes a cheerful face, but when the heart is sad, the spirit is broken.

Reflection
Someone once said, "Your smile is your heart speaking out loud."

It's true ... when the heart is full of joy, the smile simply reveals what's already overflowing. But when the soul is heavy, even the brightest smile can feel like a mask ... present on the face but absent in the spirit. A forced smile may fool people, but it never fools the heart.

In many ways, a frown is like dragging yesterday's clouds into today's sunshine. It reminds us that the condition of the heart always finds a way to show itself.

Beautiful people, real light doesn't come from pushing harder ... it comes from surrender.

When we release our burdens, fears, and hidden sadness into God's hands, He sanctifies, purifies, and restores the deep places of our soul. His love becomes our strength, His peace becomes our anchor, and His joy becomes our overflow.

Then the smile that shows up on your face isn't forced ... it's fruit. A natural, effortless reflection of heaven's presence alive within you.

Application
- Pause right now. Place your hand over your chest and say: "I surrender my heart to You, Lord. Fill me with Your joy."
- Then, smile ... genuinely ... and ask: "What blessing can I sow today with this simple expression?"
- Use that smile as your small act of Kingdom light in someone's day.

Prayer
Father, thank You that true joy comes from You. Cleanse my heart and replace what's heavy with Your peace and light. Let my smile be Your love speaking out loud today. In Jesus' name, **Amen.**

May 15

Shine

Matthew 5:14
You are the light of the world. A city set on a hill cannot be hidden.

Reflection
"This little light of mine ... I'm gonna let it shine." The gospel hymn captures a simple yet profound truth: your life was designed to shine with purpose, not to be hidden in darkness.

The song draws on the teaching of Jesus that followers are the light of the world.

Too often we dim our light: hiding our gifts, concealing our faith, shrinking when we should shine. Perhaps because we fear rejection, failure, or exposure. But your design is different. Your light is meant to illuminate, to bring hope, to break the gloom.

Don't hide your light under convenience or escape (the "bushel").
Don't let fear or criticism snuff it out.

Everywhere you go ... let your light shine.

Your light matters. In your neighborhood. In your workplace. In your home.

When you let it shine, you don't just brighten your path ... you brighten the paths of all those around you.

Application
- Identify one area today where your light is dimming (fear, silence, self-doubt).
- Choose one bold step: speak truth, act with kindness, let your faith show.
- Declare: "I will let my light shine ... not for recognition, but for revelation of light."

Prayer
Father, thank You for the light You've placed within me. Help me not to hide it, but to let it shine boldly and beautifully. When darkness surrounds, let my light be a beacon of Your love and truth. In Jesus' name, **Amen.**

May 16

Change Requires Change

Romans 12:2
Do not be conformed to this world, but be transformed by the renewing of your mind, so that you may prove what the will of God is, that which is good and acceptable and perfect.

Reflection
Change doesn't just happen by wishing for it ...
it requires real, intentional movement. Every time you change something about yourself, you are literally stepping into a different version of who you are becoming.

The well known saying is true: "Insanity is doing the same thing over and over and expecting different results." If we desire transformation, we must be willing to alter the patterns that no longer serve us.

If you want to change how you feel, you must begin by changing what you think. If you want to change what you think, you must take new actions ... choosing differently both mentally and physically.

This is exactly what Paul was teaching: transformation begins in the renewing of the mind.

God has given us His Spirit and His Word as catalysts for true change. But the responsibility rests on us to step out of old cycles and into new obedience. You cannot step into a new life while repeating old habits

Change requires change ... and when you align that change with God's truth, the result is freedom, growth, and a life that reflects His glory.

Application
- Identify one cycle you keep repeating that produces no new results.
- Surrender it to God and replace it with a new, Spirit-led choice.
- Remember: small consistent changes compound into lasting transformation.

Prayer
Lord, help me to stop repeating old cycles and expecting new outcomes. Teach me to renew my mind with Your Word and to align my actions with Your will. Give me the courage to change, knowing that You are shaping me into who I was always meant to be. **Amen.**

May 17

One Small Decision Away from Breakthrough

Proverbs 3:5–6
*Trust in the Lord with all your heart
And do not lean on your own understanding.
In all your ways acknowledge Him,
And He will make your paths straight. him, and he will make your paths straight.*

Reflection
Life changing moments rarely begin with monumental leaps. Most often, it's one small, surrendered choice that shifts everything. One decision, one step, one act of obedience can reroute an entire future.

Your choice to trust… to forgive… to pray… to act… to believe… can become the hinge that opens the door to your next season.

Beautiful people, God doesn't demand grand gestures. He honors your willingness. He looks at the posture, not the performance. That simple "yes" … whispered in faith … could be the spark that ignites transformation.

Whether it's making one call, sending one email, offering one prayer, releasing one offense, or stepping into the unknown with trembling faith … your next breakthrough may be closer than you think.

Sometimes destiny turns on the smallest decision made with the biggest amount of trust.

Your next breakthrough is one small decision away.

Application
- Pause and ask: What's the one small step God is nudging me toward? Write it down now.
- Whether you send that message, make that decision, or take that first move … do it today with faith.
- Watch how God multiplies your small faith toward something greater.

Prayer
Father, give me courage to take one small step today in alignment with Your will. Whether seen or unseen, be with me in it. Use my obedience to bring breakthrough in my life and the lives around me. In Jesus' name, **Amen.**

May 18

Our Heavenly Reconciliation

John 17:17
Sanctify them in the truth; Your word is truth.

Reflection
All our striving in life often aims outward … career, possessions, recognition. But the deeper work, the eternal work, is always within.

Our true transformation is an inside job: a heavenly reconciliation where our soul (psyche) and spirit are aligned with God's standards.

God's Word is not just information … it is transformation.

Just as soap cleanses stained garments, His Word purifies hearts clouded by sin, pride, and confusion. But this cleansing is not automatic; it requires our obedience. To be reconciled with heaven is to surrender our inner life to the Spirit's sanctifying power.

The world teaches self-help. The Kingdom teaches soul-help … allowing the Spirit and the Word to wash over us until our thoughts, desires, and actions reflect His image.

This is reconciliation: not merely peace with God, but conformity to His holiness and wholeness (spirit, soul and body).

Application
- Today, instead of focusing on fixing everything around you, ask God to fix what's within you.
- Allow His Word to do the washing, His Spirit to do the renewing, and His standards to set the measure.
- Heavenly reconciliation begins when you say, "Lord, change me from the inside out."

Prayer
Father, cleanse my heart with Your truth. Wash away the stains of sin, doubt, and disobedience. Align my soul with Your Spirit and reconcile me to Your perfect standards. Let my inner life reflect Your glory. **Amen.**

May 19

The Ride Matters

2 Corinthians 5:10
For we must all appear before the judgment seat of Christ, so that each one may receive what is due for what he has done in the body, whether good or evil.

Reflection
As a Christian, we're all headed to the same destination ... eternity with God. But how we ride matters.

Imagine you're on a plane: every passenger is going to the same place, but some are flying First Class while others are in Coach. According to Tony Evans, our Christian walk determines our "seat."

In First Class: there's more room, more comfort, more attentiveness.
In Coach: it's tighter, less comfortable, less personal attention.

Your ride is influenced by your faith, love, obedience. The way you live now affects the quality of your journey ... and how you arrive.

It's not about salvation ... it's assured. But it is about fruitfulness, faithfulness, impact.

When we live intentionally, we move toward First Class living. When we stay passive, we settle for less.

Don't treat the Christian life like basic economy; fly the class that matches the sacrifice, obedience, and passion you bring.

Application
- Ask: "Am I living like I want First Class or am I settling for Coach?"
- List three actions this week that elevate your seat: deeper prayer, more intentional service, sacrificial love.
- Declare: "I will not just arrive ... I will arrive well, having lived in the class of fullness and obedience."

Prayer
Father, thank You for my destination ... and that I'm already saved. But I pray You help me live in such a way that I ride well: with faith, love, and obedience. Elevate my journey. Make it meaningful, surrendered, fruitful. I don't just want to get there ... I want to arrive ready. In Jesus' name, **Amen.**

May 20
You Are Not The Fixer

1 Corinthians 3:7
So then neither the one who plants nor the one who waters is anything, but God who causes the growth.

Reflection
Sometimes we carry the weight of trying to fix someone else.

We believe if we just speak the right words, send the right message, serve them long enough ... we'll change them. But the truth? Only God can change a heart.

"Not by might nor by power, but by My Spirit" reminds us that human effort alone isn't sufficient.

And 1 Corinthians 3:7 teaches that while we may plant and water, it's God who brings the growth. We play a role ... but He's the One who performs the miracle.

So stop trying to assume the Savior's role ... that place is already filled. Your job isn't to fix; it's to love, pray, guide, and trust. The change you long to see isn't in your hands ... it's in God's hand.

Application
- If you've been trying to "fix" someone, pause and ask: What am I trying to control? What can only God do?
- Pray for that person today ... not to be changed by you, but transformed by God.
- Commit: "I will plant, I will water, but I release the growth to God."

Prayer
Father, thank You that You are the One who changes hearts, restores lives, and brings growth. I confess my desire to fix instead of trust. Help me to plant with compassion, water with love, and step back with faith ... knowing You do what I cannot. Use my obedience, but bring the increase. In Jesus' name, **Amen.**

May 21

Seeing Beyond the Surface

Matthew 13:29-30
He said to them, 'No; for while you are gathering up the tares, you may uproot the wheat with them. Allow both to grow together until the harvest; and in the time of the harvest I will say to the reapers, "First gather up the tares ... then gather the wheat into my barn."

Reflection
Just because you're right doesn't mean someone else is wrong ... often it means you simply haven't seen life from their lens.

In our polarized world, so many rush to judge instead of asking questions, to decide instead of understanding. We react from the angle we're standing in, forgetting that our angle is not the whole picture.

When I first started playing golf, I used to line up a putt by standing right behind the ball, looking straight toward the hole. From that one viewpoint, the path looked clear. But after playing for a while, I realized I needed to make a full 360-degree walk around the green.
Only then did I see the subtle slopes, hidden breaks, and quiet curves that I completely missed from my original position.
One perspective gave me information…
but multiple perspectives gave me revelation.

It's the same in life.

Before you judge, gather facts. Before you speak, ask questions. God alone sees the whole picture ... and He invites us to look and love deeper.

Application
- Think of a relationship where you feel strongly "right." Ask: Have I listened fully to their story?
- Choose to ask one sincere question today: "Help me understand your view…"
- Declare: "I will not assume I know it all. I will listen, learn, and walk in humility."

Prayer
Father, forgive me when I've been quick to judge and slow to understand. Give me eyes to see beyond the surface, ears to hear the heart, and a humble spirit that values truth over being right. Let me walk in love, patience, and wisdom, especially when others see differently. In Jesus' name, **Amen.**

May 22
Warned & Ready: Guard Your Soul from Silent Distractions

John 10:10
The thief comes only to steal and kill and destroy; I came that they may have life, and have it abundantly.

Reflection
From the roar of the ancient arena … "Are you not entertained?" … to the glow of streaming screens today, there is a subtle war behind our leisure: our souls are being entertained to death. The enemy doesn't always attack with obvious force … often it distracts us from the presence, peace and power of God.

Entertainment, amusement, distraction in itself isn't the problem. The issue arises when it becomes our refuge, our default, our master. As one article put it, "Entertainment is to keep us living 'in between'" … away from God's voice, away from truth.

When we replace stillness with noise, presence with feed-scrolls, worship with binge-watching, we're not just off track … we're vulnerable. We might serve the screen, the story, the thrill … rather than the Savior. Beautiful people, I've learned firsthand that when entertainment becomes easier to reach than prayer or the Word, it quietly starts taking the place only God should fill.

Today's call? Be aware. Not to kill all joy, but not to let worldly entertainment overshadow God's presence.
Let your screen-time not silence your soul-time; let your leisure not steal your destiny.

Application
- Ask: "What do I use to escape instead of turning to God?"
- Commit: Limit one entertainment habit and replace it with 10 minutes with God..
- Declare: "I choose God's presence over distraction."

Prayer
Father, forgive me for the times I chose comfort over communion, noise over Your voice, distraction over Your design. You have called me to freedom, to life. Protect me from the silent damage of unexamined entertainment. Help me to see when my soul is being rented out to amusement instead of anchored in You. Lead me back to You … to presence, purpose and power. In Jesus' name, **Amen.**

May 23
The Measure of Love Is Sacrifice

John 3:16
For God so loved the world, that He gave His only Son, that whoever believes in Him shall not perish but have eternal life.

Reflection
Love is costly. It is defined by what you are willing to give up … not merely what you are willing to receive. To love is to sacrifice.

God's love revealed itself in giving His one and only Son.
Jesus' love fulfilled itself in laying down His life.

You are made in God's image and likeness … so this same pattern is meant to flow through you. The real question isn't only, "What can I receive?" but, "What am I willing to give so someone else can rise, heal, or thrive?"

Sacrifice is not loss when it's rooted in love; it is seed, sown into people, purpose, and eternity.

When you give from your heart … your time, your resources, your compassion, your presence … you echo the sacrificial love of Christ.

You don't love merely because you are loved… you love because you are His reflection, carrying His heart into the world.

Application
- Reflect on this question: What am I giving today that mirrors Christ's sacrifice?
- Choose one act of sacrificial giving this week: maybe your time, your comfort zone, your wallet, or your presence.
- Declare: "I will measure my love by what I give .. not by what I get."

Prayer
Father, thank You for the greatest gift … Your Son. Help me live with the same sacrificial love. Remove self-interest and replace it with heart for others. Let what I give reflect Your heart. Let my life proclaim that love is more than emotion .. it's sacrifice. In Jesus' name, **Amen.**

May 24

United We Stand, Divided We Fall

Matthew 12:25
And knowing their thoughts, Jesus said to them, 'Every kingdom divided against itself is laid waste; and no city or house divided against itself will stand.'

Reflection
Like playing chess; "the pawns hate each other, while the ones playing chess are actually good friends."
This picture describes one of the oldest strategies of the enemy ... division through deception. As long as we argue, accuse, fight, and fragment, the real enemy watches on because a divided people become a defeated people.

We live in a world where battles are not always face-to-face with flesh and blood but through whispered lies, fractured relationships, and intentional isolation. The Scripture warns: any kingdom divided against itself cannot stand. The enemy doesn't need to destroy us outright; he just needs to get us to destroy each other.
Satan works to:
Divide races ... so we forget we're made of one blood.
Divide churches ... so we lose our witness.
Divide families ... so we forget our covenant and calling.
Divide minds ... so we cannot walk in peace or purpose.

But God's command is different: we must put on His full armor and stand firm ... not just against forces outside, but against the schemes that divide within. Unity is not just nice ... it's essential for our survival, our mission, and our testimony.

Application
- Ask yourself: Where am I participating in division?
- Choose one act of unity today: perhaps listen more than speak, encourage instead of compete, reconcile instead of separate.
- Declare: "I refuse to be a pawn in the enemy's game. We will stand united."

Prayer
Father, thank You for Your vision of unity ... that we would walk together, stand together, serve together. Forgive me for the times I've chosen division, for the times I've allowed fear, pride, or offense to isolate me or another. Strengthen me with Your armor, guide me in love, and bind me in purpose with my brothers and sisters. In Jesus' name, **Amen.**

May 25
The Cost of Becoming New

Romans 12:2
Do not be conformed to this world, but be transformed by the renewing of your mind...

Reflection
Transformation isn't a cosmetic fix ... it's a complete remaking of who you are internally.

The Spirit reshape us from the inside out ... renewing how we think, live, and love.

Letting go of old habits, comfort zones, familiar faces ... even long-held identities ... can feel like losing everything.

But, beautiful people, what you're leaving behind was built for a version of you that no longer exists.

The cost is steep: comfort, control, approval, understanding. But what you gain is immeasurable: a new tribe that meets you at your breakthrough, a refined comfort zone built around purpose, and an authenticity that invites others to love who you are becoming.

Paul says don't conform to your old self or the world's expectations ... let God renew your mind. This reshaping reveals God's perfect will for your life, and reveals a you that operates in deeper freedom, clarity, and grace.

Application
- Pause now. What identity are you holding onto that no longer belongs to your spiritual growth? It might be a label, a habit, a role, or a relationship.
- Offer it to God in prayer: "Jesus, I release this old me ... show me who You've called me to be."
- Then take one small step toward the person you're becoming: a kinder word, a courageous boundary, an act of faith.

Prayer
Father, let me not cling to the shell of who I've been, but be transformed ... renew my mind so I can walk boldly in who I am becoming. Fill me with new comfort, new friendships, new purpose. In Jesus' name, **Amen.**

May 26

Sow Wisely: You Get What You Give

Galatians 6:7
Do not be deceived: God is not mocked; for whatever a person sows, this he will also reap.

Reflection
In life, there's a principle at work that mirrors "karma," but on a deeper, biblical level: what you sow, you will reap. Scripture calls this the law of sowing and reaping ... a spiritual reality woven into the fabric of life that no one can outrun or override.

When you sow kindness, generosity, and love, you set in motion a harvest of favor, blessing, and meaningful connection. But when you sow anger, bitterness, or selfishness, you plant the kinds of seeds that grow into pain, distance, and regret. You can't sow darkness and expect light to return.

Here's the truth:
You can't plant weeds and expect a wheat harvest.
Your future will grow from whatever you're planting right now.

So today, be intentional with your words, your reactions, your attitude, and your energy. Every seed you plant ... good or bad ... has a future attached to it. Day by day, what you give determines what you get.

Beautiful people, your harvest will always look like your habits.
Plant with purpose.

Application
- Think about one action, word or thought today. Ask: Is this seed going into the soil of faith or the soil of flesh?
- Choose to plant something positive ... perhaps a gesture of kindness, a forgiving word, a prayer for someone.
- Declare: "I will sow wisely, so I may reap wisely."

Prayer
Father, thank You for the law You've placed in creation and our lives: that what we sow, we reap. Forgive me for the seeds of bitterness, selfishness, and neglect I've planted. Help me to sow love, generosity, patience, and faith. Let my life reflect that I understand the harvest will match the planting. Guide my hands, my words, my thoughts that I may live in the abundance of what You provide. In Jesus' name, **Amen.**

May 27
Don't Feed Your Babies the Same Lies You Ate

2 Timothy 3:15
And that from childhood you have known the sacred writings which are able to give you wisdom for salvation through faith in Christ Jesus.

Reflection
Every generation inherits something … some of it good, some of it broken. And whether we realize it or not, what we consume … lies, half-truths, fear, defeat, or faith … becomes the soil our children will grow from. If you know you've been fed the wrong things, then you carry a holy responsibility to interrupt the cycle and give the next generation something better.

Truth is more than information … it's inheritance.
When you teach firmly, kindly, and consistently, you are not just passing down lessons … you are passing down legacy.

Let them breathe something different … truth that breaks chains, not continues them … truth that frees them from the bondage you had to fight your way out of.

Instill righteous knowledge … morals rooted in Scripture, identity grounded in God's Word, values shaped by wisdom instead of wounds.

Don't feed your babies the same lies you once swallowed. Plant what you wished someone planted in you … wisdom, righteousness, courage, conviction, and freedom. Because when you choose to live intentionally … and you model truth with your life … what you hand down isn't just a family story … it's deliverance.

Application
- Make a list of lies or patterns you've believed in the past. Choose one today and declare: "I will not pass this to the next generation."
- Decide one truth to instill in a child or young person today.
- Ask: "What legacy am I leaving … bondage or freedom, fear or faith, lies or truth?"

Prayer
Father, thank You for the truth that frees. Forgive me for the lies I've believed and the patterns I may unknowingly pass on. Give me wisdom, courage, and clarity to raise up a generation rooted in You … not in yesterday's bondage. Help me to hand down your Word, your identity, your freedom. In Jesus' name, **Amen.**

May 28
God's Order: God > Jesus > Man > Woman > Children

Isaiah 3:12
O My people! Their oppressors are children, And women rule over them. O My people! Those who guide you lead you astray ... And confuse the direction of your paths.

Reflection
There is a divine order ordained by God: God → Jesus → Man → Woman → Children.

In our world today we see that when the role of man' falters, the structure begins to wobble. Because of that failing, women ... often in strength and necessity ... rise to fill the gap. Though honorable, this rise is a sign of displacement, not order restored.

In Isaiah 3 we read of a society where mature leadership has failed. Consequently: children rule, women rise, men become weak.
When men ... those called to lead with strength, integrity and sacrifice ... fail their God-given place, the result is chaos in the household, the workplace, the nation. Women step up because someone must hold the line. But make no mistake: this is not the design; it is the damage of dysfunction.

When the order is intact: men lead in humility, women follow in complementary strength, children are nurtured, and society reflects God's intent. But when ordered roles are abandoned, the ripple effects spread: unguided children, overburdened women, absent men, and the entire kingdom suffers.

Application
- Men: Ask where you've stepped back from your God-given responsibility ... and step in today.
- Women: Embrace your strength, but also release unrealistic pressure to lead where the order has fallen. Encourage restoration.
- Parent/children: Recognize the pattern in your home. Pray for order.

Prayer
Father, You have ordained men to lead in love, women to follow in strength, children to grow under care. Forgive us for the places where roles collapsed, where men fell, where chaos grew. Restore the order in the church, the family, the community. Raise up men who will lead with courage, raise women who will partner in purpose, raise children who will honor. Let Your design be seen again. In Jesus' name, **Amen.**

May 29
Disconnected Youth, Defeated Generation

Judges 2:10
All that generation also were gathered to their fathers; and there arose another generation after them who did not know the LORD nor the work which He had done for Israel.

Reflection
The easiest way to control a generation is to disconnect them from God, their family and their faith.

This stark truth highlights a strategy of isolation: take a young person away from roots, remove their community, silence their faith ... and you shape them without resistance.

When youth are spiritually orphaned ... no anchoring in God, weak family ties, lost in faith ... they become vulnerable to external narratives, peer pressure, and cultural attractions.
Studies show that faith isn't automatic ... it requires connection, community, and intentional passing on.

Beautiful people, a disconnected generation is an endangered generation. But a connected generation ... rooted in God, anchored in family, strengthened in faith ... becomes unstoppable. The enemy knows the power of unity, which is why he fights so hard to isolate. But we fight back by reconnecting. When we rebuild the links ... spiritual, relational, generational ... we don't just save a life ... we shift a legacy. The future belongs to the connected.

Application
- Ask: "Where in my life (or the life of someone I influence) is the connection to God, family, or faith being neglected?"
- Choose one action today: reach out to a young person, lead a devotional, invite someone over for family time, encourage faith discussion.
- Declare: "I will not let disconnection define a generation. I will build links ... spiritual, familial, relational ... for life to flow."

Prayer
Father, thank You for the ties You've placed in my life ... Your presence, my family, the community of faith. Forgive me for times I've let connections slip and let a generation wander. Help me today to build bridges: to You, to others, to truth. Raise up a generation anchored in You. In Jesus' name,
Amen.

May 30
Not The Woodpecker ... But The Termite

2 Corinthians 6:16
For you are the temple of the living God; just as God said, 'I will dwell in them and walk among them; I will be their God, and they shall be My people.'

Reflection
It's not the woodpecker on the outside... it's the termite on the inside that destroys us. A woodpecker on the outside makes noise, draws attention. But the termite on the inside does its damage quietly, out of sight, gradually undermining the internal structure.

Similarly, in our lives it's not always the obvious sins or crises that bring us down ... it's the subtle, unseen ones. Lies we tolerate, bitterness we harbor, un-forgiveness we carry, doubt we dismiss, or habits we ignore. We may present strength outwardly ... but inside, the foundation is rotting. Until finally the collapse comes.

Today this devotion invites you to inspect your inner man: What termites are chewing at your integrity, your faith, your relationships? What's hidden, unchecked, but weakening you? Don't ignore the whispers. Don't just blame the pressures or the enemy. Often the root issue is the internal decay: it's the weakness within ... like that stair that collapses because of the termite damage.

Friend, let truth guard us, let confession expose us, let obedience rebuild us.

Application
- Sit quietly and ask: "What has been quietly eating at me that I've ignored because I didn't see it?"
- Name one internal issue (fear, bitterness, pride, avoidance) and bring it into the light.
- Declare: "I will not let unseen damage destroy what God has built in me."

Prayer
Father, You have made me Your temple... and I refuse to allow hidden termites to destroy that dwelling. Reveal to me the unseen damage. Help me to surrender the harmful thoughts, the secret sins, the disguised assumptions. Build up what's broken, replace fear with faith, doubt with truth, passivity with obedience. May my interior be guarded, my foundation be firm, and my outward life reflect the strength You've renewed within me. In Jesus' name, **Amen.**

May 31
Love Covers a Multitude of Sins

1 Peter 4:8
And above all things have fervent love among yourselves; for love will cover a multitude of sins.

Reflection
When you're not operating in love, you're not operating in the character of Christ. You're functioning from a place Scripture clearly warns against.

Love is not sentimental or surface-level ... it is the one thing that does what nothing else can do ... cover sin. Not by excusing it, hiding it, or pretending it isn't damaging ... but by responding with mercy, truth, forgiveness, and grace.

Love is the signature of Christ's presence in a person's life.

When your words, actions, or motives lack love, you stop reflecting Christ and start mirroring something entirely contrary to His nature.
Because love sees flaws not as ammunition, but as a doorway to healing. Love doesn't demand its own way ... it lifts the value of the other person. Love pulls people together ... without it, everything pulls apart.

Beautiful people, the call is simple and serious ... keep loving. Let your love be fervent, real, costly, and consistent. Let your relationships carry the covering that only love can give. Because the moment you step outside of love, you step outside the heart of Christ and draw closer to what opposes Him.

Application
- Ask: "Where have I acted without love today ... checked out, cleaned up, removed myself?"
- Choose one relationship to extend genuine love ... not just polite words, but intentional forgiveness, service or kindness.
- Declare: "I will not operate in anything less than love, for it is the attribute of Christ and covers many sins."

Prayer
Father, fill me with Your love ... the kind that covers, that restores, that forgives. Let my life not be driven by self-defense, offense, or accusation, but by Your grace. If I have acted without love, forgive me and remake me. Let me walk today in the character of Christ, so that when people see me they see love ... and through that love they see You. In Jesus' name, **Amen.**

June 1
Grace: God's Resources At Christ's Expense

Ephesians 2:8
For by grace you have been saved through faith; and this is not your own doing, it is the gift of God.

Reflection
When we say grace, we're pointing to something beyond what we could ever earn … it is the very resources of God made available because of Christ's sacrifice. Grace is God giving us something we don't deserve.

God has resources … unlimited, eternal, life-giving resources … that were not purchased by us, but by the expense of Christ.

Christ paid the cost so that we might receive what we could never earn. Our past failures, our weaknesses … they're not permanent roadblocks … they're the backdrop against which this grace shines.

Grace isn't just about arriving at heaven; it's about living now in the fullness of what Christ purchased. When you grasp this, your identity, your purpose, your resources all shift.

You don't live trying to earn your way to God's favor … you live because God's resources are given at Christ's expense.

Your faith isn't founded on your merit … it's founded on His mercy.

Application
- Meditate: "What part of God's resources do I need today?" Might it be forgiveness, peace, wisdom, strength?
- Write it down: "Because Christ paid the cost, I receive _____."
- Declare: "I live by grace … not by my performance, but by the cost Christ paid and the resources God freely gives."

Prayer
Father, thank You for grace … Your inexhaustible resources purchased at such great cost by Christ. Help me to believe that I am rich in You because You have given, not because I earned. Use me as a vessel of Your grace so that others see not only what You've done for me but what You're doing through me. In Jesus' name, **Amen.**

June 2

Let Go and Let God

Isaiah 43:18-19
Remember not the former things, nor consider the things of old. Behold, I am doing a new thing; now it springs up ... do you not perceive it?

Reflection
Don't be a prisoner to your past ... it was a lesson, not a life sentence.

When you're stuck re-living yesterday, you miss what God wants to do today.

Real faith isn't proven when everything makes sense ... it's revealed when you trust Him even when you don't understand. Fear is "what if". Faith is "even if".

Your peace isn't about the absence of problems; it's the presence of trust.

So stop striving to solve every question, and start resting in the One who knows all things.
Let it go, and let God.

God can't pour new blessings into hands still clinging to old battles. At some point, you've got to release what was so you can receive what is. The door you're afraid to close is the very thing blocking the one God is ready to open.

So loosen your grip, lift your hands, and let Him lead. Yesterday is over, and your future is undefeated.
Let it go ... so God can let it grow.

Application
- Write down one memory or regret from your past that keeps pulling you backward.
- Say out loud: "I release it to You, Lord. I leave it behind. I press toward what You have ahead."
- Whenever that memory resurfaces this week, remind yourself: "This is a lesson, not my sentence."

Prayer
Father, thank You that You are always doing a new thing. I release the weight of past failures, regrets, and what-ifs. Fill me with Your peace that surpasses understanding. Help me to trust You with the unknown, walk forward in confidence, and live free from my yesterday. In Jesus' name, **Amen.**

June 3
Lessons in the Fall

Proverbs 24:16
For though the righteous fall seven times, they rise again.

Reflection
The more I fall, the more I figure out.
Every stumble is not just a mistake ... it's a lesson.

With each fall you learn a bit more about yourself, your heart, your motives, and your direction.

When you fall:

You see where your boundaries were weak.
You realize how your reliance may have been on the wrong things.
You recognize where your faith needs to deepen.

Because of those falls, you grow in wisdom, character, resilience.

God doesn't waste your failures; He uses them.
It's not a loss ... it's a lesson, because failure isn't final.

So don't fear the fall. Let it sharpen you, not shame you.

What's most important is that we grow through whatever we go through in life.

Application
- Reflect on one recent fall ... what did it teach you? What insight did you gain?
- Write that lesson down and identify one change you'll make because of it.
- Declare: "I will not hide from the fall ... I will learn and rise."

Prayer
Father, thank You that You are working even in my falls. Help me to see the lessons in each stumble ... so I don't just bounce back, but grow up. Give me eyes to learn, a heart to change, and the strength to rise rooted in Your purpose. In Jesus' name, **Amen.**

June 4
What Happens Inside Matters Most
In Honor of Jerry Perry

Proverbs 23:7a
For as he thinks within himself, so he is.

Reflection
It's not what you do on the outside, or even what happens to your body, that shapes your life the most. It's what happens inside ... in your soul, your spirit, and your thought life ... that is what truly defines you.

Jesus taught us to pray, "on earth as it is in heaven" (Matthew 6:10). That isn't only about global events; it's about the condition of your inner world. Whatever takes root in the soul eventually shows up in the body. Peace in the heart leads to stability in the life and the body. But anxiety, resentment, or fear on the inside will eventually wear down the outside ... manifesting as stress, high blood pressure, or even depression.

God's design is wholeness. God's design is for oneness with His Peace. When your inner life is surrendered to Him, He guards your heart with peace that surpasses understanding (Philippians 4:7). That inner peace becomes a shield, not only protecting your soul but also blessing your body.

Application
- Take inventory of your thought life today. Are your inner conversations full of faith and peace, or fear and worry?
- Practice surrender: every anxious thought, give to Christ in prayer and replace it with His promises.
- Protect your peace. Guard what you allow into your mind through conversations, media, or environments.

Prayer
Lord, help me to see that what happens inside matters most. Transform my thoughts, calm my anxieties, and anchor my soul in Your truth. Let my inner life reflect heaven so that peace, joy, and strength flow into every area of my body and my walk. May others see not stress or worry in me, but the evidence of a soul at rest in You. **Amen.**

June 5

To Me and Through Me

Philippians 2:13
For it is God who is at work in you, both to will and to work for His good pleasure.

Reflection
In our early days of faith it felt natural to ask: What can God do for me? We looked for blessings, miracles or upward movement.
But maturity changes the question. It shifts to: What does God want to do in me ... and through me?

True faith isn't just about what we receive ... it's about what God shapes in our character, our motives and our purpose. When we internalize that fact that we are vessels, not just beneficiaries, then our lives become testaments for God's glory. It's not just for me, but to and through me.

When God uses you, He isn't simply adding success to your life ... He is transforming your life into a message for His glory and a blessing for others.

Mature belief means less focus on the "promises" and more focus on the "process." Less on the "what I get" and more on the "who I become." And in this becoming, others are impacted for the better.

The real victory is when God's work in your heart becomes God's work in the lives of others. When you surrender to the process, you don't just receive His grace ... you become a channel of it. Let Him move through you.

Application
- Reflect: "Am I asking God to do for me, or am I asking Him to do in me and through me?"
- Choose one area where you'll shift from receiving to serving: maybe a spiritual gift, a mentoring role, an act of compassion.
- Declare: "My life is not only about what I obtain, but about what I become and how I give."

Prayer
Father, thank You for Your blessings and provisions ... but more than that, thank You for what You are doing in me and through me. Help me to shift my vision from "for me" to "through me." Shape my heart, refine my purpose, and use my life as a vessel of Your will. Make me mature in faith, rich in purpose, and generous in impact. In Jesus' name, **Amen.**

June 6
Jesus: My Master, Savior, Ruler, Redeemer, Provider

Isaiah 54:5
For your husband is your Maker,
Whose name is the Lord of hosts;
And your Redeemer is the Holy One of Israel,
Who is called the God of all the earth.

Reflection
Jesus is everything to me ... and He can be everything to you too.

He is my Master who leads and guides.
He is my Savior who rescues and renews.
He is my Ruler over all things, high above every power.
He is my Redeemer who buys me back and sets me free.
He is my Provider who supplies my deepest needs with grace and mercy.
When you let Jesus take each of these places in your life, you don't live by accident ... you live by purpose.

You don't wander ... you're guided.
You don't hunger ... you're fed.
You don't call ... you're rescued.

Jesus is not just a part of your life ... He is your life. When He becomes your Master, you finally stop being mastered by everything else. When He becomes your Savior, shame loses its voice. When He becomes your Ruler, fear loses its authority. When He becomes your Redeemer, your past loses its power. And when He becomes your Provider, lack loses its grip.

Application
- Pause and say: "Jesus, be my Master, Savior, Ruler, Redeemer, and Provider."
- Choose one role (Master, Savior, Ruler, Redeemer, or Provider) that you're least comfortable accepting today. Invite Him into that role.
- Record: How did seeing Jesus in that role change my perspective or response today?

Prayer
Father, thank You for Jesus. For every role He fulfills in my life. Help me believe Him as my Master, trust Him as my Savior, follow Him as my Ruler, receive Him as my Redeemer, and depend on Him as my Provider. Fill me with peace and purpose as I walk in these truths today. In Jesus' name, **Amen.**

June 7
Master Your Desires to Manage Your Destiny

Proverbs 25:28
*Like a city that is broken into and without walls
Is a man who has no control over his spirit.*

Reflection
In order to manage your destiny, you must first learn to manage your desires. Desires will either discipline you or destroy you. They will either push you toward God's purpose or pull you away from it. Destiny is not random. Destiny is shaped by decisions ... and decisions are shaped by desires.

You can't walk into the future God designed while being controlled by desires God never ordained. Unmanaged desires create impulsive choices, unstable emotions, compromised faith, scattered focus, lost time, and a life drifting away from purpose. But when your desires are surrendered to God, your destiny aligns with Heaven's design.

Samson had an anointing but lacked discipline ... and his unmanaged desires delayed his destiny.
Esau had a birthright but lacked restraint ... and one moment of appetite cost him a lifetime of blessing.
David had a calling but for a moment lost control ... and his desire brought consequences he never expected.

When the Holy Spirit governs your desires: your appetite changes, your focus sharpens, your relationships shift, your purpose becomes clearer and your future becomes protected. You cannot have destiny without discipline. You cannot have promise without restraint. You cannot have purpose without boundaries. Master your desires ... and God will trust you with your destiny.

Application
• Identify one desire or habit that threatens your focus or purity.
• Ask the Holy Spirit to help you bring that desire under God's control.
• Set one practical boundary today ... emotionally, spiritually, or physically.

Prayer
Father, help me manage my desires so I can walk boldly in the destiny You designed for me. Shape my appetite, purify my motives, and strengthen my discipline. Give me the wisdom to recognize distractions and the courage to set boundaries. Align my desires with Your will so my destiny brings You glory. In Jesus' name, **Amen.**

June 8
Stop Letting Satan Romance You to Death

2 Timothy 4:3–4
*For the time will come when they will not endure sound doctrine…
and will turn away their ears from the truth and will turn aside to myths.*

Reflection
We have systematically compromised and romanticized the Word of God. We have diluted Scripture until it tastes sweet enough for the flesh … and weak enough for the devil to swallow whole.

The enemy has found his way in … not through force … but through flirtation. Satan doesn't attack with obvious evil, he seduces with almost-truth. He whispers soft lies wrapped in an ear tickling emotional language. He offers comfort without conviction…pleasure without purity…grace without repentance…freedom without holiness. And slowly, subtly, silently…we let him romance us to death.

This generation loves inspiration more than instruction, affirmation more than transformation and comfort more than correction. We crave messages that feel good … instead of truth that makes us good. We want God's blessings without God's boundaries.

We have turned Scripture into poetry … when it was written to be power. We have turned the Gospel into therapy … when it was meant to be deliverance. We have turned holiness into an option … when God called it by command. When the church dilutes the Word … darkness grows boldly. When Christians compromise truth … the enemy gains territory. When we trade conviction for convenience …we forfeit our authority.

Application
- Ask God to reveal any area where you've been compromising biblical truth.
- Identify one lie the culture has romanticized and replace it with Scripture.
- Read Scripture daily, not just what comforts you, but what challenges you.

Prayer
Father, forgive us for romanticizing Your Word and compromising Your truth. Awaken my spirit. Sharpen my discernment. Strengthen my conviction. Silence every seductive lie of the enemy and anchor me in Your Word. Keep me from deception and help me walk in holiness, clarity, and courage. In Jesus' name, **Amen.**

June 9
Sin Separates; Obedience Unites

Isaiah 59:2
But your iniquities have made a separation between you and your God, and your sins have hidden His face from you so that He does not hear.

Reflection
Sin kills ... not always in an immediate, visible way, but it kills connection, purpose, and life. Sin builds walls between us and God; it isolates, alienates, and separates the temple from the awareness of the Holy Spirit.

On the other hand, obedience to God gives life. It restores connection, it lays down the path of unity or oneness with God, with others and with our purpose. When we choose obedience, we choose life ... we choose fellowship with God.

You don't simply avoid what's wrong ... you embrace what's right.
You don't just stop from falling ... you stand up in alignment.

Obedience isn't legalism ... it's relationship.
It's the act of saying: "I surrender, You lead, I will follow."

When you stop being defined by your sin, and begin being driven by His voice ... then true life floods in. Walls come down. Separation ends.

Sin builds distance, but obedience builds intimacy. When you choose God's way, you're not just avoiding separation ... you're stepping back into the intimacy your soul was created for. Choose the path that leads you home.

Application
- Identify one sin, habit, or thought-pattern that has been distancing you from God.
- Confess it, surrender it, and step into obedience ... however small that step may be.
- Declare: "I will not let sin define my separation; I will let obedience define my unity."

Prayer
Father, I recognize the walls I've built by sin and the hollowness it's brought. Forgive me. Grant me the strength and humility to obey You ... not just in parts of my life, but fully. Let Your life flow through me, connection be restored, unity be renewed. I choose to live, to walk in You, and to be one with You. In Jesus' name, **Amen.**

June 10
God Never Asked You to Audition

Romans 8:38–39
For I am convinced that neither death, nor life, nor angels, nor principalities, nor things present, nor things to come, nor powers, nor height, nor depth, nor any other created thing, will be able to separate us from the love of God, which is in Christ Jesus our Lord.

Reflection
We've all felt it ... that quiet pressure to perform for love.
To prove ourselves.
To show God and people why we "deserve" to be chosen.

Maybe someone in your past made you feel disposable ... like their affection had to be earned and belonging had to be bought with perfection. Those wounds whisper lies: "Do more. Be better. Try harder."
But hear me clearly: God never asked you to audition.
His love is not a role you compete for ... it's a gift you receive.

Nothing you've done, nothing you fear, nothing you struggle with ... and nothing you're still becoming ... can separate you from His love. You don't stand before Him as a performer ... you stand before Him as a son, a daughter, fully known and fully loved.

Take the mask off. Lay the checklist down.
Let your life be shaped not by striving but by surrender.
Serve from overflow, not insecurity. Worship from identity, not fear.
God's love doesn't wait for your perfection ... it meets you in your mess.

Application
- Begin your day by declaring, "I am fully loved by God without performing for it."
- Identify one area where you feel pressure to prove yourself and release it to God in prayer.
- Do one simple act of service today purely from gratitude, not striving.

Prayer
Father, thank You for loving me without conditions or auditions. Help me release every burden to prove myself and rest in the truth that I am already fully known and fully loved. Remove the masks, quiet the pressure, and shape my life through surrender, not striving. Let my worship and service flow from gratitude, identity, and Your unshakeable love. In Jesus' name, **Amen.**

June 11
True Freedom

2 Corinthians 3:17
Now the Lord is the Spirit, and where the Spirit of the Lord is, there is freedom.

Reflection
Freedom is not the absence of rules or restrictions ... it is the presence of the Spirit of Peace.

Many chase freedom through money, material, pleasure, or independence ... but that only leads to new chains. Real freedom is found in the Spirit of God.

When the Spirit is present, you are free from the weight of the Law, free from the power of sin, and free from the opinions of people.

This freedom doesn't mean living without boundaries ... it means living within God's perfect design, where joy, peace, and love abound.

The Spirit doesn't just free you from something; He frees you for something ... to walk in your divine calling, to reflect Christ, and to live unashamed as a son or daughter of God.

True freedom isn't found in doing whatever you want ... it's found in becoming who God created you to be.
When the Spirit takes His rightful place in your life, the chains fall, the noise quiets, and your soul finally breathes. Freedom isn't an escape ... it's alignment. It's living fully, boldly, and joyfully in the presence of the One who sets you free.

Application
- Ask the Holy Spirit daily to fill your heart and guide your steps, because freedom is tied to His presence.
- Reflect: am I living in the Spirit's liberty, or am I still bound by fear, sin, or people-pleasing?
- Choose one area where you've felt bound, and surrender it to the Spirit today ... trusting Him to break the chain.

Prayer
Father, thank You for bringing freedom into my life. Break every chain of sin, fear, and performance, and let me walk in the liberty of Your presence. Where You are, there is freedom ... so fill me, guide me, and let my life reflect Your truth. In Jesus' name, **Amen.**

June 12
One With God

Genesis 1:26
Then God said, 'Let Us make man in Our image, according to Our likeness…

Reflection
We serve an amazing God … the Creator of heaven and earth … who chose to make us in His own image (imago Dei).

This means we were designed not only to reflect His character, but also to share in His creativity and innovation. To be human is to carry divine fingerprints.

God's design is threefold: Spirit, Soul, and Body.

Spirit (Ruach) … the breath of God within us, our direct connection to Him.
Soul (Psyche) … our mind, will, and emotions, shaping how we think, choose, and feel.
Body (Earth) … the vessel formed from dust, the temple through which we live out God's purposes in the physical world.

When all three align under God's authority, we live whole, balanced, and powerful lives. But when the soul rules over the spirit, or when the body dictates the direction, disorder follows.
True life flows when the Spirit leads, the soul agrees, and the body obeys.

We were made to mirror God, not just in appearance, but in function … walking in love, truth, creativity, and authority.

To know who you are, you must first remember whose image you bear.

Application
- Ask yourself: Is my spirit leading, or am I being ruled by my flesh or emotions?
- Align your day by inviting God's Spirit to govern your soul and body.
- Use your creativity today as a reflection of God's image in you … whether in work, relationships, or worship.
  -

Prayer
Father, thank You for making me in Your image and likeness. Breathe Your Spirit (Ruach) fresh into me today. Bring my soul and body under Your authority, so that all of me reflects all of You. May my life be a living testimony of Your amazing design. **Amen.**

June 13
Joy Cultivated in Christ

Nehemiah 8:10
The joy of the Lord is your strength.

Reflection
Joy isn't something we stumble into; it's something cultivated within.

Too often we chase after joy in people, possessions, or circumstances, only to find it slips away as quickly as it came.

But joy is not a treasure at the end of a journey ... it's a masterpiece crafted daily through our mindset, our choices, and our fellowship with God.

The world can't give it and the world can't take it away.

Real joy is birthed in the presence of the Lord, where peace steadies our hearts and strength flows into our souls.

When we stop waiting for joy to "find us" and instead allow God to grow it in us, we realize joy has been here all along ... an inside job directed by the Spirit.

When the Spirit of the Lord fills your heart, joy becomes more than a feeling ... it becomes your foundation.

Rest in His presence, and you'll find strength for every season, steadiness for every trial, and peace for every step.

Application
- Choose to rejoice in the Lord now ... let His joy be your strength today.
- When circumstances weigh on your spirit, turn your heart toward God and let joy rooted in Him renew your strength.
- Serve others from a heart of joy and gratitude ... because the strength of the Lord works through your gladness.

Prayer
Father, thank You that Your joy isn't dependent on my circumstances but on Your presence. Fill me now with the joy of the Lord, let it become my strength, and sustain me through every season. Teach me to trust You, rejoice in You, and live from a heart overflowing with Your life and peace. In Jesus' name, **Amen.**

June 14

Heaven in Your Design

Psalm 139:14
I will give thanks to You, for I am fearfully and wonderfully made; Wonderful are Your works, And my soul knows it very well.

Reflection
God did not just create humanity ... He placed His design into our very bones.

Look closer: the human spine has 33 vertebrae, the same number of years Jesus walked the earth, carrying the weight of love and redemption. The 12 ribs on each side mirror the 12 tribes of Israel and the 12 disciples of Christ. Heaven's design is etched into our frame.

The vagus nerve runs from brain to heart to gut ... calming storms within the body ... shaped like a cross. Every time peace enters when chaos surrounds, it's not random; it's His presence.

Jesus rose on the third day, and science confirms that fasting for three days renews the body as old cells die and new life begins. Resurrection is not just history ... it's biology. Your heart beats in a holy rhythm. Your brain ignites in prayer. Your tears carry different chemistries in joy and grief. Even your bones hold memory. The body itself worships, whether or not your lips do.

We are not just flesh and blood ... we are walking prophecy, temples of dust and divinity, fearfully and wonderfully made.

Application
- Pause today to marvel at God's design in your body. Worship Him for the intricate ways He knit you together.
- Recognize that every breath, heartbeat, and tear is a reminder of His presence within you.
- Treat your body as a living tabernacle ... care for it, honor it, and use it for His glory.

Prayer
Father, thank You for writing Heaven into my design. Help me to see Your fingerprints in every rhythm of my body, every beat of my heart, every spark of my mind. May I never forget that I carry both dust and divinity, and that Your presence is woven into the very core of who I am. **Amen.**

June 15

Built For Eternity

James 1:3–4
Knowing that the testing of your faith produces endurance. And let endurance have its perfect result, so that you may be perfect and complete, lacking in nothing.

Reflection
Nobody enjoys being tested. But in God's kingdom, testing is never wasted.

Every trial you face is doing more than causing pain ... it is producing endurance. Just like muscles grow stronger under pressure, your faith grows tougher through trials.

Even Israel had to learn this. In the wilderness, God tested them ... not to break them, but to reveal what was in their hearts and to strengthen their trust in Him for the journey ahead. What looked like hardship was actually preparation.

Endurance is not just surviving the storm; it's standing firm until God has finished His work in you.

James reminds us that endurance has a purpose: to mature us, to complete us, and to ensure we are lacking nothing for what lies ahead.

Without endurance, we stay shallow. With it, we become steady, strong, and unshakable.

God is not in a hurry, but He is intentional. Each test is shaping you into someone who can carry the weight of His calling without collapsing under it. The process may feel slow, but the result is a life built to last.

Application
- When challenges come, remind yourself: "This test is training me." Instead of asking, "Why me?" ask, "What is God producing in me through this?"
- Lean on God's strength, not your own ... because endurance is a fruit of faith, not willpower.
- When trials arise, choose endurance ... trust that God is using this season to strengthen your faith and prepare you for what's ahead.

Prayer
Father, thank You for the trials that train me. Even when I don't understand, I choose to trust that You are building endurance in me. Shape me into a believer who is mature, complete, and lacking nothing, so my life can glorify You. **Amen.**

June 16
Anointed for Peace

Psalm 23:5
You have anointed my head with oil;
My cup overflows.

Reflection
I never truly understood what this scripture meant.

Many of us have read Psalm 23 and thought "anoint my head with oil" was just a poetic way of saying God keeps us healthy. But the shepherd imagery goes far deeper.

Sheep are vulnerable. Flies lay eggs in their nostrils that hatch into worms, driving them to beat their heads against rocks in torment. Their ears and eyes are constantly attacked by pests. To protect them, the shepherd anoints their heads with oil ... covering them so that the insects cannot penetrate. With the oil comes peace.

We too suffer mental torment. Worry, anxiety, intrusive thoughts, shame, and fear can pound against our minds until we feel like beating our heads against a wall.

But our Good Shepherd offers His oil ... His Spirit, His Word, His presence ... to protect us. His anointing forms a barrier, calming our minds and centering our hearts. He doesn't just relieve the torment ... He gives us overflowing peace.

Application
- When anxious or tormenting thoughts rise, pause and pray: "Lord, anoint my head with oil."
- Create a daily habit of reading Scripture as an "anointing," letting God's Word cover your mind.
- Ask the Holy Spirit to guard your thoughts and renew your mind, so peace, not torment, fills your heart.

Prayer
Father, thank You for being my Shepherd. When tormenting thoughts attack, anoint my head with the oil of Your Spirit. Protect my mind, calm my fears, and give me peace that overflows into every part of my life. I receive Your covering today and trust in Your faithful care. In Jesus' name, **Amen.**

June 17

Call To Transform, Not Perform

Matthew 23:27–28
Woe to you, scribes and Pharisees, hypocrites! For you are like white washed tombs which on the outside appear beautiful, but inside they are full of dead men's bones and all uncleanness. So you, too, outwardly appear righteous to men, but inwardly you are full of hypocrisy and lawlessness.

Reflection
Don't miss the presence of Christ and His Spirit within you by focusing only on checking religious boxes. It is possible to keep commandments, follow traditions, and still miss Christ Himself.

The gospel is not about doing ... it is about becoming.

Becoming holy.
Becoming sanctified.
Becoming like Christ.

Outward works may fool people, but they can never fool God. He searches the heart and examines the mind. He is not impressed by performance; He is after transformation.

Think of it like the poem that says: "Don't spend your life chasing butterflies, but spend your life becoming a beautiful garden, and the butterflies will come to you." In the same way, don't spend your life chasing the appearance of righteousness ... become righteous from the inside out, and your life will bear fruit naturally.

True faith is not about completing a checklist. It is about allowing Christ to transform you until you reflect His love and His light in everything you are.

Application
- Let your heart be changed inwardly, not just your outward actions.
- Stop trying to impress people ... let God transform you inside out.
- Live from genuine holiness, not a spiritual checklist.

Prayer
Father, keep me from chasing empty works and outward appearances. Transform me from the inside out. Teach me to become love, to become light, and to live as a true reflection of Christ in this world. **Amen.**

June 18

The Strength of Stillness

Psalms 46:10
Cease striving and know that I am God; I will be exalted among the nations, I will be exalted on the earth.

Reflection
Sometimes the toughest fight is simply choosing to be still… choosing stillness instead of strain.

Being still isn't a passive surrender; it's a bold act of faith. When everything inside you wants to spin the wheels, move to action, plot the course, or fix the outcome, God calls you to stop the striving.

In the stillness you refuse to hurry … you trust that He is God, that His timing, path, and power are sufficient. You stop the noise long enough to hear the whisper of His voice, to feel the calm of His presence and to recognize that you are not alone.

True strength often shows not when you're doing more, but when you're doing less and trusting more. Stillness is not weakness … it is surrender that strengthens. When you stop striving, God starts leading. Be still, and let Him be God.

Application
- Find a quiet place today and pause for 5 minutes … no phone, no agenda, simply be still with God.
- Ask yourself: "What part of my life am I trying to control instead of surrendering?"
- Write it down and consciously release it … declare: "I cease striving; I know You are God."

Prayer
Father, help me embrace stillness when the world urges me to strive. Teach me to trust Your timing, to rest in Your sovereignty, and to walk in the calm of Your presence. When I feel pressure to act, remind me: You are God. In Jesus' name, **Amen.**

June 19

The Hard Path Builds the Unshakable Life

James 1:12
Blessed is the man who perseveres under trial; for once he has been approved, he will receive the crown of life which the Lord has promised to those who love Him.

Reflection
Every time you choose the narrow road instead of the easy escape, you are laying bricks on the foundation of an unshakable life.

Each time you reject mediocrity and embrace the higher calling God has placed on you, you are making a deposit into eternal wealth ... riches that don't flow to those who beg for change, but to those who, in faith and discipline, build with their own hands under the guidance of the Master Builder.

The world teaches shortcuts. It tells you to fit in, to survive, to grasp for quick wins. But God calls you higher. He calls you to master your thoughts like a king commands his army, and to shape your destiny with discipline, patience and faith.

Success is not an accident, and freedom is not coincidence. Wealth ... spiritual or otherwise ... follows our values, and values are forged in silence, in obedience and in the invisible hours when no one is clapping for you. These moments of hidden discipline are the hammer and chisel of destiny.

As you rise daily in faith and repetition, the Spirit of God reshapes your mind until His will becomes your will, His vision becomes your vision, and His strength becomes your strength.

Application
- Identify an escape you choose too easily ... and take God's higher path today.
- Choose one daily discipline to strengthen your spirit and mind.
- Declare: "I am a builder, not a beggar ... in Christ, I am unshakable.

Prayer
Father, thank You for calling me higher. Help me to embrace the hard path that builds strength, character, and unshakable faith. Teach me to master my thoughts, emotions, and actions so that my life reflects Your power and discipline. May I live with clarity, purpose, and consistency, becoming proof of Your grace and strength in this world. In Jesus' name, **Amen.**

June 20
A Problem for Every Solution

1 Corinthians 15:33
Do not be deceived: Bad company corrupts good morals.

Reflection
Albert Einstein once said, "Stay away from negative people they have a problem for every solution."

Scripture had already warned us of this truth: who we surround ourselves with shapes our mindset and our faith. Negative people drain faith, distort vision, and multiply doubt. They see impossibility where God has promised possibility.

Jesus often withdrew from the crowds, not because He didn't care, but because He understood the power of environment. Negativity is contagious. Just as faith can move mountains, fear and constant complaint can build walls around your destiny.

God has called you to be a light, but you must guard that light from voices that constantly shadow it. Staying away from negativity doesn't mean abandoning people … it means protecting your spirit so you can still love them without being shaped by their outlook.

Surround yourself with people of faith, hope, and courage. Life is too short to let someone else's fear become your ceiling.

Application
- Examine your circle: Do they build your faith or drain it?
- When you encounter negative people, choose compassion without agreement. Don't let their storm become your atmosphere.
- Speak life where others speak death … be the solution, not the problem.

Prayer
Father, give me discernment to recognize the voices that drain my spirit. Help me to love people without being pulled into negativity. Surround me with encouragers, faith builders, and truth-tellers who point me toward You. May my life be a source of solutions and light in a world full of problems.
Amen.

June 21
A Father's Holy Weight

Proverbs 20:7
The righteous man walks in his integrity;
How blessed are his sons after him.

Reflection
Fatherhood is more than provision ... it is presence, covering, and legacy.

A paycheck may sustain the home, but it is your presence that shapes the souls. Children learn God's character by watching the man placed before them ... hopefully displaying love that forgives, strength that protects, truth that instructs, and grace that restores. A father's voice becomes their first compass. A father's walk becomes their first picture of integrity. A father's consistency becomes their first lesson in trust.

You may not be perfect ... and God never asked you to be, but what He calls you to is faithfulness ... faithful to show up, faithful to lead, faithful to repent when needed, and faithful to carry the holy weight of being both protector and priest in your home. The authority God has given you is not a burden ... it is a blessing that shapes generations. When a father lives under the Father's authority, his children inherit more than his last name ... they inherit spiritual stability, emotional strength, and a legacy of righteousness that will outlive him.

Application
- Show up consistently, knowing your presence carries a weight no one else can replace.
- Lead your home with integrity so your children see God's character reflected through you.
- Pray daily over your family, covering them as the protector and priest God has called you to be.

Prayer
Father in Heaven, thank You for entrusting me with the gift and responsibility of fatherhood. Teach me to lead with love, to stand firm in truth, and to walk faithfully so that my children see You in me. Strengthen every father who bears this holy weight, and may we leave behind legacies that honor You. **Amen.**

June 22

Shut the Door and Pray

Matthew 6:6
But you, when you pray, go into your inner room, close your door and pray to your Father who is in secret, and your Father who sees what is done in secret will reward you.

Reflection
When you step into that secret place, the first battle you'll face is not the devil ... it's your own wandering thoughts. Prayer is not passive. It is an act of the will. Suddenly, your to-do list grows, distractions surface, and your mind runs everywhere but to God. That's why Jesus said, "Shut your door." Shut the door to your emotions, your worries, and your wandering mind. Still your spirit and fix your attention on Him.

God meets you in that secret place, not in the noise. And when you practice living there, faith grows unshakable. Doubt loses its grip. You begin to see that God has been in the middle of your circumstances all along.

Prayer is not just an event ... it becomes a lifestyle. If you'll start your mornings by opening the door of your life fully to God, you'll walk through your day enlightened by His presence.

Prayer without surrender is just spiritual fog. But when you live as a true child of God ... walking in the light, confessing sin, forgiving freely, and staying obedient ... Jesus' words become true: "Everyone who asks, receives." (Matthew 7:8).

Shut the door, silence the noise, and pray like His child.

Application
- Set a daily secret-place moment ... even five minutes ... to shut the door and meet with God without distraction.
- When your thoughts wander, gently redirect them by whispering His name or repeating a short Scripture.
- Begin each day with surrender ... asking God to lead your thoughts, choices, and steps as His child.

Prayer
Father, help me to shut the door on distractions, pride, and disobedience. Teach me to pray with a clean heart and a surrendered spirit. May my private prayers be marked with purity, and may my public life carry the imprint of Your presence. **Amen.**

June 23
The Gift of Giving

Proverbs 11:25
The generous man will be prosperous, And he who waters will himself be watered.

Reflection
Giving is not just something you do for others … it is a self-serving gift to yourself as well.

When you give out of a heart surrendered to God, you're not losing … you're positioning yourself to receive from the fountain of His provision and blessing. You are planting a seed.

The generous person 'waters' others, and in doing so, his own life is refreshed and sustained.

True giving is more than a transaction … it is alignment with the character of God, who gave first. Because you give, you participate in what God is doing: you become a channel … and channels are blessed.

So next time you hesitate, remember: your act of giving is also an act of receiving … receiving the joy, the purpose, the blessing, and the growth God intends for you.

Application
- Choose one thing today you can give … time, money, encouragement, presence.
- As you give, remind yourself: "I'm not only blessing them; I'm receiving from God's work through me."
- Reflect tonight: How did I feel giving? What changed inside me?

Prayer
Father, thank You for the privilege of giving … that You entrust me with good things to release to others. Help me to give from the abundance of my heart, not out of compulsion or fear. May every act of generosity I perform also deepen my own faith, increase my own joy, and draw me closer to You. Let my giving reflect Your nature, empower others, and enrich my soul. In Jesus' name, **Amen.**

June 24

Integrity Over Impressing

Proverbs 11:3
*The integrity of the upright will guide them,
But the crookedness of the treacherous will destroy them.*

Reflection
"A man with no humility and integrity can only impress small minds with his worldly possessions." — Edmond Mbiaka

The older you get, the more you realize that real greatness has nothing to do with what a man owns and everything to do with who a man is.
A man without humility and integrity can only impress small minds …
because real ones see past the possessions and look straight at the character.

In a world obsessed with image, status, and shiny things, God still measures a person by: their heart, their honesty, their humility, their obedience, their consistency, their private decisions and their unseen sacrifices. You can fool people with possessions, but you cannot fool God.

Integrity is who you are when no one is watching. It is the quiet yes to righteousness and the silent no to compromise. Integrity is choosing the right thing even when the wrong thing pays more. Integrity is staying honest even when lies seem easier. Integrity is remaining humble even when success grows louder. Integrity is walking straight even when the path curves.

Possessions impress the immature, but character impresses Heaven. You don't need to shine for people … just stay true before God. Your character will take you where your charisma never could.

Application
- Identify one area where your integrity is being tested … money, relationships, habits, honesty, intentions.
- Ask God to strengthen your humility and your character.
- Choose one action today that aligns your private life with God's standards.

Prayer
Father, give me an un-compromised spirit. Make my character stronger than my reputation and my humility deeper than my accomplishments. Guard my heart from pride, dishonesty, and superficial living. Shape me into a person of truth, honor, and integrity. Let my life impress Heaven more than it ever impresses people. In Jesus' name, **Amen.**

June 25
The Power of Showing Up

James 2:26
For just as the body without the spirit is dead, so also faith without works is dead.

Reflection
Sometimes the greatest act of faith isn't a grand performance ... it's simply showing up.

As a hospice chaplain, my calling is not simply to preach, but to simply show up: to sit beside the dying, hold trembling hands, offer a listening ear, a calm prayer, or silent presence when words fall short. In those moments ... presence overrules performance ... you become a living expression of God's love and dignity.

There's a story of Muhammad Ali, on January 19, 1981, who found a young man poised on a ninth-floor ledge in Los Angeles. The crowd below shouted "Jump! Jump!" but Ali leaned out, looked him in the eye, and said: "You're my brother. I love you." With compassion and presence he walked him down to safety.

What this shows us: you never know whose life you might save ... not with a sermon, not with an argument, but with presence: "I see you," "I care," "I'm here."

Faith without action is empty; your "presence" becomes the conduit of God's love.
When you show up, you stand in the gap for someone who may feel unseen. When you stay present, you become part of their rescue story.

Application
- Ask: Who in my life needs to know: "I see you. I care. I'm here"?
- Choose one person today. Send a text, make a call, visit...even if briefly... and simply say those words.
- Reflect afterward: How did showing up impact you? How did it impact them?

Prayer
Father, give me courage to show up in the lives of others. Help me be present, compassionate, and real. Let my faith manifest in love and in deeds, so that someone who feels unseen will know they are seen. Use me as Your vessel of rescue, presence, and hope. In Jesus' name, **Amen.**

June 26
Energy Multiplies When We Reflect Light Together

Romans 14:19
So then we pursue the things which make for peace and the building up of one another.

Reflection
Energy doesn't simply add up ... it multiplies when believers come together to reflect light, truth, and love.

When two people choose peace instead of strife, encouragement instead of criticism, and humility instead of pride ... something powerful happens. Just as a seed reproduces more of its kind, what we pour out gains momentum when mirrored by others, creating exponential impact that neither could achieve alone.

The spiritual momentum we generate doesn't just bless individuals .. it blesses the community, the body of Christ, and magnifies God's light in this dark world.

True "Kingdom synergy" isn't about superficial connection or convenient agreements. It's about ordinary people ... with ordinary flaws ... committing to unity, love, and spiritual growth together. In that unity, God's design for fellowship ... the deep, sacred communion and shared purpose often called koinonia ... comes alive.

When we reflect light together ... in humility, in peace, in mutual edification ... we become part of a greater work: building God's Kingdom, strengthening His people, and bringing hope and power where there was none.

Application
- Today, be intentional about reflecting God's truth, love, or light back to someone you meet.
- Notice how your faith multiplies when you lean into connection and shared encouragement.
- Today, let your light meet someone else's need ... and watch how together you build peace, hope, and faith that reach far beyond yourselves.

Prayer
Father, thank You for the spiritual synergy You create when hearts align. Help me to be a wellspring of grace and light, and to connect with others in ways that multiply our joy, faith, and hope. In Jesus' name, **Amen.**

June 27
Light Your Corner

Matthew 5:14–16
*"You are the light of the world. A city set on a hill cannot be hidden…
Let your light shine before men…"*

Reflection
"It is better to light one small candle than to curse the darkness."
— Eleanor Roosevelt

When the world feels heavy with chaos, confusion, or corruption, remember this: You don't have to fix everything … just be the candle. Be the hope. Be the love. Be the light someone needs today. Light your corner.

Darkness gets louder every day. People complain more than they pray. Voices curse the darkness but never challenge it. But Jesus didn't call us to curse the night…He called us to shine.

Instead of complaining about what's wrong, be what's right. Instead of spreading noise, speak light. Instead of cursing the darkness, become the flame that reminds others hope still burns.

One candle doesn't seem like much… until it enters a dark room. Darkness doesn't negotiate. It doesn't resist. It doesn't fight back. It simply flees. Even a single candle pushes back the shadows. Imagine what happens when we all light ours together … homes change, communities brighten, churches awaken, and the world starts to glow with Kingdom hope.

You are not responsible for the entire world, but you are responsible for your corner of it. So shine. Let God use your flame to ignite someone else's faith.

Application
- Identify your "corner": home, job, ministry, friendships, or online space.
- Choose one way to shine today … kindness, generosity, integrity, truth, or encouragement.
- Silence your complaints for 24 hours and replace them with prayer and light.

Prayer
Father, make me a light in dark places. Remove the spirit of complaint and fill me with the spirit of courage. Help me shine boldly, love deeply, and carry Your presence everywhere I go. Use my small flame to ignite hope in others. In Jesus' name, **Amen.**

June 28
The Gift of Serenity

Philippians 4:7
And the peace of God, which surpasses all comprehension, will guard your hearts and your minds in Christ Jesus.

Reflection
Serenity means a state of being calm, peaceful, and untroubled … both inwardly and outwardly.

The dictionary calls it peacefulness, tranquility, calmness of mind. But spiritually, serenity is something deeper. Serenity is when your heart is still even when life is not. It's the inner quiet that comes from trusting God, not from controlling circumstances.

Most people chase serenity by changing what's around them. But Kingdom serenity comes from letting God change what's happening within you.

Storms may rage. Winds may blow. Life may shout. But serenity whispers: "God is here. God is near. God is in control." Serenity is not the absence of storms … it is the steady confidence of knowing Who is in the boat with you.

Paul said:
"Be anxious for nothing… pray about everything… give thanks in all things…" and in return, God gives peace that surpasses understanding.

True serenity is spiritual maturity. It's the fruit of trust. It's the mark of someone who has learned to let God be God. You cannot control everything. You just need to rest in the One who controls it all.

Application
- Identify the area of your life currently disturbing your peace.
- Bring it to God in prayer … specifically and honestly.
- Practice stillness for 2–3 minutes today: breathe, quiet your mind, invite God's presence.

Prayer
Father, teach me the peace that passes understanding. Quiet my mind, steady my heart, and anchor my spirit in You. Help me release control, surrender fear, and trust Your presence in every storm. Let serenity rise within me … not from circumstances, but from Your nearness. Guard my heart and mind today. In Jesus' name, **Amen.**

June 29
Love That Disciplines

Proverbs 13:24
He who withholds his rod hates his son,
But he who loves him disciplines him diligently.

Reflection
Love without correction is not love at all ... it is neglect disguised as kindness.

There is a story of a death row inmate's last letter to his mother that reminds us that silence in the face of wrongdoing is never neutral. In the letter, he tells his mother that she should be on death row as well, because she never corrected him as a child. What we refuse to confront today may grow into chains tomorrow.

Parents, mentors, and leaders are entrusted with the sacred responsibility of shaping lives. Correction may feel uncomfortable, but it is an expression of love. To discipline a child is to say, "I love you too much to let you destroy yourself." God disciplines those He loves (Hebrews 12:6), not to harm them, but to keep them from paths that lead to destruction.

When we avoid correction ... whether out of fear, guilt, or a desire to keep peace ... we unknowingly pave the way for greater pain. The truth is, boundaries build safety and discipline produces freedom.

Love that refuses to correct will eventually reap regret, but love that disciplines will bear the fruit of life.

Application
- Parents: Ask yourself if your silence is enabling, not protecting. Correction today may save your child tomorrow.
- Mentors and leaders: Don't withhold truth because it may sting; speak it in love to build up, not tear down.
- Personally: Receive God's correction as a sign of His deep love for you ... proof that He is committed to your growth.

Prayer
Father, thank You for loving me enough to correct me. Give me the courage to lovingly discipline those I lead and the humility to receive Your discipline in my own life. May my love never be silent when truth must be spoken.
Amen.

June 30

Marriage: Built to Last

Psalm 127:1
Unless the Lord builds the house, they labor in vain who build it; Unless the Lord guards the city, the watchman stays awake in vain.

Reflection
Marriage is not construction ... it is consecration.

A counselor cannot "fix" two people like a repairman; they can only help them uncover, reconcile, and invite God into their hearts. Healthy marriages begin with healthy individuals. That's why wise premarital counseling looks at each person's story ... childhood to present ...before bringing them together as one.

Statistics show us how fragile marriage can be when it is built on human strength: almost half of all first time marriages fail, and second marriages struggle even more. Yet God never designed marriage to be built on compatibility alone. He designed it to be built on Him. Unless the Lord builds the house... the foundation will crack.

God's design for marriage is threefold: Reflect His image in how we treat one another. Reproduce a godly heritage that multiplies His glory. Reign together against Satan, who is the real enemy ... not your spouse.

Conflict is inevitable. Differences are guaranteed. But God uses marriage as His workshop ... refining us, shaping our character, and teaching us grace. The goal is not performance, but connection. Not a "have to" life, but a "thank You" life.

Application
- If single or engaged, commit to personal growth and healing before entering marriage; a whole marriage starts with whole people.
- If married, take 100% responsibility for your actions, and choose compassion over criticism.
- Daily invite God to build your home, reflect His image, and protect your marriage from the enemy's schemes.

Prayer
Lord, I thank You that marriage is Your design and Your gift. Teach me to reflect Your love, reproduce godly heritage, and reign with my spouse against the true enemy. Build my house on Your foundation, and refine me in love so my marriage brings You glory. In Jesus' name, **Amen.**

July 1
Authentic by Design

Psalm 139:14
I will praise You, for I am fearfully and wonderfully made; Marvelous are Your works, and my soul knows it very well.

Reflection
There's a difference between what God creates and what man manufactures.

Consider fabrics: cotton, silk, linen, and wool are natural fibers made by God. They breathe, endure, and often increase in value with age. They are costly because they are authentic, and when heat is applied, they refine rather than crumble.

On the other hand, man-made fibers ... polyester, nylon, synthetics ... are cheaper, quicker, and easier to produce. Yet under pressure or fire, they melt, burn, and lose integrity. They are imitations that cannot withstand the test of time or heat.

So it is with life. When you live in God's design ... rooted in His Spirit, truth, and Word ... you are like natural fibers: strong, durable, authentic, and valuable. Pressure only refines you. But when life is built on shortcuts, imitation faith, or man's way over God's way, it cannot endure the fires of trial.

God doesn't want you stitched together with synthetic or man made substitutes ... He designed you as a masterpiece of His creation, woven with His Spirit.

Don't exchange His authenticity for cheap imitations. Choose the fabric of faith that endures.

Application
- Live God-made, not man-made ... choose the identity He crafted, not the world's imitation.
- Let pressure refine you ... real faith gets stronger in the fire.
- Reject shortcuts ... stay woven in God's truth, not synthetic substitutes.

Prayer
Lord, thank You for making me fearfully and wonderfully. Keep me from settling for man-made imitations of purpose or identity. Weave me with strength, authenticity, and truth, so that when life's heat comes, I will stand firm in You. In Jesus' name, **Amen.**

July 2
The Kingdom Within

Luke 17:21
For behold, the kingdom of God is within you.

Reflection
The Kingdom is not just around you ... the Kingdom is within you.
Jesus wasn't pointing to a place ... He was pointing to a presence, a reality that begins on the inside before it ever shows up on the outside.

To live in the Kingdom, you must know three things: Know God. Know Self. Know Freedom. Know God ... because He is the source of your identity, power, and purpose. The more deeply you know Him, the more clearly you see everything else.
Know Self ... because you cannot walk in authority if you don't know who you are.
Identity is not discovered in culture, comparison, or compliments ... identity is discovered in Christ.
Know Freedom ... because the Kingdom begins in a liberated heart. You can sit in church and still be bound. You can be successful and still not be free. Freedom is not the absence of restriction; it is the presence of Christ ruling within.

When the Kingdom is alive inside you: your mind transforms, your decisions sharpen, your peace strengthens, your confidence deepens, your purpose becomes clear and your life bears Kingdom fruit.
The Kingdom is not a future destination ... it is a present transformation.
And once the Kingdom lives in you, it begins to flow through you.

Application
- Ask God to reveal any area inside you where His Kingdom is not ruling yet.
- Reflect: "Do I truly know God, know myself in Christ, and know freedom?"
- Declare Luke 17:21 over your life today: "The Kingdom of God is within me."

Prayer
Father, let Your Kingdom rule within me. Reveal Yourself to me in deeper ways. Show me who I am in You, and break every internal chain that keeps me from living free. Establish Your truth in my mind, Your peace in my heart, and Your authority in my spirit. Let the Kingdom within me transform the world around me. In Jesus' name, **Amen.**

July 3
Called to Be "Twice-Born" in a Once-Born World

John 3:3
Jesus answered him, 'Truly, truly, I say to you, unless one is born again, he cannot see the kingdom of God.

Reflection
Today, simply saying you are a Christian doesn't hold the same weight it once did ... because many are once-born (physically born) but never twice-born (spiritually reborn).

The term "twice-born" describes those who experience both their first physical birth and a second, spiritual birth from God's Spirit.

True saints are those who have passed from death to life, from simply believing about Christ to living in Him.

When you claim a faith that changed nothing inside you, you're still operating in the wilderness mindset ... believer in name only.

God calls us to more than identity ... He calls us to transformation. If He is your everything, your life should reflect that reality. Don't be content with spiritual infancy.

Rise up. You were created for impact, for maturity, for life in the kingdom that's real.

Application
- Reflect: Write down one area of your life where you say you're Christian, but your behavior shows otherwise.
- Pray: "Lord, birth in me what was never alive before. Make me alive in You."
- Choose one decisive action today that reflects your new birth ...perhaps share your faith, love someone sacrificially, serve anonymously.

Prayer
Father, thank You for making me new. If I've lived only in my physical birth, forgive me. Create in me a fresh spiritual birth...open my eyes, change my heart, renew my purpose. Let me walk as one who is truly alive in You, deeply rooted, forever transformed. In Jesus' name, **Amen.**

July 4

When a Nation Forgets God

Proverbs 14:34
Righteousness exalts a nation, But sin is a disgrace to any people.

Reflection
"If God doesn't judge America harshly,
then He owes Sodom and Gomorrah an apology."
— Billy Graham

Billy Graham didn't say that for shock value. He said it as a warning. A nation cannot reject God, redefine truth, glorify wickedness, and expect peace, blessing, or protection. When a nation forgets God, it invites confusion. When a nation mocks God, it invites judgment. And when a nation replaces God, it invites destruction.

Sodom and Gomorrah weren't judged because they sinned ... every nation sins. They were judged because they refused to repent. They were judged because righteousness was abandoned, truth was despised and God was no longer honored.

America is in the same spiritual tension. We celebrate what God calls sin. We mock what God calls holy. We legalize what God condemns. We silence what God commands. We exalt pleasure and kill purity. We elevate self and sideline Scripture.

But here is the good news: Before God judges a nation, He warns it. And right now, God is raising people who stand for righteousness, preach truth without flinching and live as lights in a dark generation.

Application
• Identify one area where culture has influenced you more than Scripture.
• Pray for America ... its leaders, its churches, and its spiritual condition.
• Commit to living righteously in an unrighteous generation.

Prayer
Father, have mercy on our nation.
Forgive us for rejecting Your ways and despising Your truth. Raise up a remnant who will stand in righteousness without fear. Begin revival in our homes, our churches, and our hearts. Help me live boldly, love deeply, and walk purely in a world that has forgotten You. Heal our land, Lord.
In Jesus' name, **Amen.**

July 5
No Free Rent

2 Corinthians 10:5
Take every thought captive to the obedience of Christ.

Reflection
"I refuse to let anyone's thoughts…or my own…steal my peace in God."

One of the greatest battles in the Christian life happens in the mind. The enemy doesn't always attack your body or your bank account … he attacks your thoughts. Because whoever controls the mind controls the mood, the decisions, the peace, and the direction of your life.

People will try to live in your head. Old memories will try to live in your head. Fear, insecurity, assumptions, anxiety, and imaginary scenarios will try to set up a full apartment complex in your mind. But today you declare: "NO FREE RENT." If it didn't come from God, if it doesn't align with Scripture, if it steals your peace, if it lowers your worth,
if it questions your identity, if it distracts you from destiny … it cannot stay.

Your mind is not a dumping ground. Your spirit is not a storage unit.
Your peace is not public property. God gave you authority over every thought that tries to trespass in your mind. You don't have to let every opinion, every comment, every emotion, or every attack move in.

The Holy Spirit is the landlord of your mind. And with Him in charge, you have the power to evict every lie, every fear, every negative voice, and every unhealthy attachment. Guard your mind. Protect your peace. Set spiritual boundaries. And refuse to let anything or anyone live rent-free in a place God designed for His presence.

Application
- Identify one thought, fear, or voice that's been "living rent-free" in your mind. Evict it today.
- Replace it with a Scripture, especially 2 Corinthians 10:5.
- Declare: "My mind belongs to Christ. No free rent."

Prayer
Father, thank You for giving me authority over my thoughts. Help me guard my mind with Your truth. Evict every lie, fear, distraction, or voice that does not come from You. Fill my mind with Your peace, Your Word, and Your presence. Today I declare: my mind is Yours, and nothing gets to live here for free. In Jesus' name, **Amen.**

July 6
Ask. Seek. Knock.

Matthew 7:7
Ask, and it will be given to you; seek, and you will find; knock, and it will be opened to you.

Reflection
Jesus didn't just tell us to ask once. He said:
ASK and keep on asking.
SEEK and keep on seeking.
KNOCK and keep on knocking.

Spiritual persistence is the doorway to divine breakthrough. Most people don't miss what God has for them because it's hidden … they miss it because they stop pursuing too soon.

Some believers pray…but never seek. Some seek…but never knock. Some knock…but never asked God first.
Kingdom success requires all three. ASK … Bring it before God. Submit it. Surrender it. SEEK … Look for wisdom, guidance, strategy, and understanding. KNOCK … Put your faith into motion. Walk through the doors God opens.

God honors persistence…not stubbornness. Spiritual hunger…not pride. Dependence…not force. God honors faith.
Every breakthrough has a process attached to it.
Every answered prayer has a step of obedience tied to it.

Your blessing may be one more ask away. Your clarity may be one more moment of seeking away. Your open door may be one more knock away. Don't stop now. God responds to the persistent.

Application
- What do you need to ask God for again?
- What do you need to seek with fresh focus?
- What door do you need to knock on … today?

Prayer
Father, teach me to ask boldly, seek diligently, and knock faithfully. Break every spirit of hesitation, fear, or passivity. Give me clarity as I pursue Your will and courage as I execute what You show me. Open every door designed for me and close every door that would distract me. Strengthen my persistence and align my pursuit with Your purpose. In Jesus' name, **Amen.**

July 7
Cheerful Obedience

Jeremiah 17:10
I, the Lord, search the heart,
I test the mind,
To give to each person according to his ways,
According to the results of his deeds.

Reflection
In the Kingdom of God, it's not just about what you do ... it's about the heart posture behind it.

Paul reminds us, "God loves a cheerful giver" (2 Corinthians 9:7). The same principle applies to every act of obedience. God is not impressed with reluctant compliance; He delights in joyful surrender.

Jeremiah 17:10 tells us that God searches the heart and tests the mind. We can fool people with performance, but we cannot fool the One who sees our motives. True obedience is not just about the action ... it's about the spirit in which the action is carried out.

Think about how a parent feels when a child obeys with joy versus when they obey with grumbling. One brings delight; the other only reveals resistance. In the same way, cheerful obedience not only honors our earthly parents, but it also pleases our Heavenly Father.

God is looking for sons and daughters who obey with glad hearts, not out of duty, but out of devotion.

Application
- Examine your heart posture: Are you obeying reluctantly or cheerfully?
- The next time you give, serve, or obey God, do it with joy ... seeing it as an act of love, not a burden.
- Ask God to purify your motives, so your obedience is filled with love and truth.

Prayer
Father, thank You for seeing beyond my actions and into my heart. Teach me to obey You with cheerfulness and joy. May my giving, my serving, and my obedience flow from love, not reluctance. Let my life bring delight to You as I walk in cheerful obedience. **Amen.**

July 8

Where Attention Flows, Energy Grows

Colossians 3:2
Set your mind on the things above, not on the things that are on earth.

Reflection
Your energy is not random ... it follows the trail of your attention.

What you continually dwell on shapes your emotions, your outlook, and even the atmosphere around you. The Word teaches us to take every thought captive (2 Corinthians 10:5) because where the mind goes, the heart and life will follow.

This means you must be intentional about directing your attention toward joy, gratitude, healing, prosperity, abundance, love, and compassion.

You don't just wait to "feel" these things; you cultivate them by fixing your focus on God's truth. If you meditate on fear, scarcity, and pain, that is the energy that multiplies. But when you set your attention on Christ and His promises, you train your spirit to attract and release joy, peace, and blessing.

Energy flows where your attention goes. So be wise with your focus. Practice thanksgiving. Speak life. Visualize healing. Lean into love. Align your thoughts with heaven ... and your energy will flow in heaven's direction.

Focus on heaven so your energy follows God, not distractions.
Guard your thoughts because whatever you dwell on grows.
Speak life and your spirit will shift in the right direction.

Application
- Redirect your thoughts today toward one heavenly truth you want to grow in your life.
- Choose gratitude over negativity the moment your mind starts drifting.
- Speak one life-giving affirmation that aligns your energy with God's promises.

Prayer
Lord, teach me to set my attention on You and Your promises. Help me guard my mind from distractions that drain my energy. Let my focus bring forth joy, gratitude, healing, abundance, and love in my life and in the lives of those around me. May my energy be aligned with heaven's flow, every day. In Jesus' name, **Amen.**

July 9
The Power of Oneness

John 17:21
"...that they may all be one; even as You, Father, are in Me and I in You, that they also may be in Us, so that the world may believe that You sent Me."

Reflection
God's design for humanity has always been oneness.

Jesus prayed that we would be one with the Father, one within ourselves, and one with others. True peace flows from this divine order of unity.

One with God ... This is the foundation. Apart from Him, we are fractured. In Christ, our spirit is reconnected to its Source, and we live out of His presence and power.

One with Self (Spirit, Soul, and Body) ... Many live in inner conflict, pulled between what the Spirit desires, what the soul craves, and what the body demands. Wholeness begins when the Spirit leads, the soul agrees, and the body follows. A as matter of fact... the etymology of the word peace means to be whole or one.

One with Others ... From unity with God and self flows reconciliation with people. We can't walk in true fellowship with others if we're disconnected from God or divided within ourselves.

Oneness is not sameness ... it is alignment. It is the harmony of heaven reflected in our relationships, our inner life, and our connection to the Father. Where there is oneness, there is strength, clarity, and testimony. The world sees Christ when we are united to self and others.

Application
- Ask yourself: Am I aligned with God, or am I drifting in independence?
- Examine your inner life: Where is there tension between spirit, soul, and body? Invite the Spirit to lead.
- Pursue peace with others, remembering that unity is not optional... it's a witness.

Prayer
Father, make me one with You, whole within myself, and reconciled with those around me. Bring my spirit, soul, and body into harmony under Your Spirit. Let my life be a reflection of the unity You desire for Your people.
Amen.

July 10
The Call to Overcome

Revelation 2–3
He who has an ear, let him hear what the Spirit says to the churches.

Reflection
Everyone in life has something to overcome in order to walk in the peace and abundance of God.

The Seven Churches of Revelation remind us that every believer has a strength, a struggle, and a spiritual assignment to overcome. God wasn't exposing them ... He was inviting them higher.

Ephesus had truth but lacked love ... overcome distraction. Smyrna suffered ... overcome fear. Pergamum held faith ... overcome compromise. Thyatira showed love ... overcome corruption. Sardis had reputation ... overcome deadness. Philadelphia was faithful ... overcome weariness. Laodicea had wealth ... overcome lukewarmness. Different churches. Different battles. Same command: "To him who overcomes..."

Overcoming is the doorway to every promise God made ... Tree of Life, Crown of Life, Hidden Manna, White Garments, Pillars in God's Temple, and even the privilege to sit with Christ on His throne.
You do not overcome by trying harder. You overcome by drawing nearer.

Whatever your struggle today ... fear, compromise, fatigue, old wounds, apathy, sin, or self-sufficiency ... God gives you the strength to rise above it. Overcoming is not optional. It is the pathway to peace, promise, and abundance.

Application
- Identify the one area God is calling you to overcome in this season.
- Read one promise from Revelation 2–3 and declare it over your life.
- Pray: "Lord, show me what to release, what to return to, and what to hold fast."

Prayer
Father, show me what I must overcome to walk in Your peace and abundance. Strengthen my heart, awaken my spirit, and lead me toward the promises You have prepared. Make me an overcomer by Your Spirit and not my strength. In Jesus' name, **Amen.**

July 11
Don't Miss Today's Blessings

Isaiah 43:18–19

Do not call to mind the former things, Or ponder things of the past. Behold, I will do something new...

Reflection
Don't let yesterday's disappointments distract you from the blessings of today.
Yesterday may have wounded you. Yesterday may have shocked you. Yesterday may have drained you. But yesterday does not have permission to define today ... unless you hand it the pen.

Disappointment is dangerous because it subtly steals your vision. It blinds you to what God is doing right now. It keeps your heart stuck in moments God has already moved beyond. And if you're not careful, you can mourn yesterday so deeply that you miss the miracles standing right in front of you.

God says, "Do not call to mind the former things." Why?
Because constantly replaying the past robs you of the present. And God works in the now. His mercies are new every morning. His grace is sufficient for today. His blessings are loaded daily. But you can't receive what's new if your hands are still gripping what's old.

The enemy wants to distract you with disappointment; God wants to deliver you into destiny. Today is where God is working.

Don't miss what God is doing because you're staring at what didn't happen.

Application
- Identify one disappointment from yesterday that still lingers. Release it to God in prayer.
- Write down one blessing you recognize today ... something God is doing right now.
- Commit to practicing "present gratitude" throughout the day.

Prayer
Father, release me from the weight of yesterday's disappointments. Heal every place in my heart where the past still has a grip. Open my eyes to see the blessings and opportunities You've placed in front of me today. Give me faith to embrace the new thing You are doing. Let me walk in gratitude, expectation, and clarity. Today is Yours and so am I. In Jesus' name, **Amen.**

July 12
Just Can't Help It
In Honor of Rev. Dorceal Duckens

Acts 4:20
As for us, we cannot help speaking about what we have seen and heard.

Reflection
As my brothers Duckens would say " I got a case of the " Can't-Help-its"

When you encounter something extraordinary, silence is impossible. Think about the times you couldn't help but tell others ... a new discovery, a new birth in the family, an answered prayer, or a breakthrough moment. The disciples knew this firsthand. After healing the lame man at the temple gate, Peter and John were confronted by the religious leaders. Instead of retreating, they boldly declared that it was all done in the name of Jesus.

Their courage came not from clever words or personal confidence, but from being filled with the Holy Spirit. They had walked with Jesus, witnessed His resurrection, and experienced His transforming power. That encounter was too powerful to keep hidden. They proclaimed, "We cannot help speaking about what we have seen and heard."

The same is true for us. When Christ has changed your life ... redeemed your past, given you hope, and filled you with His Spirit ... how can you keep silent? Witness isn't just an obligation; it's an overflow of gratitude and joy. A heart touched by God naturally becomes a mouth that testifies about His Goodness.

Application
- Reflect on one way God has personally shown His love or power in your life this week.
- Share that testimony with someone today ... a friend, coworker, or even a stranger.
- Pray for boldness like Peter and John to speak truth with love and confidence.

Prayer
Dear Jesus, You are the only name by which I am saved. Fill me with Your Spirit so that my life overflows with joy, courage, and gratitude. Give me boldness to speak about what You've done in me and through me, and let my witness point others back to You. **Amen.**

July 13
Be Patient in the Process

Luke 21:19
By your endurance you will gain your lives.

Reflection
There are moments when your vision feels cloudy and progress seems slow, yet the call of a Kingdom believer is unchanged: keep moving anyway.

Choose gratitude and expectation in every season, because God knows how to redeem every delay. Christ in you empowers you to speak life, pray boldly, stand in faith, and stay committed even when you can't see results yet.

Your life is like a planted tree… it only produces when rooted in Spirit and anchored in truth. No material gain can satisfy your soul. Only Jesus … the Bread of Life … gives eternal weight to your goals. Faith, worship, prayer, and obedience aren't extras; they are the lifeline that reconnects you to your God-nature and aligns you with Heaven's purpose.

And above all, patience is your spiritual posture. Patience matures your faith, carries you through testing, and prepares you for blessing. Delay is not denial … it is development. What feels like a setback is often God strengthening you for what's ahead.

Dreams, like seeds, must be buried before they break through. Flowers endure winter before they bloom. Your dreams must endure seasons of silence before seasons of manifestation. Wait well. Be patient… and trust that God's timing will bring forth the fruit of your faith.

Application
- Endure the waiting … patience is the soil where your faith grows.
- Stay rooted in Christ … prayer, worship, and obedience keep your spirit alive.
- Trust God's timing … delays are preparation, not punishment.

Prayer
Father, teach me to wait with worship, to endure with gratitude, and to believe that every delay is working for my good. Help me to remain rooted in You, the Bread of Life, so that patience may produce the fruit of faith in me. In Jesus' name, **Amen.**

July 14
From Venting to Victory

Proverbs 16:24
Gracious words are a honeycomb, sweet to the soul and healing to the bones.

Reflection
Venting can feel like relief ... but science warns us: it may actually make things worse.

According to recent research, when we repeatedly express frustration without seeking a solution, we deepen negative neural pathways in our brain ... wiring ourselves into a cycle of helplessness, reactivity, and anxiety.

That means our venting habits can reshape our brains ... making stress and anger the default. What starts as emotional release can lead to emotional bondage.

Relationships suffer too. Constant venting places heavy emotional strain on listeners. Emotions are contagious. When you're perpetually airing frustration, your stress begins to spread ... leaving your loved ones emotionally drained.

True healing doesn't come from venting; it comes from clarity, resolution, and truth-laced release. Romans 12 calls us to renew our mind ... not to rehearse our wounds, but to align our hearts with hope and healing.

Beautiful people, your words are either deepening wounds or delivering healing. Choose speech that uplifts, clarifies, and restores. When you trade venting for virtue ... frustration for faith ... and reaction for revelation ... your soul heals, your relationships breathe, and your mind is renewed.

Application
- Recognize when you're venting out of habit, not seeking freedom.
- Pause. Ask: "Is this venting helping, or just reinforcing a negative loop?"
- Shift your posture ... from venting into the void to seeking clarity with intention.

Prayer
Father, help me resist the comfort of venting and fear-driven emotions. Renew my mind, so my words build, not break. Transform my heart to seek clarity and resolution. Replace venting with healing conversation, and let my life reflect Your peace. **Amen.**

July 15
The Battle for Your Mind

Romans 12:2
And do not be conformed to this world, but be transformed by the renewing of your mind...

Reflection
We've entered an age where entertainment tempts us, our feelings rule us and pleasure often overshadows purpose. Like I stated previously, when a man discovers his purpose, he stops chasing entertainment and begins seeking alignment with God's will. It's this shift ... from fleeting pleasures to meaningful purpose ... that births true fulfillment.

Yet, this transition requires training. You must train your mind to be stronger than your feelings, or else you'll lose yourself. Emotions are real, but they're fleeting; they can't be the foundation of your decisions. When feelings dictate your choices, your values will shift with your moods ... one moment hopeful, the next, hopeless.

But when the mind is renewed by Scripture ... anchored in truth ... it becomes a steadfast compass, guiding you through emotional storms. You begin to choose faith over fear, purpose over pleasure, character over comfort.

The wisdom of Proverbs paints it vividly:
"A man without self-control is like a city broken into and left without walls." ...Proverbs 25:28 (NASB1995) Without inner discipline, we become defenseless ... vulnerable to temptation and chaos. A renewed mind doesn't ignore feelings ... it discerns them. It filters emotions through the lens of truth and refuses to be ruled by impulse.

Application
- Reflect: Are you living from your feelings or from your purpose in Christ?
- Choose one area where emotions have guided you, and intentionally apply biblical truth instead.
- Speak: "I feel ____, but I will not be led by this feeling." Use this daily to guard your heart and mind.

Prayer
Father, renew my mind. Strengthen me to live from my calling, not my comfort. Help me to choose what lasts ... faith, purpose, and godly character ... over momentary pleasures. Build in me a city of self-control, where walls stand firm and my spirit is anchored in You. **Amen.**

July 16
Guarding Your Energy

Proverbs 4:23
Above all else, guard your heart, for everything you do flows from it.

Reflection
Your energy is your wealth.

God entrusted you with a soul, a mind, and a body that carry His Spirit, and not everyone deserves unlimited access to that gift. Like money in a budget, your energy must be stewarded wisely.

Jesus Himself often withdrew to solitary places to pray (Luke 5:16), showing us the power of boundaries and guarding your energy.

Too often we spread ourselves thin, people-pleasing, over-explaining, and exhausting our strength on those who cannot or will not receive us. But your spiritual health requires discernment. You don't owe everyone your intimacy, your vulnerability, or your emotional resources. Some connections are aligned with your healed self, while others only bond to your broken self. God calls you to release expired ties and keep your frequency pure.

This is not selfishness ... it is stewardship. To guard your energy is to protect the flow of God's Spirit in your life. To watch your energy budget is to say "yes" to emotional maturity, healthy boundaries, and divine purpose.

Your worth is not measured by how much you give away, but by how faithfully you honor the image of God in you.

Application
- Set boundaries wisely ... not everyone deserves access to your energy.
- Protect your spiritual flow ... guard your heart so God's presence isn't drained by unhealthy connections.
- Choose stewardship over exhaustion ... honor God by managing your emotional and spiritual

Prayer
Lord, thank You for the gift of life and the divine energy You have placed within me. Teach me to guard my heart with wisdom, to set healthy boundaries, and to spend my energy on what glorifies You. Free me from people-pleasing, over explaining, and unhealthy attachments. Surround me with relationships that are life-giving, reciprocal, and rooted in truth. In Jesus' name, **Amen.**

July 17
Life Is Not About Magic, It's About Management

1 Corinthians 4:2
Moreover, it is required of stewards that one be found trustworthy.

Reflection
Too often we wait for life to "magically" change. We pray for breakthroughs but neglect the discipline of stewardship.

Life is not about magic ... it's about management. God has entrusted you with time, talent, treasure, and testimony, and how you manage them determines your fruitfulness.

Think of the parable of the talents (Matthew 25:14–30). The servants weren't rewarded because something magical happened to their resources. They were rewarded because they managed wisely what was placed in their hands. The one who buried his talent lost it ... not just because he lacked faith, but because he also failed in management.

God can multiply, but He requires you to steward. A poorly managed blessing can feel like a curse. Without discipline, abundance slips through your fingers. Without boundaries, opportunities fade. Without gratitude, joy is lost.

The miracle you seek is often locked inside the management of what you already have.

Faith opens the door, but stewardship keeps it open. Trust God for provision, but honor Him by managing it well.

Application
- Practice daily discipline with what God has placed in your hands.
- Strengthen your stewardship so blessings don't slip through unmanaged cracks.
- Manage well first, and you'll see God multiply what you honor.

Prayer
Lord, teach me to be a faithful steward of all You have entrusted to me. Remove from me the illusion of magic, and give me the wisdom of management. Help me to order my time, my gifts, and my resources in ways that honor You and bless others. In Jesus' name, **Amen.**

July 18
Get Comfortable Being Uncomfortable

James 1:2–3
Consider it all joy, my brothers, when you encounter various trials, knowing that the testing of your faith produces endurance.

Reflection
Comfort is the enemy of growth. If you want to grow, you must learn to get comfortable being uncomfortable.

This life ... especially the Kingdom life ... is about learning to be comfortable with being uncomfortable, because discomfort is the environment where God develops you. It's struggle that builds muscle... not comfort. And if you're going to build spiritual, emotional, and mental muscle, you must embrace the struggle .. not run from it.

Resistance is not always the devil. Sometimes resistance is God's gym. Pressure is God's training ground. Stretching is God's preparation.
There's an old saying:
"Struggle is the meaning of life. Defeat or victory is in the hands of God, but struggle itself is man's duty and should be his joy."

Why? Because struggle is where transformation happens. Struggle is where character is forged. Struggle is where faith grows, pride dies, patience matures, and strength is born. God never develops anyone in comfort.

Your level of reward in life will always be tied to your level of sacrifice. No sacrifice ... no progress. No surrender ... no power. No stretching ... no breakthrough.

Application
- Identify an area where you've been choosing comfort over calling.
- Ask: "What discomfort is God using to develop me right now?"
- Embrace one intentional stretch today ... spiritually, mentally, physically, or emotionally.

Prayer
Father, thank You for loving me enough to grow me. Give me the courage to embrace discomfort, the wisdom to discern Your hand in the struggle, and the strength to surrender to Your process. Build my endurance, deepen my faith, and produce the character You desire in me. Help me choose sacrifice over comfort and growth over ease. Make the struggle my training ground, not my stumbling block. In Jesus' name, **Amen.**

July 19
Seated in Heavenly Places

Ephesians 2:6
And raised us up with Him, and seated us with Him in the heavenly places in Christ Jesus.

Reflection
Your true position isn't defined by your paycheck, your address, or your title. In Christ, you are already lifted ... raised up and seated with Him in heavenly places.

This isn't just a future promise of eternity; it's a present reality of authority, identity, and perspective. We just have to align our lives and act accordingly ... Holy !

When the world tries to pull you into fear, temptation, or distraction, remember where you are seated. You're not beneath circumstances ... you're above them in Christ. You're not at the mercy of the enemy ... you share in the victory of Jesus.

Living "seated in heavenly places" means carrying heaven's perspective into earth's problems. It means walking in authority, not insecurity.

It means living from victory, not for victory.
Don't fight for the seat ... live from it.

Your life changes when you stop chasing position and start living from the one God already gave you.

Application
- Start today by affirming: I am seated with Christ in heavenly places.
- When challenges rise, pause and ask: How would I respond if I truly believed I was above this in Christ?
- Let your prayers flow from authority, not anxiety.

Prayer
Father, thank You for raising me up in Christ and seating me in heavenly places. Help me to walk in that identity daily. Teach me to see from Your perspective, to live in Your authority, and to carry heaven into every situation I face. In Jesus' name, **Amen.**

July 20

The Power of Humility

James 4:10
Humble yourselves in the presence of the Lord, and He will exalt you.

Reflection
True greatness isn't about how high you rise, but how low you're willing to bow. "A great man is always willing to be little." — Ralph Waldo Emerson Humility is the doorway God uses to pour power, wisdom, and favor into your life. It keeps your heart soft, your spirit teachable, and your life usable in God's hands.

In the Kingdom, elevation always begins with surrender. Promotion always begins with posture. And favor always follows those who know how to kneel before they stand.

Pride closes doors. Humility opens them. Pride resists correction. Humility receives it. Pride takes credit. Humility gives God glory. Pride destroys calling. Humility deepens character.

Jesus ... the greatest man who ever lived...washed feet, served people, embraced the lowly, and submitted to the Father's will. He didn't just teach humility ... He embodied it.
When you walk in humility: God can trust you with more. Heaven can shape your heart. People can feel your love. Wisdom comes easier. Peace flows deeper. Growth happens faster. Humility is not thinking less of yourself... it's thinking of yourself less and thinking of God more. If you want God to elevate you, learn to bow before He lifts you.

Application
- Identify one area where pride has been resisting God's voice or people's wisdom.
- Pray for a teachable spirit in your relationships, assignments, and decisions.
- Practice humility this week through service, listening, or apologizing quickly.

Prayer
Father, give me a humble heart. Remove every trace of pride, stubbornness, and self–reliance. Make me teachable, gentle, and willing to bow low so You can lift me up in Your timing. Use my life as a vessel You can trust. Let humility shape my character and guide my decisions. In Jesus' name, **Amen.**

July 21
Steward Your Temple

1 Corinthians 10:31
Whether, then, you eat or drink or whatever you do, do all to the glory of God.

Reflection
Food is meant to be beneficial, not detrimental. God designed food to fuel your body, strengthen your mind, and support your calling ... not to destroy your health or shorten your purpose. There is a reason the saying goes: "Make your food your medicine, or your medicine will become your food."

The truth is simple:
Many battles people fight spiritually, mentally, and emotionally are made harder because their bodies are exhausted, inflamed, or out of balance. The body is not separate from your spiritual walk ... your body is the temple where the Spirit of God dwells.
What you put in your body affects the energy you give to your assignment. What you consume either fuels clarity or feeds chaos. God didn't just redeem your soul...He wants access to your habits.

You cannot pray for healing while repeatedly poisoning the temple.
You cannot ask for strength while feeding your body weakness.
You cannot ask for clarity while consuming things that fog your mind.
This is not condemnation...this is Kingdom stewardship. If God trusted you with a body, He expects you to honor it.

Making better choices is spiritual warfare. Choosing health is obedience. Discipline is worship. Take care of the temple...not for vanity, but victory.

Application
- Identify one eating/drinking habit that is harming your temple...commit to changing it today.
- Add one life-giving habit: water, fresh foods, movement, rest.
- Pray before eating and ask, "Does this serve my body or sabotage it?"

Prayer
Father, thank You for the body You've given me. Teach me to steward it well. Give me wisdom, discipline, and self-control in what I eat and drink. Remove every unhealthy craving that weakens my body or distracts my purpose. Help me treat my health as worship and my habits as obedience. Strengthen me so I can fulfill the assignment You placed on my life. In Jesus' name, **Amen.**

July 22
The Diligence of Self-Discipline

Luke 9:23
And He was saying to them all, 'If anyone wishes to come after Me, he must deny himself, and take up his cross daily and follow Me.'

Reflection
Greatness is never built in a day ... it is built daily.

Self-discipline is the diligence of small, consistent choices that shape who you are becoming. Something as simple as making your bed each morning is not just about neatness ... it's a small victory that sets the tone for larger victories.

From making the bed, to reading Scripture, to eating better, drinking water, and exercising, these daily disciplines ripple into other areas of life. Small habits create momentum, and momentum produces transformation.

When Jesus commissioned His followers, He didn't say, "Go make Christians." He said, "Go make disciples." A disciple is a disciplined follower of Christ ... someone committed, consistent, and not lukewarm. Discipline is the proof of devotion.

Even the word discipline traces back to chastisement ... correction that trains us. To embrace discipline is to embrace God's training, shaping us into disciples who reflect His character. The world may define success differently, but one truth stands: I've never seen an unsuccessful disciplined person.

Master the little things, and watch God multiply the big things.

Application
- Start small. Identify one daily habit that honors God and commit to it faithfully.
- Shift your mindset: see discipline not as punishment, but as preparation.
- Remember: discipline in the physical (habits) strengthens discipline in the spiritual (faithfulness).

Prayer
Lord, teach me the diligence of self-discipline. Help me to embrace small daily victories that lead to lasting transformation. Correct me where I resist Your training, and shape me into a true disciple who follows You with consistency, not convenience. **Amen.**

July 23

Freedom Starts on the Inside

John 8:36
So if the Son makes you free, you will be free indeed.

Reflection
Freedom… it's not where you physically are. It's about where you spiritually are. You can be standing in a palace and still be bound. You can be sitting in a prison and still be free. Because true freedom has nothing to do with location…and everything to do with internal liberation.

Some people travel the world and never escape themselves. Others never leave their neighborhood and walk in a freedom money can't buy and walls can't contain. Freedom is not a place. Freedom is a posture of the soul.

Real freedom is when: your mind is no longer chained to old lies. Your heart is no longer enslaved to old wounds. Your spirit is no longer controlled by fear, shame, guilt, or people. Your identity is no longer tied to what happened to you. You stop running from who God called you to be. Freedom happens the moment Christ steps into your spirit and breaks what life tried to lock down. Because the truth is… bondage begins internally long before it shows up externally. And freedom begins spiritually long before you ever see it physically.

You can't measure freedom by space. You measure it by Spirit.
When Christ sets you free: Your mind thinks different. Your heart loves different. Your walk carries authority. Your voice carries truth. Your spirit carries peace, and your life carries God. Freedom is not an address you move to…it is a transformation you grow into.

Application
• Ask: "Where am I physically free but spiritually bound?"
• Identify one area of internal bondage … fear, bitterness, shame, etc…
• Declare God's truth over that area today.

Prayer
Father, thank You that true freedom comes from You alone. Break every internal chain that has held my heart, mind, or spirit captive. Release me from old wounds, old lies, and old versions of myself. Fill me with the freedom Your Son died to give me. Help me walk as someone spiritually free, no matter where I stand physically. In Jesus' name, Amen.

July 24

Full Custody, Not Visitation

Colossians 3:3
For you have died, and your life is hidden with Christ in God.

Reflection
The call to follow Christ is not a call to convenience ... it is a call to the cross. Jesus said, "If anyone wishes to come after Me, he must deny himself, and take up his cross daily and follow Me" (Luke 9:23). To die to self means more than avoiding sin; it means voluntarily surrendering your whole life, just as Christ willingly laid down His. John the Baptist declared, "He must increase, but I must decrease" (John 3:30).

That's the heart of discipleship: a voluntary step back so that Christ can fully step forward in us. The tragedy is that many treat Christ like a weekend visitor instead of the rightful Lord of their lives. But Jesus will not settle for visitation rights ... He desires full custody. He bought us with His blood and longs for complete access, not partial permission.

Dying to self may feel like loss, but it is the doorway to true life. When you put to death anger, greed, lust, pride, and selfish ambition ... as Colossians 3 teaches ... you make room for compassion, kindness, humility, forgiveness, and love. Death to self is not the end of life; it is the beginning of abundant life in Christ.

Christ wants to be more than just a resident, He wants to be President in your life.

Application
- Ask yourself: Am I giving Christ full custody, or just visitation in certain areas of my life?
- Identify one area where self still sits on the throne. Lay it at the cross today.
- Practice daily "decreasing" ... choosing God's will over your own in prayer, decisions, and actions.

Prayer
Lord, I willingly lay down my life at the cross. I don't want to give You partial permission ... I give You full custody of my spirit, soul, and body. Teach me to die to self so that Christ may fully live in me. Increase in me as I decrease, until my life reflects only You. **Amen.**

July 25
Don't Be Like the Dead Sea

Proverbs 11:25
A generous person will prosper,
And one who gives others plenty of water will himself be given plenty.

Reflection
The Dead Sea is one of the most unique places on earth. Nothing can live there. Its salt and mineral levels are so high that no fish can swim, no plants can thrive, and no life can survive. It's also the lowest point on earth ... resting in a valley right next to the Holy Land of Jerusalem.

The Dead Sea has one problem: water flows in, but nothing flows out. It is a cul-de-sac, hoarding everything it receives. And because it never gives, it can never sustain life.

This is a mirror for us spiritually. Life is not about what we can gather, but about what we can give. Jesus said the greatest among us will be a servant (Matthew 23:11). Abundant life isn't about receiving more, but about pouring out more ... your time, your love, your resources, your presence.

The Kingdom principle is simple: what flows in must also flow out. If you refresh others, God promises you will be refreshed. If you hoard, your spirit dries up like the Dead Sea. True prosperity comes not from keeping, but from giving.

If you ain't giving, you ain't living.

Application
- Ask yourself: Am I a channel or a cul-de-sac? Does life flow through me or stop with me?
- Look for one opportunity today to refresh someone else ... with encouragement, generosity, or prayer.
- Remember: You cannot out give God. The more you pour out, the more He pours in.

Prayer
Lord, keep me from being like the Dead Sea. Let my life flow outward with generosity, love, and service. Teach me to give freely, knowing You refresh those who refresh others. May my life never become stagnant, but always alive with the flow of Your Spirit. **Amen.**

July 26
Helping People Is Godlike

Luke 6:36
Be merciful, just as your Father is merciful.

Reflection
Helping people is Godlike. When you step into someone's struggle…When you lift a burden off a weary heart…When you encourage a discouraged soul…You are not just being kind…you are reflecting the very heart of God.

Helping people is not a side assignment in the Kingdom; it is the Kingdom. Every time Jesus moved with compassion, healed the broken, fed the hungry, touched the untouchable, or comforted the hurting…He showed us exactly who God is. When we help people, we join Him in His work.

God is merciful … so we show mercy. God is gracious … so we extend grace. God is generous … so we give freely. God is patient … so we slow down and love deeply. God lifts … so we lift. You never look more like your Father than when you're helping someone who cannot repay you.

Heaven notices every act of kindness. Every quiet sacrifice. Every unseen moment of compassion. Every time you choose to love, comfort, support, or strengthen someone else…you carry the fingerprints of God. Here's the beauty: helping people doesn't just bless them…it transforms you. It softens your heart, deepens your character, and aligns your spirit with God's nature.

To help is to love. To love is to live out the Gospel … to live out the Gospel is to be Godlike.

Application
- Identify one person today who needs help … emotionally, spiritually, or practically.
- Offer something simple but meaningful: a prayer, a call, a meal, a listening ear, or an encouraging word.
- Ask God daily: "Show me who to help, and how to help."

Prayer
Father, thank You for helping me in ways I don't even see. Make my heart look like Yours. Teach me to love, serve, and lift others with compassion and grace. Use my hands to help, my words to heal, and my presence to comfort. Let my life reflect Your nature in how I treat people. Make me a living expression of Your mercy. In Jesus' name, **Amen.**

July 27
Be Still & Let God Fight

Exodus 14:14
The Lord will fight for you while you keep silent.

Reflection
Some battles aren't yours to fight. Some storms aren't yours to calm. Some enemies aren't yours to confront. These situations require one thing from you: Be still. Be quiet. Be calm. Let God fight.

Israel stood trapped ... Red Sea in front, Pharaoh behind ...no weapons, no strategy, no escape plan. And God spoke one of the most powerful instructions in Scripture: "The Lord will fight for you while you keep silent."

Sometimes silence is not weakness ...it is warfare.
It is the posture of someone who trusts God more than their emotions.

You don't have to argue to be understood.
You don't have to fight to be validated.
You don't have to defend yourself to be protected.
You don't have to respond to everything sent your way.
There are moments when God says, "I got this. Step back and let Me step in."

Your silence creates space for God's strength. Your calm makes room for His victory. Your stillness becomes the stage for His supernatural intervention.

You fight by standing still. You win by staying quiet. You overcome by letting God go before you.
Sometimes the greatest faith is doing nothing but trusting everything.

Application
- Identify the battle you've been trying to fight in your own strength.
- Release it to God today ... fully.
- Practice silence: refuse to argue, defend, or stress over what God has already handled.

Prayer
Father, thank You that You fight for me. Teach my heart to be still when I want to react and silent when I want to defend myself. Give me the faith to step back so You can step in. Fight every battle I cannot fight, calm every storm I cannot control, and lead me through every Red Sea that stands in my way. I trust You. In Jesus' name, **Amen.**

July 28
Bob & Weave: Lessons From My First Coaches

Proverbs 24:16
Though a righteous man falls seven times, he rises again.

Reflection
My mom and my dad were my first sparring partners. They taught me how to bob and weave. Not in a boxing ring…but in life. They didn't just teach me how to fight…they taught me how to recover, how to adjust, how to stay light on my feet, and how to move with wisdom when life swings hard.

Bob and weave means: Don't take every hit head-on. Don't let every attack land. Don't stand still in the face of adversity. Learn to move with grace under pressure. Learn to survive the rounds life didn't warn you about.

The righteous fall … but they don't stay down. They rise because they learned how to move, how to shift, how to duck, how to respond, and how to stand back up.

Life will throw punches. People will swing wild. Trials will hit harder than expected. But the lessons God plants in you … through parents, mentors, pastors, pain, and experience … teach you how to navigate the blows.

Bob: avoid what's not worth your energy. Weave: move around what's meant to distract you. Strike: only when God says fight. Stand: only by the strength God gives.
Sometimes the greatest technique in life isn't throwing harder punches … it's moving with discernment.

Application
- Identify the "punches" you've been taking head-on instead of learning to move with wisdom.
- Ask God to give you discernment … what to dodge, what to confront, and what to release.
- Honor those who taught you resilience … your parents, mentors, or role models.

Prayer
Father, thank You for the people You used to shape my resilience. Teach me how to move with Your wisdom, respond with Your strength, and endure with Your grace. Help me bob and weave through every attack, distraction, and unexpected blow. Strengthen me for every round of life, and keep my spirit steady under pressure. In Jesus' name, **Amen.**

July 29
What the Thief Comes to Steal

John 10:10
The thief comes only to steal and kill and destroy;
I came so that they would have life, and have it abundantly.

Reflection
What does the thief come to steal?
Not your stuff. Not your possessions. Not your titles. The enemy reaches for something far more valuable. Your Peace. Your Power. Your Provision.

Because if the enemy can steal your peace, he can break your focus.
If he can steal your power, he can weaken your walk.
If he can steal your provision, he can shake your trust in God.
The enemy doesn't need to take everything from you ...
he just needs to take the part of you that keeps you anchored in God.

Jesus didn't say the thief comes "to bother you." He said the thief comes only to steal, kill, and destroy. That means every attack has a target. Every distraction has an assignment. Every moment of chaos comes with an intention: to disconnect you from the abundance Jesus promised.
Don't give your peace away so cheaply. Don't hand over your fellowship with God because of a moment, a mood, a comment, or a conflict.

Protect your peace like it's treasure. Protect your power like it's sacred.
Protect your provision like it came from Heaven ... because it did.

What Jesus gives is abundant, overflowing, and eternal.
What the thief takes is temporary, deceptive, and destructive.

Application
- Identify one area where your peace has been under attack. Name it.
- Ask: "What am I giving away that God told me to guard?"
- Set a spiritual boundary today ... refuse to lose your peace over people, situations, or fears.

Prayer
Father, thank You for the abundant life You promised in Christ. Open my eyes to recognize every scheme of the thief. Strengthen me to guard my peace, protect my fellowship with You, and refuse every distraction sent to steal what You've given. Restore anything the enemy has tried to take, and anchor my heart in Your abundance. In Jesus' name, **Amen.**

July 30
Joy Inside, Happiness Outside

Philippians 4:4-5
Rejoice in the Lord always. I will say it again: Rejoice!
Let your gentleness be evident to all. The Lord is near.

Reflection
Anger is a thief.

It steals clarity, disturbs peace, and blinds you to the deeper reality God has placed within you …joy that cannot be shaken.

Happiness might paint your face with a smile, but it fades like a sunset. It's fleeting, conditional, and tied to circumstances. Joy, on the other hand … is an inside job, it runs deeper … formed in the soul, rooted in the Spirit, and sustained by God's presence. Happiness is a coat you wear; joy is the garment woven by faith.

Happiness shines in moments of comfort, but joy thrives in seasons of purpose. When your life is anchored in God's calling, pressure cannot break you and storms cannot move you. Joy becomes your stability, your anchor, your inner victory.

When anger sidetracks your emotions, it distracts you from joy's eternal trajectory. Scripture teaches us to be slow to anger because anger disrupts the harmony the Spirit is shaping inside you. Gentleness, patience, and peace allow joy to rise and reign.

Application
- Take a moment today to distinguish between what makes you momentarily happy and what fills you with lasting joy.
- Check your heart: Are anger or irritation crowding out your capacity to rejoice in God.
- Choose joy. Whether your external world is calm or chaotic, open your heart to the deep joy God offers.

Prayer
Father, teach me to refuse anger's distraction and welcome Your joy inside. Let my countenance reflect Your peace even when my circumstances do not. May my inner joy become a quiet strength that overflows … even when the world demands happiness, grant me something more … unspeakable joy rooted in You. **Amen.**

July 31
The Gift of Joy Carriers

Proverbs 17:22
A joyful heart is good medicine, But a broken spirit dries up the bones.

Reflection
Some people are like unpaid therapy, they show up, shine their light, make us smile, and never ask for anything in return. They don't fix everything ... but somehow they make everything feel lighter.

These people are joy carriers ... souls God uses to refresh others without even trying. Their presence brings peace. Their laughter brings healing. Their spirit brings encouragement. They don't demand attention; they give it. They don't drain the room; they brighten it. They don't take from you; they lift you up. Their joy becomes someone else's sunshine.

In a world where negativity spreads faster than hope, people like this are divine gifts. Sometimes they walk into your life for a season, sometimes for a lifetime ... but their impact outlives their presence.

God places joy carriers in our lives not only to bless us, but also to teach us. To teach us that: Gratitude is contagious. Presence is powerful. A simple smile can be ministry. Joy is medicine God prescribes through people.

God also calls you to be that person for someone else. Someone needs your light. Someone needs your laugh. Someone needs your words, your presence, your encouragement. Someone needs the sunshine you carry.

The joy God puts in you is never meant to be hoarded. It's meant to be shared ... because joy shared becomes healing multiplied.

Application
- Think of one "joy carrier" God placed in your life. Thank God for them.
- Send that person a message, call, or prayer of gratitude today.
- Ask God to make you a joy carrier to someone who needs encouragement.

Prayer
Father, thank You for the people who carry joy into my life ... those who lift me, love me, and lighten my spirit without asking for anything in return. Bless them with the same encouragement they bring to others. And Lord, make me a carrier of joy. Fill my heart with a light that refreshes, heals, and restores those around me. Let my smile be medicine. Let my presence bring peace. Let my joy be someone's sunshine today. In Jesus' name, **Amen.**

August 1
Unity: Gang Up on the Problem, Not Each Other

Genesis 11:6
And the LORD said, 'Behold, they are one people, and they all have the same language. And this is what they began to do, and now nothing which they purpose to do will be impossible for them.

Reflection
When God looked down at that unified people in Babel, He saw the danger of unity turned inward. They were together, aligned, speaking the same language ... but they were united for the wrong purpose. Their unity wasn't built on God's mission; it was built on their own agenda.

Yet notice what God said: "Now nothing which they purpose to do will be impossible for them." Their unity equipped them for power ... not just good, but whatever their purpose happened to be. That means:

Unity is powerful.
Unity is neutral.
Unity can build a kingdom for Christ ... or a tower for self.

As followers of Christ, we are called into true oneness.
Not for ourselves ... but for His Kingdom. We are to gang up on the real problem (sin, darkness, division, injustice), not each other. When we scatter our strength by fighting amongst ourselves, the enemy wins.
When we align our hearts with God's purpose and stand together, there is nothing the Kingdom cannot do.

Application
- Ask: "Are we united around God's purpose ... or around our comfort, preferences, or personalities?"
- Identify one relationship or team-slice in your life that is fragmented. Take one step toward reconciliation or cooperation today.
- Choose one Kingdom-mission you can do together (with one other believer, your church team, or ministry). Make unity your strength, not your excuse.

Prayer
Father, thank You for the power of unity rooted in You. Forgive us for when our unity served ourselves instead of Your purpose. Knit our hearts together around Your mission. Help us gang up on the real problems ... not one another. Use our unity to accomplish what seems impossible, for Your glory. In Jesus' name, **Amen.**

August 2
Don't Play in the Gray

Matthew 6:22
The lamp of the body is the eye; if therefore your eye is single, your whole body will be full of light.

Reflection
The enemy's strategy is simple: keep you confused, distracted, and estranged from God's clarity. He doesn't always come with horns and chains ... he often whispers subtle lies, blurs truths, and tempts you into the "gray zones" where moral boundaries are unclear.

He wants your gaze off God and on the world, on your worries, on what feels right in the moment. But Scripture warns us: when your "eye" (your focus, your spiritual vision) is undivided, your whole being is filled with light (Matthew 6:22). The Word is our lamp ... its truth cuts through confusion, exposing the path ahead (Psalm 119:105).

To live in the gray is to walk half-blind. To live in the light is to move with purpose, conviction, and peace. The world may serve darkness, distort truth, and revel in confusion. But we are called out of darkness into His marvelous light.

Don't settle for moral ambiguity. Don't trade clarity for ease. Seek God's righteousness, stay fixed on His Word, and cultivate spiritual disciplines that sharpen your vision.

Application
- Recognize a "gray area" in your life ... something you've tolerated because it seems harmless.
- Ask the Spirit to expose the lie behind it.
- Replace ambiguity with God's truth ... meditate on relevant passages, speak them out loud.

Prayer
Father, break every gray zone that clouds my vision. Grant me an undivided heart, a single focus on You, and courage to walk in Your light. Remove the distractions, distortions, and confusion that try to steal my gaze. May I never1 serve darkness but live fully in Your truth. In Jesus' name, **Amen.**

August 3
Who's Driving?

Romans 8:14
For all who are being led by the Spirit of God, these are sons of God.

Reflection
Every day you wake up, one question determines the entire course of your life: Who is driving?

God created you as a spiritual being made in His image. You are not a body that has a spirit … you are a spirit who lives in a body and possesses a soul. When your life is out of alignment, it's usually because the wrong part of you is behind the wheel. Here is God's design: Your Spirit is the driver, Your soul is the passenger and Your body is being escorted

But here's what most people do: They let their body (cravings, impulses, urges) drive…or they let their soul (emotions, memories, moods) take control…while their Spirit rides in the back seat, ignored and unheard. This is how people end up spiritually lost. When your body drives, you live by appetite. When your soul drives, you live by emotion. When your spirit drives, you live by truth.

You were created for Spirit-led living. The Holy Spirit leading your spirit… your spirit guiding your soul and your soul instructing your body. This is divine order. When the Spirit drives, your decisions are clearer, your discernment is sharper, your reactions are calmer, your purpose is steadier, and your life becomes anchored in God instead of tossed by feelings.

Application
- Before responding, pause and ask: "Who's driving right now … my spirit, my soul, or my body?"
- Feed your spirit daily with prayer, Scripture, worship, and obedience.
- Bring your soul (thoughts & emotions) under spiritual order … don't let feelings steer your decisions.

Prayer
Father, bring my entire life into divine alignment. Let my spirit … led by Your Spirit … guide every decision, every reaction, and every step I take. Help me silence my emotions when they try to lead, and discipline my body when it tries to control. Teach me to live Spirit-driven, not soul-driven or flesh-driven. Holy Spirit, take the wheel. Lead me into truth, peace, wisdom, and obedience. In Jesus' name, **Amen.**

August 4
Wait for the Wind

Isaiah 40:31
Yet those who wait for the LORD Will gain new strength; They will mount up with wings like eagles, They will run and not get tired, They will walk and not become weary."

Reflection
When God opens your eyes; you will realize that waiting is not physical... it is spiritual. It's not sitting still. It's staying sensitive. Waiting on the Lord is not inactivity; it is alignment. It is learning to wait on the wind of the Spirit.

Eagles do not exhaust themselves flapping. They rise when the wind rises. They move when the air moves. They soar when the currents shift. That's what it means to wait on God.

You are not waiting for circumstances. You are not waiting for people. You are not waiting for timing. You are not even waiting for opportunities. You are waiting on the presence of His Spirit.

Waiting means: Don't move without His whisper. Don't speak without His breath. Don't decide without His peace. Don't run without His wind beneath you. This is why waiting renews strength ... because you're no longer moving in your power. You are moving in His.

Some people wait on signs. Some wait on confirmations. Some wait on perfect conditions. But Scripture calls us to wait on the Lord Himself ... His presence, His prompting, His Spirit. When you learn to wait spiritually, your life stops being forced and starts being lifted.

Application
- Before decisions, pause and ask: "Holy Spirit, are You in this?"
- Practice listening prayer ... sit in silence and invite His presence.
- Examine your motives: Am I moving because God is leading, or because I am rushing?

Prayer
Father, teach me to wait for You, not just for outcomes. Open my eyes to recognize the movement of Your Spirit. Make me sensitive to Your presence, patient in Your timing, and obedient to Your leading. Help me to move like the eagle ... not in my own strength but lifted by the Wind of Your Spirit Let Your peace guide me, Your voice steady me, and Your timing lead me into every next step. In Jesus' name, **Amen.**

August 5
Goliath Was the Gift

1 Samuel 17:37
And David said, 'The LORD who delivered me from the paw of the lion and from the paw of the bear, He will deliver me from the hand of this Philistine.

Reflection
When God wanted to make a king out of David, He didn't give him a crown …He gave him Goliath. Because before David could sit on a throne, he had to conquer something that looked impossible. This is God's pattern with greatness: He prepares you in private…but He promotes you through a problem.

We pray for elevation, but God often answers with opposition. We ask for purpose, and God releases pressure. We want the crown, but God sends a giant. Why? Because greatness is not discovered on mountaintops … it's forged in battles. Goliath wasn't David's punishment. Goliath was David's platform. The giant wasn't there to destroy him; the giant was there to announce him.

Every person God has ever used greatly had to face something greater than themselves. God increases your capacity by increasing your challenges.
He strengthens your faith by stretching your fight.
He grows your character by allowing battles that force you to rely on Him.

When God wants to make you great, He gives you great obstacles to overcome. Your Goliath is not the end of you …Your Goliath is the making of you.

Application
- Identify the "Goliath" in your current season …what challenge is stretching your faith right now? Instead of praying the problem away, ask God what He wants to build in you through it.
- Speak victory over your situation:
- "The same God who delivered me before will deliver me again."

Prayer
Father, thank You for every challenge that shapes me.
Teach me to see obstacles as opportunities and giants as gateways to destiny. Strengthen my faith, sharpen my courage, and remind me that You have already prepared me for this moment. Help me face my Goliaths with confidence, knowing they are forming the king, warrior, and leader inside of me. In Jesus' name, **Amen.**

August 6
Righteousness Over Loyalty

1 Corinthians 15:33
Do not be deceived: 'Bad company corrupts good morals.

Reflection
Today, people often treat loyalty as the highest virtue ... even above righteousness. They misuse the word to mean blind agreement, expecting friends to side with them whether they are right or wrong. But true loyalty doesn't mean standing with someone in their sin or error; it means loving them enough to point them toward truth.

Jesus never compromised righteousness to preserve relationships. He corrected His disciples, confronted religious leaders, and stood firmly on His Father's will ... even when it cost Him loyalty from the crowds.

Loyalty without righteousness becomes bondage. But when loyalty is rooted in truth, it builds trust that lasts.

Real friends don't just agree; they sharpen one another like iron. Choose righteousness first ... even if it costs relationships ... because God honors integrity over popularity.

Loyalty without righteousness is empty.

True loyalty stands with others in truth, not in compromise.

Choose righteousness ... it always outlasts popularity.

Application
- Reflect: Do I value righteousness over blind loyalty?
- Act: Speak truth in love to someone, even if it risks tension.
- Declare: "I will honor God's truth above man's approval."

Prayer
Lord, help me never to compromise righteousness for false loyalty. Give me the courage to stand in truth and the wisdom to love others enough to speak it. **Amen.**

August 7
HALT Before You Fall

1 Peter 5:8
Be of sober spirit, be on the alert. Your adversary, the devil, prowls around like a roaring lion, seeking someone to devour.

Reflection
Charles Stanley often reminded us of a simple but powerful acronym: H.A.L.T.

When you are Hungry, Angry, Lonely, or Tired, you are more vulnerable to temptation, poor decisions, and spiritual drift.

Hungry: Physical or spiritual hunger can leave us grasping for quick fixes instead of waiting on God's provision.

Angry: Unchecked anger opens the door to sin (Eph. 4:26–27).

Lonely: In isolation, the enemy whispers lies and magnifies despair.

Tired: Fatigue weakens our defenses and dulls discernment.

The wisdom is clear: when these warning signs rise, halt. Pause. Pray.

Invite God's strength. Don't push through in your own power ... lean into His. Guard your heart when you are weak, and you will find His strength made perfect.

H.A.L.T. is heaven's reminder to pause when you're weak. Guard yourself in these moments, and you'll discover God's strength to keep you standing.

Application
- Reflect: Which of the four (Hungry, Angry, Lonely, Tired) tends to trip you most?
- Build a plan: memorize a verse or practice a pause when that state arises.
- Declare: "When I am weak, then I am strong in Christ."

Prayer
Lord, help me recognize the moments when I'm most vulnerable. Teach me to halt before I fall. Strengthen me when I am hungry, angry, lonely, or tired ... and remind me that Your grace is sufficient. **Amen.**

August 8
Wisdom in Small Things

Proverbs 6:6–8
Go to the ant, you sluggard; consider her ways and be wise! She has no commander, overseer, or ruler, yet she stores her provisions in summer and gathers her food at harvest.

Reflection
Solomon beckons us to learn from one of nature's smallest creatures ... the ant.

Though tiny and unsupervised, the ant demonstrates instinctive diligence, initiative, and foresight. She prepares when the season is favorable, storing provisions so that she won't be caught off-guard when scarcity arrives.

We are confronted with a poignant contrast: God-shaped humans, gifted with reason and destiny, often lack the ant's proactive wisdom. The ant labors not out of obligation but from instinct. She works without supervision, knows the cycles of seasons, and safeguards her future.

This should move us to ask:

Where are we idle?
Where have we delayed preparation or neglected foresight?
Are there spiritual or practical areas where we need to store up ... through prayer, planning, or purpose ... so that we can thrive in harder days?

Destiny favors the diligent; what you store in the light will sustain you in the dark.

Application
- Prepare today with diligence so tomorrow does not catch you unready.
- Take initiative in the areas God has entrusted to you instead of waiting for someone else to push you.
- Develop the discipline to recognize your seasons and act wisely before the moment of need arrives.

Prayer
Father, forgive me for moments of idleness and complacency. Teach me to emulate the ant's diligence .. working wisely and preparing strategically. Let me walk in initiative and foresight, cultivating spiritual and practical fruit that sustains through every season. In Jesus' name, **Amen.**

August 9
Procrastination Isn't Your Friend

Psalm 90:12
So teach us to number our days, that we may present to You a heart of wisdom.

Reflection
Procrastination isn't just laziness ... it's a battle between your brain's craving for comfort and your God given capacity for purpose.

The limbic system seeks quick relief, while the prefrontal cortex pushes you toward long-term goals. When comfort overpowers calling, you delay what God has entrusted to you.

But delay has a cost: temporary relief, followed by guilt, stress, and missed opportunities. Scripture reminds us life is short ... we don't have time to keep negotiating with procrastination. It's not your friend; it's a thief of purpose.

Break big tasks into steps.

Set boundaries.

Use tools like timed focus attention.

Most importantly, surrender fear and perfectionism to God.

The first step is often the hardest, but faith walks forward even when feelings hesitate.

Procrastination feels like a friend, but it's a thief.
Take the first step today ... purpose is waiting on the other side of obedience.

Application
- Identify one task you've been delaying and take the first small step today.
- Declare: "I will not let comfort steal my calling."
- Remember how fleeting life is ... choose today to invest your time in what really matters, not what merely feels comfortable.

Prayer
Lord, help me steward my time with wisdom. Break procrastination's grip on my mind and replace it with focus, discipline, and faith. Teach me to walk in purpose today. **Amen.**

August 10
Who You Are in Christ, and Who Christ Is in You

Galatians 2:20
I have been crucified with Christ; and it is no longer I who live, but Christ lives in me; and the life which I now live in the flesh I live by faith in the Son of God, who loved me and gave Himself for me.

Reflection
You cannot live out a godly life until you know two inseparable truths: who you are in Christ, and who Christ is in you. These truths are the foundation for your identity, your power, and your purpose.

To know who you are in Christ is to grasp that your value, your acceptance, and your destiny are not determined by your performance or your past ... but by the cross. You are forgiven, adopted, justified, loved, and seated with Him "in heavenly places" (Ephesians 2:6). You are a new creation (2 Corinthians 5:17). Your identity is secure because He is your identity.

To know who Christ is in you is to recognize that His life, His righteousness, and His Spirit now indwell you. You are not left alone to imitate Christ by your own strength ... you have His life flowing through your spirit. Through Him you can walk in power, holiness, and intimacy with the Father.

When those two realities unite in your heart, you stop living by fear, insecurity, or striving ... and begin walking as a son or daughter, empowered by the Spirit.

Application
- Reflect on "who you are in Christ" ... pick one truth (forgiven, adopted, new creation) and meditate on that today.
- Reflect on "who Christ is in you" ... ask the Spirit to reveal how Jesus' life works in you (e.g. peace, love, strength).
- Speak out both realities ... declare them aloud in faith whenever you feel weak or unsure.

Prayer
Father, thank You that in Christ I am forgiven, accepted, and made new. Help me know not only who I am in You but who You are in me. Fill me with the life of Christ so that I walk today in power, love, and confidence ... not by my strength, but by His. **Amen.**

August 11
The Download of Wisdom

Joshua 1:8
This book of the law shall not depart from your mouth, but you shall meditate on it day and night, so that you may be careful to do according to all that is written in it; for then you will make your way prosperous, and then you will have success.

Reflection
Spending time with God is more than devotion… it's a download. When you open your Bible, when you pray, when you sit still long enough to listen, the Holy Spirit begins transferring wisdom, clarity, peace, and strategy into your spirit. Just like a device must be plugged into a power source to update, your soul must be plugged into God to grow.

God tells Joshua that if he meditates on the Word and obeys it, then he will prosper and succeed. The success was not in Joshua's strength … it was in Joshua's connection. Meditation opens your mind. Obedience opens your path. And staying plugged in opens your destiny.

Some people want results without relationship. They want direction without devotion. They want purpose without presence. But God does not download wisdom into people who are disconnected.

The more time you spend with Him, the more He reveals. The more you slow down, the more He speaks. The more you obey, the more He trusts you with deeper things.

Everything you need for your next season is already in Him. The question is … are you plugged in?

Application
- Set aside intentional daily time to read God's Word, with expectations.
- Approach Scripture like a spiritual download … with an open heart.
- Practice stillness. Slow down long enough to hear what God is trying to reveal.

Prayer
Father, thank You for being the source of all wisdom and understanding. Teach me to slow down, plug in, and sit still long enough to hear Your voice. As I meditate on Your Word, download into my spirit the clarity, strength, and insight I need for this season. In Jesus' name, **Amen.**

August 12
Get Off the Wrong Train

Proverbs 14:12
There is a way which seems right to a man, but its end is the way of death.

Reflection
The longer you stay on the wrong train, the more expensive it is to get home.

Whether it's a toxic relationship, a sinful lifestyle, or simply living outside of God's will, the longer you ride, the higher the price becomes … emotionally, spiritually, and even physically.

Like Jonah fleeing God's call or the Prodigal Son chasing wild living, we can all testify that delay only deepens the damage. Regret, wasted time, and unnecessary pain pile up the longer we refuse to turn around.

Yet God's grace is still sufficient.

Restoration is possible … but wisdom whispers: get off now.

Today is always the cheapest it will ever be to head back home to purpose, peace, and God's plan. Don't wait for rock bottom to teach what obedience could have spared.

Every day you stay on the wrong train raises the cost of return.

Get off now.

God's way is always the safest, surest, and cheapest path home.

Application
- Reflect: Am I riding a "train" that's leading me away from God?
- Decide: What step can I take today to get off and turn back?
- Declare: "I choose correction now over costly regret later."

Prayer
Lord, open my eyes to see where I've been heading the wrong way. Give me courage to step off the wrong path today, before the cost grows higher. Lead me back to Your will, where peace and purpose are found. **Amen.**

August 13
The Power of De-Escalation

Proverbs 16:32
He who is slow to anger is better than the mighty,
And he who rules his spirit, than he who captures a city.

Reflection
"He who angers you, conquers you." — Elizabeth Kenny
Anger is not just an emotion ... it's a battleground. Every time someone provokes you and you lose control, you didn't just lose your temper... you lost your authority. You surrendered your peace. You handed someone else the keys to your emotions.

The Bible teaches that the strongest person in the room is not the loudest, the toughest, or the most aggressive. The strongest person is the one who can rule their spirit. This is where the power of de-escalation comes in.

To de-escalate means "to reduce intensity... to calm things down... to prevent a situation from getting worse." It is not weakness ... it is wisdom. It is not passivity ... it is power under control. It is not running from conflict ... it is rising above it.

Jesus modeled this. He was insulted, rejected, accused, attacked ...yet never out of control. His restraint was not a lack of strength; it was the fullness of it. When you choose calm over chaos, you are not letting someone "get away" with something. You are choosing to protect your peace, guard your witness, and maintain your spiritual authority.

A calm spirit disarms conflict. A gentle answer turns away wrath.
A quiet mind refuses to be conquered by someone else's chaos.

Application
- Before reacting, pause and breathe ... give the Holy Spirit space to lead.
- Listen more than you speak. Anger listens to respond; wisdom listens to understand.
- Practice de-escalation techniques: calm tone, soft words, controlled body language.

Prayer
Father, give me the strength to rule my spirit and the wisdom to choose calm over conflict. Teach me to de-escalate with grace, patience, and spiritual maturity. When anger rises, silence every voice but Yours. Help me respond in ways that honor You and protect my peace. In Jesus' name, **Amen.**

August 14
Getting Over You

Ephesians 4:23–24
...that you be renewed in the spirit of your mind, and put on the new self, which in the likeness of God has been created in righteousness and holiness of the truth.

Reflection
The journey to becoming who God created you to be always begins with this truth: The journey to self is getting over you. Most people spend their whole lives trying to fix what they see in the mirror ... the body, the image, the surface, the version of themselves shaped by insecurity and presentation. But life does not change from the outside in.
It changes from the inside out.

When you stop obsessing over the physical reflection and start dealing with the person behind the reflection, you begin to truly live. The inner man. The inner woman. The soul. The spirit. The unseen place where your thoughts form, your emotions grow, and your actions are born.

Transformation starts when God begins renewing the spirit of your mind. That renewal shapes what you think ... which reshapes how you feel... which reshapes how you act ... which ultimately reshapes your entire life.

We all have something to get over. We all have something to face, something to confront, something to surrender, something to let God heal. God will not transform what we keep pretending is fine. The mirror shows you where you are. The Spirit shows you who you can become.

Application
- Spend time in honest reflection ... ask the Holy Spirit to reveal what is behind the mirror that needs healing or correction.
- Journaling prompt: "Lord, what part of me do You want to renew today?"
- Choose one internal area ... thought patterns, fears, un-forgiveness, self-doubt ... and commit it to God.

Prayer
Father, help me to stop living on the surface. Show me what is behind the mirror ... my thoughts, wounds, habits, and patterns that need Your touch. Renew the spirit of my mind. Transform my inner man. Heal what I've ignored, strengthen what is weak, and refine what is misaligned. Teach me to get over myself so I can become the person You created me to be. Change me from the inside out. In Jesus' name, **Amen.**

August 15
When the Word Hurts

Hebrews 4:12
For the word of God is living and active and sharper than any two edged sword, and piercing as far as the division of soul and spirit, of both joints and marrow, and able to judge the thoughts and intentions of the heart.

Reflection
When God's Spirit brings a word that pierces your heart, it means He's exposing something in you that must die so Christ can live more fully.

Conviction is not cruelty ... it is surgery. God's Word does not pierce us to destroy us, but to remove what keeps us from Him.

When pride rises, His Word humbles.
When bitterness festers, His Word convicts.
When selfishness lingers, His Word confronts.

Every time His truth cuts deep, it exposes the false, the fleshly, and the broken.

This pain is not punishment ... it is preparation. The Spirit wounds so He can heal, convicts so He can cleanse, and kills so He can resurrect. What He puts to death in you, He replaces with life, freedom, and power.

The sting of the Word is the beginning of sanctification. Only when the old self dies can the new creation truly live.

Application
- When Scripture convicts you, don't resist ... lean into it and ask, "Lord, what do You want to remove from me?"
- Journal areas where God's Word has recently "cut" you, and surrender them to Him in prayer.
- Remember: conviction is proof that God loves you too much to leave you unchanged.

Prayer
Father, thank You that Your Word is alive and powerful. When it cuts me, let me not run from it but surrender to it. Kill in me what does not reflect Christ, and resurrect what brings You glory. Shape me, cleanse me, and transform me into Your likeness. In Jesus' name, **Amen.**

August 16
Abound to Enlightenment

2 Peter 1:19
So we have the prophetic word made more sure, to which you do well to pay attention as to a lamp shining in a dark place, until the day dawns and the morning star arises in your hearts.

Reflection
Peter urges us to treat Scripture like a lamp in darkness ... guiding, illuminating, sustaining ... until the "morning star," Christ Himself, arises in our hearts. The Scriptures are not just words; they are divine light.

David R. Hawkins' Map of Consciousness ... presents an ascending scale of human emotional states. From the depths of shame (20), guilt (30), apathy (50), and fear (100), it climbs through courage (200), neutrality (250), willingness (310), and acceptance (350), ultimately reaching love (500), joy (540), peace (600), and the elusive heights of enlightenment (700-1000).

While Hawkins' framework neither defines nor measures our spiritual reality, it mirrors a timeless truth: what permeates your heart shapes your life. The prophetic Word becomes your lamp, and gradually, through God's grace and your faithfulness, His light transforms your consciousness ... from survival to surrender, from fear to faith, from darkness to divine illumination.

As the Word lights your path, it aligns you with the heart of God. Each step upward ... from courage to willingness, from acceptance to love ... is not earned by human effort alone, but received as you dwell in Scripture, prayer, and obedience. Let God's promises dawn in you until you are radiant ... filled with compassion, joy, peace and light.

Application
- Let Scripture guide your steps daily so you don't walk in darkness.
- Trust the prophetic word's reliability over your feelings or experiences; let it shape your convictions and actions.
- Keep Scripture close until the "morning star" of Christ's light rises fully in your heart, transforming you from within.

Prayer
Jesus, Light of the world, thank You for shining Your prophetic Word into my darkness. Teach me to treasure it daily, and let Your morning star rise in my heart. Lift me from fear and apathy, and lead me toward courage, love, joy, and peace. May Your Word transform my consciousness, not by my striving, but by Your grace. In Your name, **Amen.**

August 17
The End of Self

Jeremiah 17:10
I, the Lord, search the heart, I test the mind, to give to each person according to his ways, according to the results of his deeds.

Reflection
The reason many of us are not experiencing God as He desires is because we have not yet come to the end of ourselves.

We are still clinging to pride, sin, self-reliance and disobedience. But God will not share His glory with our rebellion.

God is holy. God is light. And in Him there is no darkness at all (1 John 1:5).

God does not step into our lives on our terms.
He does not draft soldiers into His kingdom ...
He awaits volunteers who are willing to surrender.

Until there is repentance ... a turning away from sin and a turning fully to Him ... we will not encounter the fullness of His presence.

When we reach the end of ourselves, God's beginning becomes visible.

True repentance opens the door for His Spirit to dwell richly in us, transforming our hearts and renewing our minds.

It is only when we die to self that we truly live in Him.

Application
- Ask God to search your heart and align your motives before you act.
- Surrender self-reliance ... let God examine your mind and mold your deeds by His wisdom.
- Live with integrity and transparency, knowing God sees what is hidden and will judge by the fruit of your life.

Prayer
Father, search my heart and show me what still resists You. Break down every wall of pride, every secret sin, and every false reliance. Bring me to the end of myself so that I may experience the fullness of Your life and presence.
Amen.

August 18
God Will Provide

Philippians 4:19
And my God will supply all your needs according to His riches in glory in Christ Jesus.

Reflection
God will never call you to something without also providing what you need to carry it through. If He gives the assignment, He guarantees the provision.

Look at Moses.
When God called him to deliver Israel, the path wasn't easy ... but it was always provided for. God split the Red Sea, poured out water in the wilderness, sent manna and quail daily, and covered His people with a cloud by day and a pillar of fire by night. Every need had a divine supply.

When Elijah obeyed God and went to Zarephath, he met a widow with only a handful of flour and a little oil. Yet God multiplied what she had—her jar never emptied, and her oil never ran dry. Where God sent Elijah, God supplied.

The same is true for you.

Whatever God is asking to do, He has already made provision for it.

Your part is obedience; His part is supply. He is your Source, and He can deliver more than you could ever achieve or acquire on your own.

Step into your assignment without fear; the God who called you is already standing in your tomorrow with everything you need.

Application
- Trust that God will meet your true needs ... rely on His unlimited riches in Christ rather than your own strength.
- Let this promise free you from anxiety about tomorrow so you can act in faith and obedience today.
- Use God's provision not just for yourself, but to bless others, expecting that He remains faithful to supply as you follow Him.

Prayer
Father, thank You that You are my Source. Teach me to trust Your provision and not my own strength. Remind me that if You called me to it, You will carry me through it. **Amen.**

August 19
Suddenly, The Light

2 Peter 1:19
So we have the prophetic word made more sure, to which you do well to pay attention as to a lamp shining in a dark place, until the day dawns and the morning star arises in your hearts.

Reflection
At birth, like an infant in the womb, we all begin in the dark. We grow in places unseen. We develop in silence. We are shaped where no one can watch…then one day … we encounter the Great Light. The moment the Light of Christ shines on your life, everything changes. Everything accelerates. Everything awakens. Everything in you begins to move, stretch, and break forth. Some growth happens slowly… quietly…underground.

Like the bamboo tree … which spends five years developing strong roots beneath the surface, in complete darkness…in complete silence… with no visible progress. But the moment it breaks through the soil and touches light, it explodes upward … 90 feet in 5 weeks. That's the power of the Light. This is how spiritual growth often works. We mistake the darkness for delay, but God calls it development. We think nothing is happening, but God is strengthening our roots.

Then one day…Suddenly… the Light hits us…the Word becomes real to us…the prophetic promise ignites in us…and our life takes off like bamboo. This is what Peter meant when he said the prophetic Word is a lamp shining in a dark place …It guides you through the hidden seasons until the day dawns and the Morning Star rises in your heart. God has been preparing you in the dark. But the Light is here. And when His Light hits you…prepare for sudden acceleration.

Application
- Do not despise your dark seasons…they are God's root building moments.
- Meditate, write, rehearse, pray on God's prophetic word spoken over you.
- Walk in the Light you have. Light always expands.

Prayer
Father, thank You for every season…both the hidden and the revealed. Thank You for preparing me in the dark and for shining Your great Light upon my life. Let Your Word continue to rise in my heart like a morning star. Strengthen my roots, ignite my faith, and accelerate the work You have begun in me. When Your Light shines, help me to move with expectation, boldness, and obedience. In Jesus' name, **Amen.**

August 20
The Keys to Shining Your Light

Matthew 16:19
I will give you the keys of the kingdom of heaven; and whatever you bind on earth shall have been bound in heaven, and whatever you loose on earth shall have been loosed in heaven.

Reflection
Keys open doors. Jesus has given us access to the Kingdom, but we must learn how to use the keys He placed in our hands. Just as a beacon of light shines to guide others, these keys unlock the ways we reflect God's glory in a dark world.

The 7 Keys to the Kingdom are not optional ... they are essential disciplines for every believer who wants to grow, stand strong, and shine bright:

Praise & Worship ... When you worship, you shift the atmosphere and invite heaven into your situation. Worship keeps your inner light burning.
Teaching & Preaching ... The Word of God builds faith. Sharing it with others keeps truth alive and multiplies light.
Discipleship ... Walking with others in growth strengthens the body of Christ. A true beacon doesn't shine alone ... it lights the way for those who follow.
Evangelism ... Sharing the gospel is how we carry the light into darkness. Light that isn't shared becomes hidden.
Community Service ... Meeting needs is the gospel in action. Love expressed in deeds makes the light tangible.
Fellowship ... Staying connected to the body of Christ keeps your flame from burning out. A coal by itself grows cold, but in the fire of fellowship, it stays hot.
Tithing & Giving ... Generosity keeps your heart aligned with God's kingdom. When you release what's in your hand, God releases what's in His.

Each key unlocks another dimension of kingdom living, and together they create a lifestyle that keeps your light shining. God has already placed them in your hand. The question is: will you use them?

Prayer
Lord, thank You for giving me the keys to the Kingdom. Teach me to use them daily ... not for my own glory but to shine Your light to the world. Let my worship be pure, my teaching true, my discipleship faithful, my evangelism bold, my service loving, my fellowship strong, and my giving generous. In Jesus' name, **Amen.**

August 21
Love Looks Like Sacrifice

John 15:13
Greater love has no one than this, that one lay down his life for his friends.

Reflection
Love is not mere words or feelings ... it is sacrifice. Sacrifice is the Holy Spirit's greatest expression of love.

God so loved the world that He gave His only Son.
Jesus so loved us that He gave His very life.

The Bible declares there is no greater love than laying your life down for a friend. This is love that goes beyond convenience, comfort, or personal gain.

It is love that costs.

Love not only covers but conquers all, even a multitude of sins (1 Peter 4:8).

The cross proves that truth. Christ's walk to Golgotha was voluntary ... every step toward the cross was fueled by love. And just as He laid down His life, we too must lay down our flesh if we want to rise into our higher purpose. To live in the Spirit and to love like Christ, the self must die so His life can shine through us.

The cross teaches us this:
love that doesn't cost you will never change you ... but love that sacrifices will always resurrect something in you.

Application
- True love shows itself in giving ... lay down your comfort, time, or preference to serve someone else just as Christ laid down His life for you.
- Let sacrificial love guide your daily choices ... choose others' needs above your own, even when it costs you.
- Follow Jesus' example ... love deeply and wholeheartedly, offering yourself in humility and service for the good of others.

Prayer
Lord, teach me that true love is sacrifice. Help me lay down selfishness, pride, and comfort so that I may love like Christ loves. Give me strength to crucify the flesh daily so that Your Spirit may live fully in me. **Amen.**

August 22
From Fearless in Foolishness to Fearless in Faith

Jeremiah 29:11
For I know the plans that I have for you," declares the Lord, "plans for welfare and not for calamity to give you a future and a hope.

Reflection
Fearlessness is a powerful trait ... it can lead to courage in Christ or destruction in sin. Many of us once lived fearless in foolishness ... bold in rebellion, reckless in choices, blind to God's will. But God never leaves us there. Through His Word, His discipline, and His Spirit, He calls us out of darkness into marvelous light.

To be fearless in faith is not to deny our past but to be redeemed from it. Like Jacob, who deceived but became Israel; like Paul, who persecuted but became an apostle; like David, who stumbled but was still a man after God's heart ... our failures can be the very soil where God plants His purposes. The uncovering of self is not about finding a new identity but rediscovering the one God gave you before you were born (Jeremiah 1:5). The world teaches self-indulgence, but the Spirit teaches self-discovery ... learning who you are in Christ. Foolishness is loud, prideful, and reckless; faith is quiet, steady, and secure. Foolishness lives outside God's boundaries; faith thrives within His sovereign rule.

Every decision shapes a direction. Every compromise creates a consequence. You may have scars. You may carry regrets. But they do not define you. Yesterday's foolishness can give way to today's faith. What once made you fearless in sin can now make you fearless in serving the Savior.

Application
- Trust God's promise today ... He knows the plans He has for you.
- Live as a new creation in Christ ... let your past failures become soil for God's purposes, not a measure of your destiny.
- When old fears or regrets rise, surrender them to God and step forward in faith, trusting that His plans for you are good and filled with hope.

Prayer
Father, thank You for redeeming my past and uncovering my true self in You. I give You every foolish decision, every mistake, every regret, and I ask You to transform them into testimony. Teach me to live fearless ... not in recklessness but in faith. Let my story point others to Your grace and my life bring glory to Your name. In Jesus' name, **Amen.**

August 23
Light Up the Darkness
In Honor of Darryl Mayfield

Matthew 5:14–16
You are the light of the world. A city set on a hill cannot be hidden…
Let your light shine before men in such a way that they may see your good
works, and glorify your Father who is in heaven.

Reflection
My brother Darryl Mayfield said something profound one day:
"There are a lot of Christians, but not a lot of people practicing Christianity."
This truth explains why the world feels so dark. It's not because evil
suddenly got more powerful. It's because light stopped shining. Darkness is
not the presence of evil … it is the absence of light.

Jesus didn't call us church members. He called us lights. He didn't call us
cultural Christians. He called us disciples. He didn't tell us to blend in. He
told us to shine. But many believers today carry a title without carrying a
testimony. They wear the name of Christ without walking in the nature of
Christ. They proclaim faith but don't practice it. They love worship but avoid
obedience. They embrace grace but resist transformation.

When Christians stop practicing Christianity: love grows cold, truth gets
compromised, righteousness gets silenced, holiness gets mocked, compassion
gets replaced with convenience You were not created to blend in with the
culture. You were created to interrupt the darkness. You were created to shine
with righteousness, truth, love, mercy, integrity, and power.
The world is waiting on Christians to stop being Christians in name only
and start living as Christians in practice.

Application
- Do a heart check: Am I carrying the title Christian or the testimony of one?
- Identify one area where your light has dimmed … obedience, love, integrity, compassion, boldness.
- Commit today to living out Christianity, not just claiming it.

Prayer
Father, reignite the light inside of me. Remove every layer of fear,
compromise, distraction, or comfort that has dimmed my shine.
Teach me to practice Christianity in my thoughts, words, and actions.
Make me a living witness of Your love, righteousness, and truth.
Let the world see You in me. Help me shine boldly in a dark world so all
glory goes back to You. In Jesus' name, **Amen.**

August 24
Wisdom in Action

Proverbs 3:19
The Lord by wisdom founded the earth; by understanding he established the heavens.

Reflection
Wisdom is more than knowing God's truths ... it is applying them to the messy, unfiltered moments of everyday life. Knowledge fills your mind with information; but wisdom transforms your heart and guides your steps.

God's wisdom is not meant to sit on pages, stay in sermons, or collect dust in devotionals. His wisdom walks into boardrooms, classrooms, living rooms, and hospital rooms. It enters your conversations, confronts your habits, steadies your emotions, and shapes your responses. Wisdom knows when to speak truth and when to hold your peace. It knows when to plant and when to pluck up, when to run and when to rest, when to fight and when to be still.

Wisdom is seeing the world from God's perspective and then applying that perspective to our personal lives. It is looking at your storm through God's eyes instead of your fears. It is filtering your reactions through the Spirit instead of your flesh.

But true wisdom is not microwaved. It is not discovered in comfort or claimed through pride. Wisdom is earned in the fields of trial, where your faith is stretched and your motives are exposed. It is cultivated in the soil of humility, where you learn to admit your limitations and depend on God. Wisdom shapes you and is matured by obedience.

This is the kind of wisdom that does not just change how you think; it changes who you become.

Application
- Identify one truth from Scripture you believe but haven't applied.
- Ask God in prayer: "Holy Spirit, show me how to live this truth today."
- In your next decision or interaction, pause and ask: "How would Jesus act in this moment?"

Prayer
Father, give me not just understanding, but wisdom. Help me to see life through Your eyes and to walk accordingly. May Your truths shape my actions, not merely my beliefs. In Jesus' name, Amen.

August 25
Get in the Game

Ephesians 6:12
For our struggle is not against flesh and blood, but against the rulers, against the powers, against the world forces of this darkness, against the spiritual forces of wickedness in the heavenly places.

Reflection
We've got to get in the game ... and make no mistake, it is a game.

The powers of this world have carefully cultivated chaos, confusion, and darkness. Systems are designed to distract, divide, and destroy. But as children of God, we are not spectators ... we are players on the field of spiritual battle.

The schemes of darkness should not discourage you; they should ignite you.

Every time the enemy pushes lies, you have the opportunity to stand in truth.
Every time fear rises, faith can answer.
Every time the world sinks deeper into chaos, God calls His people to rise higher in His strength.

But here's the key: you cannot win this game without God.

Strategies, strength, and wisdom apart from Him will fail. Only when you are clothed in His armor, grounded in His Word, and filled with His Spirit can you overcome the forces arrayed against you.

The world is playing for souls. Heaven calls you to step up, play hard, and shine your light in the darkest arenas. Get in the game.

Application
- Put on the whole armor of God daily (Ephesians 6:13–18).
- Recognize the world's chaos not as coincidence but as strategy ... and answer with prayer and obedience.
- Refuse to sit on the sidelines; live as salt and light where God has placed you.

Prayer
Lord, thank You for reminding me that I am not a spectator in this world but a soldier in Your kingdom. Strengthen me to rise above the chaos and stand firm in Your truth. Clothe me in Your armor, fill me with Your Spirit, and use me as a light in the darkness. In Jesus' name, **Amen.**

August 26
A Shepherd and His Sheep

Psalm 23:1–3
The Lord is my shepherd, I shall not want. He makes me lie down in green pastures; He leads me beside quiet waters. He restores my soul; He guides me in the paths of righteousness for His name's sake.

Reflection
Sheep cannot thrive without a shepherd. Unlike cattle, sheep are not driven … they are led. They move not by force but by following the familiar voice of the one who cares for them. "My sheep hear My voice, and I know them, and they follow Me" (John 10:27).

Contentment and peace flow from trusting the Shepherd. He leads us to still waters when our souls are restless. He restores us when we are broken. He gives us righteousness … not earned by effort, but imputed by grace. The shepherd does not abandon His flock in the valley of shadows. Instead, His rod protects, His staff guides, and His presence comforts.

The key to following is hearing His voice. And the key to hearing His voice is spending time in His presence. Jesus said, "No longer do I call you slaves… but I have called you friends" (John 15:15). A friend confides in you; so does your Shepherd. You can walk with confidence when God has whispered His will to you.

Psalm 23 reminds us that the Shepherd is not distant. He prepares a table for us in the presence of our enemies. He anoints our head with oil, a sign of favor and healing. And His goodness and lovingkindness follow us, not sometimes, but all the days of our life. To be His sheep is to be secure. To be His sheep is to be guided. To be His sheep is to never walk alone.

Application
- Let your heart rest today .. trust the Shepherd to lead you to green pastures.
- When you feel lost or weary, listen for His voice and follow Him.
- In seasons of fear or uncertainty, remember: you are not alone … His rod protects you, His presence comforts you forever.

Prayer
Lord, thank You for being my Shepherd. Teach me to recognize Your voice above every distraction. Lead me to still waters when I am restless, restore me when I am weary, and keep me in the path of righteousness by Your grace. I place my confidence in You, knowing Your goodness will follow me all my days. **Amen.**

August 27
With God, Any Is Plenty

Philippians 4:12-13
I know how to be brought low, and I know how to abound. In any and every circumstance, I have learned the secret of facing plenty and hunger... I can do all things through Him who strengthens me.

Reflection
Paul reminds us of a profound truth: true contentment does not rise and fall with circumstances. Whether he had plenty or was in need, he remained steadfast because his sufficiency was rooted in Christ, not in material conditions.

This reveals a powerful reality ... God's presence and peace are more than enough. His fellowship is abundance itself, a provision greater than anything we could desire or lack. In Christ, "any" becomes "plenty" ... whether it's resources, strength, peace, or provision.

Contentment in Christ is not natural ... it's supernatural and spiritual. It defies circumstances and declares Him as our greatest treasure. Learning to be content in both plenty and hunger is not something we can produce on our own. True contentment is a gift of God's grace that comes from seeing Christ as our supreme satisfaction and resting in Him above all else.

So, no matter what you face today, take heart: His presence is more than enough.

Application
- Trust that Christ is enough ... in hunger or abundance, His presence makes "any" into "plenty."
- Let gratitude replace striving for more ... be satisfied in Him, not in your circumstances.
- Rely on His strength ... through Him you can rest, rejoice, and stand firm in every season.

Prayer
Lord, thank You for being my plenty in every circumstance. Teach me to rest in You ... whether in abundance or in lack. Help me find contentment in Christ alone, and to share generously out of the overflow of Your grace. In Jesus' name, **Amen.**

August 28
Discipline Is a Must

Proverbs 22:15
Foolishness is bound up in the heart of a child, but the rod of discipline will drive it far from him.

Reflection
Discipline is not an option ... it's foundational. To raise a child, to lead a home, to steward any sphere of life, discipline must govern. But the discipline we speak of is not harshness or mere legalism. It is loving structure, correction, and training that shapes character.

Proverbs 22:6 reminds us that early training ... patterns set in youth ... leave fingerprints on the adult soul. Discipline is the molding force that helps remove folly (Proverbs 22:15). It drives out what diminishes and builds in what endures. Meanwhile, Jesus commands us to make disciples (Matthew 28). Discipleship ... life in Christ ... requires discipline: training, obedience, correction, repetition.

Discipline should flow from character, not fear. The "10 things to teach your child (requiring zero talent)" ... punctuality, work ethic, effort, posture, energy, attitude, passion, coach-ability, going extra, preparation ... are not traits only for children. They are disciplines for every believer. They cost no talent but demand consistency, sacrifice, and modeling.

When you discipline your life (and those you lead), you build an altar of integrity. You resist the chaos of culture and align yourself with God's order. Remember ... discipline produces the peaceful fruit of righteousness even when it seems painful (Hebrews 12:11).

Application
- Pick one of the 10 character disciplines and commit to practicing it.
- Reflect: Which area in your life lacks discipline ... spiritual, relational, financial?
- Ask God for grace and strength to correct that area.

Prayer
Father, thank You for showing me that discipline is not punishment but purpose. Help me to receive Your correction with humility and to live consistently in what is right. Show me where I need structure, remind me where I have slacked, and empower me to lead by example. May the disciplines I develop reflect Your order and produce righteousness in me and those I lead. In Jesus' name, **Amen.**

August 29
Covered in His Dust

1 John 2:6
Whoever claims to live in Him must walk as Jesus did.

Reflection
Ancient rabbis had a blessing for their disciples: "May you be covered in the dust of your rabbi." The meaning was simple ... walk so closely behind your teacher that the dust from his sandals settles on your clothes.

To follow that closely meant to listen, to imitate, and to absorb every word and every step.
When applied to our life in Christ, this image is powerful.

Discipleship is not observing Jesus from a distance ... it is walking right behind Him, on His path, at His pace.

The closer we follow, the more His life marks ours.

His humility becomes our humility.
His compassion becomes our compassion.
His obedience becomes our obedience.

To be "covered in His dust" is to live in daily nearness.
It is to let His words shape our thinking, His Spirit guide our steps, and His example direct our choices. As we abide in Him, we are transformed into His likeness (2 Corinthians 3:18).

The world may leave its mark on those who follow it closely ... but for those who walk near Christ, His "dust" is the evidence that we have been with Him.

Application
- Draw near to Jesus through daily time in His Word and prayer.
- Examine your steps ... are they following His path or your own?
- Seek to imitate Christ in speech, service, and sacrifice, so that others recognize His imprint on your life.

Prayer
Jesus, let me walk so closely with You that Your presence marks me. Cover me with the dust of Your steps until my life reflects Your way. Keep me near, keep me humble, and keep me walking in Your likeness. **Amen.**

August 30
End of Self, Rise in Christ

Romans 6:6
Knowing this, that our old self was crucified with Him, that our body of sin might be done away with...

Reflection
There is a powerful and painful moment in every believer's journey ... a moment when you come to the end of yourself.

All your striving, your hiding, your false securities collapse. That moment of crystal-clear self-hatred is not defeat ... it is the soil from which rebirth begins.

Like a phoenix that must burn in ashes before rising, your old self must perish before Christ's life can fully arise. The flesh, the pride, the illusions ... all must die so that only the resurrected life remains. In that surrender, you tap into the place where abiding in Christ becomes natural.

When your own strength fails, Christ's strength takes over. When your identity in self is stripped away, your identity in Him begins to shine.

You were never meant to live in your own power.
He is your power.
To rise is to let Him raise you.

Application
- Identify one area where you are still trying to live by your own strength or identity.
- Confess that to God; in honest prayer say, "Lord, I surrender this ... I submit this to You, that it might die."
- Meditate on Galatians 2:20 or Romans 6:6. Speak it out loud. Let Christ live in you.

Prayer
Father, I come to the end of me. Let all my striving, my pride, my fleshly ambitions die today. Raise in me the life of Christ. Let Your resurrection power flow through my ashes so that I may soar, not by my strength, but by Yours. In Jesus' name, **Amen.**

August 31
What Temptation Tests

James 1:13
Let no one say when he is tempted, 'I am being tempted by God'; for God cannot be tempted by evil, nor does He Himself tempt anyone.

Reflection
Temptation is more than a momentary pull ... it is a spiritual test. It presses against the treasures you hold in your soul: faith, identity, righteousness, godly character. When you are tempted, it's not just an external lure ... it's a challenge to see whether you'll retain those spiritual possessions under pressure.

James 1:13 reminds us that temptation does not come from God. The enemy, through external pressure or internal desire, seeks to fracture your inner life ... to get you to surrender what you hold sacred. When Jesus faced temptation in the wilderness, Satan aimed at His identity, His purpose, His trust in the Father.

You must ask:
Am I faithful to the life of Christ within me, even when everything around me screams otherwise? The test is not whether you feel strong but whether, at your core, you remain anchored to Him.

When temptation assaults, your spiritual possessions ... your faith, your convictions, your reverence for Christ ... are all on trial. Will you yield, or will you defend those treasures? The good news: through Christ, you don't face the test alone, and a way of escape is always provided.

Application
- Recognize the test: when temptation arises, identify which part of your spiritual life is being challenged (trust, identity, purity, love, etc.).
- Stand guard: speak Scripture, pray, call on the Spirit, and refuse the lie.
- Ask for escape: trust that God provides a way out (1 Corinthians 10:13).

Prayer
Father, thank You that You do not tempt me but that You remain faithful. In this moment of trial, guard my soul. Don't let me lose what You have placed within me. Grant me strength to hold fast to Christ in me, and give me wisdom and escape through Your Spirit. In Jesus' name, **Amen.**

September 1
Righteous Hearted

James 5:16b
The effective prayer of a righteous man can accomplish much.

Reflection
Not everyone who prays touches Heaven. Jesus Himself said, "Not everyone who says to Me, 'Lord, Lord,' will enter the kingdom of heaven, but the one who does the will of My Father" (Matthew 7:21). Words alone are not enough. What God responds to is not empty repetition but a heart aligned with Him.

To be righteous-hearted is to let God's Word shape your motives, your desires, and your choices. The psalmist declared, "Through Your precepts I get understanding; therefore I hate every false way" (Psalm 119:104). A righteous heart loves truth and turns away from deception.

Isaiah reminds us that God's Word never returns void (Isaiah 55:11). When a righteous heart prays God's Word with faith, Heaven moves. The fervent prayer of a righteous person is not powerful because of eloquence, but because it flows from alignment with God's will.

This is the secret:
Righteousness fuels effectiveness.
Holiness opens Heaven's ear.

A righteous-hearted life makes prayer more than words … it makes it partnership with God.

Application
- Ask the Spirit to search your heart before you pray (Psalm 139:23–24).
- Build your prayers on Scripture, not just feelings.
- Pursue righteousness in your lifestyle, knowing your prayers flow from your walk.

Prayer
Lord, make me righteous-hearted. Purify my motives, cleanse my desires, and align my will with Yours. Let my prayers be effective not because of me, but because of You. May my life reflect Your Word, and may my heart be a place where truth and righteousness dwell. In Jesus' name, **Amen.**

September 2
Our Daily Bread

Matthew 6:11
Give us this day our daily bread.

Reflection
When Jesus taught us to pray for "daily bread," He was inviting us into a rhythm of daily dependence. Bread was never just food; it was a picture of God's provision for every aspect of our lives ... physical, emotional, and spiritual.

This prayer reaches all the way back to the wilderness, where God fed Israel with manna. It was a supernatural provision ... it arrived every morning ... it was enough for that day and it could not be stored or hoarded. God was training His people to trust Him daily and to wake up each morning with open hands. To look to Him ... not to their own reserves.

The same is true for us. We want a week's worth of peace at once, a month's worth of clarity, a year's worth of answers. But God gives strength, wisdom, grace, and guidance in daily portions. Not because He is withholding ... but because He is drawing us near. Dependence is the doorway to relationship. Just as manna sustained Israel's bodies, the Word sustains our souls. You cannot live today off yesterday's revelation any more than Israel could eat yesterday's manna. The Bread of Life must be taken in fresh. Scripture must be consumed daily. His presence must be sought continually.
The wilderness manna was more than food ... it was a prophecy of the spiritual discipline we still need: You must gather every morning.

What manna was to Israel's survival, God's Word is to your transformation. Yesterday's portion will not carry you through today. Feed on His Word daily, and you will discover what Israel learned in the desert: the God who provides each morning will sustain you every step of the journey.

Application
- Begin each morning asking God for your "daily bread" ... both provision and spiritual strength.
- Reflect: Am I trusting God for today, or am I anxious about tomorrow?
- Declare: "God is my Provider; His mercies are new every morning."

Prayer
Father, thank You for being my Provider. Give me what I need for today ... food for my body, strength for my soul, and wisdom for my walk. Teach me to depend on You daily and to find satisfaction in Your presence. **Amen.**

September 3
The Key of Prayer

Matthew 7:7
Ask, and it will be given to you; seek, and you will find; knock, and it will be opened to you.

Reflection
Prayer is one of the keys that unlocks Heaven's treasures.

God has promised to supply all our needs according to His riches in glory, but often those blessings remain unopened because we never turn the key. Prayer doesn't twist God's arm … it aligns our hearts with His will and opens the storehouses of grace, wisdom, peace, and provision already prepared for us.

Just as a key gives access to what's already ours, prayer unlocks the treasures of God's presence and power. When we neglect prayer, we live like spiritual beggars sitting outside a treasury. But when we pray in faith, we discover that Heaven's vaults are never empty, and God delights to give generously to His children.

Prayer is not just words … it's the key that unlocks Heaven's treasure. Use it daily, and walk in the fullness of God's provision and presence.

The door is not locked… it is waiting on your knock. Heaven is not silent… it is waiting on your ask. Prayer is the key God placed in your hands to access what He has already prepared. When you ask, seek, and knock in faith, you are not trying to convince God … you are aligning with Him.

Use the key. Pray boldly. Stand on truth. Heaven is waiting on your voice.

Application
- Reflect: Am I living as if God's treasure is locked away, or am I daily turning the key of prayer?
- Begin each day with a prayer of access: "Father, unlock in me what You have already prepared."
- Declare: "Prayer is my key, and Heaven is not closed to me."

Prayer
Lord, thank You for giving me the key of prayer. Teach me to use it faithfully, not neglectfully. Open Heaven's treasure over my life and align my heart with Your will so that I may walk in Your abundance. **Amen.**

September 4
God Is Near When You Call

Psalm 145:18–19
The Lord is near to all who call upon Him… He will fulfill the desire of those who fear Him.

Reflection
God is not distant. He is not hard to reach. Scripture tells us plainly: the moment you call, He draws near. Prayer is not a ritual … it is a sacred reminder that Heaven is closer than your next breath.

Psalm 145 reveals a God who responds, a Father who listens, and a Provider who delights in meeting the needs of His children. When you lift your voice in humility, you are not talking into the air … you are stepping into the presence of the God who fulfills the desires of those who fear Him. Prayer pulls you into alignment with His heart, His will, and His provision.

You were never meant to do life alone. Peace in chaos, wisdom for decisions, joy in hardship, and strength in weakness are treasures only God can give, and He releases them to those who call upon Him with reverence and trust. Prayer is the posture of dependence that keeps the supply line open. When you pray daily, you remain connected to the Source of all strength and sustenance.

Do not wait for desperation to drive you to your knees… we must be proactive in building this sacred relationship. Call on Him now. Call on Him daily. Heaven is not silent or empty … God is near, and His storehouse is full.

Application
- Call on God daily, trusting that His nearness brings the peace and strength you cannot produce on your own.
- Let prayer be your first response, not your last resort, knowing God delights to fulfill the desires of those who seek Him.
- Surrender your needs, fears, and desires to Him each day so your heart stays aligned with His will and His provision.

Prayer
Father, thank You for drawing near when I call. Teach me to seek You daily, not only in need but in love and devotion. Fulfill Your purpose in me, and provide every spiritual and natural supply I require. Keep my heart aligned with Your will as I learn to trust You more deeply. In Jesus' name, **Amen.**

September 5
Trust Me, I Have It Under Control

Psalm 46:10
Be still, and know that I am God; I will be exalted among the nations, I will be exalted in the earth.

Reflection
God's whisper to us is simple: "Trust Me. I have everything under control."

We often see only fragments of our story, while He sees the whole. We feel pressure from what looks uncertain, delayed, or broken, but God sits enthroned above time and circumstance. God sits high and looks low. His plans are never at risk. His promises are never in jeopardy.

Trust does not mean having all the answers; it means knowing The Answer. The Lord invites us to be still, to surrender the illusion of control, and to rest in the truth that He is faithful.

Every storm is subject to His command. Every need is met by His provision. Every step is guided by His hand. Our role is not to figure out every detail but to stay close to Him in obedience, faith, and peace.

When life feels overwhelming, remember this: God is not overwhelmed. He has already gone ahead of you, making crooked places straight.

So be still, breathe deep, and release the weight you were never meant to carry. God has already secured what you are worried about, settled what you are praying about, and strengthened you for what you are walking through. Stillness is not inactivity … it is faith at rest. When you quiet your soul before Him, you will discover the truth your storm tried to hide: God is in control, and He will be exalted in your life.

Application
- Pause today and pray: "Lord, I trust You with what I cannot control.
- Write down one situation that worries you and commit it to God in prayer.
- Remind yourself daily that surrender is not weakness … it is worship.

Prayer
Father, thank You that nothing in my life is outside of Your control. Teach me to rest in Your sovereignty and trust Your timing. When I feel anxious or uncertain, remind me that You are God, and You are faithful. I place every burden into Your hands. In Jesus' name, **Amen.**

September 6
Sheep or Shepherd

John 10:11
I am the good shepherd; the good shepherd lays down His life for the sheep.

Reflection
Everyone in this world is either a sheep or a shepherd ... a follower or a leader. Sheep need guidance, protection, and provision. Shepherds carry responsibility, direction, and sacrifice. Both roles are vital, and both are honored in God's kingdom.

The challenge comes when shepherds grow weary of sheep who do not yet understand or follow. But frustration is not the way of Christ. Jesus, the Good Shepherd, laid down His life for the sheep ... even for the stubborn, the slow, and the straying. He did not abandon them for their weakness but guided them with patience and love.

If you are called to lead, remember: not everyone will lead with you. Some are simply called to follow. And if you are called to follow, remember: it is not weakness but wisdom to trust the shepherd God has placed before you.

Sheep need shepherds. Shepherds need sheep. Both need the Chief Shepherd, Christ Himself, who alone guards, guides, and gathers us all.

Whether you lead or follow, your life only finds its strength when it stays close to the Shepherd. Stay near His voice, and you will never lose your way.

Application
- If you are a leader, shepherd with patience, remembering that growth takes time.
- If you are a follower, submit with humility, knowing that every shepherd is under Christ.
- Ask God daily: Am I being faithful in my role as sheep, shepherd, or both?

Prayer
Lord Jesus, my Good Shepherd, thank You for guiding me with patience and love. Teach me to follow well when I am a sheep, and to lead well when I am a shepherd. Keep me humble, keep me faithful, and keep me near Your voice.
Amen.

September 7
The War Within

Romans 7:23
But I see another law at work in my body, waging war against the law of my mind, and making me a prisoner of the law of sin which dwells in my members.

Reflection
The fiercest battles are not always fought against external foes ... but within. Paul's words uncover a tension every believer feels: the flesh pulling one way, and the renewed mind pulling another. Your spirit longs for righteousness, yet your flesh craves for what opposes it. This struggle is not a sign of failure; it is evidence that God is at work in you ... awakening you to the reality of the spiritual warfare inside your own members.

But this war is not hopeless. Romans 8 reminds us that the Holy Spirit is our strength, our strategy, and our supernatural advantage. The internal battle is not about your destruction ... it is about your transformation. It is the process of crucifying the false self so the true self in Christ can rise. It is reclaiming territory in your thoughts, desires, and identity ... while tearing down every lie that tells you your weakness defines you.

Victory does not come by avoiding the war but by stepping into it with the Spirit as your guide. Peace is not the absence of conflict; it is the fruit of winning the battles with the God within. The only path to growth, freedom, and holiness is through the very battlefield God is leading you to conquer.

Application
- Identify one area where your flesh constantly battles your faith ... be honest with God about it.
- Declare that the Holy Spirit is greater: "Spirit, I surrender this battlefield to You."
- Arm yourself daily with Scripture ... Ephesians 6 and 2 Corinthians 10 ... to demolish thoughts that oppose God and your peace.

Prayer
Father, I acknowledge the war within .. the pull of sin versus the heart that wants You. I surrender this fight to the Holy Spirit. Equip me with Scripture, strength, and grace to take every thought captive for Christ. Redeem my internal chaos into victory, that my soul may rest in Your peace. In Jesus' name, **Amen.**

September 8
Freedom Is an Inside Job

John 8:36
So if the Son makes you free, you will be free indeed.

Reflection
Freedom is not granted by external circumstances, achievements, or possessions … it is born on the inside through Christ.

Real freedom is not about doing whatever you want; it is about being who God created you to be, unhindered by sin, shame, or the approval of others.

Your behavior should be a reflection of your internal freedom through Christ. Outward deeds do not create freedom, but true freedom in Christ produces deeds that shine as evidence of what's happening in the heart. This is why Paul reminds us that "where the Spirit of the Lord is, there is liberty" (2 Corinthians 3:17). Sustainable freedom is not based on momentary victories or temporary feelings … it is rooted in the finished work of Jesus.

Freedom is not something you chase; it is something Christ plants within you. External change cannot produce internal liberation, but internal transformation will always produce external fruit. When Jesus sets you free, your identity shifts, your desires realign, and your actions begin to mirror the freedom God has already declared over your life. Walk in that truth. Live from that truth. Because the liberty Christ gives is not fragile or fleeting … it is complete, enduring, and undeniable. You are free indeed. When you rest in Him, the chains of fear, addiction, guilt, and performance are broken. Your freedom is secure not because of what you do, but because of what Christ has already done.

Application
- Live from your identity in Christ, not from the labels or limitations others have placed on you.
- Reject anything … habit, mindset, relationship … that tries to pull you back into chains God has already broken.
- Practice daily surrender so the Holy Spirit can continue producing the visible fruit of an inwardly free life.

Prayer
Lord Jesus, thank You for setting me free from the chains of sin and the weight of my past. Help me to walk daily in the liberty You provide, letting my actions reflect the freedom I have inside. May my life be a living testimony that true freedom is only found in You. **Amen.**

September 9
Sacrifice Required

Ecclesiastes 1:18
Because in much wisdom there is much grief, and increasing knowledge results in increasing pain.

Reflection
Freedom is never free ... it always requires sacrifice. In the Christian walk, sacrifice is the pathway to life. God so loved us that He gave His Son. Jesus so loved us that He laid down His life. And if we are to follow Him, we too must pick up our cross daily (Luke 9:23).

True compassion also carries a weight. The very word compassion means "to suffer with." To love deeply is to enter into the pain of others, to carry their burdens, and to let your heart break for what breaks God's heart. Freedom in Christ produces a new kind of suffering ... not slavery to sin, but empathy for others' chains.

Sacrifice, then, is both the cost of our salvation and the mark of our sanctification. Without it, love becomes shallow and freedom becomes selfish. But with it, our lives echo the Cross: a willingness to endure hardship so that others may experience healing, wholeness, and hope.

Every time you choose the Cross over comfort, you are becoming more like Christ. Wisdom will hurt you before it heals you, because God stretches what He intends to strengthen. Love will break you before it builds others, because compassion carries a cost. But sacrifice is the currency of transformation; it is the soil where true freedom, true maturity, and true purpose grow. If you want resurrection power, you must first embrace the crucified life..

Application
- Reflect on one comfort you can sacrifice this week to draw closer to Christ or to serve someone else in need.
- When you feel the weight of another's suffering, let it move you to prayer and action, not despair.
- Remember that compassion is costly, but it reflects the very heart of Christ, who suffered with and for us.

Prayer
Father, thank You for showing me the way of sacrifice through the Cross. Teach me to embrace sacrifice not as loss but as love. Give me the courage to suffer with others in compassion, and to carry my cross with joy, knowing that in You, freedom is always worth the cost. In Jesus' name, **Amen.**

September 10
In His Likeness

2 Corinthians 3:18
And we all, with unveiled face, beholding as in a mirror the glory of the Lord, are being transformed into the same image from glory to glory, just as from the Lord, the Spirit.

Reflection
The purpose of salvation is not only forgiveness …it is transformation. God's desire is to shape us into the likeness of His Son, Jesus Christ (Romans 8:29). To follow Christ is to be changed, from the inside out, until our thoughts, words, and actions bear His reflection.

Jesus described this process in John 15: we are the branches, He is the vine. Our fruitfulness comes not from striving, but from abiding. As we remain connected to Him … through prayer, obedience, and His Word … the life of Christ flows to us and through us … while reshaping us.

This likeness is not about outward appearances or religious performance. It begins in the renewing of the mind (Romans 12:2), the putting off of the old self, and the putting on of the new (Colossians 3:9–10). It is cultivated when we choose humility over pride, service over status, obedience over convenience (Philippians 2:5–8).

To live in Christ is to walk as He walked (1 John 2:6). Each day, the Spirit chisels away at what is unlike Him and polishes what reflects His glory. Transformation is not instant … it is a journey "from one degree of glory to another." Transformation begins when revelation gives birth to imitation.

Application
- Spend time daily abiding in Christ through prayer and Scripture.
- Ask the Spirit to renew your mind, replacing old thought patterns with truth.
- In every decision, ask: Does this make me look more like Jesus?

Prayer
Lord, thank You for calling me not just to believe, but to become. Transform me from the inside out. Teach me to abide in You, to think with Your mind, to walk in Your steps, and to love as You loved. Shape me daily into Your likeness until others see Christ in me. **Amen.**

September 11
Love Set Apart

1 Thessalonians 4:3–4
For this is the will of God, your sanctification... that each of you know how to possess his own vessel in sanctification and honor.

Reflection
Whether you are married, engaged, dating, or waiting, consecration is the foundation of real love. To consecrate means to set apart as sacred unto God. Relationships flourish when both people see themselves ... and each other ... as God's first.

For the married, consecration looks like prayerfully covering your spouse, speaking God's Word over their life, and remembering that they belong to the Lord before they belong to you. For the unmarried, consecration means preparing your heart, your habits, and your life as an offering to God now ... before you share yourself with another.

Love that is set apart does not demand control. It points upward, not inward. When Christ is first, the relationship becomes holy ground. Prayer replaces pressure. Sacrifice replaces selfishness. Purity replaces compromise.

Whether you are walking alone or with a partner, the call is the same: set your love apart for God. A consecrated relationship isn't built on emotions alone, but on the eternal foundation of Christ.

Application
- Married: Pray daily for your spouse's protection, growth, and purpose.
- Unmarried: Pray daily for your future spouse ... or for strength and joy in your current season.
- Both: Commit your love life to God. Put Him first in affection, decisions, and direction.

Prayer
Lord, teach me to consecrate my love to You. If I am married, help me cover my spouse in prayer and honor them as Your child. If I am unmarried, help me prepare my heart and life to glorify You in singleness or in marriage to come. May every relationship I enter be set apart for Your glory. In Jesus' name, **Amen.**

September 12
Birthed Out of the Darkness

Isaiah 45:3
I will give you the treasures of darkness and hidden wealth of secret places, so that you may know that it is I, the LORD, the God of Israel, who calls you by your name.

Reflection
Every beginning starts in darkness. Seeds push through hidden soil before breaking into light. A child forms in the secret place of the womb before drawing its first breath. Even creation itself began with darkness covering the deep before God spoke, "Let there be light."

Darkness in life does not always mean death; sometimes it means development. God often does His deepest work in unseen places. Your waiting season, your struggle, your midnight hour may feel hidden … but it is the very place where purpose is forming.

When you feel surrounded by darkness, remember: resurrection came out of a tomb, and salvation came out of a cross. Everything God births passes through hiddenness before it is revealed in glory.

So do not despise the darkness; it is the womb of what God is preparing in you. What feels buried is often being planted, and what seems hidden is being shaped for a greater unveiling. God does His finest work in places no one sees, and when the appointed time comes, He brings treasures out of the very shadows you prayed to escape. Trust the God who calls you by name … for He is forming glory in the dark that will one day testify of His light.

Application
- Embrace the hidden seasons as preparation, not punishment.
- Trust that God is working in what you cannot see.
- Look for the "treasures of darkness" He promised … wisdom, character, and faith.

Prayer
Father, thank You for the seasons of darkness that shape me. Teach me to trust You when I cannot see, and to believe that hidden places are birthing holy purpose. Let what is forming in secret be revealed in Your time, for Your glory. In Jesus' name, **Amen.**

September 13
On Earth as It Is in Heaven

Matthew 6:10
Your kingdom come. Your will be done, on earth as it is in heaven.

Reflection
When Jesus taught His disciples to pray, He didn't point their eyes only to the skies ... He pointed them to the ground beneath their feet. The Lord's Prayer isn't about waiting to escape to Heaven; it's about Heaven breaking into earth right now. Not one day... but today!

Too often, believers reduce God's kingdom to a future promise, when Christ declared it as a present reality. To pray "on earth as it is in heaven" is to invite God's order, peace, and power into your marriage, your finances, your workplace, your city, and your own heart.

Heaven is not distant ... it is near. The Spirit within you is the same Spirit who hovered over creation, raised Jesus from the dead, and fills the throne room of Heaven. That same Spirit empowers you to live holy, healed, and free on this side of eternity.

Heaven is not waiting for a someday version of you ... Heaven is ready to break into your life today. When you pray "on earth as it is in heaven," you are inviting God to make your life a living intersection where His glory meets human experience. You become a carrier of His peace, a vessel of His power, and a witness of His kingdom here and now. So walk in expectation, live in alignment, and believe boldly: wherever you surrender to God's will ... Heaven touches earth.

Application
- Begin your day by praying: "Lord, let my life today reflect Your Kingdom on earth."
- Look for one area of your daily life (home, work, relationships) where you can invite Heaven's order, peace, or love.
- Refuse to postpone joy, holiness, or purpose ... Heaven starts here.

Prayer
Father, let Your kingdom come in my life today. Transform my words, my decisions, and my environment so they reflect Heaven's order and Your will. May I live in such a way that when others see me, they catch a glimpse of Heaven on earth. In Jesus' name, **Amen.**

September 14
When the Lights Went Out, Power Showed Up

Acts 1:8
But you will receive power when the Holy Spirit has come upon you; and you shall be My witnesses both in Jerusalem, and in all Judea and Samaria, and even to the remotest part of the earth.

Reflection
On September 14, 2025, something amazing happened at St. John's UMC Downtown Houston. Just three minutes before the 9:00 a.m. service, the entire area lost electricity. The sanctuary, filled with people, went dark. But instead of panic or confusion, something greater happened … a Greater Power showed up … The Holy Spirit !

With no lights, no electricity, and no microphones, the Spirit of God lit the room. Faith was activated … Hearts were united … and worship did not stop. The absence of man's power made room for God's Dýnamis Power … for the explosive strength of the Spirit to take over. Sometimes God allows the lights to go out to remind us that He is the Greatest Generator in the world. When human resources fail, His Spirit never does. That morning, the darkness only magnified the brightness of His presence.

Similarity, when human power shuts down … divine power takes over. But to be filled with that power, something in us must die. Pride, control, and self-reliance must step aside so the Spirit can take over. When we die to self, the Holy Spirit rises in power, and what looks like darkness becomes the very space where God's glory shines brightest.

Application
- Remember that true power isn't in electricity, technology, or resources … it's in the Holy Spirit.
- When things shut down around you, choose faith over panic.
- Ask God to use your "power outages" in life to activate deeper faith and dependence on Him.

Prayer
Father, thank You for showing me that when the lights go out, You are still shining. Thank You for the reminder that my strength and supply come from Your Spirit, not from the systems of man. Teach me to lean on Your Dýnamis power in every season of lack, every unexpected outage, and every moment I feel weak. May my life be a witness that the Greatest Generator in the world is still alive in me. In Jesus' name, **Amen.**

September 15
You Get What You give

Matthew 7:12
In everything, therefore, treat people the same way you want them to treat you, for this is the Law and the Prophets.

Reflection
Whatever you want or desire from God is what you should be giving away to others. If you long for love, sow love. If you desire forgiveness, extend forgiveness. If you hunger for encouragement, be the encourager. Many people miss their blessings because they misunderstand or ignore the principle of sowing and reaping.

God built this principle into creation itself. A farmer cannot plant corn and expect a harvest of wheat. Likewise, we cannot plant bitterness and expect joy, or withhold generosity and expect abundance. What we scatter is what we gather.

Blessings are not accidents. They are often the harvest of seeds planted in faith, watered with patience, and cultivated with consistency. When we learn to sow in line with what we desire from God, we step into His divine cycle of increase and blessing.

If you want God to multiply something in your life, plant it in someone else's. The harvest you're praying for is hidden in the seeds you're willing to release. When you sow with intention, generosity, and faith, you position yourself under the flow of God's increase. Your future is not determined by chance but by the seeds you choose to scatter today. Sow well… because God always honors the seed.

Application
- Identify what you are longing for from God. Are you sowing that very thing into others?
- Be intentional today: plant seeds of kindness, forgiveness, or generosity where you can.
- Keep in mind: the harvest may not come overnight, but God is faithful.

Prayer
Father, thank You for the law of sowing and reaping. Forgive me for the times I have expected harvests from seeds I never planted. Teach me to sow love where I want love, to sow forgiveness where I need forgiveness, and to sow generosity where I need provision. May my life reflect Your abundance as I trust You for the harvest. In Jesus' name, **Amen.**

September 16
Built Low to Rise High

James 4:6
God is opposed to the proud, but gives grace to the humble.

Reflection
"Humbleness is the root from which nobleness grows. Low is the foundation on which high is built." — Unknown

In the Kingdom, elevation never begins in the spotlight ... it begins in the soil. Promotion is born in places no one applauds. Everything God grows, He first buries. Everything God raises, He first humbles. The seed must go down before it can come up. Jesus stooped to wash feet before He ascended to the right hand of the Father. David learned worship, warfare, and wisdom in obscurity before he carried the weight of a crown. Joseph was faithful in a pit, in Potiphar's house, and in prison before he ever stepped into Pharaoh's palace.

Humility is not weakness ... it is strength under surrender. It is the posture that keeps you grounded when God lifts you, anchored when God accelerates you, and balanced when God blesses you. The higher God desires to take you, the deeper He must first establish your roots.

Pride builds towers; humility builds foundations.
And God only builds destinies on what can hold His weight.

So embrace the low places, the quiet seasons, the unseen assignments. Stay low before God, and He will take you places pride could never enter, sustain you in rooms arrogance could never keep you, and trust you with influence your character is prepared to carry.

Application
- Ask God to show you areas where pride may be blocking growth.
- Choose humility today by serving where no one applauds.
- Trust that God sees the low place and honors it in due time.

Prayer
Father, teach me to walk in true humility before You. Remove pride from my heart and deepen my roots in obedience and surrender. I trust You with my elevation and my timing. Lift me only as You see fit, for Your glory alone. In Jesus' name, **Amen.**

September 17
The Power Already Within You

John 8:36
So if the Son makes you free, you will be free indeed.

Reflection
KRS-One really hit the nail on the head. The dark forces of this world are not above God, the Universe, or Nature. They may influence systems, shape narratives, distort perceptions, and manipulate minds, but they are never supreme. They operate within limits. They move under permission. They are subject to the One who created all things and sustains all things.

The real battle has always been internal. Long before oppression shows up in society, it starts in the soul. Long before bondage becomes physical, it becomes mental. Control begins in the mind ... how you think, what you believe, what you accept as truth. That is why seeking God matters more than ever. When you seek Him, you discover what the world never wanted you to know: that power has already been placed inside you. God given authority. God given identity. God given purpose. God given spiritual resilience that cannot be enslaved unless you surrender it.

This is why God sent His Son. Not to trap us in religion or ritual, but to emancipate us from internal captivity. To free us from the chains we cannot see ... fear, deception, addiction, insecurity, hopelessness, and every lie that tells us we are less than what Heaven declared. Jesus came to break mental strongholds, open spiritual eyes, and liberate the captive areas of our lives that no system or society could ever reach.
Freedom begins with truth: *"You shall know the truth, and the truth shall make you free."* Awakening begins with surrender ... releasing the false self so the true self God created can rise. Liberation begins when you realize Heaven has already deposited something powerful within you ... and hell's greatest strategy is to keep you unaware of it.

Application
- Examine where your thinking may still be bound instead of free.
- Seek God today for truth that renews your mind and restores clarity.
- Walk boldly, knowing God has already placed power within you.

Prayer
Father, thank You for the freedom found in Your Son. Break every mental, emotional, and spiritual chain that limits my thinking. Help me walk in truth, authority, and purpose, fully awake to what You have already placed within me. In Jesus' name, **Amen.**

September 18
A Good Man Leaves an Inheritance
In Honor of Charles Potter

Proverbs 13:22
A good man leaves an inheritance to his children's children, but the wealth of the sinner is laid up for the righteous.

Reflection

When it says a "good man leaves an inheritance to his children's children", this isn't just about money or property.

It means the man who lives with wisdom, integrity, and faith builds something lasting ... not only for his children, but for his grandchildren. His legacy spans generations.

The contrast is clear: the sinner accumulates wealth, but it doesn't settle with his heirs; it "is laid up for the righteous." In other words, the one who lives well invests not only in his season ... but in seasons to come.

What sort of "inheritance" are you building? Is it material only ... or does it include values, faith, character, and purpose? The real treasure isn't what you leave ... it's who you are when you leave it.

A good man's greatest inheritance is not what he owns, but what he passes on. Long after possessions fade, faith, character, and wisdom continue to speak across generations. That is the legacy that truly honors a life well lived.

Application
- Ask yourself: What inheritance am I building ...only for my children, or for my grandchildren too?
- Choose one value you'll invest today that won't vanish with time ... honesty, generosity, love, faith.
- Declare: "I will live not just for my season, but for the generations to come."

Prayer
Father, thank You for the promise and power of legacy through You. Help me to live wisely, to walk faithfully, and to build an inheritance that lasts ... spiritually and materially. May what I leave behind bless generations, point to You, and reflect Your goodness. In Jesus' name, **Amen.**

September 19
Purpose Is the Impact You Leave

1 Peter 4:10–11
As each one has received a special gift, employ it in serving one another… so that in all things God may be glorified through Jesus Christ.

Reflection
"Your purpose is not what you do … it's what happens to people when you do what you do." — Unknown

Purpose was never about job titles, degrees, or positions. It has always been about impact. Anyone can perform a task, but only a purpose driven person can shift an atmosphere.

Your gift is the vehicle, but your impact is the evidence. It is the healed heart after the conversation. It is the clarity someone gains through your guidance. It is the strength someone finds because you showed up with faith, love, and excellence.

Purpose is the echo you leave in someone's life long after the moment has passed. Do not just do what you do; do it with intention, with the Spirit, and with the awareness that God uses you as a catalyst for transformation.

Your assignment is bigger than your activity. Your calling is bigger than your career. Your purpose is the change created each time you show up as who God called you to be.

Purpose is fulfilled when your life points others to God. When you serve with the gifts He has given you, lives are changed and God is glorified. Don't measure your purpose by position or productivity … measure it by the impact of love, truth, and transformation you leave behind.

Application
- Consider how your daily actions are impacting others.
- Approach your work today with intention and spiritual awareness.
- Allow God to use you as an instrument of transformation.

Prayer
Father, thank You for calling me to a purpose greater than a position. Help me live with intention and love so that my life reflects Your light. Use my words, actions, and presence to bring healing, clarity, and transformation to others. In Jesus' name, **Amen.**

September 20
The Eyes, Ears, and Heart of Christ

Galatians 6:2
Bear one another's burdens, and thereby fulfill the law of Christ.

Reflection
Alfred Adler captured the essence of empathy when he said: "Seeing others with the eyes of another, listening with the ears of another, and feeling with the heart of another."

Empathy is more than sympathy. Sympathy acknowledges pain, but empathy steps into it. It is a Christlike quality ... Jesus didn't just observe our struggles; He entered into them. He saw the world through our eyes, heard our cries, and felt our deepest sorrows. On the cross, He bore not only our sin but also our pain, grief, and loneliness.

To live empathetically is to allow the Spirit of Christ to reshape how we perceive others. It means slowing down long enough to see the invisible, to hear the unheard, and to feel what others feel. This isn't weakness; it's Kingdom strength. It builds bridges, heals wounds, and fulfills the law of love.

When you choose to carry even a portion of someone else's weight, you reflect the heart of Christ. Empathy turns compassion into movement and love into healing. In bearing one another's burdens, you don't just help others ... you fulfill the very law of Christ.

Empathy is love in action ... the heartbeat of Christ expressed through us.

Application
- Pause today and ask: Am I really listening to those around me? Or am I rushing to speak?
- Pray that God would give you "eyes to see and ears to hear" (Matthew 13:16) the needs of others.
- Look for one opportunity today to practice empathy ... whether it's a coworker, family member, patient, or stranger.

Prayer
Father, open my eyes to see others as You see them. Open my ears to truly hear their cries. Open my heart to feel their joys and sorrows. Help me bear the burdens of my brothers and sisters so that Your love may flow through me. May I walk in the footsteps of Jesus, who carried our pain and gave us His peace. In His name I pray, **Amen.**

September 21
Live Together or Perish Together

1 John 4:7–8
Beloved, let us love one another, for love is from God; and everyone who loves has been born of God and knows God. The one who does not love does not know God, because God is love.

Reflection
Dr. Martin Luther King Jr. once said, "We must learn to live together as brothers or perish together as fools." His words echo the truth of Scripture: love is not an option for believers, it is the foundation of our life in Christ.

Division, hatred, and pride destroy communities, families, and nations. Satan thrives where there is strife, but God's Spirit moves where there is unity. The Bible reminds us that when brothers dwell together in unity, it is "like the dew of Hermon" and there the Lord commands His blessing (Psalm 133).

Living together as brothers and sisters does not mean uniformity, but it does mean humility, forgiveness, and the willingness to prefer others above ourselves. If we reject that call, we risk perishing as fools … lost in selfishness, blinded by pride, and cut off from the blessings of God.

When we choose love, we choose life. Unity is not a suggestion … it is the atmosphere where God's presence rests and His blessings flow. If we are to reflect the heart of Christ, we must lay down pride, embrace one another with grace, and walk together as true brothers and sisters. For in loving one another, we do not simply avoid perishing … we reveal God to a world desperate for Him.

Application
- Examine your relationships: are there grudges, offenses, or divisions that need to be reconciled?
- Remember that your brother or sister in Christ is not your enemy. The true enemy is Satan, who seeks to divide.
- Make one intentional act of unity today: a phone call, a prayer, an apology, or an encouraging word.

Prayer
Father, forgive me for the times I have allowed pride, anger, or selfishness to divide me from my brothers and sisters. Teach me to love as You love, to forgive as You forgive, and to walk in unity as a testimony of Your kingdom on earth. May my life reflect the truth that we are one family in Christ. In Jesus' name, **Amen.**

September 22
Letting Go of Being Right

Philippians 4:6-7
Do not be anxious about anything, but in every situation, by prayer and petition, with thanksgiving, present your requests to God. And the peace of God, which transcends all understanding, will guard your hearts and your minds in Christ Jesus.

Reflection
Investing time in proving you're right can quietly cost you what matters most. It shifts your focus from preserving peace to winning an argument, often leaving relationships strained, emotions drained, and spiritual clarity diminished.

Not every disagreement needs your defense, and not every misunderstanding requires correction. Wisdom is shown in discernment ... knowing when to speak and when to let go. Sometimes strength looks like restraint, not response.

Inner peace is a divine gift that must be protected. When we insist on being right, we may gain a momentary victory but lose joy, focus, and alignment with what truly matters. True wisdom chooses peace over pride and purpose over persuasion.

Let God's peace matter more than proving your point. When you release the need to win, you create space for the Holy Spirit to guard your heart and mind. Choose peace over pride, and you'll find yourself standing firmly in what truly lasts.

Application
- Before responding, ask if speaking will bring peace or simply prove a point.
- Choose to release one argument today in order to protect your inner peace.
- Redirect your energy toward what builds relationships and honors God.

Prayer
Father, I confess how often I cling to being right instead of seeking peace. Help me to surrender that need. Teach me to protect my soul, to grow through tension, and to speak from love. Grant me the wisdom to know when to let go ... and the courage to do it. In Jesus' name, **Amen.**

September 23
Freedom Ain't There

2 Corinthians 3:17
Now the Lord is the Spirit, and where the Spirit of the Lord is, there is liberty.

Reflection
Freedom ain't there. It's not in the money, the fame, or the power. It's not found in relationships, possessions, or fleeting pleasures. Many chase these things hoping to find liberty, but they only discover new chains ... chains of debt, addiction, pride, or brokenness.

Real freedom cannot be bought, earned, or manufactured by the world. Real freedom is the alignment of spirit, soul, and body under the Lordship of Christ. When your spirit is alive in Him, your soul is at rest, and your body follows in obedience.

Jesus declared that freedom is not found in "things" but in truth. And that truth is found in Him. He alone breaks the chains of sin, heals the wounds of the soul, and restores the body for His glory. Anything less will leave you searching in empty wells that cannot satisfy.

True freedom is not a destination you chase ... it's a Presence you carry. Wherever the Spirit of the Lord is welcomed, chains lose their grip, lies lose their power, and old bondages lose their authority. The world can offer thrills, but only Christ offers liberty. When you let His Spirit rule your inner life, the freedom you've been searching for on the outside begins to rise from within.

Freedom ain't out there ... it's in Him, and when He dwells in you, you are free indeed.

Application
- Identify one area where you've been seeking freedom in "things" rather than in Christ, and surrender it to Him in prayer today.
- Spend time in the Word daily, letting truth align your spirit, soul, and body.
- Ask God to show you what true freedom looks like in your life ... not defined by what you have, but by who you are in Him.

Prayer
Lord, remind me daily that freedom isn't in money, fame, power, or pleasure. Freedom is in You alone. Align my spirit, soul, and body under Your truth, so I may walk in the liberty that Christ purchased for me. Help me live as one truly free, bearing witness to Your glory. In Jesus' name, **Amen.**

September 24
The Equation of Divine Alignment

Ephesians 4:23–24
...and that you be renewed in the spirit of your mind, and put on the new self, which in the likeness of God has been created in righteousness and holiness of the truth.

Reflection
Like I stated before, true success is never an accident, and God's blessings are not coincidences ... they flow naturally when your inner life aligns with His divine design. When God shapes us inwardly, our outward actions align with His righteousness ...and through that alignment, His blessings naturally flow.

God doesn't reward religious performance ... He honors internal transformation. When your mind is renewed, your heart refined, your character centered on Christ, your life's equation adds up to Kingdom impact. Blessings aren't just outcomes; they are the result of living in step with God's truth and power.

Divine alignment is not something you chase ... it is something you become. When your mind is renewed by truth and your heart is anchored in Christ, your life begins to reflect God's will naturally and consistently. You stop striving for blessings and start walking in obedience, and in that obedience, favor follows.
As your thinking changes, your choices shift. As your character aligns with Christ, your actions produce Kingdom fruit. This is the equation of divine alignment ... a renewed mind, a surrendered heart, and a life lived in step with God's will.

Application
- Evaluate your daily routines and thoughts ... are they shaping outward actions or reflecting divine transformation?
- Commit your inner life to the Spirit's renewal: "Lord, transform me from the inside out."
- Notice how your relationships, service, and opportunities begin to reflect His blessings organically.

Prayer
Father, reshape my heart and mind by Your Spirit so that my life reflects Your righteousness. Let Your blessings flow ... not because I've earned them with performance ... but because You've transformed me from within. Teach me to live the equation of divine alignment. In Jesus' name, **Amen.**

September 25
Don't Open the Door

Galatians 5:19–21
Now the deeds of the flesh are evident, which are: immorality, impurity, sensuality, idolatry, sorcery, enmities, strife, jealousy, outbursts of anger, disputes, dissensions, factions, envying, drunkenness, carousing, and things like these, of which I forewarn you, just as I have forewarned you, that those who practice such things will not inherit the kingdom of God.

Reflection
Just like in the movie Sinners, the enemy has no authority over you unless you invite him in. Sin is that invitation. It cracks the door for Satan to step into your life and wreak havoc. What begins as a small compromise often grows into a stronghold that separates you from the peace and fellowship of God.

Sin never produces life. It always produces death ... death to peace, death to joy, and separation from the presence of God. The enemy's strategy has not changed since the Garden: temptation, invitation, destruction. But through Christ, you are no longer a slave to sin. His Spirit empowers you to say no to the deeds of the flesh and yes to righteousness.

When you refuse to open the door to sin, you close the door to the enemy's influence. The fruit of sin is pain and punishment, but the fruit of the Spirit is peace and freedom. God doesn't just call you to avoid sin ... He calls you to abide in Him, so His presence fills the places where sin used to reign.

Application
- Identify one area where temptation tries to "knock" on your heart's door and surrender it to God in prayer today.
- Replace sinful invitations with godly ones ... invite the Holy Spirit in through worship, scripture, or prayer before the enemy has a chance.
- Remember: every choice is either an open door for peace or an open door for pain ... choose to walk in the Spirit.

Prayer
Lord, I thank You that the devil has no power over me unless I give it to him. Help me to guard the doors of my heart and mind, to resist the invitations of sin, and to invite Your Spirit in daily. Fill me with Your peace, and let my life bear the fruit of righteousness. In Jesus' name, **Amen.**

September 26
The Blessing of Being a Blessing

Acts 20:35
In everything I showed you that by working hard in this manner you must help the weak and remember the words of the Lord Jesus, that He Himself said, 'It is more blessed to give than to receive.

Reflection
On September 26th, 2025, I went into Ramsey #2 Prison with Jubilee Ministries to minister, pray, preach, and teach the inmates. My intention was to pour into them, to give encouragement, and to be a vessel of hope. Yet in the mystery of God's economy, I received more than I gave.

The men were alert and receptive to every word, every prayer, and every encouragement. Their hunger for truth and openness to God's Spirit reminded me that ministry is never one directional. When we give, God often multiplies the return back into our own souls.

Every time we step out to bless others, God steps in to bless us in ways we never expect. What we give away in love, compassion, and service does not diminish us ... it enlarges us. At Ramsey #2, I thought I was going to pour out, but God used those men to pour back into me. This is the divine exchange of the Kingdom: when you become a blessing, you step into the flow of God's own heart. And in that flow, you discover that the greatest gift is not what you give or what you receive ... it's who you become in the process

The Kingdom of God runs on this paradox: in giving, we receive; in serving, we are strengthened; in pouring out, we are filled. What was meant to be a blessing for others became an even greater blessing to me. Truly, it is more blessed to give than to receive.

Application
- Look for opportunities today to give your time, prayer, or encouragement.
- Remember: when you bless others, you position yourself to be blessed.
- Keep your heart open: often the people you seek to help will minister to you in unexpected ways.

Prayer
Lord, thank You for reminding me that giving is never loss in Your Kingdom. Thank You for the brothers at Ramsey Prison, whose faith and openness ministered to me as much as I ministered to them. Teach me to live with a giving spirit, trusting that You will always return more than I release. In Jesus' name, **Amen.**

September 27
Washed Away

Psalm 103:12
As far as the east is from the west, so far has He removed our wrongdoings from us.

Reflection
On September 27th, 2025, I had the opportunity to facilitate a forgiveness ceremony at Ramsey #2 Prison in Rosharon, Texas. What a glorious day it was!

The inmates were invited to write down all the sins they needed forgiveness for and the names of those they needed to forgive. Then, they placed those papers into a bowl of water and watched as the words dissolved and disappeared. In that simple but powerful act, they saw a picture of God's mercy ... sins washed away, offenses removed, and burdens lifted.
That day was not just symbolic. Men gave their lives to Christ and others rededicated themselves to Him. Forgiveness broke chains that iron bars never could. It was living proof that when we let go of what weighs us down, God sets us free.

Forgiveness is Heaven's cleansing river ... when we release what has held us, God removes what once defined us. What happened at Ramsey #2 was more than a ceremony; it was a resurrection. In that room, guilt lost its grip, shame lost its voice, and grace rewrote stories in real time. The same God who washed their papers clean is the God who washes our souls clean. When we surrender the past, He separates us from our sins as far as east is from west and opens the door to a freedom no prison can contain.

Application
- Take time today to write down the sins you need God to forgive and the names of those you need to forgive. Then destroy the paper as a reminder that Christ has already washed it away.
- Remember: forgiveness is freedom ... for yourself and for others.
- Keep short accounts with God and people. Don't carry what He's already removed.

Prayer
Father, thank You for the cleansing power of forgiveness. Thank You that in Christ, my sins are dissolved and remembered no more. Give me the courage to release others from the debts I've been holding onto. May my life be a testimony that true freedom comes through forgiveness. In Jesus' name, **Amen.**

September 28
Free Behind Bars
This is a dedication to Ramsey #2 Unit in Rosharon Texas
(Jubilee Ministry Sept 26-28, 2025)

John 8:36
So if the Son makes you free, you will be free indeed.

Reflection
There are many people physically imprisoned by the judicial system in the United States and across the world. Yet the real truth is this: even more people live imprisoned outside of the judicial system.

There are walls built in the mind ... strongholds of fear, shame, addiction, bitterness, and unbelief ...that prevent countless souls from experiencing real freedom and lasting peace. Some men and women physically locked behind penitentiary walls have found more freedom in Christ than those walking freely on the streets every day.
True freedom is not measured by where your feet can travel but by where your soul can rest. It is possible to be "outside" and still be bound, and it is possible to be "inside" and yet live free. Freedom comes only through Christ, who breaks the chains no earthly judge can see.

Freedom is not defined by steel doors, razor wire, or court sentences ... it is defined by the presence of Jesus Christ. At Ramsey #2, I witnessed men who the world calls "inmates" stand taller in spiritual freedom than many who walk unshackled in society. Their chains fell not because their circumstances changed, but because Christ stepped into their cell and claimed their hearts. This dedication is a reminder to every soul ... inside or outside prison walls ...that true liberation is found only in the One who breaks invisible chains.

Application
- Examine your own life: Are there invisible chains still holding you captive?
- Pray for God to tear down mental strongholds and renew your mind with His truth.
- Remember: freedom is not found in a place, but in a Person ... Jesus Christ.

Prayer
Lord, I thank You that true freedom comes from You alone. Tear down every wall in my mind that keeps me bound. Break the chains of fear, bitterness, and shame. Help me to walk in the freedom that Christ purchased for me, no matter where I am. In Jesus' name, **Amen.**

September 29
Stay Light So You Can Take Flight

Hebrews 12:1
Let us throw off everything that hinders and the sin that so easily entangles, and let us run with perseverance the race marked out for us.

Reflection
"Stay Light So You Can Take Flight" is one of my signature quotes from my spiritual clothing line at www.*blasé One.com*. It carries a double meaning ... stay light in weight and stay light in brightness ...because both are tied to the spiritual weight you permit to rest on your soul.

Spiritual heaviness dims your glow. Emotional weight hinders your lift. Burdens like sin, guilt, shame, fear, and doubt don't just slow you down; they ground you.

To stay light is to live unburdened, refusing to let yesterday's clouds steal today's sunshine. When we cast off what entangles us, we rise into who God created us to be ... bold, bright, and free. Just as a lamp was never designed to be hidden, neither were we meant to walk around dimmed by invisible weights. Our calling is not just to survive life's journey, but to illuminate it ... to reflect the brilliance of the Son everywhere we go.

Anything that entangles your soul will eventually entangle your purpose. But the same Spirit who came "to set the captives free" still lifts hearts, breaks chains, and restores brightness. When you release what weighs you down, God releases what lifts you up. Stay light ...so you can take flight.

Application
- Reflect: What spiritual weight ... sin, shame, anxiety ... is holding you down today?
- Act: Confess and repent, asking, "Lord, free me from this."
- Declare: "I am light. I choose to stay free. I refuse every chain."

Prayer
Heavenly Father, strip me of all weights that hinder my spiritual flight ... sin, fear, regret, shame. Revive my spirit with Your light. Help me walk freely, shining brightly as Your reflection. May my life illuminate the path for others and glorify You. In Jesus' name, **Amen.**

September 30
Disciplined Growth

Hebrews 12:11
No discipline seems pleasant at the time, but painful. Later on, however, it produces a harvest of righteousness and peace for those who have been trained by it.

Reflection
Many of us grew up in environments marked by struggle, scarcity, and survival. And because of that history, we naturally want to shield our children from the pain we endured. We want to give them comfort, convenience, and opportunity. But here's the problem: in trying to remove every difficulty, we may also remove their development. You can give so much that you unintentionally take away the very things God wants to use to grow them.

Hebrews 12:11 tells us plainly … discipline isn't pleasant. Nobody shouts "hallelujah" when God pulls the belt out. Discipline doesn't feel good, but it does us good. God uses discipline to produce righteousness and peace … to shape our character, strengthen our faith, and grow us into spiritual maturity. See, discipline is the divinely designed tool that God uses to develop His children.
God loves us too much to let us stay weak. He will allow hardship, not to hurt you, but to help you. Not to destroy you, but to develop you. Because God knows what we often forget: comfort rarely creates character. Ease doesn't produce endurance. Convenience never cultivates conviction. Growth comes when we face the hard things, not when we avoid them.
The struggles you push through become the strength you walk in. The pain you endure becomes the platform God stands on. And the discipline you embrace today becomes the fruit you enjoy tomorrow.

Application
- Identify one area where you've avoided necessary struggle … whether for yourself or your child.
- Choose to embrace discipline instead of rescuing from discomfort.
- Ask God for wisdom and strength to grow through the hard, not around it.

Prayer
Father, thank You that You see the long view. Forgive me when I've tried to spare my children, or myself, every difficulty, thinking comfort was best. Help me choose the "hard" that builds character, integrity, and godly peace. Teach me to embrace discipline … even when it hurts … because I know You work through it for my good. May my choices today, even the difficult ones, yield a harvest of righteousness and peace. In Jesus' name, **Amen.**

October 1
The Hard That Builds

Hebrews 12:11
Now no chastening seems joyful at the time, but painful. Later on, however, it yields the peaceful fruit of righteousness to those who are exercised by it.

Reflection
Life isn't going to be easy; we all have a "hard" to choose. The difference is which hard will we bear ... the hard that destroys, or the hard that builds.

Marriage is hard. So is divorce. Being obese is hard. So is being fit. Being in debt is hard. Being disciplined with money is hard. You're going to face hardship either way; the question is what kind. One is temporary pain with negative consequences; the other is temporary discipline with long-term gain.

Hebrews 12:11 reminds us that discipline ... though painful ... produces something far better: righteousness and peace. Proverbs says a person without self-control is like a city with no barriers ... easy to overrun. And Proverbs 4:5 calls us to choose wisdom and understanding and hold fast to truth.

So when you're faced with two "hard paths," ask: Which hard leads to growth? Which hard lines up with God's truth and purpose? Choose the hard that builds strength, character, peace, and maturity ... not just what feels easier in the moment.

Application
- Think of an area in your life where you're avoiding "hard" (finances, relationships, health, discipline).
- Decide which "hard" you're willing to accept now that yields long-term benefit (e.g. discipline instead of comfort, serving instead of being served, patience instead of instant gratification).
- Use Scripture to remind you when the hard gets heavy. Meditate on Hebrews 12:11 and Proverbs 25:28.

Prayer
Father, thank You for reminding me that every path has its challenges. Give me wisdom to choose the hard that builds me up rather than tears me down. Help me to endure discomfort when needed, to exercise self-control when it's tough, and to lean into discipline over ease. Strengthen my resolve to walk the path of growth, not just comfort. In Jesus' name, **Amen**.

October 2
Don't Lose Your Soul Chasing The Gold

Mark 8:36
For what shall it profit a man, if he shall gain the whole world, and lose his own soul?

Reflection
We live in a culture addicted to "more" … more money, more accolades, more comfort, more success. Many believe the more we accumulate, the more satisfied we'll be. But Jesus warns that "gaining the whole world" means nothing if it costs us our soul.

The soul is your eternal essence … your character, purpose, relationship with God. It's what lasts. The world is fleeting. All the glory, all the trophies, all the wealth … if they are pursued above God, they are slipping sand beneath your feet.

True life isn't measured by what you possess, but by what possesses you … what motivates you, what you treasure, what you live for. When your chase is for gold above God, you risk losing your way … and yourself. But when your life is anchored in Christ, rooted in eternal values, even material blessings serve a greater purpose rather than being a trap.

As C.S. Lewis once said, "Aim at heaven and you will get earth thrown in. Aim at earth and you will get neither." Don't lose your soul chasing what won't last. When God is your treasure, nothing in this world can bankrupt you.

Application
- Evaluate your priorities. What are you pursuing above all else …. wealth, status, comfort?
- Ask: If I gained everything I want today, would I still be close to God?
- Realign your goals. Shift from "God bless my plans" to "God shape my priorities."

Prayer
Father, forgive me when I've let the pursuit of gain overshadow the preservation of my soul. Show me what I treasure more than You. Help me keep my eyes fixed on eternity, not the temporal. Let my life be a testimony that success rooted in You doesn't cost me my soul … but enriches it. In Jesus' name, **Amen.**

October 3
Beyond the Classroom

Colossians 2:2-3 (NIV)
2 My goal is that they may be encouraged in heart and united in love, so that they may have the full riches of complete understanding, in order that they may know the mystery of God, namely, Christ, 3 in whom are hidden all the treasures of wisdom and knowledge.

Reflection
Mark Twain once said: "I have never let my schooling interfere with my education." That's profound.

Formal education, degrees, and grades are valuable ... but they don't guarantee wisdom, character, or spiritual growth. Real education often comes self seeking outside the classroom: even through failure, relationships, hardships, observation, and moments when you simply have to discern what is true.

Proverbs tells us that true knowledge begins with revering God. When wisdom is pursued with humility, understanding follows. And Colossians reminds us that in Christ are hidden treasures of wisdom and knowledge ... things no classroom can fully teach.

So your education is more than what your transcript shows. Your richer lessons could be in your mistakes, in seasons of waiting, in grief and triumph, in seeking, in listening, in loving, in failing, and getting back up.

Application
- Reflect: What is one lesson life has taught you recently that no class ever could?
- Seek wisdom daily: read Scripture, listen to God, ask questions, stay curious.
- Value character over credentials. Let God grow in you what can't be stamped or graded: humility, compassion, resilience.

Prayer
Father, thank You for lessons that go beyond the classroom. Help me to see Your teaching in every season of my life ... through success, failure, joy, sorrow. Teach me to pursue wisdom and understanding above grades, recognition, and approval. May my life reflect depth, character, and spiritual maturity. In Jesus' name, **Amen.**

October 4
Saved, But Still in Chains

Isaiah 58:6
Is this not the fast which I choose, To loosen the bonds of wickedness, To undo the bands of the yoke, To let the oppressed go free, And break every yoke?

Reflection
It's possible to be saved but not delivered. To be forgiven, yet still bound. To confess Christ with your lips, but still walk daily in cycles of sin, addiction, anger, pride, or generational chains.

For a season of my life, I was that lost man ... saved, but not sanctified. I thank God daily for His patience, for His Spirit's persistence, for His mercy that waited on me.

Salvation is the door, but deliverance is the journey. Sanctification ... the process of being made holy ... is what separates us from who we were and molds us into who God called us to be. And it's not just about us. Our sons, daughters, nephews, nieces, students ... all are watching. The patterns we refuse to break, they may inherit. But the deliverance we walk in, they can also inherit.

God desires not just to save you but to set you free ... free from every yoke, every curse, every chain. He is patient, but tomorrow is not promised. The time to surrender is now.

Application
- Identify one area in your life where you're saved but still bound ... something you know doesn't align with God's will.
- Fast and pray (Isaiah 58:6). Ask God to loosen the bonds and break the yokes in your life.
- Seek accountability. Share your struggle with a trusted brother or sister in Christ who can walk with you.

Prayer
Father, thank You for saving me. But Lord, I don't want to just be saved ... I want to be delivered. I want to be sanctified. Break the chains in my life that keep me bound. Destroy every generational curse, every hidden sin, every yoke that hinders me from walking fully in Your freedom. Use me as a vessel to show my children, my family, and my community that Your deliverance is real. In Jesus' name, **Amen.**

October 5
The Enemy Inside

2 Corinthians 10:3–5
For though we walk in the flesh, we do not wage battle according to the flesh, for the weapons of our warfare are not of the flesh, but divinely powerful for the destruction of fortresses. We are destroying arguments and all arrogance raised against the knowledge of God, and we are taking every thought captive to the obedience of Christ.

Reflection
Many times, the greatest enemy we face isn't external ... it's internal. While we watch for the threats outside the gate, we often ignore the battles raging within our own walls. Jealousy, pride, division, bitterness, and un-forgiveness destroy us from the inside out before oppression even reaches our door.

History reminds us of the weight of systemic injustice, but Scripture reminds us that bondage also begins in the heart. We cannot heal if we keep tearing each other down. We cannot build if envy and strife are still our architects. We cannot demand freedom if we remain chained by sin, un-forgiveness, or self sabotage.

True revolution begins in the mirror. Before we can transform systems, we must allow God to transform our souls. Victory is not just in changing laws but in changing lives. And freedom is not just escaping oppression but breaking every internal chain that keeps us from living as the royalty God declared us to be.

Application
- Today, examine your own heart. Ask: Am I building or breaking? Healing or harming? Uniting or dividing?
- Choose one area of inner struggle (jealousy, bitterness, pride, comparison, un-forgiveness) and surrender it to God in prayer.
- Remember: you can't conquer the enemy outside until you first overcome the enemy within.

Prayer
Father, open my eyes to the battles within me. Show me the places where I've been my own worst enemy ... through pride, envy, bitterness, or fear. Teach me to walk in healing, unity, and love so that my life reflects the freedom Christ died to give me. May my revolution begin in the mirror, and may Your Spirit make me whole from the inside out. In Jesus' name, **Amen.**

October 6
Blessed to Be a Blessing

Luke 6:38
Give, and it will be given to you. They will pour into your lap a good measure ... pressed down, shaken together, and running over. For by your standard of measure it will be measured to you in return.

Reflection
Every blessing that finds its way into our hands ... every resource, every opportunity, every open door, every encouragement ... carries an assignment attached to it. God never blesses us to build dams; He blesses us to build rivers. What flows to us is meant to flow through us. When we refresh others ... through a kind word that lifts their spirit, a listening ear that reminds them they matter, a prayer that strengthens their soul, or a gift that meets a need ... we step into God's divine cycle of blessing. Our generosity becomes a mirror of His heart, reflecting His goodness into the world. Like a lamp that refuses to hide beneath a basket, our joy and our giving illuminate more than our own path ... they spark fire in someone else's darkness.

But here's the mystery of the Kingdom: giving is not loss. It is multiplication. It is not subtraction; it is sowing. Scripture makes it clear ... when we water others, God Himself becomes the One who waters us. He pours back into our laps, "pressed down, shaken together, and running over," exceeding what we released. The measure we pour out becomes the measure He pours back in.Refreshing others isn't just a duty ... it's divine reciprocity. It's God allowing us to participate in His nature, His generosity, and His abundance. Blessings do not grow when we clutch them ... they grow when we give them away.

This is the Kingdom rhythm: Give freely. Love boldly. Sow generously ... and watch God multiply what you release.

Application
- Reflect: Who can I refresh today ... spiritually, emotionally, or practically?
- Act: Send an encouraging message or perform a small act of kindness with each encounter.
- Declare: "Blessed to be a blessing ... I sow refreshment into others today."

Prayer
Heavenly Father, thank You for refreshing me with Your love and grace. Teach me to pour out what I've received ... comfort, kindness, hope ... so that others might be encouraged through me. May Your blessings multiply through every generous gesture. In Jesus' name, **Amen.**

October 7
Spiritually Intelligent

1 Corinthians 2:14
But a natural man does not accept the things of the Spirit of God, for they are foolishness to him; and he cannot understand them, because they are spiritually appraised.

Reflection
Spiritually intelligent people don't just hear with their ears; they discern with their hearts. They feel what's not said. They sense what's not shown. They protect their peace like it's sacred ... because it is.

True growth means choosing healing over hiding, alignment over unhealthy attachment, and purpose over pain. This requires discernment ... a Spirit-led sensitivity to what God is saying beneath the noise of life. In order to comprehend spiritual things, you must be spirit filled.

The natural mind can't grasp this. To the world, protecting peace looks weak, releasing attachments looks foolish, prioritizing purpose over pain looks unrealistic. But the Spirit reveals truth beyond appearances. But the Spirit reveals truth beyond what audible. To walk in discernment is to live Spirit-first, not our five senses first. It's to value inner alignment with God over external approval.

Spiritual intelligence is not about being clever; it's about being connected. Connected to God's Spirit. Guided by His whisper. Rooted in His peace.

Application
- Start your day with quiet: ask God for discernment, not just information.
- Before reacting, pause and ask: "What is God revealing beneath the surface here?"
- Protect your peace by setting boundaries where your spirit feels drained.

Prayer
Father, thank You for the gift of discernment. Teach me to live spiritually intelligent ... not swayed by noise or appearances, but led by Your Spirit. Help me protect the peace You've given me, and choose healing, alignment, and purpose over pain. Make me sensitive to what You are saying in every season, and keep my heart rooted in You. In Jesus' name, **Amen.**

October 8
A Temple Divided Cannot Stand

1 Corinthians 3:16
Do you not know that you are a temple of God and that the Spirit of God dwells in you?

Reflection
You are not just flesh and bone ... you are a temple.

God designed you to be a dwelling place of His Spirit, a house of prayer, peace, and power. But a divided temple cannot stand. When fear replaces faith, or when idols rise to rule the heart, cracks begin to form. Anxiety steals peace, sin steals clarity and fellowship ... and soon the temple weakens from within.

The enemy doesn't always need to storm the gates of your life ... he only needs to divide your inner walls. A double-minded heart, a distracted soul, or a spirit swayed by vanity creates disunity where God designed wholeness, fellowship and unity with Him. Jesus warned that a house divided against itself will fall. The same truth applies to your life as God's temple.

Yet there is hope ... grace is a healing balm. Christ restores what is broken and unites what is divided. The Spirit brings peace to anxious thoughts, healing to weary hearts, and wholeness to fractured souls. The key is alignment: bringing your mind, body, and spirit under the authority of Heaven's plan. Confess and repent...and come back into fellowship with God.

Application
- Take a quiet moment to examine your inner temple: What thoughts, fears, or idols may be causing division in your spirit?
- Write down one area of inner conflict and surrender it in prayer to God.
- Commit to daily practices (prayer, Scripture, worship) that align your soul with God's truth, strengthening the unity of your temple.

Prayer
Father, I thank You that I am Your temple and that Your Spirit dwells within me. Forgive me for the ways I have allowed fear, doubt, or idols to create division in my heart. Heal the cracks within me. Align my soul with Your truth, and let Your peace guard my mind and spirit. May my life stand strong as a whole and holy temple that brings glory to You. In Jesus' name, **Amen.**

October 9
The Point of No Return

Genesis 19:17
As soon as they had brought them outside, one of them said, 'Escape for your life! Do not look behind you, and do not stay anywhere in the plain; escape to the mountains, or you will be swept away!

Reflection
There comes a moment many of us face ... a breaking point when we realize that staying where we are is no longer an option. Whether it's staying in a relationship, a mindset that suffocates, a habit that drains life, or a fear that shrinks your spirit ... the familiar "safe" place can feel like a prison. You might think you can manage, that you'll hold on forever ... but something inside finally cracks, and you recognize: this is not living ...I'm dying inside. It's not a call to triumph or a flashy victory. It's about honoring the life God has given you and choosing not to let the brokenness win. That moment ... when hope outweighs comfort, and your soul won't settle for less ... that is your point of no return. You leap not because you're sure you'll soar, but because you're sure you must go or let go ... or your soul won't ever breathe again.
As Paulo Coelho wrote, "When you walk away from something that no longer grows you, you are not losing ... you're choosing." The point of no return is not a moment of defeat but a moment of destiny. It is the holy decision to stop looking back, to stop living small, and to stop surrendering your soul to what was. When God calls you out, it's because there is nothing left for you behind ... only ahead. Step into the mountain of your becoming, because forward is the only direction where your freedom, your healing, and your future can live.

Application
- Reflect on your life right now: is there an area where you've been holding on out of familiarity or fear ... even though it's killing your joy?
- Name it clearly ... don't just sense the pain; identify what you need to "leap" away from.
- Pray for the courage to take that leap, trusting God to meet you on the other side and breathe new life into your spirit.

Prayer
Father, I recognize the place I'm in ... familiar, but suffocating. Grant me the courage to say "no more," even when I can't see the whole path ahead. Help me to lean not on my own strength, but on Yours. If staying here is death, let me step into life. Teach me to trust Your promise that every leap of faith becomes a foothold for new freedom. In Jesus' name, **Amen.**

October 10
Peace Through Righteousness

Isaiah 48:22
There is no peace," says the Lord, "for the wicked.

Reflection
Let me let you in on a little secret that's in the Bible: there is no peace apart from righteousness.

No matter how much success, noise, or music surrounds you your life; real peace is reserved for those who walk in right standing with God. In God's eyes all sin is considered wickedness… there is no gray area.

Isaiah 48:22 makes a bold statement: "There is no peace… unto the wicked." What does that mean? From what commentators say, the "wicked" are those who rebel against God … those in which the external may look fine, but inwardly there is disobedience, hardness, pride, or separation from God. Remember separation form God ultimately means separated from Peace.

The peace God defines isn't dependent on circumstances … wealth, acclaim, or applause … but on righteousness, obedience, and relationship with Him.

Without this alignment with God's ways, the soul remains restless: guilty conscience, dissatisfaction, fear, or shame may lurk beneath the surface. The wicked may have moments of rest, but not the abiding peace that comes only from walking with God.

Application
- Examine your life: are there areas where you've said you follow God, but your actions or heart are out of alignment?
- Choose one area of disobedience or pride to bring before God. Confess, repent, and align your steps with His truth.
- Let your peace not be based on what you have or what you achieve, but on whether your heart is right with God.

Prayer
Father, thank You for Your truth. Forgive me when I've sought peace in externals … money, comfort, praise … while neglecting my walk with You. Help me to live in righteousness, to obey Your Word, and stay rooted in Your presence. Let my heart be aligned with Your will so that I might walk in the peace that only You provide. In Jesus' name, **Amen.**

October 11
The Mirror That Demands Change

James 1:23-24
23 For if anyone is a hearer of the word and not a doer, he is like a man who looks at his natural face in a mirror; 24 for once he has looked at himself and gone away, he has immediately forgotten what kind of person he was.

Reflection
Many spend their days staring out the window ... judging others, comparing lives, and pointing fingers. Yet we often walk past the mirror and refuse to see ourselves as we truly are. James exposes this spiritual contradiction: hearing God's Word is like looking in a mirror ... seeking ourselves clear and honestly. But if we walk away unchanged, we forfeit the power that reflection was meant to bring.

Seeing flaws without correction is empty religion. Knowing truth without living it is spiritual self deception. God's Word doesn't just illuminate ... it demands transformation. Only when we put the Word into action ... cleaning what's dirty, correcting what's crooked, surrendering what's stubborn ... do we begin to reflect Christ's image. The danger is that we can become experts at analyzing others while ignoring the logs in our own eyes. But God calls us higher: to look honestly, respond humbly, and act obediently.

Real growth begins the moment the mirror stops being a threat and becomes an invitation. Don't turn away from what God reveals ... step into it. For it is not the glance that changes you, but the obedience that follows.

Application
- Pause ... Before judging someone today, ask: "What's God showing me about my own life?"
- Reflect ... Choose one area revealed by God's Word where you've gained conviction. Don't just glance ... look deeply.
- Act ... Take deliberate steps to remove that log ... repent, seek accountability, or surrender the area to God.

Prayer
Father, thank You for the mirror of Your Word that reveals truth in me. Forgive me for quick judgment of others while I ignore the logs in my own heart. Give me the courage to look honestly ... then obey what You show me. May I not just be a hearer, but a doer ... reflecting Your mercy, humility, and love. In Jesus' name, Amen

October 12
Kindness, Not Weakness

Romans 12:21
Do not be overcome by evil, but overcome evil with good.

Reflection
History has often misread kindness as weakness. Open hands were mistaken for emptiness; humility was exploited as if it meant inferiority. Yet true kindness is not the absence of strength ... it is the decision to utilize your strength differently.

From the generosity given of Africa's lands and wisdom, to the hospitality of the Aztecs, to the open hearts of native peoples ... nations lived in rhythm with creation and with one another. Yet their kindness was met with conquest, betrayal, and chains. Still, the witness of their story is this: kindness has never been weak. David showed King Saul this kind of kindness... even though Saul tried to kill him. David knew vengeance was the Lord's.

The Kingdom of God reveals the same truth. Jesus Himself was mocked as powerless when He refused to call down angels at His arrest, when He stayed silent before His accusers, when He stretched out His hands in surrender. But His humility was His victory, and His kindness became our salvation.

To choose mercy over vengeance, peace over violence, and love over fear is to walk in divine strength. Kindness is not weakness ... it is Kingdom power under control.

Application
- Today, choose one act of kindness where you could instead demand your own way.
- Reflect on how Jesus' humility brought freedom, and how your kindness can bring healing in places of brokenness.
- Respond to one situation today with kindness instead of asserting your way. Let humility guide your strength, just as Jesus did.

Prayer
Father, help me to see kindness the way You see it ... not as weakness but as strength wrapped in mercy. Teach me to lead with humility, to overcome evil with good, and to reflect the power of Christ who chose love over conquest. May my life tell the story that kindness is not weakness ... it is victory. In Jesus' name, **Amen.**

October 13
The Quiet Power of Knowing Who You Are

Colossians 3:3
For you have died, and your life is hidden with Christ in God."

Reflection
There's a quiet power in knowing who you are in Christ ... an unshakable strength that doesn't need to announce itself. When your identity is rooted in Him, you are no longer driven by the need to prove, perform, or be seen. You stop chasing every room, every opportunity, and every voice of validation because you understand something deeper ... your value was settled at the Cross. True confidence doesn't shout ... it simply stands, anchored in the One who defines you.

When you build within ... cultivating character, discipline, integrity, and faith ... you carry a presence that speaks louder than any platform or promotion. People feel the weight of someone whose soul is grounded in God. The world runs itself ragged trying to be noticed, applauded, or affirmed, but the child of God rests in assurance. Your gift may open doors, but it is your identity in Christ that keeps you standing in those rooms with grace, humility, and authority.

When you know who you are ... and whose you are ... you walk differently. You think differently. You choose differently. You no longer need to prove yourself ... you simply *express* the self Christ has formed in you. And in that quiet confidence, Heaven's authority becomes your strength, and your life becomes a living testimony of God's glory.

Application
- Spend 10 minutes today affirming your identity in Christ through Scripture (e.g., 1 Peter 2:9).
- Choose to walk in one space today without striving for recognition.
- Declare: "I am secure in Christ. My life speaks for itself."

Prayer
Father, thank You for the quiet strength of identity in You. Teach me not to chase rooms but to carry Your presence into every room. Let my inner life reflect Your Spirit so that who I am speaks louder than what I do. In Jesus' name, **Amen.**

October 14
The Origin of the Word Helper

Genesis 2:18
Then the Lord God said, 'It is not good for the man to be alone; I will make him a helper suitable for him.

Reflection
The word helper in Genesis is richer than our English ears may first hear. The Hebrew word is ʿēzer (עֵזֶר), rooted in ʿāzar (עָזַר), meaning to help, to support, to strengthen. This word appears 21 times in the Old Testament, and most often it describes God Himself: "My help comes from the Lord" (Psalm 121:2).

That truth changes everything. If God Himself is called ʿēzer, then the "helper" described in Genesis cannot mean weakness, subordination, or lesser value. Instead, it points to strength, partnership, and necessity. Eve was created not as an afterthought, but as an indispensable counterpart to Adam ... equal in worth, unique in function, designed to complement him.

The phrase ʿēzer kĕnegdô literally means "a help corresponding to him." It paints a picture of balance: one who stands face to face, adequate and sufficient, strengthening where the other is lacking. Just as God's help empowers His people to flourish, Eve's role was to empower Adam so that together they could fulfill God's mandate.

This means that in God's design, the role of "helper" is not about hierarchy ... it's about mutual strength and divine partnership. It is a reflection of God's own character in human relationships.

Application
- Honor the divine design of partnership by valuing strength, equality, and mutual support in your relationships.
- Recognize and celebrate the God-given gifts in others that complement your weaknesses and empower your purpose.
- Model God's character by becoming a source of help, strength, and encouragement to those connected to your calling.

Prayer
Lord, thank You for showing us that true help is strength, not weakness. Teach me to value the helpers You place in my life, and to be one who strengthens and supports others. May my relationships reflect Your heart of partnership, love, and mutual purpose. In Jesus' name, **Amen.**

October 15
Love Beyond Convenience

1 Corinthians 16:14
Let all that you do be done in love.

Reflection
Society teaches us to love for convenience ... when it's easy, comfortable, when feelings are strong, when gain is visible. But the Bible invites us into a higher love ... a love rooted in covenant, self sacrifice, humility, and perseverance.

Christ's love for the Church wasn't conditional on her performance or perfection; He gave Himself. That is the model of true love ... not defined by what you get, but by what you give. True love lasts through seasons of joy and seasons of pain. It stays when emotions fade, when fame dims, when hardship comes.
When you shift from "who will love me?" to "how can I love?", you move from dependency on external affirmation to having Christ's love reveal His presence in you. Biblical love is not about romance, but character. It's not served by flip-flopping based on mood, but by quiet commitment.

Real love isn't measured by how it feels, but by how it endures. When you choose to love beyond convenience, you step into the very heart of Christ ... where commitment outweighs comfort and sacrifice speaks louder than emotion. This is the love that transforms relationships and reveals Jesus to the world.

Application
- Examine your current or past relationships: have there been moments when you looked for convenience over covenant?
- If married or in a committed partnership, recommit today: not to what makes you feel good, but to what glorifies God through sacrifice, forgiveness, loyalty.
- Practice love as an act of the will today: choose humility, delay gratification, give grace even when hurt. Let your love reflect God's love.

Prayer
Father, thank You for showing me what real love looks like in Christ. Forgive me when I've treated love as something to be received for benefits or comfort rather than something I am called to give. Help me to live a love that is sacrificial, covenantal, humble, faithful. May Your love in me reflect Your glory, not just in good times, but especially in tough ones. In Jesus' name, **Amen.**

October 16
From Perform to Transform

Ephesians 4:22-24
...to put off your old self... and to be renewed in the spirit of your minds, and to put on the new self, created after the likeness of God...

Reflection
God is not impressed by performance. He is moved by transformance (neologism). The world teaches us to measure worth by deeds, applause, and outward appearance. But God looks deeper: "The Lord sees not as man sees, since man looks at the outward appearance, but the Lord looks at the heart" (1 Samuel 16:7).

Performance can fool people, but it cannot fool God. True freedom is an inside job ... Christ dwelling in you, reshaping your heart, renewing your mind, and producing the fruit of the Spirit (Galatians 5:22–23). Your behavior is not the source of your freedom; it is the reflection of it.

Transformation is the Spirit's work, not our stage play. Religion says, "Do more." Grace says, "Become more." When Christ lives in you, the Kingdom of God is not just around you ... it is within you (Luke 17:21). And when the Kingdom is alive within, your light cannot be hidden.

The difference is eternal: man grades performance, but God measures transformance. Outward works without inward renewal are empty. But when God gives you a new heart and a new spirit (Ezekiel 36:26–27), your life overflows with love, peace, joy, and lasting fruit that points back to Him.

Application
- Today, instead of striving to impress people, invite God to renew your mind and measure your worth by who you are becoming in Christ.
- Let your actions flow from inward transformation, not outward performance, so that your life reflects the fruit of the Spirit.
- Choose to live from the inside out, allowing God's Kingdom within you to shine through in love, peace, and joy.

Prayer
Father, thank You that my worth is not in how I perform but in who I am becoming in Christ. Transform me from the inside out. Search my heart, test my mind, and align my deeds with the freedom and life I have in You. Let Your Kingdom live in me and shine through me. In Jesus' name, **Amen.**

October 17
One Human Family, One Origin

Genesis 1:27
So God created man in His own image, in the image of God He created him; male and female He created them.

Reflection
The Christian truth that we are all made in the image of God (Genesis 1:27) lines up beautiful with the scientific reality that we all share a common origin. Being created by God means every single person carries dignity, purpose, identity ... no one more original than another.

Galatians 3:28 reminds us that in Christ, distinctions of ethnicity, skin, background, status ... all of that falls away. When it comes to our spiritual identity, we are one in Him. This unity doesn't erase diversity; instead, it grounds it. Differences become expressions of God's creativity, not markers of superiority or shame.

In a world where division, racism, pride, and prejudice still try to define people, knowing our shared beginning as one human family should shift how we see and treat one another. It's evidence that no one is more "original" than you ... though some may claim superiority based on appearance, wealth, skin tone, or background.

Remember: variations ... skin tone, features, etc. ... are just adaptations shaped by climate, geography, migration. They don't change our value; they only make us more beautiful in diversity.

Application
- Recognize the dignity in every person you meet. Treat others as fellow image bearers of God.
- Celebrate human diversity. Allow differences to enrich your understanding and compassion rather than divide you.
- Reject any lie that says you are less original, less worthy, or less made in God's image because of how you look or where your ancestors came from.

Prayer
Father, I thank You that You made humanity in Your image. Thank You that we all share a common origin and a shared dignity. Help me to see others as You see them ... as Your creation, worthy, loved, valuable. Break down any walls of prejudice, superiority, or shame in my heart. May my life reflect unity, love, and the truth that in Christ, we are one people, one family, with Your image stamped on every face. In Jesus' name, **Amen.**

October 18

Guard Your Legacy

Proverbs 4:23
Watch over your heart with all diligence, for from it flow the springs of life.

Reflection
One minute of anger, lust, or greed can undo decades of diligence, trust, and integrity.

What seems small in the moment can leave scars that last a lifetime. That single decision, driven by impulse, can dismantle the very foundation you've worked so hard to build.

This is why Scripture calls us to guard our hearts with diligence. Character is not forged in grand gestures, but in daily choices.

One moment of patience over rage, one act of integrity over temptation, one breath of restraint over reckless indulgence … these are the bricks that preserves a legacy.

Pause. Inhale. Exhale. Let that breath protect your vision, not destroy it.

Legacy is not built in a day … but it can be lost in a moment. Guard your heart, guard your habits, and guard your yes.

May you guard your heart with divine wisdom, stand firm in holiness, and build a legacy that honors God in every moment.

Application
- Reflect: Where are you most vulnerable to anger, lust, or greed?
- Pause: Practice one "sacred pause" today … choose prayer over impulse.
- Declare: "I will not let one moment undo what God is building in me."

Prayer
Father, give me the strength to guard my heart and the wisdom to pause before I act. Protect my legacy from being shattered in a single moment of weakness. May my daily choices reflect patience, integrity, and the character of Christ. **Amen.**

October 19

The Call Back to Surrender

Galatians 2:20
I have been crucified with Christ; and it is no longer I who live, but Christ lives in me; and the life which I now live in the flesh I live by faith in the Son of God, who loved me and gave Himself up for me.

Reflection
In today's church culture, the word commitment has often replaced the word surrender. But these two words are not the same.

Commitment is something I do. It reflects my effort, my choice, my decision to remain faithful on my terms. I stay in control. Surrender is something God receives. It is me laying down control, giving up my rights, and yielding completely to His authority. Commitment feels empowering because it lets me set the boundaries. Surrender feels costly because it demands everything. Yet the Gospel never calls us to mere commitment ... it calls us to crucifixion of the self.

Jesus said: "Whoever does not carry his own cross and come after Me cannot be My disciple" (Luke 14:27). Following Christ is not about making a commitment to try harder ... it's about surrendering all and letting Him live through you.

When the church exchanges surrender for commitment, we end up with: Shallow discipleship ... thinking effort, not grace, sustains us. Consumer Christianity ... serving as long as it's convenient. Control issues ... resisting God's redirection. But Paul makes it clear: "Present your bodies as a living and holy sacrifice, acceptable to God" (Romans 12:1). God isn't just asking for commitment; He's calling you to surrender.

Application
- Ask yourself: Am I "committing" parts of my life to Christ, or am I surrendering my whole life to Him?
- Today, choose one area (finances, relationships, time, habits) where you've been in control ... and surrender it to God's lordship.
- Remember: God doesn't want weekend visitation rights. He wants full custody of your life.

Prayer
Lord, forgive me for offering You commitments on my own terms. Teach me the way of surrender. I place my life fully on the altar today ... not in part, but whole. Take control, lead me, and use me for Your glory. **Amen.**

October 20
Saved From Foolishness

Ephesians 2:4–5
But God, being rich in mercy, because of His great love with which He loved us, even when we were dead in our wrongdoings, made us alive together with Christ (by grace you have been saved).

Reflection
Like Denzel once admitted, I too have done foolish things ... choices that could have cost me my life, my freedom, or my future. But here's the truth: But God.

Grace and mercy stepped in where judgment was deserved. God's unchanging hand reached down into the chaos of my decisions and steadied me. His patience covered my rebellion. His love pursued me even when I wasn't looking for Him.

That's the miracle of salvation. We aren't saved because we never stumbled ... we are saved because Christ lifted us out of our foolishness and placed us in His marvelous light. Where there could have been death, He gave life. Where there could have been loss, He gave purpose. Where there could have been despair, He gave joy.

If we are honest, many of us should not have survived our own decisions ... but God. His mercy intercepted our mess, His grace outran our folly, and His love rewrote the ending we deserved. Salvation is the testimony that foolishness didn't win ... because Christ stepped in and saved us from ourselves.

Application
- Reflect: Write down one "But God" moment in your life ... a time when His grace and mercy kept you from what could have destroyed you.
- Share your testimony. Someone else may need to hear how God rescued you from foolishness to faith.
- Live in gratitude daily. Begin your mornings by thanking God for specific mercies.

Prayer
Father, thank You for Your grace and mercy that carried me through my foolishness. Thank You for sparing me from dangers seen and unseen. I am grateful for the light and love I have found in Christ Jesus. Keep me walking in Your truth, rooted in gratitude, and bold enough to share my testimony. In Jesus' name, **Amen.**

October 21
Awake from the Prison of Distraction

1 Thessalonians 5:6
So then, let us not sleep as others do, but let us keep awake and be sober.

Reflection
You're not bored ... you're asleep.

Society has constructed a prison and labeled it "freedom." Boredom isn't merely a lack of stimulation; it's a symptom of spiritual slumber. The world drowns us in distractions ... screens, noise, continuous stimulation ... while our souls quietly drift into emptiness. Boredom in an overstimulated life is not a failure of entertainment ... it is conditioning.

True spirituality is the awakening ...not just escaping the noise, but putting faith-driven questions to our habits, our cultural prisons, and the systems that quietly drain life from us. Remember the parable of the wise man who recognized the threat and escaped before judgment came (Luke 12:20–21). Escape doesn't mean a physical exodus ... it means reclaiming our minds, renewing our spirits, and choosing mindfulness over autopilot.

When you reconnect with presence ... through nature, purposeful living, and stillness ... boredom dissipates. You stop merely existing in a prison designed by others. Instead, you unlock your heart, step into awareness, and begin to truly live.

Application
- Notice when boredom creeps in ... not as an absence of things to do, but as spiritual numbness.
- Pause: Turn off the distractions. Sit in silence. Ask: What's running in my mind? What is shaping my habits ... fear, habit, or awareness of God?
- Engage: Seek presence today through mindful prayer, walking in creation, or stillness with God. Choose awareness over autopilot.

Prayer
Father, awaken me from my spiritual slumber. Shake me from the denial that distraction equals freedom. Help me recognize the prisons built around me ... screens, habits, noise ... and give me the courage to open the door and step out. Rekindle purpose in my soul. May boredom evaporate when I reconnect with Your presence, nature, and the life You've breathed into me. In Jesus' name, Amen.

October 22
Mastery Through Calm

Proverbs 25:28
Like a city whose walls are broken through is a person who lacks self-control.

Reflection
Self-control is strength. Calmness is mastery.

When someone else's thoughtless action, rude comment, or careless mood tries to derail you, you can either react ... in anger, resentment, or bitterness ... or you can stand firm. Your mood doesn't have to shift with every wind. You don't have to hand others the keys to your emotional state.

The Bible describes self control as part of the fruit of the Spirit. It's not just about restraining wrong behavior; it's about your inner world being governed by truth, peace, maturity, and the Spirit's calm. A person lacking self-control is like a city without walls ... vulnerable to attack, easily invaded, unprotected.

The Holy Spirit gives us the strength to respond rather than react, to remain grounded, to think before we speak, to remain steady in the storms. Emotional discipline isn't suppression; it's alignment ... aligning your reactions to wholeness, wisdom, and what God says.

Application
- Notice triggers. What kinds of situations, words, or people tend to shift your mood? Write them down.
- When you feel a reaction rising, pause. Take a breath. Pray for the Spirit's intervention: "Lord, guard my heart and mind."
- Replace impulsive reactions with wise responses. Ask: "What is true? What is kind? What brings honor?"

Prayer
Father, I thank You that You give me the power, love, and self discipline that I need. Help me not to shift at the whims of others or give them control over my mood. Guard my heart, renew my mind, steady my emotions. May I learn to respond rather than react. May Your peace reign in my soul; may Your Spirit grow self control in me. In Jesus' name, **Amen.**

October 23
Transformed by Choice

Colossians 3:10
Put on the new self who is being renewed to a true knowledge according to the image of the One who created him.

Reflection
Your life does not change by chance; it changes by choice. Transformation is not accidental ... it is intentional. Many believe that time alone will heal, or that luck will suddenly shift their path. But without deliberate decisions, time only repeats old patterns, and luck remains an illusion.

The Greek word Paul uses for "transformed" in Romans 12:2 is metamorphoō ... the same root word where we get metamorphosis. Just as a caterpillar does not stumble into becoming a butterfly, your transformation in Christ requires process, patience, and submission. It begins with renewing your mind daily through God's Word, aligning your thoughts with His truth, and choosing obedience over convenience.

Fate doesn't shape your future ... faith does. And faith is always expressed in choices: what you think, what you say, what you do. Every small decision to follow Christ builds a life that reflects His will. Transformation happens not because you waited, but because you chose.

Application
- Daily Decision: Ask yourself each morning, What one choice can I make today that aligns with God's truth? Then do it.
- Mind Renewal: Replace one negative or worldly thought with a promise from Scripture. Write it down and revisit it throughout the day.
- Obedience Practice: When tempted to follow emotions or old habits, pause and pray: "Lord, transform me in this moment. Help me choose Your way."

Prayer
Father, thank You for calling me not to conform but to be transformed. I surrender my mind, my heart, and my will to You. Help me to make choices that align with Your Word and reveal Your will. Teach me to choose wisely, boldly, and faithfully each day. May my life become a testimony that true transformation is not by chance but by Christ. In Jesus' name, **Amen.**

October 24
What Does Your Attitude "Smell" Like?

Ephesians 4:31-32
Let all bitterness and wrath and anger and clamor and slander be put away from you, along with all malice. Be kind to one another, tenderhearted, forgiving one another, as God in Christ forgave you.

Reflection
What if we actually smelled like our attitude? It sounds humorous, but there's truth in that image. Our attitude reveals what we carry inside: bitterness, pride, envy, gratitude, joy ... they all have a spiritual aroma.

Scripture warns us about bitterness, anger, slander, malice ... all of which "stink" spiritually and influence others negatively. Ephesians 4:31-32 tells us to put these away and instead to clothe ourselves with kindness, tenderheartedness, forgiveness. These are the fragrances of a heart aligned with Christ.

What others perceive in your spirit or atmosphere is often just what's been growing within: unconfessed hurts, envy, pride, or unhealed wounds. But also, what could shine out: gratitude, faith, joy, compassion.

Your attitude carries a scent long before your words ever arrive. You can't hide what's living in your heart... it shows up in your tone, your posture, your reactions, and the atmosphere you create. When Christ transforms the inner life, the outer life begins to smell like grace. Choose today to release what stinks and embrace what reflects Him, so your life leaves a fragrance that draws others closer to God, not pushes them away.

Application
- Do a heart check. What are the attitudes you "wear" frequently ... bitterness, pride, envy, or grace, gratitude, kindness?
- Confess any attitude that would "smell bad." Ask God to help you remove bitterness, slander, anger. Replace it with kindness, forgiveness, love.
- Think: if your attitude was an aroma, would someone near you take a step back or lean in?

Prayer
Father, thank You that the state of my heart matters ... not just for me but for those around me. Reveal to me any attitude that smells of bitterness, envy, or pride. Help me to lay them down. Fill me with Your fragrance ... joy, gratitude, love. May others sense Your presence in me. May my attitude be a blessing, not a burden. In Jesus' name, **Amen.**

October 25
When You Move, The Way Appears

2 Corinthians 5:7
For we walk by faith, not by sight.

Reflection
Rumi said, "As you start to walk on the way, the way appears." This is a sacred truth of faith: many times we are called to move forward …despite not seeing the full path, despite uncertainty, even when the next step feels risky.

The Bible affirms this process. We are told to walk by faith, not by sight (2 Corinthians 5:7) …which means trusting God with our unseen steps. Our word becomes a lamp, lighting the next step when it's dark; we move forward even though we can only see a few feet ahead (Psalm 119:105). And God promises, when we acknowledge Him—when we commit our ways to Him … He will make the path straight (Proverbs 3:6).

When you step forward in faith, God's presence begins to reveal what was hidden. Doors open. Clarity comes. Confirmations appear. The way doesn't always appear first; but your obedience helps it form.

Faith is not waiting for the road to be revealed; it's trusting the One who builds the road beneath your feet. When you step, God shows. When you move, God makes a way. Your obedience becomes the bridge between where you stand and where God is taking you. Keep walking… the path will meet you as you go.

Application
- Identify one area in your life where you feel unsure, but sense God calling you forward (a decision, a step of faith, a leap).
- Pray and move. Even a small step counts … maybe it's speaking up, starting something new, letting go of fear to follow a conviction.
- Use Scripture to guide your movement. Let God's promises be your map when you don't have sight.

Prayer
Father, thank You that You are faithful even when I cannot see the full path. Give me courage to step forward in faith, trusting that as I move, You will make the way. Help me lean on Your Word as my lamp, and keep my eyes fixed on You, not my fears. May I walk in obedience, trusting You with my steps. In Jesus' name, **Amen.**

October 26
More Than 24 Hours: The Power of Divine Teamwork

Matthew 4:18–22 and Mark 1:16-20
After His baptism, Jesus began gathering His first disciples ... ordinary men ... to walk, learn, and multiply His mission together. They left their nets and followed Him immediately.

Reflection
On the surface, we all have just 24 hours in a day ... that's undeniable. But when we join hands in a team united by a shared mission, those 24 hours expand. Why? Because you gain more than people ... you gain the collective strength, wisdom, time, and anointing of every teammate.

Jesus demonstrated this beautifully. Right after His baptism ... before miracles, before crowds, before preaching the Sermon on the Mount ... He began building a team. Even the Son of God, in His chosen human limitation, showed us the divine strategy of multiplication: do it with others. He called fishermen, not scholars; ordinary workers, not the elite ... proving that kingdom impact is not about qualifications, but about willingness.

Teamwork in the Kingdom is not about personal glory ... it is about collective obedience. It's hearing Christ say, "Come, follow Me," and being willing to leave behind comfort, predictability, and isolation so that together we can walk out His mission.
God already knows our limitations ... our time, our capacity, our weaknesses, our blind spots. That's exactly why He calls us into community. When we link arms with others who share the same vision, we carry one another's burdens, sharpen one another's gifts, and multiply one another's reach. Alone, we add. Together, we multiply. This is the Kingdom way.

Application
- Reflect: Are you trying to bear the load alone today?
- Connect: Go to someone who shares your calling ... mentor, volunteer, pray together, or simply encourage one another.
- Multiply: Let God use your gift within a team ... for a church, a ministry, a mission ... that multiplies impact beyond your working hours.

Prayer
Father, thank You for the gift of teamwork. Just as Jesus gathered His disciples, help me build spiritual partnerships that extend our impact. Show me where I'm trying to do life alone and give me the grace to invite others in. May we together multiply time, talent, and purpose for Your Kingdom. In Jesus' name, **Amen.**

October 27
Be Still and Know : From Beta to Alpha:

Psalm 46:10
Cease striving and know that I am God;
I will be exalted among the nations, I will be exalted on the earth.

Reflection
Your brain is always active, sending electrical signals we call waves. When you are in beta waves (12–30 Hz), your mind is on high alert ... planning, problem-solving, multitasking. Beta is necessary for daily living, but when it dominates, it can leave you anxious, restless, and overworked.

God, however, often meets us in the alpha waves (8–12 Hz). Alpha is the rhythm of calm focus, creativity, and inner stillness. It's the state your brain enters in prayer, worship, and meditation on God's Word. It is here that the noise of life quiets, and your soul can hear His voice clearly.

The world trains us to live in beta mode ... always performing, always pushing. But Scripture calls us into alpha rest ... to abide in Christ, to walk in His peace, to let His Spirit renew us from the inside out. Jesus Himself modeled this rhythm: withdrawing from the crowds, resting in His Father's presence, and then returning empowered for ministry.

Real transformation happens when you learn to move from constant performance to Spirit-led presence. Beta helps you do; alpha helps you be. And God is more interested in who you are becoming than in how much you are performing.

Application
- This week, schedule five minutes daily to silence distractions, breathe deeply, and meditate on a single scripture, allowing your mind to shift from beta busyness to alpha stillness.
- Notice when your life feels consumed by performance and ask, Am I striving, or am I abiding?
- Choose one activity (walking, journaling, worship) where you can intentionally slow down and let God recalibrate your inner life.

Prayer
Lord, I confess that I often live in the noise of constant performance. Teach me to enter into Your rest, where my mind and heart align with Your Spirit. Help me to live from Your presence, not my pressure ... from Your peace, not my performance. May my doing flow out of my being in You. **Amen.**

October 28
It's All a Gift

James 1:17
Every good and perfect gift is from above, coming down from the Father of lights, with whom there is no variation or shadow due to change.

Reflection
Everything good in your life ... every talent you possess, every breath you take, every opportunity you've been given, every relationship that strengthens you, every moment that lifts your spirit ... all of it is a gift from God. You didn't earn it. You didn't manufacture it. You didn't orchestrate it. You simply received it.

James reminds us that God is the Father of lights ... meaning His goodness does not flicker, fade, or shift with circumstances. His gifts flow from a perfect Source with perfect consistency. That means every blessing in your life has divine fingerprints on it.

And here's the truth, gifts were never meant to terminate on us. We are blessed to be a blessing. What God places in your hands is meant to flow through your heart. When you recognize the Source, you stop boasting and start stewarding. You stop comparing and start appreciating. You stop hoarding and start sharing.

Gratitude becomes the doorway to elevation. It changes how you see your life, your struggles, and your story. A grateful heart can find joy in small moments and purpose in hard ones. Even secular studies confirm what Scripture has already declared: gratitude lifts your altitude. It strengthens mental health, deepens emotional resilience, and awakens spiritual clarity. When you understand that everything is a gift, you walk lighter, love deeper, give freer, and praise louder ... because pride dies where gratitude lives. Gratitude isn't just healthy ... it's holy. It turns blessings into worship.

Application
- Today, list three "gifts" you often take for granted and thank God for each.
- Ask, "Who can I bless with one of these gifts today?"
- Declare: "All I have is from You, Lord ... and I release it in Your name."

Prayer
Father, thank You for the good and perfect gifts You've granted me. Forgive my pride and help me use these gifts to reflect Your love and grace. Cultivate my heart in gratitude so that I may live in Your perfect altitude, honoring and sharing Your blessings. In Jesus' name, **Amen.**

October 29
Don't Build Your Barns First

Luke 12:20–21
But God said to him, 'You fool! This very night your soul is required of you; and as for all that you have prepared, who will own it now?' So is the one who stores up treasure for himself, and is not rich toward God.

Reflection
Society tells us that comfort is king, that accumulation equals success. But Jesus cuts through that noise. In His parable of the rich fool, the man hoarded wealth ... even planning to rest in abundance ... only for God to call him "fool" when death arrived unexpectedly.

You're not bored ... you might just be asleep. Our lives are often stuffed with distractions, possessions, and convenience. Yet, like the rich fool, we can wake up one day to find that our treasures neither feed our souls nor guarantee our tomorrows.

True freedom doesn't come from barns full of stuff ... it's found in being "rich toward God." That means investing in relationships, surrendering distractions, stewarding your spirit, and embracing purpose beyond the hollow comforts that numb our souls. When your heart is awake, boredom flees. You step out of the prison of autopilot into the fullness of life God designed.

Application
- Inventory your soul: What are you hoarding ...time, habits, consumption, comforts ... that keep you spiritually asleep?
- Surrender it: Ask God to help you release those things and reorient toward Him.
- Reinvest: Engage in practices that enrich your spirit ... prayer without distraction, generous living, moments in creation, deep connection with others.

Prayer
Heavenly Father, forgive me for building my barns first ... my comfort, my distractions, my busyness. Awaken my soul to Your presence. Help me to be rich toward You, storing up treasures that last. Free me from the prison of distraction and lead me into true life and purpose. In Jesus' name, **Amen.**

October 30
Single and Rooted in Worth

Psalm 139:14
I will give thanks to You, for I am fearfully and wonderfully made; Wonderful are Your works, And my soul knows it very well.

Reflection
Your worth is not determined by whether you wear a wedding ring, hold someone's hand, or carry someone's last name. Worth rooted in relationships is fragile ... but worth rooted in Christ is unshakeable. Your identity is anchored in something far deeper than companionship. It is grounded in who God designed you to be, the character you cultivate, the calling you pursue, and the wholeness you embrace.

Culture often treats singleness like a waiting room or a deficiency, as though being partnered validates your existence. But God's Word tells a different story. You are already chosen, already loved, already enough. Your value doesn't rise because someone claims you ... and it doesn't fall because no one has. You are "fearfully and wonderfully made," complete in Christ, not incomplete without another person.

Scripture gives us example after example of individuals who walked through seasons of solitude yet stood in divine purpose. Joseph was alone in a pit, alone in a foreign land, alone in a prison cell ... and God still called him successful because the Lord was with him. Paul advanced the Kingdom in singleness. Jesus Himself lived fully, purposefully, joyfully without earthly marriage. Singleness is not a pause on your life ... it is a platform for your growth. This season is not punishment ... it is preparation. God uses it to strengthen your confidence, clarify your calling, deepen your roots, and purify your desires. The goal is not to wait for someone to complete you, but to become someone who is whole, rooted, and radiant in Christ.

Application
- Refuse to measure yourself by worldly categories ... rest in Christ.
- Focus on values, character, and growth rather than external approval.
- Encourage others to see themselves as God sees them: whole and complete.

Prayer
Father, thank You for reminding me that my worth is found in You alone. Deliver me from the lies of comparison and the pressure of labels. Teach me to value myself according to Your truth ... that I am fearfully and wonderfully made, loved beyond measure, and chosen for a purpose. May my life reflect growth and a heart that beats after You. In Jesus' name, **Amen.**

October 31
Light in the Darkness

John 1:5
The Light shines in the darkness, and the darkness did not comprehend it.

Reflection
Darkness is real. We all walk through seasons where life feels heavy, unclear, cold, or overwhelming. The beauty of the Kingdom is this, darkness never has the final word … Light does. And not just any light… Christ's light, shining in you, around you, and before you.

These truths echo through history:

"Darkness cannot drive out darkness; only light can do that." — **MLK**
"In the midst of darkness, light persists." — **Gandhi**
"The night is darkest just before the dawn." — **Thomas Fuller**
"My dark days made me strong… or maybe I already was strong, and they made me prove it." — **Emery Lord**

Hatred never heals. Negativity never lifts. Only God's love can break cycles of darkness. Even when you can't see your way through, God's light doesn't disappear … sometimes it just appears small. Divine Spark breaks through darkness. When things feel the worst, you might be moments away from breakthrough. Darkness often intensifies right before God shifts something. Sometimes God lets darkness test you, not to break you, but to reveal you.

God is not intimidated by the darkness around you … and neither should you be. The darker the night, the brighter His light shines. The brighter His light shines, the clearer your purpose becomes. You were created to shine. You were built for hard seasons.
You carry the Light the world desperately needs.

Application
- Identify the "dark area" in your life right now ..fear, confusion, stress, loss.
- Speak John 1:5 over it: "The Light shines in this darkness."
- Choose one candle-sized act of light today … kindness, forgiveness, prayer, gratitude, or encouragement.

Prayer
Father, thank You that darkness is never stronger than Your light. Shine in my mind, my heart, and my circumstances. Help me carry Your presence into dark places with courage and hope. Make me a candle in this world … a steady, quiet, unshakeable light for Your glory. In Jesus' name, **Amen.**

November 1
Windows and Mirrors

Matthew 7:3–5
Why do you look at the speck that is in your brother's eye, but do not notice the log that is in your own eye? Or how can you say to your brother, 'Let me take the speck out of your eye,' and behold, the log is in your own eye? You hypocrite, first take the log out of your own eye, and then you will see clearly to take the speck out of your brother's eye.

Reflection
People are quick to look out the windows of life and pass judgment on others, but slow to look in the mirrors they pass by every day. Windows make it easy to see other people's flaws, but mirrors confront us with our own flaws.

Jesus warned against the danger of pointing out specks in someone else's eye while ignoring the logs in our own. Self-reflection is not weakness .. it is spiritual maturity. When we choose to examine ourselves honestly, God uses the mirror of His Word to reveal what needs cleansing, healing, and surrender. Only then can we see clearly enough to help someone else.

The truth is, judging others is easier than confronting the hidden pride, bitterness, or un-forgiveness within us. But transformation begins when we stop being window watchers and start being mirror gazers. God's grace is big enough to change anyone, but He starts with the one willing to look in the mirror first.

Application
- Pause at the Mirror … Each morning, when you see yourself in the mirror, pray: "Lord, show me what needs to change in me today.
- Stop Window Watching … Resist the temptation to criticize others quickly. Instead, ask God: "Am I guilty of the same thing?
- Lead by Example … Let your transformation be the testimony that speaks louder than your judgment.

Prayer
Lord, forgive me for the times I've judged others while ignoring my own faults. Teach me to look honestly into the mirror of Your Word and allow Your Spirit to transform me. May I walk in humility and grace, so that when I do speak into the lives of others, it comes from a place of compassion and clarity. In Jesus' name, **Amen.**

November 2
Sin Is Poison to the Elevated Soul

James 4:1
What causes fights and quarrels among you? Don't they come from your desires that battle within you?

Reflection
To an elevated consciousness, sin reveals itself not as a mere misstep, but as poison. Once your soul awakens to higher spiritual truth, sin becomes unmistakably corrosive ... a toxin that dulls clarity, stunts growth, and stifles purpose. Sin becomes weight on your conscious when you are awakened.

A higher awareness sees sin for what it is: venom. It distorts perceptions, clouds judgment, and throttles spiritual ascent. Sadly, many remain unconscious ... drinking poison while denying its effects, never realizing that what they believe brings freedom is actually binding their soul.

When we awaken spiritually, sin's poison no longer masquerades as pleasure or escape ... it becomes unmistakably hazardous. On that journey upward, we refuse what harms, embrace what restores, and guard against the subtle trap of Satan, the flesh and the world.

Once your soul is awakened, you can no longer treat poison like nourishment. Sin may still tempt, but it no longer deceives ... it exposes itself as the very thing that weakens your spirit and dims your light. Choose holiness not out of fear, but out of awareness, guarding your soul so it can continue to rise, see clearly, and live fully in God's truth.

Application
- Reflect: Is there a recurring sin or habit you've become numb to ... a spiritual poison you no longer recognize?
- Pray: Ask God to awaken your awareness ... light the darkness so you can see what's numbing your soul.
- Act: Identify one area to renounce today. Replace it with Scripture, prayer, worship, or fellowship that revitalizes your spirit.

Prayer
Heavenly Father, awaken me to the poison lurking in my life ... those habits and sins I've grown blind to. Elevate my consciousness, so I see sin as You see it. Give me courage to reject its lure and embrace what brings healing, clarity, and divine life. In Jesus' name, **Amen.**

November 3
The Obstacle Is the Way

James 1:2–4
Consider it all joy, my brothers and sisters, when you encounter various trials, knowing that the testing of your faith produces endurance. And let endurance have its perfect result, so that you may be perfect and complete, lacking in nothing.

Reflection
Many times the obstacles in life become the doorway to the blessings in life. This is more than a motivational phrase ... it is a spiritual reality.

The very obstacle you face is often the tool God uses to shape you, stretch you, and prepare you. What feels like resistance is actually divine redirection. What looks like a blockade is often a bridge to the next level of your calling.

Moses faced the Red Sea, but that sea became the pathway to Israel's deliverance. David faced Goliath, but Goliath became the doorway to his destiny as king. Even Jesus faced the cross, the greatest obstacle of all ... and it became the way of salvation for the world.

The obstacle doesn't signal God's absence ... it confirms His presence. He is not asking you to avoid the difficulty but to go through it, knowing He is with you. What the enemy meant for harm, God transforms into the very means of your breakthrough.

Application
- Identify one obstacle in your life right now. Instead of asking God to remove it, ask Him what He wants to teach you through it.
- Write down one biblical example of someone whose obstacle became the pathway to their purpose.
- Practice gratitude by thanking God not just for the victories, but also for the resistance that builds your endurance.

Prayer
Lord, thank You that the obstacles in my life are not wasted. Help me to see every challenge as a doorway to deeper faith and greater purpose. Give me courage to face what is in front of me, trusting that You will turn it into the way forward. I believe that what stands in my way is shaping me for what You have prepared. In Jesus' name, **Amen.**

November 4
Forgiven As I Forgive

Matthew 6:12
...and forgive us our sins, as we have forgiven those who sin against us.

Reflection
I sometimes wonder if people truly understand the Lord's Prayer. When we pray, "and forgive us our sins, as we have forgiven those who sin against us.," we are not merely asking God for His mercy ... we are setting the terms by which we want Him to deal with us.

This prayer only works if forgiveness flows both ways. If we come to God while clinging to bitterness or harboring resentment, we are essentially saying, "Lord, treat me as I treat others." Many Christians stumble here, desiring God's forgiveness while refusing to extend the same grace to others.

Imagine God granting the very prayer request of those who still walk with un-forgiveness in their hearts: "Lord, forgive me just like I forgive others." Would we be found forgiven ... or still bound? Forgiveness is not optional; it is commanded, demanded, and modeled by Christ Himself.

Forgiveness is the bridge between God's mercy and our freedom. What we release in others, God releases in us. To pray this prayer with integrity is to choose mercy every time ... because the forgiven must become the forgivers.

Application
- Self-Examine: Before you pray, search your heart. Who are you holding hostage through un-forgiveness?
- Release Quickly: Do not delay. Choose to forgive, even if the hurt runs deep. Forgiveness is not excusing the wrong, but freeing yourself from its chains.
- Pray With Integrity: When you pray the Lord's Prayer, let your words reflect your actions. Forgive as freely as you want to be forgiven.

Prayer
Father, search my heart and expose any un-forgiveness hiding within me. Teach me to release offenses as quickly as You release mine. I do not want to live bound by bitterness or self
deception. I choose to forgive those who have wronged me, just as Christ forgave me on the cross. Lord, make my prayers true, my forgiveness real, and my heart clean before You. In Jesus' name, **Amen**

November 5
Created to Create

Genesis 1:27
So God created man in His own image, in the image of God He created him; male and female He created them.

Reflection
To be made in the image of God means far more than physical appearance ... it speaks to the divine imprint upon our very being. We are fashioned with the capacity to reflect His nature in the earth. God is the Creator, and in His wisdom, He placed within us a spark of creativity to shape, build, speak, write, imagine, and bring forth good fruit that glorifies Him.

Every time you write a poem, start a business, cook a meal, or even encourage someone with your words, you are demonstrating the Creator's DNA within you. These moments, though they may feel ordinary, are extraordinary because they mirror God's ongoing work of creation. You were not designed simply to consume life, but to contribute to it ... to leave a mark that points others back to Him.

Creation didn't stop in Genesis; it continues daily through the people of God who live with intention, faith, and vision. When you walk in your creative purpose, you don't just make something new ... you reveal the God who made you new.

Application
- Ask yourself: What am I building today that reflects the image of God in me?
- Use your gifts ... whether small or great ... to create something that blesses others.
- Remember: creativity is not optional for believers; it's part of our calling.

Prayer
Father, thank You for creating me in Your image. Remind me today that I was made to create ... to bring beauty, order, and life wherever I go. Teach me to use my gifts to glorify You and to serve others. In Jesus' name, **Amen.**

November 6
Trained for Greater

1 Samuel 17:39–40
But David said to Saul, 'I cannot go with these, because I have not tested them.' And David took them off. Then he took his stick in his hand and chose for himself five smooth stones from the brook… and his sling was in his hand.

Reflection
David's courage before Goliath did not come from sudden bravery .. it was forged in the field. While tending sheep, he fought off lions and bears. Those unseen battles became the very training ground that prepared him for a public victory. What seemed like ordinary labor was actually extraordinary preparation.

The same is true for us. The struggles we face, the weight we carry, and the daily responsibilities we endure are not wasted … they are training. Struggle builds spiritual muscle, and affliction sharpens our faith. God uses hidden seasons to equip us for visible assignments.

When David rejected Saul's armor, he showed us that our preparation is unique. We cannot wear another's methods or mimic their tools; we must trust the training and gifting God has given us. Your sling and stones may look small, but in the hands of God, they are powerful enough to topple giants.

Your training in secret will sustain you in public. Trust the process, use what God has placed in your hands and in your heart … and step forward with confidence … because you have been trained for greater.

Application
- Value the Small Battles: Recognize that the daily struggles you face are preparing you for greater victories.
- Trust Your Training: Don't despise your unique journey. God has equipped you with specific experiences and gifts for your calling.
- Use What's in Your Hand: Like David, lean into the tools, skills, and gifts God has given you … they will make room for you.

Prayer
Father, thank You that nothing in my life is wasted. Help me see that even my struggles and afflictions are preparation for greater works. Give me the courage to trust the training You have placed me in and the confidence to use the gifts You have given me. May my sling and stones be enough in Your hands to defeat the giants I face. In Jesus' name, **Amen.**

November 7
Joy Beyond Happiness

John 15:11
I have told you these things so that My joy may be in you and that your joy may be complete.

Reflection
Family, let's talk truth … "happy" and "joy" are not the same, and understanding this difference brings true freedom.

The word happy originates from "hap", meaning chance, fortune, or that which just occurs. Happiness relies on circumstances … an event, blessing, or pleasant moment that happens. But because it's tied to the fickleness of life, it's fleeting. Soon after it arrives, it slips away. That's why you find yourself chasing happiness through new experiences, new stuff, or new highs.

But friends, true joy is not transactional. It is not bought or stumbled into. It's internal. It's your posture before God, rooted in who He is and the covenant relationship you share. Unlike happy … which dies when your mood shifts … joy endures in the storms.

God offers joy. It is a gift, not a gimmick. It remains when circumstances change. It doesn't vanish when life gets heavy. It is cultivated in the soil of your relationship with Christ, sustained by His Spirit.

Ask yourself … are you chasing the fleeting flowers of happiness, or are you grounded in the river of God's joy?

Application
- Identify a moment today when you felt "happy." Ask yourself … was it circumstantial or anchored in God?
- Declare a simple truth: "Lord, I want Your joy, not temporary happiness."
- Root yourself in Him … spend time in His presence, not looking for a feeling, but seeking His face.

Prayer
Heavenly Father, let Your joy … not mere happiness … be my strength today. Teach me to rest in You, not in fleeting moments, and to trust that true joy flows from an unshakeable relationship with You. **Amen.**

November 8
Strength in His Joy

Nehemiah 8:10
...Do not be grieved, for the joy of the Lord is your strength.

Reflection
Family, happiness may come and go, but joy is eternal. The kind of joy Jesus carried wasn't based on circumstances … it was anchored in His delight to do the will of the Father. Psalm 40:8 declares, "I delight to do Your will, O my God." That delight, that joy, was His strength even as He faced the cross: "for the joy set before Him, He endured…" (Hebrews 12:2).
Here's the truth: the joy of the Lord doesn't just make you smile … it makes you strong. It is strength in weakness, calm in chaos, and endurance in suffering. When the cares of this world rise up to choke your faith (Mark 4:19), His joy gives you power to push through.

Every blessing, every answered prayer, every testimony you carry is not the end of the story …it's the starting line. God's goal is not just to fill you with good things but to fill you with Himself so that His strength flows through you. Jesus said, "From your innermost being will flow rivers of living water" (John 7:38). That's strength that overflows … not borrowed, not temporary, but sustained by His Spirit. And here's the beauty: when you live hidden in Christ (Colossians 3:3), joy becomes as natural as breathing. You don't even have to try to "look strong." His joy carries you, lifts you, and shines through you, often blessing others without you realizing it. So when you feel weak, discouraged, or worn down … don't look to your circumstances for strength. Look to His joy. That joy will uphold you, renew you, and empower you to keep walking by faith.

Application
- When you feel weary, declare out loud: "The joy of the Lord is my strength."
- Write down three ways God has shown His goodness to you this week and let those reminders fuel your joy.
- Choose to shift your focus from what drains you to the One who sustains you.

Prayer
Lord, thank You that Your joy is my strength. Teach me to delight in Your will as Jesus did. When life feels heavy, remind me that Your joy lifts burdens, breaks chains, and renews my spirit. Let my life overflow with living water, so that others may see the strength that comes only from You. In Jesus name, **Amen.**

November 9
Be A Conduit And Not A Cul-de-Sac

John 7:38
He who believes in Me, as the Scripture said, 'From his innermost being will flow rivers of living water.

Reflection
What God pours into us was never meant to stay with us. When we truly believe in Him, everything He pours into us is meant to flow out of us. We are called to be conduits, not cul-de-sacs. A cul-de-sac traps what enters; a conduit lets it flow freely to bless others.

The Lord's teaching was never meant to puff us up with knowledge, but to shape us into humble servants. God's purpose is not just to make us better versions of ourselves, but to make us reflections of His Son. The life of Christ was defined by continual outpouring … giving away of Himself, spending Himself, serving and blessing others.
God's desire is not merely that we appear as beautifully fruit hanging on a tree. He wants to make us nutritious fruit, pressed and poured out to refresh and sustain others. In God's kingdom, spiritual life is not measured by worldly success but by surrender … by how much He can accomplish through us.

Are we willing to live lives poured out? To stop chasing self-satisfaction and instead become His hands, His feet, His mouthpiece? For every seed we plant, He promises a multiplied return. The abundant life is found not in hoarding blessings but in pouring them out to others.

Application
- Shift the Focus: Ask daily, "Am I a conduit or a cul-de-sac of God's grace?"
- Pour Out Intentionally: Look for opportunities to serve, encourage, and bless … even in small, hidden ways.
- Plant Good Seeds: Every word, every action is a seed. Choose to sow life-giving, refreshing seeds into others.

Prayer
Lord, make me a conduit of Your living water. Forgive me for the times I have held on to blessings You meant to flow through me. Teach me to pour out my life for others the way Jesus poured out His life for me. Let my words, my hands, and my steps refresh those around me. May the seeds I plant bear fruit that brings glory to You and blessing to Your people. In Jesus' name, **Amen.**

November 10
Go Get It and Come Back With It

Deuteronomy 11:24
Every place on which the sole of your foot steps shall be yours.

Reflection
God has given us promises, but He also requires us to walk into them. He requires us to move in faith and courage in order to obtain the promise. It's not enough to just dream about victory ... you must go after it in faith. When David pursued the Amalekites after they raided Ziklag, he didn't sit still and cry. He prayed and inquired of the Lord, received direction, and then went to recover everything that was stolen (1 Samuel 30:8,18).

Faith without works is dead. The blessing is already spoken, the victory already secured in Christ ... but it takes faith, obedience, courage, and persistence to go get it and come back with it. Whether it's peace, joy, healing, restoration or a dream; God is calling you to move forward, not sit back. His Word equips you, His Spirit empowers you, and His promise assures you.

God's promises are activated by movement. What He has spoken is already yours, but possession comes when you step out in faith. Move forward with courage, obey His direction, and trust that every step taken in faith places you on promised ground.

Application
- Identify one area in your life where you've been passive ... waiting, but not moving.
- Pray for direction, then take a step of faith this week toward reclaiming what God has promised.
- Keep your testimony in mind: don't just go get it ... come back with it to encourage someone else.

Prayer
Lord, give me the faith and courage to rise, pursue, and reclaim every promise You have for my life. Help me not to sit in fear or defeat, but to move boldly in obedience. May my testimony be proof that when You send me, I can go get it and come back with it. In Jesus' name, **Amen.**

November 11
Professing Is Not Possessing

Matthew 7:21–23
Not everyone who says to Me, 'Lord, Lord,' will enter the kingdom of heaven… Then I will declare to them, 'I never knew you; depart from Me.

Reflection
There's a profound difference between someone who simply professes Christianity and someone who truly possesses Christ. The one may know all the right words, even attend church faithfully. But the one who possesses Christ has made Him Lord of their life; and transformation is evident in word and deed.

As Billy Graham put it, "Professing faith in Jesus Christ is clearly not the same as possessing Christ… People can have religion but not know Christ. It's having Christ that counts."

The Apostle James echoes this: mere intellectual assent to Christ doesn't save ("Even the demons believe … and shudder.") … what matters is a faith alive enough to change and transform a life.

Those who truly possess Christ are known by the Spirit's fruit in their lives … love, joy, peace, patience, kindness, goodness, faithfulness, gentleness, self-control (Galatians 5:22–23). Their transformation flows from relationship, not religion.

Application
- Self-Examination: Ask yourself … "Do I merely profess faith, or do I truly possess Christ in my heart?" Be honest before God.
- Invite the Spirit's Work: Spend time in prayer asking the Holy Spirit to illumine your life and produce Christlike fruit.
- Live it Out: Identify one area … speech, forgiveness, compassion … where your life can better reflect possessing Christ, not just professing Him.

Prayer
Lord Jesus, forgive me for the times I have merely professed faith without letting You possess my heart. Fill me with Your Spirit. Let my life bear the fruit of Your presence: love, kindness, humility, endurance. I want not just to say Your name, but to live by Your power. Help me know You more deeply and reflect You more clearly in all I do. In Your precious name, **Amen.**

November 12
The Power of "I AM"

Proverbs 23:7a
For as he thinks within himself, so he is.

Reflection
The two most powerful words you can ever say are "I AM."

Why? Because whatever follows shapes your identity, your atmosphere, and your destiny. Every "I AM" plants a seed into your mind and spirit ... either cultivating life or reinforcing defeat.

When you say, "I am tired," or "I am not enough," you are sowing seeds that weaken your faith. But when you say, "I am blessed," "I am chosen," "I am strong in the Lord," you are declaring God's truth over your life. These words do not just float in the air ... they carry creative power, commanding your soul, body, and spirit into alignment with God's will.

Jesus reminds us that His words are spirit and life. When we speak words filled with truth, we are breathing life into our future. Our declarations shape our identity, influence our emotions, and frame the world we walk into. Be intentional about your "I AMs" ... because they are more than words; they are the blueprint of your becoming.

Application
- Guard Your Mouth: Before you speak, ask yourself: "Am I planting life or death with this 'I AM'?"
- Daily Affirmations: Begin your mornings declaring God's truth: "I am a child of God. I am forgiven. I am equipped. I am victorious."
- Shift Your Thoughts: Since thoughts shape words, discipline your mind with Scripture. Let your inner conversation agree with what God has spoken over you.

Prayer
Father, thank You for giving me the power of words and thoughts. Forgive me for the times I have spoken death over myself. Today I declare that I am loved, I am chosen, I am victorious, and I am Yours. Let my words align with Your truth so that my life reflects Your Spirit and Your power. In Jesus' name, **Amen.**

November 13
True Life

1 John 5:12
He who has the Son has the life; he who does not have the Son of God does not have the life.

Reflection
In our world, success is often measured by what we own... our wealth, fame, power, or prestige. Yet all of these can be hollow. Even Satan tempted Jesus with material wealth and dominion over all the world, seeking to lure Him with earthly glory (Matthew 4:8–9) . But Jesus refused, declaring, "Worship the Lord your God, and serve Him only" .

True life isn't found in material gain ... it's found in relationship with Christ. Possessing the Son means holding onto real, unshakable life. As John writes, eternal life isn't just added time ... it's a restored, abundant life anchored in the presence of Jesus .

When we truly have the Son, we gain His strength, peace, and purpose. Even life's storms become meaningful, for "the Son of God takes the tribulations of your life and actually turns them for your good" . That same life breathed into Christ sustains us ... and no worldly treasure can match it or give what The Holy Spirit gives.

True life is not something we chase ... it is Someone we receive. When we have the Son, we have everything that truly matters ... life, purpose, and peace that cannot be taken away. Without Him, even the world's greatest gains leave us empty, but in Christ, we are fully alive.

Application
- Rest in His Life ... Before your day begins, breathe deeply and affirm: "I have the Son. I have life."
- Re-center Your Heart ... When material worries or worldly pressures arise, remind yourself: true success is knowing Him, not having more.
- Live from Life, Not Chasing It ... Ask God today to help you walk from a place of rest and assurance, not striving or performance.

Prayer
Lord Jesus, thank You that in You I have life ... eternal, abundant, and secure. Help me fix my eyes on You today, not on what I lack or crave. When temptation whispers, remind me that You are my all sufficient treasure. Let me walk in Your strength, guided by the life only You can give. In Your precious name, **Amen.**

November 14
From Spectators to Disciples

Hebrews 5:14
But solid food is for the mature, who because of practice have their senses trained to distinguish between good and evil.

Reflection
One of the greatest challenges in the church today is not attendance ... it's the depth of obedience. Many come to worship services, hear sermons, and enjoy fellowship, but their spiritual roots remain shallow. Without personal study of God's Word and intentional discipleship, believers remain vulnerable: easily swayed by cultural trends, spiritual fads, and false teaching.

Jesus never called us to be spectators; He called us to be disciples. Disciples don't just hear the Word ... they live it, practice it, and let it shape their thinking and behavior. A church filled with spectators may be full of people but empty of power. A church filled with disciples, however, is rooted, resilient, and reproducing.

If we want to stand firm in these times, we must move beyond casual Christianity into committed discipleship. That means more than Sunday attendance ... it means a daily walk with the Word, a lifestyle of obedience, and a willingness to grow into maturity.

Application
- Feed Daily on the Word: Set aside time each day to read and meditate on Scripture, not just to know it, but to apply it.
- Seek Discipleship: Find or build a community where accountability, teaching, and spiritual growth are prioritized.
- Move Beyond Milk: Challenge yourself with deeper study, prayer, and service. Refuse to remain a spiritual spectator ... step into the calling of a disciple.

Prayer
Lord, forgive me for the times I've been a spectator instead of a disciple. Give me a hunger for Your Word and a desire to grow deeper in faith. Strengthen my roots so I will not be swayed by culture or false teaching. Shape me into a disciple who not only knows Your truth but also lives it out daily. In Jesus' name, **Amen.**

November 15
Focus Sets the Frequency

Colossians 3:2
Set your mind on the things above, not on the things that are on earth.

Reflection
Wherever your focus goes, your life flows.

Just as a radio tunes into a certain frequency by what it is dialed to, your spiritual focus determines the "frequency" you operate on. Fix your eyes on problems, and you will vibrate with worry. Fix your eyes on pleasures, and you will vibrate with distraction. But fix your eyes on Christ, and you will walk in peace, clarity, and power.

The mind is not neutral ... it is a tuner. What you meditate on shapes your attitude, emotions, and even your atmosphere. That is why Scripture commands us to think on things that are true, honorable, pure, lovely, and praiseworthy (Philippians 4:8). God designed us to rise or fall according to the frequency of our focus.

Jesus Himself modeled this. Even amid betrayal, ridicule, and the cross, His focus remained on the Father's will and the joy set before Him. That focus tuned His life to heaven's frequency, empowering Him to endure suffering and fulfill destiny. When we align our thoughts with God's truth, our lives emit a frequency that attracts grace, peace, and strength for every battle.

Application
- Ask yourself honestly: What has my mind been tuned to this week ... fear, stress, or faith?
- Practice redirecting your focus by meditating on a single Scripture each day.
- Guard your "mental tuner" ... limit distractions and saturate your environment with God's Word, worship, and prayer.

Prayer
Father, thank You for giving me the ability to choose where I set my focus. Forgive me for the times I've tuned in to fear, doubt, or negativity. Help me to fix my eyes on You, that my life may resonate with the frequency of faith, love, and hope. May my focus stay on heaven's wavelength so that Your presence and peace flow through me daily. In Jesus' name, **Amen.**

November 16
Training Wheels and The Teacher Within

2 Timothy 3:16-17
All Scripture is God-breathed and useful for teaching, rebuking, correcting and training in righteousness, so that the man of God may be thoroughly equipped for every good work.

Reflection
The Bible is like training wheels. Basic Instructions Before Leaving Earth. It provides guidance, structure, and reveals God's character, His promises, and His commands. But there is more. The written Word is essential ... but it is not the final horizon. It is a guide to something greater.

There is a deeper internal understanding that is not just found on a page or scroll. This understanding is revealed to the soul only by the Holy Spirit. This is revelational knowledge. The Holy Spirit fulfills the role of the greatest teacher you will ever have. He illuminates, interprets, applies, and leads beyond what you can see with your eyes.

However, to sit in the front row of this class with the Holy Spirit, there are requirements: faith, love, obedience, and service. These are not optional extras; they are the qualities that unlock spiritual insight and allow the Spirit to work deeply in your heart. Without them, the Bible remains powerful, but some of its deeper layers, its personal whispers to your soul, remain hidden.

Application
- Faith: Approach your Bible time believing God intends to speak to you, not just inform you.
- Love: Let your love for God and for others drive your reading. When motivation is love, understanding is more receptive.
- Obedience: When the Holy Spirit reveals something, respond. Even in small ways. Obedience builds trust with God, opening more revelation.

Prayer
Father, thank You for giving me the Bible as my guide. Thank You for Your Holy Spirit, Who reveals truth to my soul beyond the words on a page. I ask now for faith to believe, a heart full of love, for obedience in the small and big things, and a life marked by service. May my soul be enlarged by Your Spirit, and may I walk in the deeper understandings You have for me. In Jesus' name, **Amen.**

November 17
The Rhythm of God

1 Corinthians 14:33
For God is not a God of confusion but of peace, as in all the churches of the saints.

Reflection
All of creation moves to a divine rhythm. The waves crash and recede, the sun rises and sets, the heart beats and rests … each one a testimony that God designed life in balanced cycles of order and harmony. Even our thoughts and actions flow in waves. When they align with the God within us, they become rhythmic expressions of beauty, vitality, and peace.

But when our thoughts grow unbalanced … filled with fear, envy, or disorder … the rhythm falters. Just as an instrument out of tune produces dissonance, unbalanced living produces ugliness, disease, and failure. God calls us back to His rhythm, where our inward life matches His Spirit and our outward actions flow in grace and balance.

Jesus walked in perfect rhythm. He withdrew to pray, then served with power. He spoke with authority, then rested in silence. His life shows us that strength comes not from constant motion but from a balanced harmony with the Father. To walk in His rhythm is to move with heaven harmony.

Let your life become a wave of balanced light … reflecting the perfection of the Creator's rhythm.

Application
- Observe your daily rhythm: where is there imbalance … too much noise, not enough prayer, too much striving, not enough rest?
- Intentionally align one area of your life with God's balance this week (e.g., adding silence, gratitude, or worship).
- Each day, speak beauty and life into your thoughts to replace fear and disorder.

Prayer
Father, thank You for the perfection of rhythm woven into Your creation. Forgive me for the times my thoughts and actions have been unbalanced, producing chaos instead of peace. Teach me to walk in harmony with Your Spirit, to think beauty, and to live in the balanced waves of Your light. May my life reflect Your rhythm, bringing health, joy, and order. In Jesus' name, **Amen.**

November 18
Consistency Beats Creativity

1 Corinthians 4:2
Moreover, it is required of stewards that one be found trustworthy.

Reflection
Many entrepreneurs and visionaries chase the "next big idea." They believe the breakthrough will come from a flash of creativity, an innovative twist, or a trend no one else has seen. But the truth is deeper and simpler: it's not brilliance that builds trust, it's consistency.

A consistent message, consistent branding, and consistent follow up will always outlast the occasional spark of inspiration. Creativity can grab attention, but consistency keeps it. Trust is the fruit of steady faithfulness.

This isn't just true in business ... it's biblical. God calls His people to be faithful stewards, not flashy innovators. The early church grew not because the apostles constantly reinvented their approach, but because they consistently devoted themselves "to the apostles' teaching and to fellowship, to the breaking of bread and to prayer" (Acts 2:42).

Consistency may feel boring. But in the kingdom of God, faithfulness compounds into fruitfulness. Over time, consistency makes you unforgettable because it proves your character.

Application
- Where in your life have you relied on creativity instead of consistency?
- What "boring" habit of faith (prayer, Scripture reading, serving) needs more of your commitment this week?
- In your work, ministry, or business, identify one area where doubling down on consistency could build trust.

Prayer
Lord, thank You for showing me that faithfulness matters more than flashes of brilliance. Teach me to be consistent in my walk with You, in my service to others, and in the work You've placed in my hands. May my steady obedience bring glory to You and build trust with those around me. **Amen.**

November 19
Passing the Baton

2 Timothy 2:2
The things which you have heard from me in the presence of many witnesses, entrust these to faithful people who will be able to teach others also.

Reflection
Every relay race requires a baton pass, and the church is no different. The mission of God has always depended on one generation declaring His works to the next. Yet today, many young people see the church as irrelevant, judgmental, or out of touch. At the same time, many congregations fail to intentionally mentor and equip new leaders, leaving a dangerous gap in the relay of faith.

The truth is, the Gospel is timeless ... even if methods must shift. Jesus did not call the church to merely preserve traditions but to make disciples in every generation. That means we must listen as much as we teach, create authentic relationships across generational lines, and invite young people not just to watch but to lead.

When churches hoard leadership, they die with the last leader still holding the baton. But when we equip, empower, and release the next generation, the mission of God runs forward with strength. The question is not whether the baton will be passed ... but how.

Application
- Bridge the Gap: Seek to understand and engage with younger generations rather than dismiss their questions or culture.
- Mentor Intentionally: Identify younger believers and invest time, wisdom, and encouragement into their growth.
- Release Leadership: Don't just train new leaders ... trust them with responsibility. Let them run their leg of the race with the baton of faith.

Prayer
Father, thank You for every generation You have called to Yourself. Forgive us when we fail to pass the baton faithfully. Give me a heart that listens, mentors, and releases others into their calling. May I be faithful in declaring Your works to the next generation so that the mission of Christ continues with power and purpose. In Jesus' name, **Amen.**

November 20
Invincible Ignorance vs. Visible Wisdom

James 1:22
But prove yourselves doers of the word, and not merely hearers who delude themselves.

Reflection
Oswald Chambers once wrote, "A fanatic is one who entrenches himself in invincible ignorance." How true this rings in our generation. Many people today ... Christians included ... cling tightly to traditions, rituals, and even denominational identities, mistaking them for righteousness. Like the Pharisees of old, they justify their behavior on the basis of their forefathers' customs rather than on Christ and His love.

The danger is subtle but deadly: when religion becomes routine without righteousness, we deceive ourselves. James warns us not to be merely hearers of the Word. Knowing Scripture without living it out is no different than gazing into a mirror and then forgetting who you are. True wisdom is not in defending tradition ... it is in obeying Christ.

Christ Himself is the standard. Love is the measure. Anything less is hypocrisy dressed in religious clothing. To follow Him is not to cling to ignorance but to grow in wisdom, humility, and action. Our faith must take form in how we live, how we treat others, and how we love beyond measure.

Application
- Where have I been holding onto traditions or opinions that are not rooted in Christ?
- Am I content with "knowing about" God, or am I actively becoming like Christ through obedience and love?
- Today, how can I embody the Word ... not just recite it ... in my home, workplace, or community?

Prayer
Father, deliver me from the trap of ignorance masked as tradition. Teach me to be a doer of Your Word and not a hearer only. Where I've justified myself by anything less than Christ, forgive me. Fill me with Your Spirit so that my actions are aligned with Your love. Let my life reflect not empty religion but holy righteousness, grounded in Jesus. In His name, **Amen.**

November 21
A Weight to Heavy to Carry

1 Peter 3:18
For Christ also suffered once for sins, the righteous for the unrighteous, to bring you to God. He was put to death in the body but made alive in the Spirit.

Reflection
Our salvation is anchored in the love and the suffering ... the passion and the suffrage ... of Christ. In ancient Israel, sin's weight could be carried only by the high priest once a year, in elaborate atonement rituals behind the veil. But as Christians today, we no longer have bear that burden of waiting on a Priest. We no longer have to carry the weight of our sins until the High Priest goes into the Holies of Holies.

You and I stand free.
Christ has already carried our sins to the cross ... our only job is to confess and repent. We don't depend on yearly rituals; Christ's sacrifice has made a way for us directly into God's presence.

We weren't part of the world before Christ, but now live in the light of His cross, redeemed by His suffrage and enveloped in His love.
Because of this, we can live a life of gratitude ... lightened by the burdens Christ already bore. The penalty of sin is death ... and Christ has already carried the weight of that death to the cross.

Application
- Release Your Burden ... Quietly in prayer, offer your sins and struggle to Jesus, trusting that He has carried them wholly.
- Enter His Presence Freely...No veil now stands between you and God. Enjoy communion with the Father throughout your day ... unfettered and assured in His unconditional welcome.
- Live in Grateful Rest ... Let your deeds and words flow from the freedom of forgiveness. Serve, speak, and love from the abundance of grace, not obligation.

Prayer
Heavenly Father, thank You for lifting the weight of my sins ... my shame, guilt, and burden are no longer mine to bear. I rejoice that Jesus entered the Holiest place for me, not as a priest once a year, but as the eternal High Priest who pleads for me forever. May my life reflect the freedom You've given ... walking in grace, living in love, and loving others as You loved me. In Jesus' precious name, **Amen.**

November 22
Forged in the Fire, Beautified from Brokenness

Roman 5:3-5
3 And not only this, but we also exult in our tribulations, knowing that tribulation brings about perseverance; 4 and perseverance, proven character; and proven character, hope; 5 and hope does not disappoint, because the love of God has been poured out within our hearts through the Holy Spirit who was given to us.

Reflection
True beauty is not born of ease. It is not sculpted in the calm or carved by comfort. The most beautiful souls are shaped in the shadows: through brokenness, grief, loss, struggle. They are those who, though defeated, do not deny their wounds but allow them to teach, to soften, to refine.
The Scriptures tell us that suffering has purpose. It produces perseverance. Perseverance builds character. Character births hope. And hope does not disappoint.

When life breaks us, God doesn't abandon the pieces; He uses them. He takes what is fractured, and by His grace … turns it into something whole. Psalm 34:18 says He is near to the brokenhearted; He saves those crushed in spirit. This journey … the wrestling, the mourning, the nights of emptiness … can leave scars. But those scars, touched by grace and love, become proof. Not of defeat, but of victory. Strength born in gentleness. Light born from darkness. Love grown through triumph.

Application
- Name one hardship or painful experience you are still carrying. Write it down. Acknowledge its weight.
- Remember that each trial, each loss, however painful, has the potential to refine you. Ask God to show you what He is producing in you through it: perseverance, compassion, wisdom, gentleness.
- Let your brokenness deepen your empathy. Reach out and speak life into someone else whose pain you recognize.

Prayer
Lord, thank You that You do not waste my pain. Thank You that despite the darkness, You are shaping me, refining me, molding me into something more compassionate, more real, more like You. Help me to receive Your grace in my brokenness. Give me courage to face what I fear, patience to endure what I cannot change, and faith to trust that You are working all things together for my good. May I emerge from this fire with a heart of compassion, strength in gentleness, and light that shines from within. In Jesus' name, **Amen.**

November 23
Depth Determines Connection

Proverbs 20:5
A plan in the heart of a man is like deep waters, but a man of understanding draws it out.

Reflection
"People can only meet you as deeply as they have met themselves." Depth is not about age, status, or intellect ... it's about how far a person has allowed God to search their heart. Shallow souls live on the surface, afraid of still waters where reflection is clear. But those who have wrestled with God in prayer, confronted their weaknesses, and embraced His grace carry a depth that cannot be faked.

Jesus Himself often met people at the level they were ready to receive. To some He spoke plainly, to others He used parables, and to His disciples He revealed mysteries of the Kingdom. He knew that depth of revelation is always tied to depth of readiness.

When we expect others to understand the fullness of our journey, we must remember: they can only meet us where they have met themselves. That's not a limit to love ... it's a call to compassion. Just as God is patient with our growth, we are called to extend patience to others.

Depth shapes connection. Those who have gone deep with God carry wells of understanding, but not everyone knows how to draw from them. Walk in wisdom, extend patience, and remember ... true connection flows where depth has first been formed in the heart.

Application
- Identify a relationship where you've felt misunderstood or unseen. Ask God to give you patience with that person's level of growth.
- Commit yourself to going deeper in Christ through prayer, study, and obedience, so you can love others from a place of maturity.
- Instead of frustration, choose compassion. Pray that God will lead them into deeper waters at the right time.

Prayer
Father, search my heart and take me deeper in You. Teach me to release the need for others to fully understand me, and to extend grace where depth is lacking. May my walk with You draw me into deeper waters so that I can meet others with patience, wisdom, and love. In Jesus' name, **Amen.**

November 24
Why Consistency Is Everything

Galatians 6:9
And let us not lose heart in doing good, for in due time we will reap if we do not grow weary.

Reflection
Motivation is a spark, but consistency is the flame. Anyone can start, but few keep going when the excitement fades. That's why consistency is the bridge between where you are now and where you want to be.

David didn't defeat Goliath in one day of practice ... he had been consistent in the fields, faithfully slinging stones while tending sheep. Daniel didn't become a man of wisdom overnight ... he prayed three times a day, no matter what decree was signed against him. Jesus Himself showed us this rhythm, consistently withdrawing to pray, teaching faithfully, and obeying the Father step by step until the cross.

Small, daily obedience compounds over time, like deposits in a savings account that grow with interest. Each prayer, each step of faith, each act of obedience might feel small, but together they build a life of strength, faith, and fruitfulness.

Consistency is not perfection ... it's perseverance. You may stumble, but the key is to keep showing up. God honors steady faith, not just fleeting bursts of passion.

Application
- Make It Non-Negotiable: Choose one habit that aligns with your faith (prayer, Scripture reading, serving) and treat it as essential as breathing.
- Keep It Simple: Don't complicate it ... start small and manageable. A verse a day, a five-minute prayer, a single act of kindness.
- Anchor It to Routine: Attach it to something you already do (pray while making coffee, read Scripture before bed).

Prayer
Father, thank You for reminding me that consistency is the pathway to growth and transformation. Forgive me for the times I started strong but gave up too soon. Strengthen me with steady perseverance to keep showing up, even on the hard days. Help me see that each small, faithful act matters in Your eyes. Teach me to sow daily so that in due season, I will reap a harvest that brings You glory. In Jesus' name, **Amen.**

November 25
The Courage to Continue

Galatians 6:9
Let us not lose heart in doing good, for in due time we will reap if we do not grow weary.

Reflection
"Success is not final, failure is not fatal: It is the courage to continue that counts." — Winston Churchill

This truth is deeply spiritual, because God never measures you by what happens to you ... He measures you by how you handle what happens to you.

Success is not the finish line. Failure is not the end of the story. The real test of spiritual maturity is the courage to keep going when life hits, when plans fail, when doors close, when people walk away, and when you don't feel strong. Everyone loves success ... but success is seasonal. Everyone fears failure ... but failure is not permanent. The only thing that carries you from promise to fulfillment is courageous endurance.

Moses failed before he delivered. Joseph was betrayed before he rose. David fell before he reigned. Peter denied before he preached. Paul suffered before he conquered. Jesus was crucified before He was glorified.

Your story is no different. You will have victories. You will have failures. But neither defines you. God looks for the one who continues.

Keep going. Keep believing. Keep sowing. Keep trusting. Keep continuing. Your "due time" is closer than you think.

Application
- Identify one area where you've been tempted to give up.
- Ask God for renewed courage to continue.
- Revisit one promise God made you and reaffirm your faith in it.

Prayer
Father, give me the courage to continue despite setbacks, obstacles, or discouragement. Strengthen my heart, steady my mind, and renew my faith. Help me rise after every failure, stay humble in every success, and remain faithful in every season. Let me walk with endurance until I reap the harvest You promised. In Jesus' name, **Amen.**

November 26

Enlightenment as a Way of Life

In Honor of Alde Lewis

2 Peter 1:19
So we have the prophetic word made more sure, to which you do well to pay attention as to a lamp shining in a dark place, until the day dawns and the morning star arises in your hearts.

Reflection
Manly P. Hall reminds us: enlightenment isn't a place you arrive at … it's a posture you choose. "The path to enlightenment is not a destination, but a lifelong commitment to self-improvement." — Manly P. Hall

In the same way, spiritual transformation isn't a one-time event but a lifelong journey of refining our mindset, character, and alignment with God's truth. Each moment, whether in error or elevation, invites us to learn, unlearn, grow, and reflect His light.

Transformation begins through daily, Spirit-driven renewal of our thoughts … not by reaching a fixed finish line.

Paul describes this process as renewal: setting aside worldly motivated thinking and letting God reshape our perspectives to a Christ consciousness. It's not about rushing to perfection, but cherishing the daily commitment to become more Christlike.

Enlightenment is not something you reach … it is something you live. When you daily attend to God's Word, His light keeps rising within you, guiding your steps and reshaping your heart. Stay committed to the journey, because a life aligned with His truth is a life continually becoming brighter.

Application
- Pause now and breathe. Identify one area of your thinking or behavior needing refinement … maybe pride, impatience, or fear.
- Then, journal one intentional step to shift that mindset … perhaps memorizing a verse, offering forgiveness, or serving someone.
- Take that step today.

Prayer
Father, I release my old patterns and ask You to renew my mind moment by moment. Teach me humility, patience, and wisdom as I walk this journey of becoming. Let each day reflect more of You. In Jesus' name, **Amen.**

November 27
Love from the Level of Healing

2 Corinthians 3:18
But we all, with unveiled face, beholding as in a mirror the glory of the Lord, are being transformed into the same image from glory to glory, just as from the Lord, the Spirit.

Reflection
Everyone can only love, listen, and understand at the level of their own healing, maturity, and self-awareness. When someone fails to grasp your depth, it doesn't always mean rejection … it may simply mean they don't have the capacity to receive it at that time. Just as a child can only eat what their body can handle, people can only receive the measure of truth their soul has room to digest.

This is why Jesus could be misunderstood by His own disciples at times. Yet He never dimmed His light. He kept teaching, kept loving, kept praying for them until their eyes were opened. In the same way, your responsibility is not to shrink back but to keep shining.

Those who have walked through their inner battles will see you clearly. Others may still be learning, stumbling, or growing. Love them where they are. Pray that they become all God has called them to be. As you do this, remember … you too are still becoming.

Application
- Don't take others' inability to understand you personally; instead, see it as part of their process.
- Choose to love people at their level of growth while you keep pursuing yours.
- Pray for discernment to know when to explain and when to simply let your life be the testimony.

Prayer
Father, thank You for the grace to grow in healing, wisdom, and maturity. Help me not to be offended when others can't grasp my heart or my depth. Instead, give me patience to love them where they are, just as You loved me when I was immature and blind. May I keep shining my light, walking in grace, trusting that You are leading us all on the journey to overcome and become. In Jesus' name, **Amen.**

November 28
You Were Created for Connection
In Honor of Cortez Tolbert Jr. … Aka Smiling Jack

Genesis 2:18
Then the LORD God said, 'It is not good for the man to be alone …

Reflection
Solitude is not the design. When God declared "it is not good for the man to be alone," He broke with His pattern of creation. Everything else He made was "good" … but people were made for more than just existence. They were made for relationship.

This truth doesn't stand only for marriage … it stands for all of us. We were designed for companionship, community, and connection. We are meant to sharpen one another ("Iron sharpens iron…" Proverbs 27:17) .

When we remove ourselves from fellowship …when we stop showing up, calling in or reaching out … we starve the part of us that was made for people. We were never meant to walk alone.

In honoring the memory of those we've lost … we're reminded: presence matters. Being there, being counted, being connected … it's how disciples are sharpened, how hope is held, how the Church is alive.

Today, ask yourself: Am I in community? Am I showing up? Am I letting someone see me … and letting myself see someone else? Because the life God wants for me and for you isn't just survival … it's relationship.

Application
- Reach out to one person today whom you haven't called or seen in a while.
- Invite them into connection … simple message, quick visit, genuine presence.
- If you feel alone, pray: "Lord, bring me into community. Show me the helper You have placed around me."

Prayer
Father, thank You for creating me for more than existence … I was made for relationship with You and with others. Forgive me for the times I've hidden, isolated, or withdrawn. Bring me into community. Give me courage to show up, to connect, to love. Let me be the helper You designed me to be … and let me receive the help You placed around me. In Jesus' name, **Amen.**

November 29
Rules to Upgrade Your Life

1 Timothy 4:7–8
Discipline yourself for the purpose of godliness; for bodily discipline is only of little profit, but godliness is profitable for all things, since it holds promise for the present life and also for the life to come.

Reflection
Transformation does not happen by accident ... it is built by choices. Every day, we are given opportunities to either reinforce habits that keep us stuck or cultivate disciplines that upgrade our lives and bring us closer to Christ's best for us. The world sells shortcuts, but God's Word calls us to stewardship: of our bodies, our minds, and our relationships. Think of these 10 rules as anchors of wisdom, both practical and spiritual. Lifting weights strengthens your body, but it also reminds you to carry burdens with resilience. Eating real foods teaches you to value what truly nourishes, not what simply entertains. Facing your fears mirrors David running toward Goliath, refusing to let intimidation dictate destiny. Positive self-talk aligns your inner voice with God's truth instead of the enemy's lies. Lifelong learning keeps you humble and teachable, just like the Bereans who searched the Scriptures daily. Prioritizing sleep honors the Sabbath principle of rest, trusting that God works while you sleep. Lowering screen time frees your attention from distraction so you can focus on what matters most. Waking up with gratitude tunes your heart to God's blessings before you even face the day's battles. Enjoying the present moment is a reminder that "this is the day the Lord has made." And choosing your circle carefully is wisdom straight from Proverbs: "Bad company corrupts good morals." When practiced with intention, these rules not only upgrade your life ... they align your habits with heaven.

Application
- Choose one rule to practice today ... start where you need growth most.
- Anchor it in Scripture to keep your habit aligned with God's truth.
- Invite accountability by sharing your commitment with a trusted person.

Prayer
Lord, thank You for giving me both wisdom and discipline to live a life that honors You. Help me to see that even the smallest daily choices shape the trajectory of my destiny. Teach me to embrace these rules not just as self-improvement, but as acts of stewardship and obedience. Strengthen me to face fears, guard my circle, and live with gratitude and presence. May my upgraded life reflect Your glory and inspire others to do the same. In Jesus' name, **Amen.**

November 30
Supported From the Inside Out

Psalm 46:10
Be still, and know that I am God.

Reflection
I wasn't always someone who made room for meditation, prayer, or grounding practices. Slowing down felt unfamiliar ... even uncomfortable. But over time, I've learned that stillness is not weakness; it is a form of spiritual strength. In the quiet, God does work that noise can never accomplish.

When we calm our nervous system, regulate our breathing, and sit attentively in God's presence, we create space for restoration. Stillness allows our hearts to realign, our thoughts to settle, and our spirits to receive direction. The world praises constant motion and endless productivity, but God invites us into a different rhythm ... one where rest renews purpose. As Jesus said, "Come away and rest for a while" (Mark 6:31).

Caring for yourself is not selfish ... it is stewardship. God designed us to be vessels, and vessels must be tended to if they are to pour well. When we allow Him to restore us from the inside ... mentally, emotionally, and spiritually ... strength rises naturally on the outside. From that inner support, we lead with clarity, love with patience, and live with a steadiness that only God can give.

Application
- Practice daily stillness: Set aside a few minutes each day to sit quietly before God, focusing on your breath and His presence.
- Honor rest as obedience: Schedule intentional pauses to restore your mind and body, trusting God to sustain what you release.
- Lead from overflow: Before pouring into others, allow God to strengthen you internally so your actions flow from renewal, not exhaustion.

Prayer
Lord, teach me the power of stillness. Quiet my anxious thoughts and help me find grounding in Your presence. Restore me from the inside out, so I may lead, love, and live with the peace that only You provide. **Amen.**

December 1
Refined in the Fire

Isaiah 48:10
Behold, I have refined you, but not as silver; I have tested you in the furnace of affliction.

Reflection
Affliction is not abandonment ... it is refinement.

Just as a blacksmith places gold and silver in the fire to remove impurities, God places His children in seasons of heat to purify our hearts and shape our character. The fire is never meant to destroy you, but to burn away everything that is destroying you ... and that does not reflect His character.

Like the blacksmith who keeps the metal in the furnace until he can see his own reflection, God keeps us in the fire until His image shines back through our lives. Affliction, pain, and struggle are not wasted; they are the divine forge where you are prepared for greater purpose and eternal glory. The real question is not whether you are in the fire, but whether you will let the fire form Christ within you.

The fire you are in is not proof of God's absence ... it is evidence of His attention. He is not punishing you; He is perfecting you. Stay in His hands, endure the heat, and trust the process ... because when the refining is complete, what emerges will bear His image, His strength, and His glory.

Application
- Examine your trials: Are they the result of disobedience or the tool of refinement?
- Invite God to use your affliction to remove pride, sin, or worldly thinking from your heart.
- Remember ... when His reflection becomes visible in you, you are ready for promotion into your next assignment.

Prayer
Father, thank You for the refining fire. Forgive me for resisting the seasons of affliction meant to shape me. Burn away my impurities, my sin, and my selfish thinking, until Your reflection is seen in my life. I trust that the fire is not to destroy me, but to prepare me for my heavenly purpose. In Jesus' name, **Amen.**

December 2
Take Responsibility, Stop Complaining

Philippians 2:14–15
Do all things without complaining or arguments; so that you will prove yourselves to be blameless and innocent, children of God above reproach in the midst of a crooked and perverse generation, among whom you appear as lights in the world.

Reflection
The Israelites saw God part the Red Sea, drown Pharaoh's army, and provide manna from heaven ... yet they still complained. What they thought was frustration with Moses was really unbelief toward God. Complaining is more than words; it reveals the condition of the heart.

Like Adam in the garden, we often avoid responsibility. Instead of saying, "I disobeyed," Adam blamed Eve ... and even God Himself for giving her to him. Complaining is the easy road because it shifts blame outward instead of examining our own heart.

But the truth is this: when we murmur about leaders, family, or circumstances, we are really questioning God's wisdom and care. Complaints choke out gratitude, blind us to God's provision, and delay our growth. The Israelites had bitter water at Marah, but instead of seeking God in prayer, they turned against Moses. How quickly they forgot the God who delivered them was also the God who would sustain them.

The next time life feels bitter, instead of turning on others, turn to God. He knows your need. He holds your life in His hands. He alone can turn bitter waters into sweet refreshment.

Application
- Check Your Heart: When you feel like complaining, ask: Am I really upset with people, or am I frustrated with God's timing and provision?
- Take Responsibility: Own your mistakes without excuses. Repent quickly.
- Pray Instead of Complain: Replace complaints with petitions.

Prayer
Father, forgive me for the times I've complained against others when in truth my heart was doubting You. Teach me to take responsibility, to stand before You with honesty, and to trust that You will meet every need. Help me to lay down excuses, stop blaming others, and walk in gratitude and faith. May my words reflect trust, not grumbling, and may my life shine as a light in this world. In Jesus' name, **Amen.**

December 3

Set the Setting

In Honor of B.Tjuri Turner

Galatians 5:22–23
But the fruit of the Spirit is love, joy, peace, patience, kindness, goodness, faithfulness, gentleness, self-control; against such things there is no law.

Reflection
A thermometer simply tells you the temperature of a room ... but a thermostat actually sets the temperature in the room.

As believers, we are called to be like thermostats; we aren't called to simply mirror culture or reflect the mood of those around us. We are called to set the setting ... to be salt that preserves, light that shines, and Spirit-filled witnesses who bring the presence of Jesus wherever we go. God doesn't simply want visitation rights; He wants full custody of our lives.

That means every space you enter ... your home, your workplace, your church, even casual conversations ... becomes an opportunity to shift the atmosphere in God's favor.

Light pushes back darkness. Love pushes back hate. Joy pushes back despair. Peace calms anxiety.

Remember ... the light of the lamp isn't for the lamp itself ... it's for those who are around the lamp. Your presence should radiate the fruit of the Spirit, so that others are drawn not to you, but to Christ in you.

Application
- Before entering a room today, whisper a prayer: "Lord, let Your Spirit set the atmosphere through me."
- Choose one fruit of the Spirit to "wear" intentionally ... love, joy, peace, patience, kindness, goodness, faithfulness, gentleness, or self-control.
- Reflect at the end of the day: Did I mirror the environment I walked into, or did I set the setting with Christ's presence?

Prayer
Father, take full custody of my life. Make me more than a thermometer that reflects ... make me a thermostat that sets the tone with Your Spirit. Let my presence bring light in dark places, love where there is hate, and joy where there is despair. May the fruit of the Spirit always be evident in me, for Your glory. In Jesus' name, **Amen.**

December 4
Three Solutions

Proverbs 3:5–6
Trust in the Lord with all your heart and do not lean on your own understanding. In all your ways acknowledge Him, and He will make your paths straight.

Reflection
Life presents us with countless challenges, but God always provides a way forward. Often, the answer comes down to three choices: accept it, change it, or leave it.

Some things we must accept ... they are outside of our control, and God is using them to shape us. Like Paul's "thorn in the flesh" (2 Corinthians 12:7–9), acceptance reminds us His grace is sufficient.

Other things we must change ...whether it's our attitude, habits, or circumstances, God gives us authority to act, wisdom to decide, and courage to move forward.

Sometimes, we must simply leave it ... walk away from what drains, distracts, or destroys our peace, and trust God to handle what we cannot.

The key is discernment. Leaning on God allows us to know when to accept, when to act, and when to release. Without His guidance, we often cling to what we should leave or resist what we should accept. But when we surrender the problem to Him, He directs our steps with clarity and peace.

Application
- Pray for Discernment: Ask God, "Is this for me to accept, to change, or to walk away from?"
- Embrace What You Can't Control: Instead of resisting, let it teach you reliance on His grace.
- Act Where You Can: Don't complain about what you have the power to change ... start today.

Prayer
Father, thank You that every problem I face comes with a solution in You. Teach me to accept what I cannot change, to boldly change what I can, and to walk away from what is not Your will for me. Give me wisdom, courage, and peace as I trust in Your guidance. In Jesus' name, **Amen.**

December 5
To Love and Let Go

Matthew 19:29
And everyone who has left houses or brothers or sisters or father or mother or children or farms on account of My name, will receive many times as much, and will inherit eternal life.

Reflection
Love is powerful, but sometimes love can keep us bound to what God is calling us to release.

Many stay in jobs, relationships, or environments far too long ... not because God wants them there, but because love ties them there. Yet Scripture shows us that true love sometimes requires letting go.

God loved Jesus, and Jesus loved His life on earth, but greater glory awaited through the cross. Abraham loved his family and homeland, yet God called him to leave everything familiar for a promise that could only be fulfilled in a new place. Both reveal a truth: letting go is not loss, it is often the doorway to greater.

Sometimes the most loving thing you can do for yourself, others, and God is to release what no longer serves your growth or His purpose. Letting go is not a sign of weakness ... it is an act of trust. To love is to cherish, but to let go is to believe that God has something better beyond what you can see.

Application
- Examine Attachments: Ask God if the things or people you are holding onto are still part of His will for your journey.
- Trust the Exchange: Believe that when God asks you to let go, it is always for something greater ... new provision, new growth, new purpose.
- Obey Quickly: Don't delay obedience like Lot's wife, who looked back. Move forward in faith, trusting God's leading.

Prayer
Father, give me the strength to let go when You are calling me higher. Teach me not to cling to what is familiar if it hinders my growth in You. Help me trust that every release is an invitation to something greater in Your plan. I choose today to let go and let God, believing You hold my future in Your hands. In Jesus' name, **Amen.**

December 6
Be Still and Breathe

Psalm 46:10
Cease striving and know that I am God; I will be exalted among the nations, I will be exalted in the earth.

Reflection
Your body has a built-in "rest and digest" system ... the parasympathetic nervous system (PNS). God designed it to balance the "fight or flight" stress response. When the PNS is activated, your heart rate slows, digestion improves, your muscles release tension, and your mind quiets. It's as if God wired rest right into your design.

Science confirms what Scripture has long declared: stillness brings peace. Practices like deep breathing, gentle movement, prayerful meditation, and even time in nature activate this God-given system. But beyond biology, there is a spiritual reality ... when you slow down and breathe deeply, you make space to sense the Spirit of God within you.

Every exhale can be a release of fear. Every inhale can be a reminder of the breath of life He first gave Adam. To activate the PNS is to practice stewardship of your temple, honoring God with rhythms of calm, trust, and rest. In doing so, you discover that true peace isn't just physiological ... it's spiritual.

Application
- Practice box breathing (inhale 4 seconds, hold 4, exhale 4, hold 4) and use it as a prayer rhythm ... thinking "Lord, You are with me" on the inhale and "I trust You" on the exhale.
- Take a 10-minute walk outdoors today. As you move, thank God for creation and notice the calm He built into nature.
- At night, before sleep, release one worry with each exhale and receive God's peace with each inhale.

Prayer
Father, thank You for designing my body with rhythms of rest. Teach me to breathe with intention, to quiet my heart, and to trust that You are in control. As I slow down, let my body reset and my spirit realign with You. Fill me with Your peace that surpasses understanding, and let my very breath become an act of worship. In Jesus' name, **Amen.**

December 7
Beyond Your Ability But Within His Grace

1 Corinthians 15:10
But by the grace of God I am what I am, and His grace toward me did not prove vain; but I labored even more than all of them, yet not I, but the grace of God with me.

Reflection
God did not design your calling to be comfortable, convenient, or within the limits of your natural abilities. If it were, you would never need Him ... you could fulfill it on your own strength. Instead, He intentionally placed your calling beyond your capacity so you would lean on His sufficiency.

This truth shifts how we see our weaknesses. They are not barriers to ministry; they are the very places where His strength is perfected. When you feel inadequate, you are in the perfect position for God to show Himself strong. When you lack, His grace abounds. When you are stretched beyond what you can do, you discover what only God can do through you.

The real danger is not being weak; it is forgetting your need for Him. Our callings are impossible apart from grace. But when we abide in Him, grace doesn't just cover our shortcomings ... it empowers us to labor faithfully and fruitfully in ways we never imagined.

Application
- Identify one area of your calling that feels overwhelming or beyond your capacity. Surrender it to God in prayer.
- Remind yourself daily that God's grace is not only pardon for sin but power for living and serving.
- Ask the Holy Spirit to make you more dependent on Him than on your natural gifts, talents, or strategies.

Prayed
Lord, thank You for giving me a calling that is bigger than me. Teach me not to fear my weaknesses, but to rest in Your strength. Keep me from pride when I succeed and despair when I fail. Let Your grace empower me to walk faithfully, serve humbly, and finish well. May my life and calling testify that it was not me, but Christ in me. **Amen.**

December 8
The Church is A Hospital, Not a Hospice

Psalm 147:3
He heals the brokenhearted and binds up their wounds.

Reflection
Many people approach church wanting comfort without change. They want soothing words that make them feel good in the moment, but not the kind of truth that brings transformation. This is a dangerous mindset. A church that functions like a hospice will only keep people comfortable while their souls waste away.

But the church Jesus founded was never meant to be a hospice; it was meant to be a hospital. A place where the wounded are healed, the sinner is restored, and the broken are made whole. Hospitals can be uncomfortable … they require surgery, rehab, and sometimes painful treatments. Yet the goal is life, strength, and renewal. Likewise, the church is called to confront sin, challenge hearts, and administer the medicine of God's Word so that people might truly live and experience the freedom Christ came to give.

The church exists to heal, not to merely comfort the dying. God's truth may confront, correct, and even cut at times … but it always cuts to heal. When we embrace the church as a hospital, we allow the Great Physician to do His work: binding wounds, restoring strength, and sending us back into the world alive, whole, and transformed.

Application
- Ask yourself: Do I come to church seeking comfort or transformation?
- Allow God's Word to do the hard work of healing .. confession, repentance, obedience.
- Commit to being part of a church community that equips and restores rather than one that merely entertains or appeases.

Prayer
Lord, thank You that Your church is not a hospice for dying souls but a hospital for healing hearts. Give me the courage to embrace the process of transformation, even when it's uncomfortable. Make me whole and help me to bring the healing power of Christ to others. **Amen.**

December 9
Change Your Soil to Bloom

Isaiah 32:15-16
Until the Spirit is poured out upon us from on high, and the wilderness becomes a fruitful field, and the fruitful field is counted as a forest. Then justice will dwell in the wilderness
And righteousness will abide in the fertile field.

Reflection
Sometimes your roots are planted in soil that simply won't allow you to grow.

In the wrong soil, growth stops and blooms fade. When you're in the wrong environment … spiritually, mentally, relationally … you may need to relocate yourself so you can blossom.

God doesn't always leave you where you are for comfort. He sometimes moves you for cultivation.

Many do not grow because they stay where the soil is depleted and lacks the proper nourishment to produce growth. But when you shift to a place that supports your growth, God's Spirit turns your wilderness into a fruitful field. You don't just survive … you flourish.

Don't fear the shift. Embrace it as part of your blossoming.

Beautiful people, when God shifts your soil, it's never to diminish you … it's to develop you. Trust His placement. Where the Spirit plants you, the Spiritual fruit will prosper you.

Application
- Ask: "What environment is limiting my growth right now?"
- Identify one setting you need to change—maybe your circle, a habit, or a mindset.
- Commit: "I will step into new soil so I can bloom."

Prayer
Father, thank You for not leaving me stranded in unfruitful soil. Help me recognize when it's time to move and give me faith to trust the change. Plant me where Your Spirit can pour out and produce a harvest in my life. In Jesus' name, **Amen.**

December 10
It's Not the Arrow, It's the Archer

2 Corinthians 4:7
But we have this treasure in earthen vessels, so that the surpassing greatness of the power will be of God and not from ourselves.

Reflection
There's a saying: It's not the arrow, it's the Indian. In other words, it's not about what you have in your hand but how you use it. God is less concerned with the size of your resources and more concerned with the posture of your heart and the faith in your obedience.

Moses only had a staff, but when yielded to God, it parted seas. David only had a sling, but with faith, it brought down a giant. The boy only had five loaves and two fish, but in the hands of Jesus, it fed thousands. The lesson is clear: It's not the tool that determines the outcome … it's the God working through the tool and the vessel who is willing to trust Him.

God's power has never depended on perfect tools, only surrendered vessels.

When what you have is placed in His hands, the ordinary becomes extraordinary. Trust the Archer, not the arrow … because the greatness of the result will always point back to God, not you.

Application
- Take inventory of what God has already placed in your hand … your gifts, skills, relationships, and resources.
- Ask God to show you how to use them for His glory, not just your gain.
- Remember: God doesn't need more of what you don't have; He just asks for all of what you do have.

Prayer
Lord, teach me to stop focusing on what I lack and start trusting You with what I already have. Use my hands, my voice, my talents, and my resources as arrows guided by Your Spirit. May my obedience be the bow You draw back to hit the target of Your will. In Jesus' name, **Amen.**

December 11
What Would You Ask For?

Matthew 7:7
Ask, and it will be given to you; seek, and you will find; knock, and it will be opened to you.

Reflection
If God said He would grant you one request, what would rise from your heart first? Would it be something spiritual, emotional, relational, or material? Our answers often reveal where our treasure truly lies.

Solomon asked for wisdom ... not wealth, not fame, not victory over enemies. And God not only gave him wisdom but also added blessings he never asked for. The question forces us to pause: Is what I want most in life something only God can give, or something another person could supply? If it's the latter, perhaps our desires are too small.

God's best is not always what dazzles the eye or satisfies the moment ... it's what transforms the soul. Don't settle for what anyone else could provide. Lift your desires to the level where only God can meet them.

What you ask for reveals what you value. The problem with people is not that they dream too big and miss ... the problem is that they dream too small and hit. God invites you to ask beyond the temporary and seek what only He can give. Ask boldly, seek deeply, and knock faithfully ... because when your desires align with His wisdom, your prayers lead to lasting transformation.

Application
- Take inventory of your desires: are they rooted in eternity or just in the temporary?
- Pray for God to refine your heart so your deepest request aligns with His will.
- This week, write down one request you know only God can answer and lay it before Him daily.

Prayer
Father, reveal the true desires of my heart. Teach me to long for what only You can give ... wisdom, peace, love, and life in You. Protect me from settling for temporary satisfactions, and draw me into eternal pursuits. In Jesus' Name, **Amen.**

December 12
Come as You Are, But Don't Stay as You Are

2 Corinthians 5:17
Therefore, if anyone is in Christ, he is a new creature; the old things passed away; behold, new things have come.

Reflection
"Come as you are" is the beautiful invitation of the gospel. God opens His doors to the broken, the lost, the hurting, and the sinner without condition. But the invitation does not end there. Grace welcomes us, but grace also transforms us.

The church is not a clubhouse for comfort; it is a hospital for healing and a training ground for holiness. God calls us to lay down the sinful patterns we once practiced and step into sanctified living. To stay the same after encountering Christ is to miss the power of His Spirit working within us. Holiness is not perfection by human effort … it is surrender to the God who makes us new.

Grace meets you where you are, but it refuses to leave you there. An encounter with Christ always produces change. As Christians, we should all have a B.C. (Before Christ) and an A.D. (After Deliverance) … and they should not look the same. If anyone is in Christ, the old has passed and the new has come. Come as you are, yes … but surrender fully, be transformed, and walk in the new life He has given you.

Application
- Reflect honestly: Are there areas where you've used "God accepts me as I am" as an excuse to stay unchanged?
- Commit to one habit this week that aligns your lifestyle more with holiness and less with old patterns.
- Remember: the same grace that saved you is the grace that sanctifies you.

Prayer
Lord, thank You for welcoming me into Your presence just as I am. But don't let me stay the same. Transform me by Your Spirit. Break every tie to sinful habits, and shape me into the likeness of Christ. Make holiness not just a calling but my daily pursuit. In Jesus' Name, **Amen.**

December 13
Live For The Audience of One

Galatians 1:10
For am I now seeking the favor of men, or of God? Or am I striving to please men? If I were still trying to please men, I would not be a bond-servant of Christ.

Reflection
The world will never give you the validation your soul craves. If it rejected Jesus ... the only perfect man ... why would it fully embrace you? The cross is proof that the world's standards are broken, unstable, and inconsistent.

Validation is not found in likes, applause, or approval but in Christ alone. To keep chasing worldly affirmation is to put your worth in the hands of people who cannot even carry their own. God's voice is the only one that defines you.

Jesus' life shows us that obedience to the Father matters more than acceptance by the crowd. If you live for the approval of people, you will die by their rejection. But if you live anchored in God's love, you will stand firm no matter what the world says or does.

You were never created to live for applause, but for obedience. When God's approval becomes your anchor, the opinions of people lose their power. Choose faithfulness over fame, truth over trends, and remember ... living for the Audience of One is the only way to live unshaken.

Application
- Shift your source of worth. Each time you crave human approval, remind yourself: "My Father's voice matters most."
- Examine your motives. Ask: Am I doing this to be seen by people, or to be faithful to God?
- Anchor in Christ. Write down three truths from Scripture about who you are in Christ. Meditate on them instead of worldly opinions.

Prayer
Father, forgive me for the times I've sought validation from people more than from You. Help me to remember that if the world crucified Jesus, I cannot expect its approval to define me. Teach me to rest in Your love and let Your Word shape my identity. May I live for an audience of One ... pleasing You above all else. **Amen.**

December 14
Don't Get Distracted

Psalm 16:8
I have set the Lord continually before me;
Because He is at my right hand, I will not be shaken.

Reflection
The size of God in your life will always determine the size of everything else. When God is set continually before you, He becomes your reference point, your stabilizer, and your source of clarity. Problems don't magically disappear, but they are rightly positioned. Fear loses its dominance. Pressure loses its voice. The opinions of people no longer dictate your peace because God's presence outweighs their perspective.

Distraction doesn't usually come by removing God altogether … it comes by slowly shifting our focus. Little by little, worries grow louder, deadlines feel heavier, and people's expectations begin to compete with God's Word. When that happens, God isn't absent … He's just been crowded out. But when we intentionally magnify Him through worship, prayer, and Scripture, everything else shrinks back to its proper size.

To "set the Lord continually before me" is an act of discipline and devotion. It means choosing His truth over noise, His promises over pressure, and His presence over performance. With God at your right hand, stability replaces anxiety and confidence replaces fear. So guard your focus. Don't let distractions pull your eyes downward toward chaos … keep them lifted upward toward the One who keeps you unshaken.

Application
- Start today by praying, "Lord, be bigger in my life than anything else."
- Whenever you feel overwhelmed, pause and ask: "How big is God in this moment to me?"
- Silence unnecessary voices and elevate God's voice by dwelling on His Word.

Prayer
Father, help me not to be distracted by the noise of people or the weight of my problems. Teach me to magnify You daily so that everything else falls into its proper place. Be the greatest reality in my life, Lord, and let me walk in confidence because You are at my right hand. In Jesus' Name, **Amen.**

December 15
Compassion That Breaks Our Hearts

Matthew 9:36
When He saw the crowds, He felt compassion for them, because they were distressed and downcast, like sheep without a shepherd.

Reflection
We have to ask ourselves as Christians: Do the things that break the heart of Jesus break our hearts also? Jesus was never indifferent to the suffering around Him. His eyes saw beyond the surface, His heart felt the weight of brokenness, and His hands moved toward healing and hope.

Compassion is not pity ... it is love in action. It is the divine capacity to hurt with others and move toward them with the same mercy Christ has shown us. Compassion literally means ... " to suffer with." If our hearts remain unmoved by the pain of others, then we must examine whether we are truly walking in step with Christ. To follow Him is to be sensitive, empathetic, and responsive to the needs of the lost, the hurting, and the forgotten.

If our hearts are unmoved by suffering, injustice, or spiritual lostness, then something in us has grown calloused. Following Christ means allowing Him to shape our inner life so deeply that His burdens become ours. A heart aligned with Jesus cannot remain indifferent ... it becomes sensitive, responsive, and willing to step into discomfort for the sake of love.

Compassion is the evidence that Christ is alive within us. When His heart becomes our heart, we no longer turn away from brokenness ... we move toward it. May we allow God to break our hearts for what breaks His, and may that brokenness become the doorway through which healing, hope, and redemption flow to others.

Application
- Identify someone in your life who is struggling and take a step to show Christ's compassion.
- Pray for the Spirit to give you His eyes so you see beyond surface appearances.
- Ask yourself daily: Am I moved by what moves Jesus?

Prayer
Lord Jesus, soften my heart to feel what You feel. Break my heart for what breaks Yours. Let me not walk past the hurting without seeing them, nor hear the cries of the weary without responding. Fill me with Your compassion so that my life reflects Your mercy and love. **Amen.**

December 16
Your Story Becomes a Survival Guide

2 Corinthians 1:3–4
Blessed be the God and Father of our Lord Jesus Christ, the Father of mercies and God of all comfort, who comforts us in all our affliction so that we will be able to comfort those who are in any affliction with the comfort with which we ourselves are comforted by God.

Reflection
Every trial you've endured has a purpose bigger than your pain. What once felt like a breaking point can later become the very testimony that holds someone else together. God does not waste your tears, your setbacks, or your struggles. He redeems them, shapes them, and then uses them as a guiding light for others who are still walking through their storms.

One day, when you share your story of overcoming, it won't just be a victory report … it will be someone else's survival guide. Your scars become signposts pointing others to Jesus, the true Healer. What you thought was just about your survival becomes the seed of another person's revival.

Your pain was never the end of the story … it was the training ground for compassion. What God carried you through, He now wants to carry others through *you*. Don't hide your testimony or minimize your journey. When surrendered to Him, your story becomes proof that survival is possible, healing is real, and hope still lives.

Application
- Think of one challenge God has already brought you through. How might your testimony help someone going through the same thing right now?
- Ask God for opportunities to speak courage into another person's life using your lived experiences.
- Instead of hiding your scars, see them as evidence of God's healing power and share them with humility.

Prayer
Father, thank You for turning my trials into testimonies. Help me to see that my story is not just for me, but for the healing and encouragement of others. Give me the courage to share how You've brought me through, so that someone else may find hope, strength, and salvation in You. **Amen.**

December 17
Thank You Father, for Saving My Life

Psalm 28:7
The LORD is my strength and my shield; My heart trusts in Him, and I am helped; Therefore my heart triumphs, And with my song I shall thank Him.

Reflection
If the enemy had his way, we would have been destroyed long ago. In many cases, the choices we've made has made his job much easier. Yet God, in His mercy and grace has caused us to pivot … to turn away from destructive thoughts and actions and come back to Him.

Every breath you take is evidence that God has not given up on you. He has saved your life … He carried you when others turned their backs, and He loved you when you didn't even love yourself. The testimony of your life is not what the enemy planned, but what God has redeemed.

When you were broken, God healed. When you were lost, He found you. When you were empty, He filled you. Even in the midnight hour, when no one else was listening, He heard your cry. That's why gratitude must be more than a moment … it must become a lifestyle and a heart posture.

Application
- Reflect on a time when God "pivoted" your life away from destruction. Write it down as a testimony of His saving grace.
- Today, start your morning with three specific "Thank You, Father" statements.
- Share your story of God's faithfulness with someone who may need hope right now.

Prayer
Father, I am only here because You allowed me to be. If the enemy had his way, I would have been gone long ago. But You stepped in, You redirected me, You saved me. Thank You for not giving up on me, for hearing me in the midnight hour, for breathing life into me when others thought I was finished. My life is a testimony of Your mercy. I give You glory, in Jesus' name, **Amen.**

December 18
The Battlefield of the Mind

2 Corinthians 10:3–5
For though we walk in the flesh, we do not war according to the flesh, for the weapons of our warfare are not of the flesh, but divinely powerful for the destruction of fortresses. We are destroying speculations and every lofty thing raised up against the knowledge of God, and we are taking every thought captive to the obedience of Christ.

Reflection
The greatest battle you will ever fight is not with others, but with yourself. Every day the mind becomes a battlefield where the voices of the world compete against the voice of God. Culture trains us to chase success, status, and self gratification, while the Spirit calls us to holiness and obedience.

The enemy knows if he can capture your thoughts, he can control your life. That is why Paul tells us to "take every thought captive to the obedience of Christ" (2 Cor. 10:5). Our thoughts are not neutral ... they either align with the lies of the world or with the truth of God's Word.

Renewal comes through reprogramming. The mind shaped by the world is programmed for fear, pride, and compromise. The mind renewed by the Word of God is programmed for peace, faith, righteousness and victory. The more we meditate on Scripture, the more the Spirit rewrites the code of our thinking until Christ becomes the pattern of our thoughts.

Application
- Identify one worldly thought pattern you've believed (fear, doubt, pride, comparison). Replace it with a Scripture promise.
- Begin your day by reading or reciting a verse to program your mind with truth before the world programs you with lies.
- When negative thoughts rise, stop and declare: "I take this thought captive to Christ."

Prayer
Father, I confess that too often my mind has been shaped by the patterns of this world. Reprogram me by Your Word. Train my thoughts to line up with truth, and give me discernment to recognize the lies of the enemy. May my mind become a stronghold of peace, faith, and obedience, so that I might live out Your will in victory. In Jesus' name, **Amen.**

December 19
When Charity Becomes Toxic

2 Thessalonians 3:10
For even when we were with you, we used to give you this order: if anyone is not willing to work, then he is not to eat, either.

Reflection
Not all giving is godly.

Sometimes what we call "charity" actually becomes toxic when it robs people of the very lessons God wants them to learn. When we step in to rescue others from the natural consequences of their choices, we can unintentionally disable their growth, stunting both their character and faith.

God calls us to compassion, but also to wisdom. Jesus fed the hungry and healed the sick, but He also called people to repentance, responsibility, and discipleship. True love does not enable destructive patterns; it empowers people to walk in freedom. Toxic charity feels like kindness in the moment, but in reality, it keeps people dependent on the giver rather than on God.

Healthy generosity equips, encourages, and points people to Christ as their ultimate source. Toxic charity, on the other hand, creates cycles of dependency that keep others from rising up in faith, stewardship, and responsibility. The call of the believer is to give in ways that bring dignity, not dependency … help that heals, not help that harms.

Application
- Ask God to show you if your giving patterns are empowering or enabling.
- When you help someone, also consider how you can teach, equip, or guide them to grow.
- Reflect on Jesus' model … He gave freely, but His gifts always led people toward responsibility and transformation.

Prayer
Lord, give me wisdom in my generosity. Keep my heart tender to the needs of others, but also discerning so I do not enable cycles of dependency. Teach me how to give in ways that reflect Your love, empower responsibility, and point people back to You. May my charity bring freedom, not bondage. In Jesus' name, **Amen.**

December 20
Unshackled: From History to Destiny

Philippians 3:13
Brothers and sisters, I do not consider myself yet to have taken hold of it. But one thing I do: forgetting what lies behind and straining forward to what lies ahead.

Reflection
We often carry invisible chains ... our past mistakes, regrets, disappointments ... keeping us tethered to what was instead of launching us into what can be. Yet, destiny beckons us forward, urging us not to be so handcuffed to history that we cannot embrace the future God has planned.

T.D. Jakes hits this truth powerfully:
"When you hold onto your history, you do it at the expense of your destiny."
"You cannot embrace your destiny if you do not let go of your history."

God's Word echoes this call:
Isaiah declares, "Forget the former things; do not dwell on the past. See, I am doing a new thing!" And Hebrews reminds us of God's redemptive power: Our sufferings and past failures pale in comparison to the glory unveiled in our future.

Your history doesn't define you ... unless you let it. In Christ, the shackles of the past can't hold you. Let go. Lean in. Your true story is still unfolding.

Application
- Identify the Chains ... Write down a thought, habit, regret, or fear from your past that keeps you stuck.
- Release It ... Lay it before God in prayer and confession; trust His forgiveness and purpose.
- Take One Step of Faith ... Do one thing today that propels you toward your God-given future: start a new habit, seek a fresh calling, or declare a hope-filled truth out loud.

Prayer
Lord Jesus, forgive me for letting my past dictate my present. I confess those thoughts and habits that have kept me bound. Today, I surrender them at Your feet. Renew my mind, shift my focus, and help me step into the destiny You've prepared. Teach me to strain forward, pressing into Your purposes, unshackled and ready. In Your name, **Amen.**

December 21
Hidden Worship, Public Weapons.

Matthew 6:6
But when you pray, go into your inner room, close your door and pray to your Father who is in secret, and your Father who sees what is done in secret will reward you.

Reflection
The hidden personal worshiping life of the saint is God's training ground. It is there away from applause and recognition, that God shapes character, sharpens discernment, and equips His people with weapons unseen. Public ministry is forged in private devotion. Missionary power flows not from platforms, but from prayer closets.

Every missionary weapon … faith, love, humility, endurance, authority in the Spirit … is first learned in the unseen presence of God. The disciple who kneels in secret before the Father carries invisible strength into visible battles. Without the hidden life of worship, public service becomes hollow performance.

Like David in the fields before Goliath, the Lord trains our hands for war in solitude long before He sends us to the battlefield. What you cultivate with God in secret becomes the arsenal you carry in service to others.

This battle is won by spiritual authority, not human strength. Every lie must fall and every thought must submit to Christ. When your mind is aligned with Him, your life will move in power.

Application
- Evaluate your secret life with God … does it overflow into your public witness?
- Commit daily time for private prayer, worship, and Word, even when no one sees.
- Ask God to reveal the "missionary weapons" He is forming in you: faith, courage, patience, or compassion.

Prayer
Father, thank You for the secret place where You train and prepare me. Forgive me for times I've neglected the hidden life with You. Teach me to treasure the unseen moments of worship and prayer, knowing they shape me for every battle and mission You send me into. May my strength in public always be the fruit of my surrender in private. In Jesus' name, **Amen.**

December 22
Failure Is Part of It, and the Start of It

Proverbs 24:16
For a righteous man falls seven times, and rises again,
But the wicked stumble in time of calamity.

Reflection
Failure is not the end of the story ... it is often the doorway into your next level of growth. Proverbs reminds us that righteousness is not defined by never falling, but by the willingness to rise again. The righteous fall, learn, adjust, and get back up. The difference is not perfection ... it is perseverance.

Don't be paralyzed by the fear of falling; be paralyzed by the thought of never trying. God uses failure as a classroom. In those moments where plans collapse and confidence is shaken, He teaches us humility, dependence, and endurance. Failure exposes where we relied too heavily on ourselves and invites us to trust Him more deeply. What the world labels as defeat, God often uses as development. The world claps for winners, but heaven claps for the faithful. God measures not by trophies or titles, but by obedience and trust in Him.

The fear of failure can immobilize us, keeping us stuck in comfort rather than obedience. But faith is rarely flawless ... it is often messy, stretched, and tested. When we step out, even imperfectly, we give God room to work. Heaven is not impressed by flawless performance; it honors faithful persistence. God measures success by obedience, not outcomes.

So fall if you must ... but rise again. Each attempt refines you, strengthens you, and prepares you for what's ahead. Do your part with courage and faith, then rest in the assurance that God is working through every step, stumble, and restart.

Application
- Think about a time you failed ... what lesson did God teach you through it?
- Identify one area where fear of failure is holding you back. Take one step of faith this week.
- Remind yourself daily: failure is not fatal, and God uses it for formation.

Prayer
Father, thank You for reminding me that failure is not my enemy but a stepping stone to growth. Help me not to fear falling, but to fear standing still in disobedience. Give me courage to try, to trust, and to learn. Reward my effort as I rest in Your hands. In Jesus' name, **Amen.**

December 23
Secrets of Sincere Love

Jeremiah 33:3
Call to Me and I will answer you, and I will tell you great and mighty things, which you do not know.

Reflection
George Washington Carver once said, "If you fall in love with anything sincerely it will reveal its secrets to you." His words carry a spiritual weight beyond science and agriculture. The same principle applies to our relationship with God. Love is the key that unlocks revelation. When we sincerely love God ... beyond ritual, beyond obligation ... His Word, His Spirit, and even His creation begin to unveil their hidden treasures.

Just as Carver discovered new uses for the peanut through devotion and curiosity, the believer who falls in love with God discovers mysteries of grace, wisdom, and power not available to the casual seeker. Revelation is not random; it is relational. The more we love God with sincerity, the more the secrets of His Kingdom are entrusted to us.

Love is the door, and sincerity is the key. When our hearts are aligned with God in love, even ordinary things become extraordinary lessons. Like the disciples who walked closely with Jesus, we are invited to hear things "hidden from the wise and intelligent" but revealed to those with childlike hearts (Matthew 11:25).

Application
- Reflect: Do you love God for what He gives, or for who He is?
- Commit to pursuing God with sincerity, not performance ... letting love guide your study and prayer.
- Ask God to reveal hidden truths as you fall deeper in love with Him and His Word.

Prayer
Father, thank You for the reminder that love unlocks Your secrets. Forgive me for times I sought knowledge without seeking You. Teach me to love You sincerely, with all my heart, mind, and soul. As I fall deeper in love with You, reveal to me the mysteries of Your Word, Your Spirit, and Your creation. May my devotion open the treasures of Your Kingdom and make me a faithful steward of Your truth. In Jesus' name, **Amen.**

December 24
Handcuffed to History or Free for Destiny

Isaiah 43:18–19
Forget the former things; do not dwell on the past. Behold, I am doing something new, now it will spring forth; will you not be aware of it? I will even make a roadway in the wilderness, rivers in the desert.

Reflection
History is a teacher, but it was never meant to be a prison.

Too often, we chain ourselves to past mistakes, failures, or even past successes, as if they define the totality of who we are. When that happens, history becomes handcuffs … limiting what God desires to do in the present and through us in the future.

Your destiny is not held hostage by your history. In Christ, the past is redeemed, the present is empowered, and the future is secured. The enemy will always remind you of what you did; the Spirit always points to what God is doing. The call of God requires forward movement … pressing toward what lies ahead, not dragging the chains of yesterday.

Joseph's betrayal did not cancel his destiny in Egypt. Paul's persecution of Christians did not cancel his destiny as an apostle. Your mistakes, wounds, or even your victories do not define the fullness of your calling. God's grace not only unlocks the door … it removes the handcuffs and points you toward the path of destiny.

Application
- Identify one area where you've been dwelling on your past … whether shame, regret, or even nostalgia.
- Release it in prayer, declaring God's promise to make all things new.
- Take a tangible step toward your God-given future this week … apply for the opportunity, begin the project, forgive the person, or simply trust Him for the next step.

Prayer
Father, thank You that my destiny is not chained to my history. Forgive me for the times I've let the past handcuff my faith, my joy, or my obedience. Today, I release every regret, every failure, and even every success to You. Teach me to walk freely in the new thing You are doing. I embrace my destiny in Christ and trust that Your future for me is greater than anything behind me. In Jesus' name, **Amen.**

December 25
The Languages of Love

1 Corinthians 13:13
And now faith, hope, love, abide these three; but the greatest of these is love.

Reflection
Love is the heartbeat of Scripture. Yet in the New Testament, not all love is the same. The Greek language paints a fuller picture with four unique expressions:

Agápē … God's unconditional, covenant love. This is love that sacrifices without expecting return, perfectly demonstrated in Christ's death on the cross (John 3:16).
Phílos …The love of friendship, loyalty, and mutual encouragement, like the bond of David and Jonathan (1 Samuel 18:1).
Storgē … The affection of family, the natural bond of parent and child or brothers and sisters, seen in the household of Martha, Mary, and Lazarus.
Érōs … Romantic, passionate love, designed by God for marriage, expressed in the Song of Solomon and celebrated as a gift within the covenant of husband and wife (1 Corinthians 7).

C.S. Lewis described these as the four loves that shape human experience … affection, friendship, romance, and charity … with agape reigning as the highest. Even psychology observes similar categories, though Scripture alone points us back to the source: God is love (1 John 4:8).

Each form of love has its place, but agape love is the root and fulfillment of them all. When God's unconditional love flows through us, it strengthens friendships, unites families, and purifies romance.

Application
- Which form of love (agape, philia, storge, eros) do you experience most strongly in this season of life?
- How can you express agape love more intentionally today … to a friend, a family member, or even in your marriage?
- Reflect on the ways God has demonstrated all four loves in your own story.

Prayer
Father, thank You for showing me the fullness of love in all its forms. Teach me to walk in agape love, so that my friendships grow deeper, my family ties stronger, and my relationships purer. May every expression of love in my life reflect the heart of Jesus. **Amen.**

December 26
Why the Shift Feels Like Rejection

2 Timothy 3:12
Indeed, all who desire to live godly in Christ Jesus will be persecuted.

Reflection
Sometimes the tension you feel isn't because you did something wrong … it's because you did something right.

When you begin to heal, grow, and stand on truth, you unknowingly confront what others have refused to face within themselves. Your boundaries challenge their entitlement. Your peace disrupts their chaos. Your discipline exposes their excuses.

Rather than doing their own inner work, some people rewrite the narrative. They say you've "changed," become "cold," or grown "distant." Not because you lost love … but because you lost tolerance for dysfunction. This is the silent war … not fought with confrontation, but with projection.

Scripture prepares us for this reality. A life aligned with Christ will not always be applauded. Growth has a cost. Standing on truth often separates you from those who were only comfortable with the version of you that stayed small. But God never calls you to shrink for the sake of someone else's comfort. He calls you to be transformed.

Those who are meant to walk with you will recognize the upgrade … not resent it.

Application
• Examine whether resistance around you is a call to compromise or confirmation to stand firm.
• Release the need to explain your growth to those unwilling to grow.
• Choose alignment over approval … even when it feels lonely.

Prayer
Father, give me the courage to stand on truth without shrinking back. Help me discern between conviction and projection. Keep my heart pure, my boundaries healthy, and my walk aligned with You. **Amen.**

December 27
Purposely Bright

Philippians 2:15
Shine as lights in the world, in the midst of a crooked and perverse generation.

Reflection
To be bright on purpose means to live with intentional illumination … reflecting God's glory in a darkened world. It's not an accident, a mood, or dependent on external approval. It's a choice rooted in identity and empowered by Spirit.

In a time when shadows threaten to overwhelm, believers are called not just to survive but to shine. But many drift through life dimmed by fear, comparison, offense, or self-doubt. The world usually rewards keeping one's light hidden, playing small, staying quiet. Yet the Kingdom calls us higher.

Being bright on purpose begins within: in how you see yourself, whom you trust, and to what you surrender. If your identity is hidden, your brightness will flicker. If your faith is small, your impact will be weak. But when you recognize that your worth is in Christ … and that He has placed radiance within you … you can step forward, intentionally, with courage.

When you choose to shine … through your words, your deeds, your presence … you push back darkness. You affirm God's design in you and offer others a glimpse of what's possible. Don't wait for permission. Live as the light you were created to be.

Application
- Choose one area today where you've been dimmed by fear or doubt, and intentionally shine with confidence in Christ.
- Speak or act in a way that reflects God's light, even if the environment around you feels dark.
- Root your identity in Christ daily so your inner light stays steady, strong, and unhidden.

Prayer
Lord, thank You for placing Your light in me. Help me to live not by hiding, but by brightness on purpose. Reveal to me any shadows I still carry. Replace fear with faith. Give me courage to shine … not for myself, but for Your glory and for those around me. In Jesus' name, **Amen.**

December 28
A Beacon of Light

Matthew 5:14
You are the light of the world. A city set on a hill cannot be hidden.

Reflection
God's Light is for you; your light is for others.

To be a beacon means to shine in a way that guides, warns, and inspires. Just as a lighthouse stands tall on the shore to keep sailors from danger, you are called to be a light in a dark world ... pointing people back to God.

Psychologist Abraham Maslow spoke of self-actualization: becoming all that you were created to be. Yet long before Maslow, God's Word taught us that true fulfillment is not found in climbing human hierarchies of need, but in surrendering to God's Spirit. Real self-actualization is Christ-actualization. When His light fills you, it overflows to others.

Honesty, awareness, freedom, and trust are more than psychological pillars ... they are spiritual cornerstones. Honesty keeps your light clear. Awareness keeps your light focused. Freedom keeps your light unhindered. Trust keeps your light anchored in God.

To be a beacon of light in someone's darkness is not optional; it's the Christian's calling and command. The light of the lamp is not for lamp. You don't shine for yourself... you shine for others. And you don't shine by your own strength ... you shine because you are connected to the Source.

Application
- Stay connected to the Source: Begin each day in prayer and the Word, asking God to fill you so His light ... not your own ... shines through you.
- Shine with intention: Look for one person or situation today where your words, actions, or presence can guide, encourage, or point someone to God.
- Guard your light: Walk in honesty, awareness, freedom, and trust so nothing clouds, dims, or distracts from the light God has placed within you.

Prayer
Father, thank You for Your Light that guides me, heals me, and saves me. Help me to shine with honesty, awareness, freedom, and trust, so that others may see You through me. Make me a beacon that points the lost to safety, the broken to healing, and the weary to rest. In Jesus' name, **Amen.**

December 29
Training the Inner Man

1 Timothy 4:8
For bodily training is just slightly beneficial, but godliness is beneficial for all things, since it holds promise for the present life and also for the life to come.

Reflection
You can exercise seven days a week, 365 days a year. You can maintain the cleanest diet and eat only the best foods. You can achieve the highest degrees and even amass billions of dollars. But if you neglect your inner man, all your external achievements will mean little.

The body has limits. Wealth and education have boundaries. But godliness reaches both this life and the life to come. The inner man ... your spirit and soul ... must be fed, trained, and guarded with more diligence than your body. Otherwise, you risk premature perishing, not because your body failed, but because your soul was malnourished.

Physical health and worldly success are not wrong, but they cannot replace the eternal value of cultivating godliness. When you strengthen the inner man through prayer, the Word, and godly discipline, you build a foundation that sustains every other part of life.
Everything you build on the outside will eventually fade, but what you strengthen on the inside will carry you through time and into eternity. Train your body, pursue excellence, and steward success ... but never at the expense of your soul. When the inner man is strong, every other area of life finds its balance, purpose and its victory.

Application
- Take time today to feed your spirit with God's Word before you feed your body with food.
- Set spiritual disciplines (prayer, study, worship) with the same intentionality as physical exercise or work goals.
- Evaluate your priorities ... are you training your body and career more than your soul?

Prayer
Lord, thank You for reminding me that true strength is not found in muscles, money, or degrees, but in a soul anchored in You. Help me train my inner man daily with Your Word and Spirit. May my pursuit of godliness outweigh every earthly ambition, and may my life bear fruit that lasts beyond time into eternity. **Amen.**

December 30
Your Greatest Project

Ephesians 2:10
For we are His workmanship, created in Christ Jesus for good works, which God prepared beforehand so that we would walk in them.

Reflection
Your greatest project is you.

Your greatest work of art is not something you build with your hands, but the life you allow God to shape through your heart. Every stroke of growth, every line of discipline, every color of grace added to your story is a reflection of the Master Artist.

The truth is, God isn't finished with you yet. He specializes in renovation … taking broken vessels and making them new. The greatest creation you'll ever present to the world is not your résumé, not your business, not even your ministry … it's the new, improved version of you, surrendered and transformed by the Spirit of God.

Transformation is a process. There will be days you need to restart. Moments you need to reset. Seasons when you must refocus. That is not failure … it is faith. The only way you lose is if you give up. As long as you keep going, God keeps working.

You are the greatest project you'll ever work on.
Don't give up … the Artist is still painting.

Application
- Daily Check-in … Each day, ask: Am I letting God shape me, or am I trying to shape myself?
- Allow Restart Grace … When you stumble, don't quit. Restart. Reset. Refocus.
- Celebrate Small Progress … Remember, every step forward, no matter how small, is part of God's masterpiece.

Prayer
Father, thank You that I am Your workmanship, a project still in progress. Teach me to embrace the process of becoming, to restart when I fall, to reset when I drift, and to refocus when I grow weary. May my life reflect the masterpiece of Your love and grace. In Jesus' name, **Amen.**

December 31
Shutting the Door on Yesterday

Philippians 3:13–14
Brothers and sisters, I do not regard myself as having taken hold of it yet; but one thing I do: forgetting what lies behind and reaching forward to what lies ahead, I press on toward the goal for the prize of the upward call of God in Christ Jesus.

Reflection
Yesterday carries its weight ... failures, regrets, broken promises, and painful memories. If we aren't careful, we drag yesterday clouds over today's sunshine ... and chain ourselves to what God has already released. But grace gives us the authority to shut the door on yesterday, lock it, and throw away the key.

God never meant for you to live in the shadows of past mistakes. In Christ, your sins are forgiven, your failures redeemed, and your future secured. The Spirit invites you into a new room ... a new season, furnished not with sorrow, but with joy; not with regret, but with hope; not with fear, but with faith.

Living in the present doesn't ignore the past ... it redeems it. Nor does it fear tomorrow ... it trusts it into God's hands. Freedom begins when you release yesterday, embrace today, and walk into tomorrow without fear, because God is already there.

Application
- Take a moment to write down one regret or failure from yesterday (or your past). Pray over it, then physically tear it up as a symbolic act of shutting the door.
- Start today by furnishing your "new room" with hope: write down three blessings you're thankful for right now.
- Speak life into your future by declaring, "Tomorrow holds no fear for me, for God is already in my tomorrow."

Prayer
Lord, thank You that in You, my past no longer defines me, my present is filled with Your presence, and my future is secure. Give me the strength to shut the door on yesterday and the faith to walk in today's blessings. Replace my regrets with hope, my sorrows with joy, and my fears with peace. In Jesus' name, **Amen.**

An Author's Charge

Beautiful People,

If you have walked these pages with sincerity, you already know this book was never meant to simply be read … it was meant to **reshape how you live**.

Transformation is not an event; it is a daily decision. Every morning you wake up with a choice … to conform to the world's noise or to be renewed by God's truth. My prayer is that *THE PIVOT* has reminded you that real change does not begin around you … it begins **within you**.

I charge you to **live transformed**.
Not polished on the outside while fractured on the inside, but rooted, whole, and aligned with God's purpose. Let truth confront you, refine you, and strengthen you. Growth may be uncomfortable, but stagnation is far more dangerous.

I charge you to **stand on truth daily**.
Truth is not popular, but it is powerful. In a culture that shifts with opinions, emotions, and trends, anchor your life in what does not change. When truth governs your thoughts, your choices, and your character … clarity replaces confusion and peace replaces unrest.

Finally, I charge you to **become a light in this world**.
Light does not argue with darkness … it simply shows up. Wherever God places you … in your home, your work, your community … shine. Reflect Christ through your love, your integrity, your compassion, and your courage. The world does not need more noise; it needs more light.

This is your pivot point.
Do not turn back. Do not settle. Do not shrink.
Live awake. Live aligned. Live as one who knows the truth … and walks in it.

Pastor Everett LaMar Blaylock
A Beacon Of Light.org

Scripture Index

Old Testament

Genesis

- **Genesis 1:26** ... (June 12 • One With God)
- **Genesis 1:27** ... (November 5 • Created to Create)
- **Genesis 2:7** ... (February 25 • The Cheat Code of Breath); (April 14 • A Divine Spark Within)
- **Genesis 11:6** ... (August 1 • Unity: Gang Up on the Problem, Not Each Other)
- **Genesis 12:3** ... (February 20 • Will Your Sacrifice Be the Reason Your Family Flourishes?)
- **Genesis 19:17** ... (October 9 • The Point of No Return)

Exodus

- **Exodus 12:2** ... (April 1 • Happy New Year April Fool)
- **Exodus 14:14** ... (July 27 • Be Still & Let God Fight)
- **Exodus 20:5** ... (April 11 • Heal the Parent, Protect the Child)

Deuteronomy

- **Deuteronomy 2:3** ... (April 7 • To Get to the Promise)
- **Deuteronomy 11:24** ... (November 10 • Go Get It and Come Back With It)

Judges

- **Judges 2:10** ... (May 29 • Disconnected Youth, Defeated Generation)

Psalms

- **Psalm 16:8** ... (December 14 • Don't Get Distracted)
- **Psalm 19:14** ... (May 6 • Living by a Creed)
- **Psalm 23:5** ... (June 16 • Anointed for Peace)
- **Psalm 23:1–3** ... (August 26 • A Shepherd and His Sheep)
- **Psalm 28:7** ... (December 17 • Thank You Father, for Saving My Life)

- **Psalm 37:4** ... (January 27 • Through Devotion)
- **Psalm 37:7** ... (March 4 • Mastered by Time)
- **Psalm 46:10** ... (March 9 • A Still Pond Reflects the Sun Perfectly); (June 18 • The Strength of Stillness); (October 27 • Be Still and Know: From Beta to Alpha); (November 30 • Supported from the Inside Out); (December 6 • Be Still and Breathe)
- **Psalm 51:10** ... (February 2 • Stay Light So You Can Take Flight)
- **Psalm 90:12** ... (August 9 • Procrastination Isn't Your Friend)
- **Psalm 96:1** ... (April 5 • I Didn't Come to Go Along; I Came to Create a New Song)
- **Psalm 103:12** ... (September 27 • Washed Away)
- **Psalm 119:37** ... (February 16 • A Distracted Mind Never Builds an Intentional Life)
- **Psalm 119:105** ... (May 1 • The Greatest Love Letter Ever Written)
- **Psalm 127:1** ... (June 30 • Marriage: Built to Last)
- **Psalm 139:14** ... (March 7 • Don't Wait to Be Great); (June 14 • Heaven in Your Design); (July 1 • Authentic by Design); (October 30 • Single and Rooted in Worth)
- **Psalm 145:18–19** ... (September 4 • God Is Near When You Call)
- **Psalm 147:3** ... (December 8 • The Church Is a Hospital, Not a Hospice)

Proverbs

- **Proverbs 2:6** ... (April 10 • Mastering Your Three Currencies: Knowledge, Time, Money)
- **Proverbs 3:5–6** ... (February 19 • Appreciate the Detour); (May 17 • One Small Decision Away from Breakthrough); (December 4 • Three Solutions)
- **Proverbs 3:19** ... (August 24 • Wisdom in Action)
- **Proverbs 4:20–21** ... (January 19 • Look, Listen, and Learn)
- **Proverbs 4:23** ... (March 31 • Guarding Your Peace); (July 16 • Guarding Your Energy); (October 18 • Guard Your Legacy)
- **Proverbs 4:25** ... (January 30 • Focus: Eyes Fixed on Purpose)
- **Proverbs 4:25–27** ... (May 4 • Distractions in Disguise)
- **Proverbs 6:6–8** ... (August 8 • Wisdom in Small Things)
- **Proverbs 11:3** ... (January 31 • Integrity: Wholeness in Action); (June 24 • Integrity Over Impressing)

- **Proverbs 11:25** … (June 23 • The Gift of Giving); (July 25 • Don't Be Like the Dead Sea)
- **Proverbs 13:4** … (January 6 • Discipline Determines Destiny); (May 3 • Ambition Without Action Becomes Anxiety)
- **Proverbs 13:12** … (February 13 • The Power of Hope)
- **Proverbs 13:22** … (September 18 • A Good Man Leaves an Inheritance)
- **Proverbs 14:12** … (August 12 • Get Off the Wrong Train)
- **Proverbs 14:34** … (July 4 • When a Nation Forgets God)
- **Proverbs 15:13** … (May 14 • What's Behind Your Smile?)
- **Proverbs 16:24** … (July 14 • From Venting to Victory)
- **Proverbs 16:32** … (August 13 • The Power of De-Escalation)
- **Proverbs 20:5** … (November 23 • Depth Determines Connection)
- **Proverbs 20:7** … (June 21 • A Father's Holy Weight)
- **Proverbs 21:5** … (January 16 • You Are the Equation)
- **Proverbs 23:7** … (March 2 • Power of Thought, Word, and Presence)
- **Proverbs 23:7a** … (June 4 • What Happens Inside Matters Most); (November 12 • The Power of "I AM")
- **Proverbs 23:20–21** … (April 26 • Make Your Food Your Medicine)
- **Proverbs 24:16** … (January 5 • Rise Again); (June 3 • Lessons in the Fall); (July 28 • Bob & Weave: Lessons From My First Coaches); (December 22 • Failure Is Part of It, and the Start of It)
- **Proverbs 25:28** … (June 7 • Master Your Desires to Manage Your Destiny); (October 22 • Mastery Through Calm)
- **Proverbs 31:26–28** … (May 10 • A Mother's Sacred Influence)
- **Proverbs 31:30** … (May 11 • Vanity or Virtue)

Ecclesiastes

- **Ecclesiastes 1:18** … (September 9 • Sacrifice Required)
- **Ecclesiastes 3:11** … (April 13 • The God-Shaped Hole in Your Heart)
- **Ecclesiastes 4:9** … (March 16 • When Two Become More Than Two)

Isaiah

- **Isaiah 3:12** … (May 28 • God's Order: God > Jesus > Man > Woman > Children)
- **Isaiah 26:3** … (April 16 • A Peace of Mind vs. A Mind of Peace)
- **Isaiah 32:15–16** … (December 9 • Change Your Soil to Bloom)
- **Isaiah 40:31** … (August 4 • Wait for the Wind)
- **Isaiah 43:18–19** … (February 24 • Looking Forward); (June 2 • Let Go and Let God); (July 11 • Don't Miss Today's Blessings); (December 24 • Handcuffed to History or Free for Destiny)
- **Isaiah 45:3** … (September 12 • Birthed Out of the Darkness)
- **Isaiah 48:10** … (December 1 • Refined in the Fire)
- **Isaiah 48:22** … (October 10 • Peace Through Righteousness)
- **Isaiah 54:5** … (June 6 • Jesus: My Master, Savior, Ruler, Redeemer, Provider)
- **Isaiah 58:6** … (October 4 • Saved, But Still in Chains)
- **Isaiah 59:2** … (June 9 • Sin Separates; Obedience Unites)
- **Isaiah 63:3** … (May 9 • The Loneliness of Leadership)

Jeremiah

- **Jeremiah 17:10** … (July 7 • Cheerful Obedience); (August 17 • The End of Self)
- **Jeremiah 29:11** … (January 20 • In the Huddle); (August 22 • From Fearless in Foolishness to Fearless in Faith)
- **Jeremiah 33:3** … (December 23 • Secrets of Sincere Love)

Ezekiel

- **Ezekiel 36:26** … (March 26 • Change Born from Love)

Zechariah

- **Zechariah 13:9a** … (April 2 • Refined for Elevation)

New Testament

Matthew

- **Matthew 4:18–22** ... (October 26 • More Than 24 Hours: The Power of Divine Teamwork)
- **Matthew 5:14** ... (May 15 • Shine); (December 28 • A Beacon of Light)
- **Matthew 5:14–16** ... (June 27 • Light Your Corner); (August 23 • Light Up the Darkness)
- **Matthew 5:16** ... (February 4 • Be Bright On Purpose)
- **Matthew 5:17** ... (January 23 • The Fulfillment of the Law Is Love)
- **Matthew 6:6** ... (April 6 • Public Praise Flows from Private Worship); (June 22 • Shut the Door and Pray); (December 21 • Hidden Worship, Public Weapons)
- **Matthew 6:10** ... (March 14 • On Earth As It Is In Heaven: Roots & Reach); (September 13 • On Earth as It Is in Heaven)
- **Matthew 6:11** ... (September 2 • Our Daily Bread)
- **Matthew 6:33** ... (May 2 • Seek First); (March 10 • Your Value Isn't in Your Bank ... It's in Your Vision); (March 13 • One Purpose)
- **Matthew 6:34** ... (March 1 • The Power of Being Present)
- **Matthew 7:7** ... (July 6 • Ask. Seek. Knock.); (December 11 • What Would You Ask For?); (September 3 • The Key of Prayer)
- **Matthew 7:12** ... (September 15 • You Get What You Give)
- **Matthew 7:21–23** ... (November 11 • Professing Is Not Possessing)
- **Matthew 7:24–25** ... (March 23 • When the Storm Comes)
- **Matthew 7:24** ... (February 6 • Stop Chasing Sand)
- **Matthew 9:36** ... (December 15 • Compassion That Breaks Our Hearts)
- **Matthew 12:25** ... (May 24 • United We Stand, Divided We Fall)
- **Matthew 13:29–30** ... (May 21 • Seeing Beyond the Surface)
- **Matthew 14:23** ... (February 12 • Greatness in Solitude)
- **Matthew 16:19** ... (August 20 • The Keys to Shining Your Light)
- **Matthew 16:24** ... (January 13 • Living Beyond the Conscious)
- **Matthew 17:20** ... (April 18 • Faith Makes Miracles)
- **Matthew 19:29** ... (December 5 • To Love and Let Go)

- **Matthew 23:27-28** ... (June 17 • Called to Transform, Not Perform)
- **Matthew 25:40** ... (January 21 • Service: The Secret to Greatness)

Mark

- **Mark 8:36** ... (October 2 • Don't Lose Your Soul Chasing the Gold)
- **Mark 11:24** ... (April 19 • Faith Receives Before It Sees)

Luke

- **Luke 6:26** ... (February 9 • No Enemies?)
- **Luke 6:36** ... (July 26 • Helping People Is Godlike)
- **Luke 17:21** ... (July 2 • The Kingdom Within)
- **Luke 19:10** ... (March 17 • The Lord Saves Us From...)
- **Luke 21:19** ... (July 13 • Be Patient in the Process)
- **Luke 5:16** ... (May 7 • The Beginning of Solitude)

John

- **John 1:5** ... (October 31 • Light in the Darkness)
- **John 3:3** ... (January 4 • Die to Rise); (July 3 • Called to Be "Twice-Born"...)
- **John 3:16** ... (May 23 • The Measure of Love Is Sacrifice)
- **John 7:38** ... (November 9 • Be a Conduit and Not a Cul-de-Sac)
- **John 8:32** ... (January 12 • Truth That Heals); (May 8 • Truth Breaks Chains)
- **John 8:36** ... (July 23 • Freedom Starts on the Inside); (September 8 • Freedom Is an Inside Job); (September 17 • The Power Already Within You); (September 28 • Free Behind Bars)
- **John 10:10** ... (May 22 • Warned & Ready...); (July 29 • What the Thief Comes to Steal)
- **John 10:27** ... (April 15 • Resonating with Heaven's Frequency)
- **John 13:35** ... (March 5 • How You Love Is Your Superpower)
- **John 15:11** ... (November 7 • Joy Beyond Happiness)
- **John 15:13** ... (August 21 • Love Looks Like Sacrifice)

- **John 17:17** ... (April 29 • Standing Firm in a Shifting Culture); (May 18 • Our Heavenly Reconciliation)
- **John 17:21** ... (July 9 • The Power of Oneness)

Acts

- **Acts 1:8** ... (September 14 • When the Lights Went Out, Power Showed Up)
- **Acts 4:20** ... (July 12 • Just Can't Help It)
- **Acts 10:38** ... (January 14 • Give Freely, Live Abundantly)
- **Acts 20:35** ... (March 15 • If You Ain't Giving…); (September 26 • The Blessing of Being a Blessing)

Romans

- **Romans 8:26** ... (April 17 • Prayer That Starts in Heaven)
- **Romans 8:38–39** ... (June 10 • God Never Asked You to Audition)
- **Romans 12:1** ... (May 5 • Sacrifice: The Currency of Elevation)
- **Romans 12:2** ... (February 8 • The Smallest Shift…); (March 21 • Change Your Mind…); (May 16 • Change Requires Change); (May 25 • The Cost of Becoming New); (July 15 • The Battle for Your Mind)
- **Romans 12:9** ... (May 13 • When Kindness Is a Mask)
- **Romans 14:19** ... (June 26 • Energy Multiplies When We Reflect Light Together)
- **Romans 7:23** ... (September 7 • The War Within)

1 Corinthians

- **1 Corinthians 3:6** ... (February 18 • Just Plant the Seed)
- **1 Corinthians 3:7** ... (May 20 • You Are Not the Fixer)
- **1 Corinthians 3:8** ... (January 2 • The Rewards of Sacrifice)
- **1 Corinthians 3:16** ... (October 8 • A Temple Divided Cannot Stand)
- **1 Corinthians 4:2** ... (July 17 • Life Is Not About Magic…); (November 18 • Consistency Beats Creativity)
- **1 Corinthians 6:19** ... (April 25 • Love Yourself Enough to Care for Your Temple)
- **1 Corinthians 9:27** ... (April 9 • Choose Daily Discipline)
- **1 Corinthians 13:13** ... (February 14 • Love: The Greatest of All); (December 25 • The Languages of Love)

- **1 Corinthians 14:33** ... (November 17 • The Rhythm of God)
- **1 Corinthians 15:10** ... (December 7 • Beyond Your Ability but Within His Grace)
- **1 Corinthians 15:33** ... (January 22 • Choose Your Company Wisely); (June 20 • A Problem for Every Solution); (August 6 • Righteousness Over Loyalty)

2 Corinthians

- **2 Corinthians 1:3–4** ... (December 16 • Your Story Becomes a Survival Guide)
- **2 Corinthians 3:17** ... (June 11 • True Freedom); (September 23 • Freedom Ain't There)
- **2 Corinthians 3:18** ... (March 11 • The Ladder of Consciousness); (March 25 • The Gospel Means More Than Blessings...); (September 10 • In His Likeness); (November 27 • Love from the Level of Healing)
- **2 Corinthians 4:7** ... (December 10 • It's Not the Arrow, It's the Archer)
- **2 Corinthians 5:7** ... (January 7 • One Step at a Time); (April 3 • Ready Is a Decision...); (October 25 • When You Move, The Way Appears)
- **2 Corinthians 5:10** ... (May 19 • The Ride Matters)
- **2 Corinthians 6:16** ... (May 30 • Not the Woodpecker ... But the Termite)
- **2 Corinthians 10:3–5** ... (December 18 • The Battlefield of the Mind); (October 5 • The Enemy Inside)
- **2 Corinthians 10:5** ... (July 5 • No Free Rent)

Galatians

- **Galatians 1:6–7** ... (March 28 • The Illusion of a Compromised Gospel)
- **Galatians 1:10** ... (December 13 • Live for the Audience of One)
- **Galatians 2:20** ... (August 10 • Who You Are in Christ...); (October 19 • The Call Back to Surrender)
- **Galatians 5:17** ... (February 5 • You vs YOU)
- **Galatians 5:19–21** ... (September 25 • Don't Open the Door)
- **Galatians 5:22** ... (May 12 • Kindness Is Godly)
- **Galatians 5:22–23** ... (December 3 • Set the Setting)
- **Galatians 6:7** ... (March 8 • Be the Energy...); (May 26 • Sow Wisely...)

- **Galatians 6:9** … (January 28 • Consistency…); (March 20 • The Power of Small Acts); (April 8 • Habits Shape Your Horizon); (November 24 • Why Consistency Is Everything); (November 25 • The Courage to Continue)

Ephesians

- **Ephesians 2:8** … (June 1 • Grace: God's Resources at Christ's Expense)
- **Ephesians 2:8–9** … (March 27 • Grace Over Performance…)
- **Ephesians 2:10** … (April 4 • Build the Builder…); (December 30 • Your Greatest Project)
- **Ephesians 2:4–5** … (October 20 • Saved From Foolishness)
- **Ephesians 2:6** … (July 19 • Seated in Heavenly Places)
- **Ephesians 4:22–24** … (October 16 • From Perform to Transform)
- **Ephesians 4:23–24** … (August 14 • Getting Over You); (September 24 • The Equation of Divine Alignment)
- **Ephesians 4:25** … (January 24 • Stay Honestly Free)
- **Ephesians 4:31–32** … (October 24 • What Does Your Attitude "Smell" Like?)
- **Ephesians 4:32** … (January 25 • Compassion: The Heart That Heals)
- **Ephesians 5:8** … (March 12 • Drawn to the Light)
- **Ephesians 5:14** … (January 8 • Wake Up: Don't Be the Walking Dead)
- **Ephesians 6:12** … (August 25 • Get in the Game)

Philippians

- **Philippians 2:12–13** … (March 22 • The Only Person Coming to Save You)
- **Philippians 2:13** … (February 15 • The Will to Win); (June 5 • To Me and Through Me)
- **Philippians 2:14–15** … (December 2 • Take Responsibility, Stop Complaining)
- **Philippians 2:15** … (December 27 • Purposely Bright)
- **Philippians 3:13** … (December 20 • Unshackled: From History to Destiny)
- **Philippians 3:13–14** … (February 23 • Your Next Move Matters…); (December 31 • Shutting the Door on Yesterday)
- **Philippians 4:4–5** … (July 30 • Joy Inside, Happiness Outside)

- **Philippians 4:5** ... (January 3 • Let Your Smile Change the World)
- **Philippians 4:6–7** ... (March 19 • From Worry to Wonder); (September 22 • Letting Go of Being Right)
- **Philippians 4:7** ... (February 27 • Faith That Finds Peace); (June 28 • The Gift of Serenity)
- **Philippians 4:12** ... (January 11 • Doing Less, But Doing Better)
- **Philippians 4:12–13** ... (August 27 • With God, Any Is Plenty)
- **Philippians 4:19** ... (August 18 • God Will Provide)

Colossians

- **Colossians 1:16** ... (January 18 • For Him, Not For Us)
- **Colossians 1:18** ... (April 12 • He Is Everything to Me)
- **Colossians 2:2–3** ... (October 3 • Beyond the Classroom)
- **Colossians 3:2** ... (July 8 • Where Attention Flows, Energy Grows); (November 15 • Focus Sets the Frequency)
- **Colossians 3:3** ... (July 24 • Full Custody, Not Visitation); (October 13 • The Quiet Power of Knowing Who You Are)
- **Colossians 3:10** ... (April 20 • Spiritual Beings, Holy Assignment); (October 23 • Transformed by Choice)
- **Colossians 3:17** ... (January 9 • The Rhythm of Becoming)
- **Colossians 3:23** ... (March 18 • Hard Work Works)
- **Colossians 3:9–10** ... (February 17 • Change Habits → Change Your Life)

1 Thessalonians

- **1 Thessalonians 4:3–4** ... (September 11 • Love Set Apart)
- **1 Thessalonians 5:6** ... (October 21 • Awake from the Prison of Distraction)
- **1 Thessalonians 5:18** ... (January 26 • Gratitude: The Key to Elevation)

2 Thessalonians

- **2 Thessalonians 3:10** ... (December 19 • When Charity Becomes Toxic)

1 Timothy

- **1 Timothy 4:7–8** … (November 29 • Rules to Upgrade Your Life)
- **1 Timothy 4:8** … (December 29 • Training the Inner Man)
- **1 Timothy 5:8** … (February 1 • Winning Where It Matters Most)

2 Timothy

- **2 Timothy 2:2** … (November 19 • Passing the Baton)
- **2 Timothy 3:12** … (December 26 • Why the Shift Feels Like Rejection)
- **2 Timothy 3:15** … (May 27 • Don't Feed Your Babies the Same Lies You Ate)
- **2 Timothy 3:16–17** … (November 16 • Training Wheels and the Teacher Within)
- **2 Timothy 4:3–4** … (June 8 • Stop Letting Satan Romance You to Death)

Hebrews

- **Hebrews 4:12** … (August 15 • When the Word Hurts)
- **Hebrews 5:14** … (November 14 • From Spectators to Disciples)
- **Hebrews 12:1** … (January 15 • Remove What Stops Growth); (September 29 • Stay Light So You Can Take Flight)
- **Hebrews 12:11** … (February 21 • Discipline: The Pathway to Purpose); (September 30 • Disciplined Growth); (October 1 • The Hard That Builds)

James

- **James 1:2–4** … (April 21 • Growth Demands Challenge); (November 3 • The Obstacle Is the Way)
- **James 1:3–4** … (June 15 • Built for Eternity)
- **James 1:4** … (January 29 • Patience: The Power of the Wait)
- **James 1:12** … (February 11 • The Sacred Struggle); (June 19 • The Hard Path Builds the Unshakable Life)
- **James 1:22** … (April 27 • Knowing God by Doing His Work); (November 20 • Invincible Ignorance vs. Visible Wisdom)
- **James 1:23–24** … (October 11 • The Mirror That Demands Change)

- **James 3:13** … (April 28 • Wisdom That Speaks, Works That Show)
- **James 4:1** … (November 2 • Sin Is Poison to the Elevated Soul)
- **James 4:6** … (September 16 • Built Low to Rise High)
- **James 4:10** … (July 20 • The Power of Humility)
- **James 4:14** … (April 24 • Don't Wait; Life Moves Faster Than You Think)
- **James 5:16b** … (September 1 • Righteous Hearted)
- **James 5:19–20** … (February 29 • A Church Serious About Souls)

1 Peter

- **1 Peter 3:18** … (November 21 • A Weight Too Heavy to Carry)
- **1 Peter 4:8** … (May 31 • Love Covers a Multitude of Sins)
- **1 Peter 4:10–11** … (September 19 • Purpose Is the Impact You Leave)
- **1 Peter 5:7** … (April 23 • The Power of Letting Go)
- **1 Peter 5:8** … (August 7 • HALT Before You Fall)
- **1 Peter 5:10** … (February 7 • Struggle Is the Assignment)

2 Peter

- **2 Peter 1:5** … (April 22 • The Call to Virtue…)
- **2 Peter 1:19** … (August 16 • Abound to Enlightenment); (August 19 • Suddenly, The Light); (November 26 • Enlightenment as a Way of Life)

1 John

- **1 John 1:6–7** … (February 26 • Called to Be Light, Not Liked)
- **1 John 2:6** … (August 29 • Covered in His Dust)
- **1 John 2:16** … (March 3 • Dying to Live Divine)
- **1 John 3:8** … (March 24 • The Enemy Wants More than Casualties)
- **1 John 4:7–8** … (September 21 • Live Together or Perish Together)
- **1 John 4:20–21** … (January 17 • You Cannot Love God Without Loving Others)
- **1 John 5:12** … (November 13 • True Life)

Revelation

- **Revelation 2–3** ... (July 10 • The Call to Overcome)

Hallelujah !

Made in the USA
Coppell, TX
04 March 2026

72896629R00229